Genealogical Research
in
England and Wales

VOL. 2

Genealogical Research in England and Wales

VOL. 2

DAVID E. GARDNER

•

FRANK SMITH

Artwork by Mariel P. Gardner

BOOKCRAFT PUBLISHERS

Salt Lake City, Utah

CONTENTS

✦

A SUCCEEDING VOLUME WILL INCLUDE, AMONG
OTHER SUBJECTS, A DISCUSSION OF:

Apprentice and freemen records; reading early English script; Chancery
Proceedings, Schools and University registers; Poll Books; Feet of Fines;
Inquisitions Post Mortem and Manor Court Rolls.

HOME-THOUGHTS, FROM ABROAD

Oh, to be in England
Now that April's there,
And whoever wakes in England
Sees, some morning, unaware,
That the lowest boughs and the brush-wood shreaf
Round the elm-tree bole are in tiny leaf,
While the chaffinch sings on the orchard bough
In England — now!

And after April, when May follows,
And the whitethroat builds, and all the swallows!
Hark, where my blossomed pear-tree in the hedge
Leans to the field and scatters on the clover
Blossoms and dewdrops — at the bent spray's edge —
That's the wise thrush; he sings each song twice over,
Lest you should think he never could recapture
The first fine careless rapture!
And though the fields look rough with hoary dew,
All will be gay when noontide wakes anew
The buttercups, the little children's dower
— Far brighter than this gaudy melon-flower!

—*Robert Browning*

Corfe Castle, County Dorset, has parish registers dating back to 1653.
In earlier times the inhabitants were principally employed in stone
quarries and clay pits.

Great Malvern, a fashionable health resort, romantically situated in
Worcestershire, has parish registers dating back to 1556.

INTRODUCTION

The response to Volume 1 of this series has indicated the great need for text books relating to research in England and Wales that discuss in detail the record sources in those countries. Volume 1 dealt with a number of the record sources of genealogical value, this volume continues in that chosen direction.

The aim and reason for this volume is therefore obvious. There is little that could be added to the introduction to the first Volume, except perhaps, to include an ever increasing awareness that success in genealogical research depends to a large measure on an understanding not only of what records actually are available, but also their contents and their availability.

The obtaining of information on the types of records available has presented little problem, and the information contained in these records is, to those who have experience in research in England and Wales, perhaps already known. The difficulty has been in the determining *where* the records are presently located, and for this reason, a great deal of this volume tends to discuss the present whereabouts of the records.

An awareness of the necessity of maps in any genealogical problem has led to the inclusion of maps for each county of England and Wales. The use of these maps, together with the information relating to the records, their contents and their whereabouts, is encouraged.

Appreciation is again expressed to Archibald F. Bennett, Secretary of the Genealogical Society, Salt Lake City; L. Garrett Myers, Superintendent of the Society, and Henry E. Christiansen, head of the Society's Research Department, for their cooperation and encouragement.

Special mention is made of Mr. F. G. Emmison, County Archivist, Essex; Dr. Felix Hull, County Archivist, Kent; Mr. C. E. B. Hubbard, Birmingham; Mr. E. H. Sargeant, County Archivist, Worcestershire; Mr. R. Sharpe France, County Archivist, Lancashire; Miss Helen Thacker, F. S. G., London; Mrs. Muriel Thompson, York; Mr. Peter Walne, County Archivist, Berkshire and many others for their helpful assistance.

Special mention should also be made of Lt. Col. M. E. S. Laws, O. B. E., M. C., R. A. (Ret'd.), F. R. Hist. S., for reading the manuscript chapter on Naval and Military Records and for helpful suggestions and comments.

Grateful acknowledgement is made to our friend and colleague, Derek Harland, for reading the manuscript and assisting in its preparation for the press.

Our appreciation is also due to many kind readers in the United States, Canada, New Zealand, South Africa, Australia and Great Britain who have written so favorably regarding the contents of Volume One. It is hoped that this present volume will be as kindly received.

Chapter 1

PLANNING RESEARCH AND RECORDING RESEARCH RESULTS

Planning Research.

Success in genealogical research demands planning. The items for which searches are to be made, the period of time in which the required events are likely to have taken place — these are items that should be determined before actual research begins.[1]

If searches are contemplated at the General Register Office, Somerset House, London,[2] for specific birth, marriage, or death records, it is essential that the period in which the various events are thought to have taken place be reduced to as narrow a period as possible. This narrowing down process can be achieved usually by obtaining ages at dated events from other record sources. As much information as possible should be obtained about the relevant events before having searches made in the various record repositories, and such information should be given in the actual request letter.

Research procedure is nothing more than the correct and wise use of genealogical records. It would not be considered correct or wise to spend several days searching the census returns of a large town for a family thought to have been resident somewhere in that town, when the length of the search could be reduced considerably by obtaining a birth, marriage, or death certificate, which would give an actual street address in that town at which the family did reside. Street indexes have been prepared for census returns, and their use can reduce a several day search into one of a matter of minutes.[3]

---

1. For the rules affecting the determining of period searches, see Chapter 6, Vol. 2, A *Basic Course in Genealogy;* "Research Procedure and Evaluation of Evidence," (Salt Lake City: Bookcraft, Inc., 1958).
2. See also Chapter 7, Vol. 1 of this present series, "Civil Registration of Births, Marriages, and Deaths."
3. See also Chapter 4, Vol. 1, of this present series, "How to Trace Place and Family in the 1841 and 1851 Census Records."

Recording Research Results.

Equally as important as the planning of research, is the recording of the searches actually made, with sufficient detail to give a clear and accurate picture of the records, periods and items covered by such searches. Planning of future research will be made easier if results of previous searches have been clearly listed.

A research notebook should be kept in which details of all searches, as well as the resulting entries, can be recorded. A typical heading on a page on this notebook could read — *Results of searches in the indexes of Somerset House for the period 1838 — 1842 for the death of John Knighton. Reasons for search — to determine his age at death and the specific street address at which he died.*

Searches in census returns would require the page(s) in the research notebook to be headed, for example — *Searches in the 1851 census returns of Figheldean, Wiltshire, listing all entries of Adams and Baker. Reason for search — to find details of the family of John and Mary Adams. Mary's maiden surname was Baker, hence the interest in the Baker families.*

If the searches result in the compiling of more than one page of extracts, each page should be headed with exact details of the search. As this system becomes a part of the research program, the headings on each page can be made more brief, but care should be taken to ensure that the headings are comprehensive enough to describe the record searched.

Library call numbers, page numbers for entries taken from the 1851 census, the exact periods covered in searches of parish registers — these are essentials in the completing of details of record searches.

This program of systematic recording of search results should be logical and obvious in its necessity, but, unfortunately, there are many record searchers who do not record such details, and a scrutiny of their work, no matter how careful, often fails to show just what searches have been made. Such an omission often results in previously made searches being duplicated, simply because there is no evidence to show whether or not a certain search for a specific period has been carried out.

Not only is it important to record the periods covered in searches, but note must be made of the periods missing or illegible in any records. Parish registers and Bishop's Transcripts are often far from complete, and it is a wise policy in searching these records to prepare a list of the relevant years before beginning the search, so that, as the years are covered, they can be checked or noted with any pertinent remark. Transcripts often are found out of chronological order, and a check list of the years being searched will ensure that every year is either covered in the search or the fact that it is missing or illegible noted. The following check list of years demonstrates the use and value of such a system.

Bishop's Transcripts of Llandissilio, Montgomeryshire.
1740-1770

June 1740 to June 1741 CMB
June 1741 to July 1742 CMB
Oct 1742 to May 1743 CMB Many entries illegible
May 1743 to Dec. 1744 CMB
May 1745 to Mar 1746 CMB Faded in parts
May 1747 to Mar 1748 CMB
June 1748 to Apr 1748 CMB
Apr 1750 to Mar 1750/1 CMB Some entries torn
        etc.   etc.   etc.

This list graphically shows the condition of the particular transcripts. It may be difficult to determine without careful examination of the registers or transcripts whether or not the entries for a specific year are complete. In many of the smaller parishes, there were no baptisms, marriages, or burials for weeks, even months, resulting in a gap in the records. If, however, the parish is large, with regular and chronologically consistent entries, then a gap in the entries for a period of a month or two may suggest that the register or the transcript is incomplete. The noting of missing or illegible periods is important , as there is the real possibility of the required ancestral entry being in the missing period. In the foregoing example, note that one transcript appears to have been dated incorrectly — June 1748 to Apr. 1748 probably should read "June 1748 to Apr. 1749", and that other periods are also missing.

The following *Research Summary Sheet* is a suggested form that can be used to record details of searches in parish registers or Bishop's Transcripts. There are two sides to this form. The front shows the parishes that have been searched, the periods covered in each parish and the surnames included in the search. The reverse of the Summary Sheet indicates the conditions under which the searches were made, and allows a brief report to be made on a number of pertinent points. The obvious usefulness of this form strongly recommends its use.

SUMMARY OF SEARCHES

Date: My Name:

PERIODS SEARCHED

Parish (es)	Christenings	Marriages	Burials	Surname (s)
B.T.'s of Westhoughton	1800-1840 1802 and 1840 missing	No Marriages recorded	1800-1840 1802 and 1840 missing	{ Eckersley Cowburn Gregory Higham Cleworth Barlow Carter
P.R.'s of Westhoughton	1733-1800 (none earlier)	1733-1754 (none earlier. Marriages after 1754 at *Deane*)	1755-1800 (none earlier)	all as above
P.R.'s of Westhoughton	1733-1760	1733-1754	1755-1760	Wilkinson
B.T.'s of Flixton	1787-1840	1787-1840	1787-1840	all as above

State clearly *actual periods* searched. If different periods are searched for different surnames, show this clearly. If Bishop's Transcripts are searched, state this, carefully recording the years which are missing. Note illegibilities and all peculiarities Place of abode, trades and witnesses are vital. If married by license, so state. Search banns books where available for marriages which cannot be found in the regular marriage registers. See Overleaf.

1. Can the record(s) searched be read easily?
   Early parish registers of Westhoughton faded.

2. Did you make the search(es) personally?
   Yes.

3. Were conditions unsuitable? (i.e., minister in a hurry, funds running out, etc.)
   Conditions good.

4. Did you make a note of all the periods missing, illegible and difficult to read?
   Yes. See extracts.

5. Did you search for all items and/or surnames requested in all the periods required? If not, which items and/or surnames were omitted and for what periods.
   Searched for all required surnames.

6. Did you double-check the periods in which the ancestral entry (entries) was expected to be found?
   Yes.

7. Did you search the churchyard for helpful tombstone inscriptions.
   No. Too wet.
   No copy available in library.

The keeping of a research notebook in which details of searches, etc., can be entered is almost essential if a genealogist is to know what he has done and what he should next do. Neatness is of great value in the keeping of such a book. It allows for a simple filing and indexing system that enables ready and quick reference to be made to any of the items, any of the extracts and any of the documents filed therein.

The type and quality of paper used is also of importance. Paper of sufficient width to record a full parish entry or a full census entry should be used. The common school exercise notebook, $8\frac{1}{2}$" x $10\frac{1}{2}$", is ideal for such a purpose.

Locality Search Forms.

There will be occasions when searches for one specific item will have to be made in the registers or transcripts of a number of parishes. The Research Summary Sheet is of little use in such instances, and so a separate itemized list of the parishes and the periods covered must be kept. The Locality Search Form, Type A, is ideal for recording the progress of this type of search.

An example of this form appears on page 17 and demon-strates the use of this aid in an actual research problem. Robert Wood, the ancestor, was married at Sevenoaks, Kent in 1791, at which time he was said to be of the parish of Leigh. His children were christened at Westerham, and he was buried at Westerham, 1823, aged 51 years. His year of birth can be calculated from his age at death, namely 1772, and in accord-ance with the standards for period approximating,[4] the period 1767-1777 would be searched for his birth or christening record. The obvious starting point for the christening of Robert Wood would be at Leigh, his place of residence at the time of his marriage. Sevenoaks, Westerham, and surrounding parishes would then be searched. The names of the parishes, the periods covered, and the results of the searches can then be itemized on the Locality Search Form, Type A.

The Wood example has a number of interesting facets:

1. The periods covered in the searches are much wider than absolutely necessary for the one item of Robert Wood's chris-tening. This is because the registers of this area are easily accessible and the searching of wider periods meant little addi-tional time and effort.

2. Early in the search, a christening of a Robert Wood was found at Crowhurst, which could be ancestral. To stop the search at this point would be unwise, as there is the possibility that there may have been other Robert Woods born in neighboring par-ishes. The evidence that the Robert Wood christened at Crow-hurst in 1771 is the Robert Wood who married at Sevenoaks is only circumstantial,[5] and could not possibly be accepted with-out further searches.

   Note that a christening of another Robert Wood took place at Nutfield. Which of these christenings is ancestral is a problem that could utilize the information contained in probate records.

3. The possibility that Robert Wood's christening could have taken place when he was a few years old should not be overlooked, and in the searching for christening entries, it is policy to extend the period of search to include such a possibility.

---

4. See chapter 6, volume 2, A Basic Course in Genealogy, op. cit.
5. The process of strengthening circumstantial evidence is outlined in Chapter 3, Vol. 2, A Basic Course in Genealogy, op. cit.

FORM A.

LOCALITY SEARCHES — Kent and Surrey

OBJECTIVE OF SEARCHES:

chr. of Robert Wood, marr 1791 at Sevenoaks (of Leigh at the time) bur. 1823 aged 51 (born 1771/2). All children christened at Westerham.

PARISH SEARCHED	PERIOD(S) COVERED	REMARKS
Leigh	* 1760-1800	
Sevenoaks	* 1760-1800	
Westerham	* 1760-1840	
Crowhurst	1760-1800	A Robert Wood chr 28 April 1771 s.o. Rob't and Ann.
Titsey	1760-1800	
Tatsfield	1760-1800	
Nutfield	1760-1812	A Robert Wood chr 17 May 1771 s.o. Rob't and Sarah.
Limpsfield	1760-1800	
Sundridge	1760-1800	
Brasted	1760-1800	
Otford	1760-1800	
Burstow	1760-1812	
Gatton	1760-1800	
Caterham	1760-1800	
Farleigh	1760-1800	
Woldingham	1760-1800	
(and 25 other parishes listed on similar forms)		

THIS IS A PERMANENT PART OF THE RESEARCH FILE.
BE SURE TO KEEP IT UP TO DATE.

*Indicates the parishes in which they were known to have had connections.

FORM B

ITEM and period in which which sought → / PARISHES SEARCHED →	Trowbridge	Seend	Bremhill	Calne	Atworth	Broughton Gifford	Compton Bassett	Lacock	Potterne	Rowde	Heddington	Cricklade St. Mary	Cricklade St. Sampson	Great Cheverall	Little Cheverall	Durnford	Erlestoke	Homington	Hilperton
chr of John Dunford born 1759/60 (1755-1765)	√*	√	√	√	√	√	√	√	√	√	√	√	√	√	√	√	√	√	√
chr of John Flower 1721-1743	*	√	√	√	√	√	√	√	√	√	√	√	√	√	√		√	√	√
marr of Wm. Blair to Sarah 1788-96	√*	√	√	√	√	√	√	√	√	√	√	√	√	√	√	√	√	√	√
chr of James Bailey 1774/5 (1770-1780)	F√	A√	√	√	√	B√	√	√	√	C√	√	√	√	D√	√	√	√	√	E√
chr of Rachel Moore abt. 1794 (1789-1799)	*	√	√	√	√	√	√	√	√	√	√	√	√	√	√	√	√	√	√
marr of William Atkin to Sarah 1751-61	√*	√	√	√	√	√	√	√	√	√	√	√	√	√	√	√	√	√	√

(The word "FOUND" is written diagonally across the central cells of the chart.)

REMARKS:

A. 12 Aug. 1770. James son of Mary Bailey chr.
B. 24 Jan. 1770. James son of James Bailey and Ann Tuck. chr.
C. 3 Jul. 1774. James son of Ann Bailey chr.
D. 5 Jul. 1778. James son of Thomas and Elizabeth Bailey chr.
E. 19 Jul. 1772. James son of John and Joanna Bailey chr.
F. A James and Mary Bailey have children heere about the time the above James would have been born.
Both parish registers and bishop's transcripts imperfect for the period.
All Wiltshire wills examined on the Bailey problem.

*Indicates the parishes in which they were known to have resided.

There will be occasions when searches will be made *in the same locality, in the same parishes, for a* NUMBER OF ITEMS, rather than for one specific christening, marriage, or burial. Rather than use separate Search Forms, for each item, as in Type A, a form can be used that lists *all* items for which searches are being made.

The form on page 18 demonstrates the use of this type of form in an actual research problem. The six "loose-ends" of the pedigree, the six items for which searches are being made, can be listed on the same form, as searches for these items will be carried out in the same area.

In the first column, the objective is detailed with the period of time to be covered for the respective item. The asterisk indicates the parish(es) with which the individuals are known to have residential connections. Alphabetical references can be made to the findings of interest in any specific parish, and the entries of interest listed on the bottom of the form. As the items are found and accepted as ancestral, the form can be so marked, as in the case of the marriage of William Blair.

To use this form enables the genealogical progress of the various searches to be easily and quickly seen. It is recommended that maps be used in conjunction with these forms. As a parish has been searched, a colored ring could be drawn around the name of that parish on the map. This system of using maps gives a pictorial view of the status of the research program.

In addition to the two types of Locality Search Forms, an individual progress chart can be devised, listing the known facts and possible sources of new information about a specific individual. The items that could be considered as forming part of this individual progress chart are:

1. *Birthplace. (Parish and county)*
   Birthdate.
   Give source of information.
   If not found, list all efforts to find this birth record.
   If it occurred before 1 July 1837 use Form "A" and a map to show the places searched.
   If it occurred after 1 July 1837 give details of searches made.

2. *Marriage.* (*Date, place, denomination*)
   Are the witnesses thought to be related?
   If the marriage took place by license, has the bond and alle-gation been examined?
   Have the banns books been searched?
   List all efforts to find the marriage if before 1 July 1837 using Form "A."
   List all searches made if the marriage took place after 1 July 1837.

3. *Death or burial.* (*Parish and county*)
   Date and age at death.
   List all searches made, unless it has been found.

4. *List the probate courts pertinent to the problem.*
   List the periods searched in each court and attach a list of the Wills found and details of those which have been read.
   Have the probate courts in nearby counties been considered?
   Have the records of the Prerogative Court(s) been ex-amined? Give details of all such searches.

5. *Give details of the military service of the individual.*
   List details of the military records already searched.

6. *List any other likely clues and helpful information such as details of emigration, family tradition, unusual given names, L.D.S. Church record evidences, etc.*

Filing Research Results.

A great amount of genealogical material will be gathered in the process of research, and it is advisable, that from the very outset of research, plans are made to file the material in a well planned and orderly manner. If possible, all papers should be kept flat and not folded.

Material can be divided into sections according to the localities to which they refer, and then the material from each locality can be divided into files or binders, involving one or two surnames. Consider the following example pedigree:

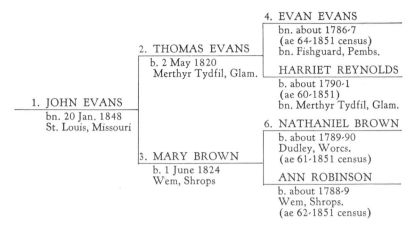

The obvious divisions in this example would be:

1. One file containing material relating to the EVANS line from County Pembroke.

2. One file containing material relating to the REYNOLDS line Glamorgan.

3. One file containing material relating to the BROWN line from Worcester.

4. One file containing material relating to the ROBINSON line from Shropshire.

Each file would contain a copy of the relevant section of the pedigree, and divisions made in each file, or binder, if necessary, for each type of genealogical record — census extracts in one section, parish register extracts arranged in the alphabetical order of the parishes, in another, and so on. As the pedigree extends and is developed, it may be necessary to have separate files for the new surnames added by the new extensions.

There is no doubt that many genealogists spend countless hours searching through file after file of material for a record they know to be "somewhere there." Genealogy demands order and neatness, both in the manner in which searches are planned and in the manner in which the material gathered as a result of the searches is filed.

Chapter 2

AN INTRODUCTION TO PROBATE RECORDS

Of all genealogical records, those coming under the heading of *probate records* are perhaps the most valuable and yet, perhaps, the least used and appreciated. Not only are the contents of these records of inestimable value, but the periods covered by them are somewhat amazing, some probate records dating as early as the fourteenth century.

GENERAL NOTES ON PROBATES.

A person having property could dispose of it in any way he chose, as long as the disposal was not contrary to law. Anciently, a *Will* itemized the way in which an individual wished to have his real estate, that is, land or interests in land, disposed of after his demise. As the medieval church objected to the devising of real estate, that is, its disposition by document, the *Testament* gradually came into being as a formal document bequeathing the personalty — that is, the personal effects, goods, chattels, credits and other moveable valuables. The disposal of real estate by Will became legal in 1540 under the Statute of Wills. The *Will and Testament* gradually merged into a single document often known as the "Last Will and Testament." Assistance in the preparation of a Will could be given by a friend or lawyer, and on the completion of this document it was retained either by its author or by a legal representative.

On the death of the testator, those named by him in the Will as executors, on learning of the existence of a Will, took it either to the appropriate probate court or its nearest representative. When the grant of probate was passed and made legal by the officials of the probate court, the person(s) named in the Will as executor(s) was empowered to dispose of the property according to the provisions of the Will.

Most Wills were made a short time before the death of the testator, although in some instances some Wills were made many years before death. Sometimes, persons made a verbal

Will on their death-bed in the presence of reliable witnesses. The death of a testator abroad might cause considerable delay before his Will was proved. When a person possessing property died without making a Will or no valid Will was found, close relatives (or in some cases, other interested parties) took legal steps to obtain power to administer the goods of the deceased.

There were many who died leaving no property or valuables. As they left nothing to be administered by their next-of-kin, no mention of them will appear in the records of a probate court. There are, undoubtedly, many cases where the disposal of property was arranged and agreed upon in the family circle before the death of the property owner, without the necessity of making a Will.

. . . many cases where the disposal of property was arranged and agreed upon in the family circle . . . without the necessity of making a Will.

It is estimated that one per-cent to ten per-cent of adults left Wills. This percentage will vary according to the locality in which a person lived. In a community of farmers and small landowners, the number of Wills left is likely to be higher than in an industrial area where the majority of the working class owned nothing of sufficient value to dispose of by Will. A higher estimate than ten per cent would be noticed in later periods as the possession of disposable property became more common. The small percentage of persons leaving Wills should not be a deterrent to the consideration of this source. There are Wills of persons who are described as laborers and even paupers.

The mastery of the complex details of probate records does not come without concentrated and determined study. Terminology must be understood and the host of different records that come under the general heading of Probate Records must be taken into consideration.

PROBLEMS OF JURISDICTION.

Before 11 January, 1858, the great majority of probates were granted in *ecclesiastical courts* by officials appointed by the Church of England. There were a number of probate courts, each having varying jurisdictions and the jurisdictions of these courts and the years they covered must be understood before probate records as a valuable genealogical source can be used effectively.

Since January, 1858, the system of probate jurisdiction is comparatively simple. In 1858 England and Wales were divided into civil probate districts, and in principal cities and towns, civil district probate registries were opened, and the former pre-1858 ecclesiastical courts were closed. These post-1858 probate records are kept in the local district probate registries and a copy of all these records, together with an annual master-index for the whole country, is kept in a central registry known as the Principal Probate Registry, Somerset House, London, W. C. 2. This chapter will deal with the pre-1858 probate records found in the *Ancient Courts of Probate*.

Some of the lists of probates recorded in certain courts have been printed, and a few of the older Wills have been printed. For the most part, however, research will have to be among the original records or their photo copies. The use of these handwritten records will present some difficulty, and in order to become acquainted with the various types of hand-writing found in probate records, the beginner might practice first, the reading of nineteenth century probate records and gradually work back to earlier periods. With practice and with the aid of text-books on old English handwriting, it will be possible to read the handwriting in Wills proved as early as the seventeenth century. Some will be able to read even earlier probate records, but others will need the help of experts, especially if the records are written in Latin.

VALUE OF PROBATE RECORDS.

The use of probate records in the compilation of family histories has been neglected by many, partly because their value has not been appreciated, and partly because the records have not been easily available. A Will often provides information that cannot be found in any other type of genealogical record. Children named in Wills may not be recorded in parish registers. A Will is perhaps the most authentic and genealogi-cally acceptable record in the information it gives about family relationship. The examples given later will demonstrate the value of this type of record.

It has been necessary to itemize in considerable detail some of the problems connected with the use of probate records and this detail may give the impression that an understanding of these records is beyond the scope of the beginning genealogist. It is stressed, however, that the use and intricacies of probate records can be mastered and the understanding of some of the finer points will increase with experience.

Chapters 2-6 include a description of the types of records appearing under the general heading of Probate Records and a description of the divisions of the ecclesiastical probate courts used prior to 1858. Chapter 9, "The Counties of England and Wales," should be studied in conjunction with this chapter, information on the probate courts of *each* county being listed there.

PRINTED RECORDS.

The excellent work of individuals and societies in the transcribing and printing of information from probate records should not be overlooked. Even their untiring efforts, however, when compared with the vast multitude of original records, has resulted in the transcription and printing of only a small percentage of such records. The experience and scholarly writing of these individuals and societies has given much information on the searching of probate records. It is hoped that those who seek data to prove and extend pedigrees and write histories will strongly support every effort to list, calendar, transcribe, edit, index and publish the names of persons and places appearing in the Calendars (sometimes called Indexes), Wills, Administrations, Act Books, and other records of probate.

The British Record Society, 120 Chancery Lane, London, W.C. 2., is one of the many publishers of probate records. The following, taken from the Preface of their 1958 publication, *Index to Wills Proved in the Prerogative Court of Canterbury, 1686-1693*, should be the concern of all who are interested in the support of this, and similar societies, in the continuation of their invaluable contribution to the field of genealogical and historical research:

> In preparing an index of Wills . . . a slip must first be written, then checked with the Probate Act Book . . . This is a long, difficult and expensive task. . . . With rising costs the Society finds it difficult to sustain its pre-war rate of output and now that voluntary help is getting scarcer . . . it can no longer pay for the preparation of the slips and for the checking. . . .

Within the original probate records are millions of names and pedigree clues, many of them hidden until the records have been adequately calendared and indexed.

The far-sighted program of microfilming the probate records at the expense of the Genealogical Society of the Church of Jesus Christ of Latter-day Saints safeguards these invaluable records from complete loss. One microfilmed copy of the original records is in the care of responsible officials in England and Wales and a second copy is in the Library of the Genealogical Society, Salt Lake City, Utah, U. S. A. These records may now be examined without inconvenience to the custodians and without damage to old and fragile documents.

PROBATE PROBLEMS.

A text book dealing with the problems and records of *each* ancient court of probate in England and Wales would require several large volumes. There is in these chapters, however, sufficient information to give an overall picture and a working knowledge of probate records. It is stressed again that there is a close relationship between these chapters and the chapter, "The Counties of England and Wales," as in that chapter, under the name of each county, details are given of the three categories closely connected with local probate records, namely:

    i. The ecclesiastical divisions in each county.

    ii. The ancient courts of probate and their jurisdictions.

    iii. The present (1959) whereabouts of probate records.

All who expect to search probate records should become thoroughly familiar with certain guide and reference books, many of which will be mentioned in this chapter. One of these, *Wills and Their Whereabouts*[1] should be obtained personally or for the local library. This excellent guide book lists details of each ancient court of probate and names Peculiars, the latter consisting of one or more parishes or places outside of the ordinary jurisdiction of a local probate court and, although many of the records mentioned have been transferred from the repositories listed, it is a valuable reference guide.

TERMINOLOGY.

One of the obstacles in the path of the user of probate records is the terminology used in such documents. Business methods varied from probate court to probate court, resulting in a variety of types of documents and books and a corresponding variety of terms to describe them. Unless these terms or titles are considered, valuable records may be hidden from the record searcher. The list that follows includes types of documents found in probate courts together with some of the terms commonly used in the records. The records themselves are dealt with more fully later.

This list might be used to locate references to important records "hidden" under an unfamiliar term in library card catalogues and indexes to books. The National Council of Social Service, London, published as Local History Series No. 9, *A Handlist of Medieval Ecclesiastical Terms* (R6A99), that might be useful to those who find an obscure term that requires definition.

---

1. B. G. Bouwens: *Wills and their whereabouts,* (London: The Society of Genealogists, 1951) 2nd ed. (Obtainable by mail from The Society of Genealogists, 37 Harrington Gardens, London, S.W.7., England. Price 12s 11d. It is recommended that $2 be sent from dollar areas). [ENG. 162].

Account — Executors and administrators of an estate might be requested, as part of an obligation made before the probate court, to render a "true and just account" of their management of the estate. These accounts are occasionally found among the records of the probate courts. (See also *Bond, Administrator, Inventory*). Books recording financial transactions of the court are also labelled accounts, sometimes fee books.

Act — The endorsement on a Will by a probate officer indicating that probate has been granted; the official recording of a grant in an Act Book. (See *Act Book*).

Act Book — A day-by-day account of the official grants of the probates of Wills and Letters of Administrations by the court. Caveats and guardianships (tuition, curation, etc.) are also to be found recorded in many Act Books. In some courts this is called a Day-Book or a Diary. Some Act Books contain details of other records such as marriage licenses, and ecclesiastical matters not related to testamentary business.

Administration — See *Letters of Administration*.

Administrator — A man who has entered in a bond before the Court and therefore vested with the right to administer an estate. An administrator may be appointed where an executor of a Will or the next-of-kin of an intestate was a minor; over a testator's estate where there was no competent executor; or over the estate of a person who left no valid Will. An Administratrix is a woman.

Admon. — A common abbreviation for *Letters of Administration*.

Assignations — An assignment to some person(s) to administer the estate; a transfer of the right from one person to another to administer the property.

Beneficiary — One who receives a benefit from property.

Bona Notabilia — A Latin term meaning "considerable goods." It usually indicates that the deceased's estate was valued at £5. (Five Pounds Sterling) or more. It is often used to denote "Having goods of £5. (or more) in diverse dioceses or peculiar jurisdictions within the province." When the deceased had *Bona Notabilia* in more than one jurisdiction, then the higher court claimed superior jurisdiction to issue the necessary grant. In effect, the bishop claimed the right to grant probate if *Bona Notabilia* was held solely within the diocese, but if in more than one diocese, then the archbishop claimed the right. In the course of time the Prerogative Courts granted probate of the goods of any person who applied, even when there was no case of *Bona Notabilia*. Act Books sometimes refer to *Bona Notabilia* by a brief phrase stating "(having &c.)" as part of the Act Book entry. An example of this is cited on page 103.

Bond — A signed, sealed and witnessed obligation, entered into at the probate court, by which a person promised to carry out the provisions of the conditions detailed in the bond. These conditions might include, among others, the execution of a Will; the administration of an intestate's estate; to render into the court, as an executor or administrator, a true and just account of the estate; to render a true and perfect Inventory; to be guardian of minors; and any other conditions that the court might impose. (See also *Administrator, Executor*).

Calendar — In a probate court the lists of the names of the Testators or Intestates (or both), for whose estates a grant has been made. Although not always alphabetical, it serves as an index to the Wills and Administrations. Some Calendars (or Indexes) contain errors and omissions.

Cathedral — The Church that contains the cathedra — that is, the official throne, seat, or chair of the bishop; hence the center of the episcopal see or diocese. Certain cathedral officials exercised jurisdiction in certain Testamentary Peculiars. In early Wills, "Mother Church" usually signified the cathedral church of the diocese where the testator lived.

Caveat — A warning notice issued by an interested person to the probate court that no action be taken in granting probate without their case being heard.

Chancellor — The Chancellor of a diocese was the Principal Officer appointed by the bishop. The Chancellor sometimes acted as Vicar-General and also as Judge if the bishop was absent or unable to act in person. Until 1546 this Official was always a clergyman, but since then a layman may be appointed to fill the position.

Chasm — A break in the records of the probate court, caused either by a loss of records or because the court was closed. (See also *Vacancy, Hiatus*). During the Civil Wars and Commonwealth (1642-1660) all courts (except the P.C.C.) became disrupted and from 1653-1660 were closed. (*See* Chapter 4, under "Example of Calendars . . . for the P.C.C.")

Codicil — A signed and witnessed addition (similar to a postscript) to the end of a Will by the testator after the Will had been made and signed.

Commissary Court — A court appointed by a superior authority and commissioned to carry out the duties assigned to it in a particular district; hence it is acting with delegated power to grant probates and Letters of Administration in a certain locality.

Consistory Court — A court of Church officials or dignitaries for deciding or determining ecclesiastical causes arising within the jurisdiction of such a court. These causes included the granting of probates and Letters of Administration.

Copyhold — The holding of land, as a tenant, the holder's title under the Lord of the Manor being recorded on the official roll of the court of the manor; the copy of the appropriate entry having been handed to the tenant, he (the tenant) is said to possess a copyhold — hence the term "copyhold" land, as distinct from leasehold and freehold; copyhold was abolished by the Property Acts of 1925.

Curation — Guardianship over orphaned minors who are usually over the age of fourteen (male) and twelve (female), but who are under twenty-one.

Day Book — A day by day account of the official grants of probates by the court. In some courts this is called an act-book or diary.

Decree — A judgment of a court. In probate calendars (especially P.C.C.), a note may appear "by decree" or "int. dec." (meaning interlocutory decree) indicating contested proceedings had taken place prior to the grant of probate. (See also *Sentence*).

Depositions — The testimony (usually in writing) given under oath. Occasionally referred to as affidavits.

Diaries — At Chichester, Sussex, after a grant of Probate or Letters of Administration was made, brief particulars were entered in probate Diaries. The references are in approximately alphabetical order and form a "day book" for the probate registry.

Diocese — The district in which a bishop has authority. An arch-diocese is the district or province in which an archbishop has authority. (See also *See, Cathedral*).

Donative — A parish totally exempt from the jurisdiction of the bishop of the diocese, as the benefice was given (i.e., the appointment of the parish minister) by the founder or patron of the parish — without the bishop presenting, inducting or instituting the parish minister. Many of these were Testamentary Peculiars (*which see*).

Dorse — The back of a document or page. Information added to the back of a doument is often known as an endorsement.

Double Probate — If, at the time of the original grant of probate, power was reserved of making a like grant of probate to one of the executor(s) who was unable to act or be present, the subsequent grant(s) of probate to the remaining executor(s) is, in some courts, designated as a Double Probate.

Esquire — Technically a person qualified to bear arms; generally used, from the 16th century onwards to denote either, correctly, such a person, or someone who was of a family of this rank. An esquire was next in social precedence below a knight. The term was also officially bestowed upon solicitors and barristers and upon persons holding a military or naval commission directly from the Crown. Today, the usage is very loose and is applied generally and indiscriminately to all males above the age of eighteen, as a matter of courtesy. (B. G. Bouwens in *Wills and their whereabouts* explains on page 77 what, in his opinion, are the meanings attached to "Esquire.")

Executor — A man appointed by the testator to execute the will. An executrix is a woman.

Folio — A leaf of a book or manuscript. References in Indexes, Calendars, Act Books, etc. may refer to a folio (and not a page) number. In many probate records the folio number is *not* strictly a page number, as a folio may, and usu-ally does, consist of a number of pages — perhaps as many as sixteen pages. To locate the record from its folio number, it is often necessary to find the folio number in the book or manuscript and then search onwards from there.

Freehold — A tenure of real property (i.e., land), held by right of inheritance, purchase, or gift, etc. Usually meaning the absolute ownership of the land, sub-ject only to the simple fee (fee simple) of allegiance to the Crown. Some Manors, however, had freehold tenants who paid a purely nominal rent but their tenure was regarded as free and not servile.

Gentleman — Technically, a person of gentle birth and next below an esquire in social precedence. An exact definition is impossible as the gentleman shaded into both the esquires and yeomen (*which see*).

Grant — The act of approval by the probate court that Letters of Administra-tion have been granted; used also to indicate that probate of a Will has been granted.

Guardianship — see *Curation* and *Tuition*.

Hiatus — A break in the records of the probate court, sometimes for several years, caused either by a loss of records or because the court was closed. (See also *Vacancy, Chasm, Inhibited*).

Holograph Will — A Will written entirely in the handwriting of the person making the Will.

Honour Court — Apparently an honour court was the jurisdiction exercised by the lord of an honour, i.e., a group of several manors, but the Honour Court of Knaresborough, Yorkshire, seems to be the only one that has surviving any records of a testamentary nature.

Indexes or Indices — Lists of Wills, Administrations, and other documents, by names of testators and intestates. (See also *Calendar*).

Inhibition — A writ to forbid a judge, archbishop, bishop, or other Official of a court, from proceeding further in a cause before him; the forbidding of probate being granted in a lower court during the visitation of the Official from a higher court. For example, an archdeacon's court was closed (i.e., inhibited) during the visitation of a bishop. A court might be inhibited for several months, during which time the probate business would be conducted in the court of the higher official. (See also *Chasm, Hiatus, Vacancy*).

Intestate — A person who died without making a Will or for whom no valid Will was found.

Inventory — A list of personal and household goods — usually including the tools of trade, etc — left by the deceased, with their appraised value. The occupation(s) of the deceased is often mentioned or inferred.

Journals — Books kept by a court for various reasons, sometimes mentioning persons and places not recorded elsewhere in the probate records.

Journeyman — A tradesman or laborer who is paid by the day (the word is derived through the French *Jour* meaning day). He may of course travel from place to place, but is just as likely to have served the same master throughout his working life.

Jurisdiction — The district over which a court claimed the right to grant probate or Letters of Administration. Such right was often subject to a variety of limitations or local exceptions. This is dealt with in full later.

Leasehold — Property, usually land or tenements, held by a lease for a given number of years.

Letters of Administration — A grant by the probate court to the next-of-kin (or some other person or persons) who applied to administer the property of a person who left no valid Will. (See also next item).

Letters of Administration-with-Will-annexed — A grant by the probate court to the next-of-kin (or some other person or persons) when the Will did not specify any executors or they were unable to act, or renounced, or had died. The Will is then attached (annexed) to the Administration Bond(s). In some courts the Will might be copied into a Register, the Act recorded in an Act Book, and the documents filed in the bundles of original Wills. However, in many courts the documents will be found recorded and filed as Letters of Administration, and not found recorded as Wills.

Limited Administrations — Cases where the grant concerning an intestate was limited to part of the estate.

Limited Probates — Cases where the grant was limited to part of the estate of the testator.

Manor — A territory, comprising the whole or part of a parish or more than one parish, held or owned by some person, not necessarily of exalted (noble) rank. A part of the manor would normally be held by the lord of the manor himself (lord here not necessarily being the equivalent of a nobleman) and the remainder allocated to tenants, some holding by a free tenure, others by unfree tenure. An essential right of the lord of the manor was the right to hold courts exercising jurisdiction over the tenants by court leet and court baron. Sometimes a manor court would possess the privilege of probate of Wills and grants of Letters of Administration and would thus be a testamentary Peculiar (*which see*) but by no means were all manors possessed of this privilege.

Minor — In England and Wales a person under the age of twenty-one years, i.e., under "legal" age.

Minute Books — Books kept by a court for various reasons. (See *Journals*).

Monitions — Usually a summons; many relate to a summons from a superior court to a lower court to send to the higher court certain documents.

Mrs. — The written form of the title or style Mistress. Up to the mid-18th century at least, it signifies any woman, married or single of "gentle" rank, e.g., to daughters of knights and esquires. After that time, it became usual to use it, in the present fashion, only for married women and widows.

Nuncupative Will — A Will made orally by a testator. Witnesses wrote the statements of the testator and were required to swear to the truth of the statements. The majority of nuncupative Wills were made by individuals in extremely poor health or those actually on their death beds.

Ordinary — A person who has immediate jurisdiction in ecclesiastical matters, such as the bishop of a diocese.

Orphans — See *Curation* and *Tuition*.

Peculiar — See *Testamentary Peculiar*.

Personalty — Personal property (goods, chattels, credits, etc.) as opposed to "real" (land) property.

Prebend — Some Collegiate and Cathedral Churches possessed a source of income that carried the title of Prebend, and the official appointed to receive such an income was known as a Prebendary. The name chosen for a Prebend was either that of a manor or a parish church belonging to the Collegiate or Cathedral Church. Many Prebendal Courts were Testamentary Peculiars (*which see*).

Probate — Evidence that a document offered as the last Will and Testament of the deceased has been accepted by the court and that the executor(s) (or others) has been granted permission to carry out the provisions of the Will. (See also *Double Probate*). (For intestates, see *Letters of Administration*).

Proved — A Will has been proved when probate has been granted, or in other words the Will has passed the seal of the court.

Real Property — Property in land, as opposed to personalty (i.e., goods, chattels, etc.).

Registers and Registered Wills — Volumes containing copies of Wills that have been proved. The Will is entered in full, but bonds and other documents attached to original Wills are not entered in the Registers. However, in the P.C.C., affidavits connected with the Wills are frequently registered.

Relict — A relict (in Latin *Relicta* or *Relictus*) is a person who is left behind after the decease of his or her spouse. Usually, but not necessarily, relates to the widow. As used in probate records — e.g., "Admon. of John Brown, deceased, granted to Mary Brown, widow, the *relict*" — the term confirms that in fact the widow mentioned is *his* widow and not just "Mary Brown, widow," who could be anyone.

Renunciation — When a person, who is named as executor in a Will, or is the next-of-kin of an intestate, declines to apply for a grant of probate or Letters of Administration, he is said to have renounced, and usually signs a document known as a renunciation. Mention is usually made in the Act Book (or elsewhere) of the renunciation.

Royal Free Chapel — See *Royal Peculiar*.

Royal Peculiar — A benefice, not necessarily a parish, but usually a royal chapel, to which the right of presentation (i.e., the appointment of the minister) is personally in the hands of the Sovereign. Such Royal Peculiars are totally outside the jurisdiction of the diocese in which they lie and were generally testamentary Peculiars.

See — The seat of the power or authority of a bishop (or archbishop); the diocesan center; hence, the rank, office, power, etc., of a bishop. (See also *Diocese*).

Sentences — A final judgment, determination and opinion. Disputed Wills, after trial by the appropriate court were entered by Sentence. There seems to have been many kinds of disputes, some trivial but others of importance. In the diocesan courts there may have been Wills proved or entered after a Sentence had been pronounced, and such cases, if properly recorded, might be found in the Bishop's and Archdeacon's Act Books, Court Books and Registers. Many Wills (together with the Sentences) are registered in the Prerogative Court of Canterbury, London, though the proceedings of the court may be filed at the Public Record Office, London, or elsewhere. (See also *Decree*).

Special Probate — Concerning grants of probate made in cases where special problems have arisen.

Surrogate — One who is substituted for another; in ecclesiastical matters (such as proving of Wills, granting of Letters of Administration, or in issuing marriage licenses), a surrogate is a deputy appointed by the ecclesiastical court to act for that ecclesiastical authority. A surrogate was often the local parish minister, appointed to deal locally wih testamentary and other matters.

Tenant — One who holds or possesses real estate by right; one who has the occupation of lands or tenements of another. (See also *Copyhold, Manor*).

Tenure — The act or right of holding real estate.

Testamentary Bond — A bond required of the executor(s) obliging him well and truly to execute the Will.

Testamentary Peculiar — A Peculiar may and usually does consist of more than one parish. A Manor consists of a part or all of a parish or several parishes. When a parish or a manor had jurisdiction over the grant of probate or Letters of Administration within itself, it is referred to as a Peculiar or Testamentary Peculiar.

Testamentary Suits — Records of disputes concerning probate records.

Testaments — see *Wills*.

Testator — A man who has made his last Will and Testament. A testatrix is a woman.

Tuition — Guardianship over orphaned minors who are under the age of fifteen (male) or thirteen (female).

Unproved Wills — Occasionally called Unprobated Wills. Wills that for some reason have never been proved. Some courts have unproved (unprobated) Wills, i.e., those for which no grant has been given and therefore have not passed the seal of the court. At York some of these are called "Re-infecta" Wills. An Unregistered Will is not necessarily an unprobated Will. An Unregistered Will usually has been proved, but not entered into a register of copy Wills.

Unregistered Wills — Wills that have been proved but not entered into a volume of copy or Registered Wills at the probate court, either because the executor(s) was not disposed to pay fees for registering, or because the probate court did not maintain registered copies at that period of time. This does not make the Will less valid, but in some cases makes it more difficult to find.

Vacancy — A break in the official business of a probate court caused by the death or resignation of the chief Official. During such a vacancy (that is, until a new Official was appointed) the court might be closed and the business carried on in another court. However, in many courts the business continued during a vacancy. (See *Chasm, Hiatus, Inhibited*).

Visitation — The official visit by an ecclesiastical dignitary or official of a higher court to a lower (or minor) court. For example, the visit of a bishop to an archdeacon's court. (See *Inhibited*).

Will — A written statement by which a person regulates the disposition of property and rights after his death. "Will" is a general term sometimes referred to as a "Last Will and Testament." However, anciently a Will set out the deceased's wishes in regard to his real property, whereas a Testament applies only to the disposition of *personalty* (which see). Wills are referred to as Registered Wills, Unregistered Wills, Copy Wills, Original Wills, Registers of Copy Wills, Testamentary Records, etc., all terms found in various courts. There are also Wills referred to as Administration-with-Will-annexed. Wills are also called — in some places — Testaments. There are also *Nuncupative Wills, Holograph Wills,* and *Unproved Wills* (which see).

Yeoman — Anciently a servant or attendant in a royal or noble household; technically, a person possessing freehold land worth 40/- (forty shillings) a year or more, qualified to serve on juries, to elect members of parliament from the shire, etc. Generally used to denote small landowners (freeholders) not of the rank of "gentleman;" tenant farmers; persons engaged in agriculture above the status of a laborer; hence vaguely, a commoner or countryman of respectable standing, especially one who cultivates his own land. [There are other definitions, such as Yeoman of the Guard, Yeoman of Signals, etc.] B. G. Bouwens in *Wills and their whereabouts* explains on page 77 what, in his opinion, are the meanings attached to "Yeoman."

ABBREVIATIONS.

The following is a list of some of the abbreviations appearing in the manuscript, printed, and microfilmed copies of probate records:

A.	Account(s)
A., Ad, Adcon., Adm., Admin., Admon., Adon., Admcon.	Administration(s)
Admr., Adminr.	Administrator(s)
A.T., A.W., Ad.w.T., Ad.w.W., Ad.-cu-T., Ad.-cu-W.,	Administration with Will Annexed
A.W.C.	Admon. with will and codicil annexed
Ad. Act. Book Admon. Act. Book	Administration Act. Book
Ad.b.n.c.-T.	Admon. (de) bonis non administratis cum-Testamentum (Admon. of goods unadministered with Will annexed) (See d.b.n.)
Bon. Not.	Bona Notabilia, a Latin term meaning "considerable goods." (See definition under Terminology earlier.)
B.M. Brit. Mus.	British Museum
Bt., Bart.	Baronet
C.	Accounts
C., C's.	Codicil(s)
Cal., Calrs.	Calendar(s)
Cath:	Cathedral (church)
Cons.	Consistory
C.D.C.	Codicil ("rare")
Comm.	Commissary
C. P. C.	Prerogative Court of Canterbury, London
Cur.	Curation, Curator
D.	Decree; Dean
D. & C.	Dean and Chapter (or Canons)
d.b.n.	de bonis non administratis ("of goods unadministered by.")
dec.. decd.	deceased.
d.m.	during minority of

D.R.	Diocesan Registry
Ecc.	Ecclesiastical
e.g.	exempli gratia (Latin for "for example")
E.I. E.I.C.	East India Company
Ex. Exors. Exex., Extrix	Executor(s), executrix
Esq., Esqre.	Esquire
Exted.	Executed
Gent.	Gentleman
Guard:	Guardian; guardianship
H.E.I.C.	Honourable East India Company
H.M.S.	Her (or His) Majesty's Ship
i.e.	id est (Latin for "that is")
Ind.	Index; indexes, indices
Ind. dec.	Interlocutory decree
I., Inv.	Inventory, inventories
Jr.	Junior
Jur.	Juratus (sworn)
Kt., Knt.	Knight
L., Ld., L.P., Lim. Prob. Ltd. Prob.	Limited probate
Mcht., Mht., Mt.	Merchant(man)
Mr.	Mister
Mrs.	Mistress (see page 31)
N.E.	No executor (named in will)
N.B.	North Britain (Scotland)
N.B. n.b.	nota bene (Latin for "note well")
Nunc.	Nuncupative will
P.A.B.	Probate Act Book
P.C. C.	Prerogative Court of Canterbury, London
P.C.Y.	Prerogative Court of York
Pec.	Peculiar
P.P.R.	Principal Probate Registry, London
P., Pd., Pr., Prob.	Probate; probate act; proved
P.r.	Power reserved of making a like grant to

Prerog., P'rog.	Prerogative (e.g., Prerogative Court of York)
P.R.O.	Public Record Office, London
Preb.	Prebend, prebendary
Pts.	Foreign parts; parts overseas; parts beyond the seas; (i.e., died outside of the British Isles)
Quoad bona	An expression (term) found in Lichfield Calendars indicating the deceased was resident outside of the jurisdiction of the court.
Reg., Regd., Rd.	Registered
Ren:	Renounced, renunciation
r., rp., rpt.	Respite(d). (See pgs 66)
S., Sent.	Sentence
Ser.	Serviceman (Army, but usually in the Navy — do not confuse "Ser." with "Sir").

Sr., Senr.	Senior
Tests. T., Test.,	Testament(s)
T.Ad.,T.W., T.-cu-ad., T.-cum-ad.	Admon.-with-Will-annexed
t.a.i.	Tanquam ab intestato i.e., "as of an intestate")
Tui., Tuon.	Tuition(s)
Vacat.	Vacancy
Vid., Vidua.	Widow
Vide	Latin for see
Vis., Visit.	Visitation
Wid.	Widow
W'.	Will
W.Ad., W.A., W.- cu(m)-Ad.	Admon.-with-Will-annexed
W.D.	Will dated.
W.P.	Will proved
Yeo.	Yeoman
Y.P.C.	Prerogative Court of York

Probate Jurisdiction.

With the exception of a few manorial and honor courts, probate jurisdiction, until January, 1858, was held in *ecclesiastical* courts. The geographical areas covered by these courts did not necessarily conform to any of the boundaries of the civil divisions of the country, although in some instances, they did bear the names of existing towns, cities and counties.

As the areas covered by probate courts was based on the various types of ecclesiastical divisions, it is obvious that a study of these ecclesiastical divisions is essential to an understanding of probate jurisdiction.

The five types of areas or divisions of the Church of England are:

Parishes: Ecclesiastically, a parish is a district served by a clergyman of the Established Church of England, known, in addition to other titles, either as the Vicar or the Rector of his parish.

Certain parishes and places that were exempt from the immediate control of the rural deans, archdeacons, bishops and sometimes archbishops were classed as being in or having peculiar jurisdiction.

Although geographically located within a county, ecclesiastically, the parish is part of the Church of England's divisions of rural deaneries.

Rural Deaneries: A rural deanery is an area consisting of a number
of ecclesiastical parishes headed by a rural dean, who is usually
one of the parish ministers within that deanery.[2] The number
of parishes in a deanery varies, although the smaller deaneries
usually have about twelve parishes.

When Bishop's Transcripts, Marriage Licenses, Probate
Records and other diocesan and archdeaconry records are filed
in order of "deaneries," the value of knowing the name of
the deanery is obvious.

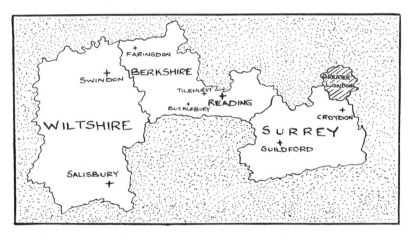

Map Illustrating Probate Jurisdictions.

Bucklebury and Tilehurst are two of many parishes in Berkshire,
and Reading is a borough comprising three parishes in the same county.
They are all in the Archdeaconry of Berks., Diocese of Salisbury.

Great Farringdon is a parish in Berkshire, but was within the
Peculiar jurisdiction of Farringdon, formerly a Prebend in Salisbury
Cathedral.

Swindon is a parish in Wiltshire, in the Archdeaconry of Wilts.,
Diocese of Salisbury.

Salisbury is a city in Wiltshire, comprising three parishes in the
Peculiar jurisdiction of the Sub-dean of Salisbury Cathedral, and the
Cathedral Close in the Peculiar jurisdiction of the Dean of Salisbury.

Guildford was a borough consisting of several parishes in Surrey,
in the Archdeaconry of Surrey, Diocese of Winchester.

Croydon is a parish in Surrey, in the Peculiar jurisdiction of the
Archbishop of Canterbury in the Peculiar Deanery of Croydon.

All the above counties are in the Province of Canterbury.

---

2. Except, until peculiar jurisdictions were abolished, for those parishes which
were known as *exempt* or *peculiar* jurisdictions.

Rural Deaneries (*continued*)

The head of the Chapter in a cathedral church of the diocese also is known as a Dean, but such an office should not be confused with that of a "rural dean." In certain dioceses, the Dean and other cathedral officials had probate jurisdiction in many parishes that were of peculiar jurisdiction.

Archdeaconries: An archdeaconry is an area consisting of a number of a number of rural deaneries (with their parishes[2]) and is headed by an archdeacon, who, if he has an office, conducts his business in the Archdeacon's Registry. Anciently in some dioceses, (notably in Wales) the bishops, for long periods, failed to appoint archdeacons, the vacant office being held by the bishop.

Dioceses: A diocese is an area or district over which a bishop has authority and consists of one or more archdeaconries (with their rural deaneries and parishes). It is also known as a *bishopric* or *see,* being the seat of power or authority of a bishop, who sometimes is referred to as the *Ordinary*.

As head of the diocese, the bishop (in Latin-*Episcopus*) has a court and this court is consequently known as the Epis-copal Court, having ecclesiastical jurisdiction over the whole diocese except for those places having *peculiar* exemption. The chief office of administration is the diocesan office or diocesan registry, and this office is usually situated in the Cathedral City, the chief city of the diocese.

Each diocese has a cathedral church, attached to which are certain clergymen who are officials. Anciently, until such courts were abolished, some of these officials had courts with peculiar jurisdiction, principally in matters of probate.

Provinces: A province is a large area over which an archbishop has authority and consists of a number of dioceses. A province is also known as an *archdiocese* or *see,* and the archbishop is sometimes referred to as the *Ordinary*. There are three prov-inces, namely:

i. The Province of Canterbury, comprising those dioceses that include the midland and southern counties of Eng-land, the Channel Islands, and, until 1920, the dioceses covering the counties of Wales.[3] (See map on page 38.) It is headed by The Most Reverend and Right Honour-able The Lord Archbishop of Canterbury, Primate of All England and Metropolitan, who claims superior jurisdic-tion throughout the whole country. His palace is at

---

3. A few parishes in North Wales at one time were in the Diocese of Chester, Province of York.

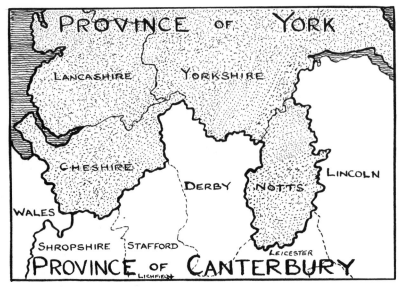

Map showing the counties adjacent to the boundary between the
Province of Canterbury and the Province of York.

Lambeth, London, where there is an excellent library and
an extensive archive. His principal offices, including the
Faculty Office, and the office of his Vicar-General, are
in Westminster, London.

It should be noted that the Archbishop is also head
of the Diocese of Canterbury with a Diocesan Office in
the City of Canterbury, Kent. It should be understood
that the archdiocesan (i.e., archbishop's) records were
kept in London and that they are separate and distinct
from diocesan (including the Episcopal Consistory and
Archdeaconry) records kept at Canterbury, Kent, and
elsewhere.

ii. The Province of York, comprising the dioceses covering
the northern counties of England[4] (see map on page 38),
and on the Isle of Man, is headed by The Most Reverend
and Right Honourable The Lord Archbishop of York,
Primate of England and Metropolitan. He is also head
of the Diocese of York. The principal offices are in the
City of York.

iii. The Province of Wales was created in 1920, prior to
which time the Welsh Dioceses were in the Province of
Canterbury.[4]

---

4. See footnote 3.

The degrees of ecclesiastical authority are as follows:

Jurisdiction.	Church Official.
PROVINCE	ARCHBISHOP
DIOCESE	BISHOP
ARCHDEACONRY	ARCHDEACON
RURAL DEANERY	RURAL DEAN
PARISH	PARISH MINISTER

In addition to the above degrees of authority, the arch-bishops, bishops, and archdeacons appointed various cathedral and other officials, deputies, etc., some of whom had certain rights in granting probate, issuing marriage licenses, etc.

A *Jurisdiction* is the district over which a court claimed the right to grant probate or Letters of Administration. Such right was often subject to a variety of limitations or local exceptions. The course of action concerning estates generally was:

i. If the estate was solely within a Testamentary Peculiar, that Peculiar Court usually made the grant.

ii. If solely within an Archdeaconry exercising testamentary juris-diction, (and some Archdeacons did not), then that Arch-deaconry Court usually made the grant.

iii. If within two or more (i.e., diverse) jurisdictions within the *same* diocese, then the grant would usually be found in the Episcopal (i.e., Bishop's) Court.

iv. If within two or more (i.e., diverse) jurisdictions within the *same* province, then the grant would usually be found in the Prerogative Court of the Archbishop.

v. If within diverse dioceses or peculiars within *both* provinces, then the Prerogative Court of Canterbury, London, claimed superior jurisdiction. The Prerogative Court of Canterbury (usually abbreviated to P.C.C.), also claimed jurisdiction over the English and Welsh estates of many persons who died out-side of the country. This not only included those who died at sea or overseas (including sailors and soldiers), but also Scottish, Irish, and foreign born persons who died possessing property in England and Wales (including the Channel Is-lands and the Isle of Man). There are, however, similar rec-ords filed with the Prerogative Court of York (usually abbrevi-ated P.C.Y.), and a few are also to be found in the minor, i.e., lower, courts.

vi. Exceptions did occur to these rules, however. There are, to name but a few, Bishop's (Episcopal) Courts that claimed jurisdiction over the estates of certain clergymen, of noblemen, and of others, and also in certain cases of litigation. There were courts that claimed jurisdiction during Inhibition and Vacancies, and occasionally grants are found in courts that claimed unusual rights, or where the next-of-kin found that one court was personally more convenient than another.

Probate jurisdiction followed the areas of ecclesiastical division as the following details show:

PECULIARS.

The smallest probate divisions were *certain* parishes, known as *Peculiars,* where the parish minister or some other ecclesiastical officer, or in certain cases, the Manorial Court had, for ages past, the peculiar right of granting probate when the deceased had property solely within the area of that *peculiar* jurisdiction.

One of the greatest difficulties which the genealogist encounters arises from the possibility that the Will of a testator, whom he wishes to trace, may have been proved in a Peculiar, and his inability to discover the whereabouts of the records belonging to the particular court.[5]

Prior to 1846, Peculiars existed in most dioceses, and in some dioceses were numerous. Holdsworth, in *A History of English Law,* Vol. 1, page 600, states "Some of these Peculiars where wholly exempt from Episcopal and even from Archiepiscopal control." Many of these small courts ceased to function many years before 1858, when the civil High Court of Justice took over the probate jurisdiction, and some of the records have been lost or their places of deposit are unknown.

There are a variety of Peculiar Courts, namely:

1. *Peculiar Jurisdiction Limited to one parish or several nearby parishes.*

Peculiar jurisdiction, in some cases, was limited to one parish, as was the case of the Peculiar Court of Good Easter, Essex, where the parish minister had the right to grant probate in that parish only. In other cases, such as that of the Peculiar

---

5. See "The Testamentary Documents of Yorks. Peculiars" (Yorks. Archael. Soc. — Record Series, — 1929), Vol. 74, pp. 46, 66, 86. [YORKS 7. Vol. 74], Also "The Churchwardens Presentments in the Oxford Peculiars" (Oxford Rec. Soc. 1928), Vol. 10, pp. vii to xi. [OXON: 2, Vol. 10].

Court of Sturminster Marshall, Dorset, jurisdiction included that parish and the nearby parishes of Corfe Mullen, Ham' worthy, and Lychet Minster.

2. Peculiar Jurisdiction covering widely separated parishes

Some Peculiars involved widely separated places in different counties. An example of this is the Peculiar Court of the Dean and Chapter of St. Paul's Cathedral, London, that had jurisdiction in several places in the City of London, and over certain parishes in the counties of Middlesex, Essex, and Hertford.

3. Peculiar Jurisdiction covering part of a parish only.

It appears that parishes containing several townships might be in more than one jurisdiction. This, however, is probably rare. The parish of Topcliffe, Yorks., is in the Archdeaconry and Diocese of York, and is *not* a Peculiar. The chapelry of Dishforth, which is a township in the parish of Topcliffe, is in the Peculiar Jurisdiction of the Dean and Chapter of York.

4. Variety of Titles for Peculiar Courts.

Many Peculiar Courts have titles relating to dignitaries of the Church of England, such as Archbishop and Bishop; and others to cathedral and other officials, such as Dean and Chapter, Dean, Sub-Dean, Prebend, Chancellor, Precentor, and Succentor; and still others to Rector and Vicar. The 1832 *Report of the Ecclesiastical Commissioners* states, "There are Peculiars of various descriptions . . . Royal, Archiepiscopal [Archbishop], Episcopal [Bishops], Decanal [Deans], Sub' decanal [Sub-deans], Prebendal, Rectorial and Vicarial; and there are some Manorial Courts."

5. Anomalous Nature of Peculiar Jurisdictions.

Sometimes it is difficult to find the actual records, and in connection with problems associated with Peculiars, B. G. Bouwens explains in *Wills and Their Whereabouts*:

> It will be noticed that the same place appears in the jurisdiction of several Peculiars — indeed one whole Peculiar is included in the jurisdiction of another. Perhaps in some cases a parish or place lies within two Peculiar jurisdictions and is quoted in both. Common ownership of several Peculiars grouped in one Court may explain other cases. (Page 75.)

The 1832 *Report* (above) mentions that "There were some [Peculiars] of so anomalous a nature as scarcely to admit of accurate description."

6. *Manorial Courts having Peculiar Jurisdiction.*

Sometimes a manor court would possess the privilege of probate of Wills and grants of Letters of Administration, if the property of the deceased was solely within that jurisdiction. It would thus be a testamentary Peculiar, but not all manors possessed this privilege. The probate records of residents of parishes that were in the Peculiar jurisdiction of Manorial Courts are available, if they were transferred from the Manor, in the probate registries or record offices. There were many that were not surrendered, like those in the Manor of Wester-dale, parish of Stokesley, Yorkshire, where some of the probates 1550-1575, are engrossed upon the manor court rolls.[6]

7. *Colleges with Courts of Peculiar Jurisdiction.*

Certain universities and colleges exercised Peculiar jurisdiction. At Oxford University, the "Chancellor's jurisdiction applied to all Members of the University and to all who were engaged in their service. In process of time . . . persons of several other descriptions became entitled to partake of the privileges of the University."[7] At Cambridge University, the "Vice-Chancellor's Court . . . had the supervision of the Wills, not only of actual members of the University, but also of the various townsmen, college-servants, tradesmen, etc.[8]

The Ledger Books among the muniments of King's College, Cambridge, a Royal Peculiar, contain enrolled probates of those who died in the precincts.[9] Eton College, Buckingham-shire, also has records testamentary.[10]

---

6. See "The Manorial Peculiar of Westerdale" and "The Manorial Peculiar of Batley," (Yorks. Archael. Soc. — Record Series, 1929), Vol. 74, pp. 46, 66, 86. [YORKS. 7., Vol. 74.].

7. An *Index to Wills* . . . *University of Oxford, 1436-1814*, (1862). [OXON. 7].

8. *Alumni Cantabrigienses,* (Cambridge, 1922), Pt. 1, Vol. 1, p. xiv. [CAMBS C. lc., Pt. 1, Vol. 1]. See also *Wills Proved in the Vice-Chancellor's Court, Cambridge,* 1501-1765. (Cambridge: 1907).

9. "The Muniments of King's College," in *Proc. Cambridge. Antiquarian Soc.,* 1933, Vol. 33, p. 94. [CAMBS. PUB. C. Vol. 33].

10. "Notes concerning records of Eton College," *Genealogists' Magazine,* (London), Vol. 5, p. 38. [ENG. PUB. V, Vol. 5].

8. Cities and Towns with Courts of Peculiar Jurisdiction.

The Court of Husting of the City of London, and the Court of the Mayor of Exeter, Devonshire, are courts that were exempt from the jurisdiction of the Ordinary (i.e., the bishop or archbishop). Similar records in other cities, and towns (boroughs), might be determined by a study of the history and records of the places concerned.

How is it possible to determine whether or not a place or parish is within Peculiar Jurisdiction?

It is best to use Lewis' *Topographical Dictionary of England,* (1831 and 1833 editions only), and *Topographical Dictionary of Wales* (1833 edition only), and find the reference to the place or parish. Generally the ecclesiastical jurisdiction given mentions whether or not it is within Peculiar jurisdiction. There are places, however, for which it may be difficult to determine the actual jurisdiction, such as extra-parochial liberties, etc., but these are rare. If Lewis states that a place is within a certain parish (without stating the jurisdiction), reference must then be made to that parish. Having found that a Peculiar jurisdiction is involved, it is then necessary to refer to Bouwen's *Wills and Their Whereabouts,* pages 79-86, in which is listed an "Index of Parishes and Townships" that includes most peculiars. This listing *does not include* the "Sarum Peculiars." Mr. Bouwen states on Page 61, "In the General Index of Sarum Peculiars is a list of parishes in the various [Sarum] jurisdictions. As it totals some 650 parishes it is not reproduced [by Mr. Bouwen] *in toto.*" This General Index for Sarum is now at the County Record Office, Trowbridge, Wiltshire. Sarum is the Latin name for Salisbury Diocese.

If the Peculiar Court does not have record of the grant, what is the next step?

As already stated, the Peculiar Court usually made the grant if the property was *solely* within that Peculiar jurisdiction. Some Peculiars were, however, from time to time, Inhibited and undoubtedly Vacancies occurred. During such times some Peculiar courts were closed. Details of the Inhibitions are given in *Wills and Their Whereabouts,* under the name of the court concerned.

If the deceased possessed property within a Peculiar and *elsewhere,* the Episcopal (Bishop's) court sometimes claimed jurisdiction, but usually the Prerogative Courts of the Arch-bishops claimed superior jurisdiction. When the records of a Peculiar court fail to disclose the grant, it might be wise to search the Episcopal Court, and failing that, the Prerogative Courts concerned. Although the deceased resided and died within a Peculiar, his property might have been *solely* within a nearby archdeaconry, and the grant might be found in that court.

Many Peculiar Courts ceased to function long before 1858, and it would seem that when such a court ceased, or was abolished, the parishes involved were incorporated within and became subject to the jurisdiction of the archdeaconry and diocese in which they were geographically situated.

COURTS OF THE ARCHDEACONS, BISHOPS, AND ARCHBISHOPS.

As already detailed under Jurisdiction on page 39, the course of action on the part of executors or next-of-kin gener-ally was determined by the location of the deceased's estate. Genealogists rarely know where the property of the deceased was located, therefore it is necessary to proceed as follows:

To Find the Ecclesiastical Jurisdiction.

Lewis' *Topographical Dictionary*[11] (1831 and 1833 Edi-tions only), under the name of each *parish,* except for Peculiars, gives the names of the archdeaconry and diocese within which each parish was situated prior to 1831 and 1833.

In Chapter 9, "The Counties of England and Wales," under each county, the names of all archdeaconries and dioceses having jurisdiction within that county are listed, including the name of the province in which it is situated.

To Find the Names of the Probate Courts.

In Chapter 9, "The Counties of England and Wales," under each county, the names of all probate courts (except Peculiars) used in that county are listed. The probates for

---

11. There are other publications that list parishes and their ecclesiastical juris-dictions, but, if the date of publication is later than 1858, jurisdictions may be given that do not apply to the pre-1858 testamentary jurisdictions.

those persons of small estates are usually found in the court of the lowest jurisdiction for the parish concerned, where, according to B. G. Bouwen "probably it involved less trouble."

The Court of the Archdeacons.

If the estate was *solely* within an archdeaconry, and if that archdeaconry exercised testamentary jurisdiction, it was customary for the grant to be made in the Court of the Archdeaconry. Some archdeaconries did not exercise testa-mentary jurisdiction, in which case the bishop of the diocese claimed jurisdiction, and grants will be found in the bishop's court. Note the following two examples:

i. If the deceased had residential connections with a parish or parishes in the Archdeaconry of Bedford, Diocese of Lincoln, it would be expected that a grant of probate would be found in the court of the Archdeaconry of Bedford.

Reference to the article for Bedfordshire in Chapter 9, under the category "Probate Records," will disclose that there was an Archdeaconry Court of Bedford exercising testamentary jurisdiction. The place of deposit of the records and details of any publications dealing with them are also mentioned.

ii. If the residential connections were in the Archdeaconry of Derby, Diocese of Lichfield and Coventry, reference to the article for Derbyshire in Chapter 9, under the category "Probate Records," will disclose *no mention* of a court named the Arch-deaconry Court of Derby, simply because that archdeaconry did *not* exercise testamentary jurisdiction. In the case of the Archdeaconry of Derby, the court of the bishop of the diocese, known as the Episcopal Consistory Court of Lichfield, exercised testamentary jurisdiction.

The Courts of the Bishops.

If an estate was in more than one archdeaconry, but *solely* within the same diocese, then the bishop's court, having jurisdiction over the whole diocese, normally would grant probate. In some dioceses, the bishop usually claimed powers of probate over the goods of all noblemen, gentlemen-at-arms, rectors, vicars, and the whole clergy within the diocese. According to J. C. C. Smith, ". . . a bishop claimed the exclusive right to issue a grant in cases where the deceased person had goods ["*bona*"] in divers archdeaconries or juris-dictions within his diocese . . . [but] as was inevitable, the bishop was apt to encroach upon the testamentary authority of his archdeacons . . ."[12] It is possible that the bishop was also apt to encroach upon the testamentary authority of other minor and Peculiar courts.

The Courts of the Archbishops.

If the estate was in more than one diocese or peculiar jurisdiction, but *solely* within the same province, then the archbishop's prerogative court, having jurisdiction over the whole province concerned, normally would grant probate.

If parts of the estate were in both provinces, or the deceased died overseas, then the Prerogative Court of Canterbury, London, claimed superior jurisdiction, and many such grants are to be found in the P. C. C. Despite this claim, however, there are a number of grants in the P. C. Y. relating to persons with estates in the Province of Canterbury and also who died overseas, presumably because the deceased had some goods within the Province of York.

The grants of probate for those of wealth are often found in the higher jurisdictions, where, according to B. G. Bouwen, ". . . but from early days people of property largely went to the prerogative courts, both as having greater weight and better care of their records in case of later dispute."

*   *   *   *   *

There is little doubt that the study of probate records is complex, and yet, with an understanding of the problems of jurisdiction, the subject can be mastered, at least to a degree where the records can be located.

It should not be thought that the standards and rules governing them are without exceptions, however. The researcher may fail to find record of a Will although it is definitely known that such a document existed and was probated in the normal manner. In the vast majority of cases, it will be possible to locate the Will in the process of determining the areas of jurisdiction and searching the records of all the courts in which the Will, in the normal run of events, could have been proven. The exception to the rule of jurisdiction is noted in the following example.

12. J. C. C. Smith, "Introduction," *Index of Wills* . . . P.C.C. (British Rec. Soc., 1893), Vol. 10. [Eng. Pub. AB. Vol. 10].

Thomas Turpin died in Eaton Bray, Bedfordshire, in 1665. From other sources it was thought that he possessed property in Eaton Bray and Edlesborough, Buckinghamshire. Eaton Bray was within the jurisdiction of the Archdeaconry Court of Bedford, while Edlesborough was within the jurisdiction of the Archdeaconry Court of Buckingham. The probate rule or standard regarding such a circumstance states that if an estate came within two archdeaconries, and those archdeaconries are within the same diocese, as in this case, then probate should have been granted in the Court of the Bishop of that diocese. In this example, the Archdeaconry Court of Bedford and the Archdeaconry Court of Buckingham came under the higher jurisdiction of the Episcopal Consistory Court of Lincoln. No record was found of any probate granted to Thomas Turpin in this court, however. It was found in the records of the Archdeaconry Court of Bedford, a court with authority inferior to that of the Episcopal Court, where the Will should have been proved, if the rules and standards of probate jurisdiction had been followed. Just why probate was granted in a lower court can only be surmized, but this example does prove that there are exceptions even to a genealogical rule.

An understanding of the problems of probate jurisdiction will make it obvious that searches for Wills and Admons. cannot be restricted to one particular court. A genealogist must be prepared to search the local courts, then consider the higher courts governing that area, and then, even take into consideration the very real possibility that the record may be found in some court not connected in any apparent way with the locality at which the deceased was known to have resided.

Probates Granted by Rural Deans.

Strictly speaking, the rural deans did not have their own probate courts. In some dioceses, however, it was customary for the rural deans to grant probate or Letters of Administration, but they were acting by virtue of a commission from either the archdeacon's or bishop's courts. After making a grant, the rural dean would transmit the documents to the court for which he was acting.

It is not necessary to find the name of the rural deanery concerned unless the records of the probate court are filed in order of rural deanery. Note the following two examples:

    i. The rural deans within the Archdeaconry of Chester, acting for the Episcopal Consistory Court of the Diocese of Chester, granted probates. As the records of this court *are not filed in deanery order,* it is not necessary to know the names of the rural deaneries.

ii. The rural deans within the Archdeaconry of Richmond, Diocese of Chester, acting for the Consistory Court of the Commissary of the Archdeaconry of Richmond, granted probates. This archdeaconry consisted of eight rural deaneries, the records of five of them being filed according to rural deanery and kept at one registry, and the records of the other three kept at another registry. It is, therefore, necessary to learn the names of the rural deaneries covering the parishes involved.

When the records are filed in rural deanery order, the probate court involved may, and usually does, have a "Deanery Book" stating the names of the parishes and the rural deanery in which each parish is situated.

Inhibitions and Vacancies.

At various times, usually during a Visitation by a superior ecclesiastical dignitary, a probate court might be inhibited, that is, closed, for several months and the business conducted in another and usually superior probate court. During a Vacancy caused by the death, deprivation or resignation of the ecclesiastical head of a jurisdiction, another court might assume control. This means that during Inhibition or Vacancy, probates were granted in another court. In many courts, however, the business continued as the officials of the inhibited or vacant court carried on the business by commission.

Some courts, such as that of the Bishop of Durham, are said to have never been inhibited, but both the Prerogative Court and the Exchequer Court of York were closed during a vacancy in the See, and all grants were made in the Court of the Dean and Chapter of York.

In former times, when the Archbishop of Canterbury died, the jurisdiction of his Prerogative Court of Canterbury and Episcopal Consistory Court of Canterbury passed to the Court of the Prior (or Dean) and Chapter of Canterbury until the Vacancy was filled. In later times, the P. C. C. was never closed, as the court officials carried on the business and the Dean and Chapter of Canterbury exercised only *pro forma,* that is, matter of form, jurisdiction.

Although differences in the handling and naming of the records occur from court to court, all courts were governed by the same statutes. As the right to transfer property goes back to ancient times, the intricacies of the various laws relating to the disposal of a deceased person's possessions is of legal rather than genealogical concern, although a knowledge of probate custom is of genealogical value.[13]

Until 1837, a Will could be made by males over the age of fourteen years, and females over the age of twelve. The Act of 1837 provided that no valid Will could be made by any person under the age of twenty-one years.[14] Until the Married Woman's Property Act of 1882, a married woman could not (with few exceptions) make a Will without her husband's consent.[15] According to English Law, the freehold property of the wife belonged to her husband and herself and the personal property passed absolutely to the husband, and certain other types of property (such as leaseholds) usually passed to the husband. After the death of her husband, the widow was permitted to make a Will.

PROBATE TECHNICALITIES.

The dates used in the Calendars (or Indexes) of probate records refer to the dates of the *grants* of probate or Letters of Administration, and *not* to the dates the Wills were *made*

---

13. For additional information see: Burns: *Ecclesiastical Law*, "Wills," (1842), also C. W. Foster: *Lincoln Wills 1505-1530*. (Horncastle: Lincoln Record Society: 1918), X, ix-xxv. and read the Introduction for information on Wills and Testaments and their connection with land, tenements, and chattels. [LINCS. 1. vol 10]. Also: J. E. Auden: "The Local Peculiar Courts of Shropshire," in the *Trans. of the Shrops. Archael. Soc.* (1929-1930) 4th Series, Vol. XII, pp. 273-325. [SHROPS. PUB. A. vol. 45]. Also: *Encyclopaedia Britannica* (*1895 and later edd.*); also read introductions and prefaces and articles found in numerous publications on probate records in magazines and books issued by genealogy, history, antiquary, archaeology and other learned societies.

14. A Will made 6 Jan 1837 and proved 2 July 1840 described Thomas Harrison of Bury, Lancs., as aged 19 years when he died 7 January 1837. It is not known whether the grant of 1840 ignored the Act or whether because the Will was made at an earlier date was considered.

15. The Will of Mrs. Mildred Gale (grandmother of George Washington) is an example of a married woman making a Will. (See illustrations on page 79.) When a marriage was considered by a spinster or a widow possessing (or likely to possess) property in her own right, she might have made an indenture (or articles of agreement or marriage settlement) concerning the right to dispose of such property. Probably as a married woman she might alter or cancel such an agreement or make a new one, if her husband was willing, concerning changes in her personal property holdings. If during her coverture (i.e., while married to her husband) she died, her widower or other interested parties would apply to the probate court for a grant *limited* so far only as concerned all rights, titles, interests, profits, monies, jewelry, stocks, securities and other properties of which she, by the articles of agreement, had a right to dispose. See also later in Chapter 5 concerning "Limited and Special Probate Records."

or the dates on which testators or intestates died. A Will usually was proved within a short time after the death of a testator, and in the case of an intestate, Letters of Administration were granted, usually, shortly after the death of that intestate. Some probates were delayed for several years, however, and cases are on record where the probates were not granted for fifteen or more years after the death of the testator or the intestate.

There is no legal requirement that a testator mention all or any members of his family in his Will, either by relationship or by name. When the eldest son or other children are not mentioned, it may be that their portions were settled either before the Will was made or left to the judgment of the executors. A man, for instance, might bequeath all his property to his wife, allowing her the sole right to provide for the children. Local custom might influence the provisions written into the Will — custom required that the citizens of London bequeath one-third to the widow, one-third to the children, thus leaving one third at the disposal of the testator.

The probate record of an intestate (the Administration Bond) rarely mentions more than two bondsmen. One of these may be a member of the family of the intestate, such as his widow, the eldest son, or the nearest relative (i.e., the next-of-kin) whose name is recorded in the Act Book as the person to whom Letters of Administration were granted. Except in unusual cases, there is no recitation of all possible heirs, as it was the duty of the administrators of the property, having been duly sworn (at the time and place of the granting of Letters of Administration) to "well and faithfully administer." Administrations, therefore, do not have as great a genealogical value as Wills, but they should not be neglected. In some pedigree problems, Admons. are the very documents that provide the required evidence.

It seems that occasionally the principal creditor of a debtor attended court and obtained Letters of Administration in an effort to control the property of the deceased and secure payment of debts. In such cases, the next-of-kin might not be mentioned unless a Renunciation of the next-of-kin has been recorded. Executors named in a perfectly valid Will, as well as the next-of-kin, might renounce their rights of executing or administering the estate. There are many reasons for such renunciations and the matter of debts of the deceased is one of them.

There is no actual clue that would indicate whether or not the next-of-kin *would* prove a Will or apply for Letters of Administration. Some probate records relate to persons with very little property. There are cases where it would seem that property was disposed of by agreement before death, or the deceased was an annuitant or pensioner, whose income ceased at death, making application for a probate unnecessary.

It is suggested by Bouwens that in order to save time, trouble, and fees, the next-of-kin of persons with a small amount of property sometimes did not seek probate at all, "it being no one's business to interfere." He also writes, "This may explain puzzling cases where no record of a Will can be found in spite of almost complete certainty that one existed."[16] If there is reason to believe however, that the deceased was an individual of means, there may be many explanations why no probate record can be found as the following examples demonstrate:

1. When seeking to extend a pedigree, the searcher often has no intimation of the names of the parents and the surnames of the maternal grandparents, uncles, aunts, and other close relatives (including "in-laws") of the deceased. If an individual had an income from relatives and died during the lifetime of those relatives, there would be little need for a grant of probate. If the ancestor died during the lifetime of an executor, an administrator, or a trustee, who had been paying him, and perhaps his children, an income from an estate, his heirs may not apply for a probate. Some years later, however, when that executor, administrator, or trustee died, perhaps leaving a portion of the estate unadministered, the heirs to that property might apply for a further grant of probate in order to gain possession of the residue of the original estate. Such a grant might be recorded under either the name of the original owner of the estate or the name of the executor, administrator, or trustee, and as none of the surnames of these individuals would be known to the searcher, the record would be hidden from the normal pattern of searches.

2. Grants of probate and Letters of Administration sometimes are found recorded in courts that did not have jurisdiction

---

16. B. G. Bouwens, op. cit. p. 4.

over the place or places where the deceased was known to have usually resided. Sometimes it appears that the next-of-kin chose a court that was personally convenient, but in other cases it would seem that the deceased had property solely within that jurisdiction even though he resided elsewhere. The deceased may have changed his abode and the grant was given in a court that had jurisdiction of the area where he died. The reasons for finding probates in courts outside of the usual jurisdiction are many and varied, as the following examples demonstrate:

   i. Elizabeth Pickford of Great Portland Street (London), and late of the county of Hertford, was the widow of Matthew Pickford. She made her Will in 1828 and mentioned in it property in Hertfordshire and also the Pickford's carrying concern (that is, furniture moving) of London. Normally her Will would be found probated in one of the local courts of the County of Hertford, or in one of the Minor Courts of London, or in the Prerogative Court of Canterbury, also in London. The probate was actually granted at Chester, nearly two hundred miles from London and Hertfordshire. No explanation has been found why the probate was granted at Chester, but it is possible that the next-of-kin was living in the area covered by the particular court in which the Will was proved, and he found it more convenient to have the local official for the Court at Chester to take care of the business.

   ii. The Will of Ann Pease, widow, formerly of Ottery St. Mary, Devonshire, but late of Craddock Lodge, Cullompton, in the same county, was neither proved in the local Devonshire courts nor in the Prerogative Court of Canterbury in London, the courts where the record might be expected to be recorded. In 1853 it was proved in the Prerogative Court of York, hundreds of miles away. The Will gives no clue why this occurred, but it might be assumed that the next-of-kin was resident in the north of England and, for the sake of convenience,, arranged to prove the Will through the local official for the Prerogative Court of York.

   iii. Thomas Slack, a provision dealer of Macclesfield, Cheshire, died in 1857. It would be expected that his Will would be proved in one of the local courts for Cheshire, and failing that, either in the Prerogative Court of York or in the Prerogative Court of Canterbury, London. Actually the Will was proved in the Lichfield (Staffordshire) Consistory Court, as his estate was *solely within the diocese of Lichfield*.

Anciently, certain probate courts held a peculiar right to probate the Wills of persons who died within their jurisdiction. An example of this is the town of Bury St. Edmunds in County Suffolk, where, in early times, the Abbot had jurisdiction over the property of strangers (visitors) dying within the town.

Chapter 3

WILLS, ADMINISTRATIONS AND INVENTORIES

1. WILLS.

The Will and Testament, as already mentioned, gradually merged into a single document, often known as the "Last
Will and Testament." This "Last Will and Testament" is a
statement, usually written, by which a person stipulates the
manner in which, after his death, his property is to be disposed
and, in some case, the rights of others over the family are
detailed. In it there is usually named at least one executor (or
executrix) who, as soon as possible after the death of the
testator (or testatrix) arranged for the Will to be proved.
Occasionally, when one of the executors was a minor (i.e.,
under twenty-one years of age), the remaining executor(s)
went to a probate court and received a grant, which authorized
the under-age executor(s) to come, after reaching the age of
twenty-one years, and receive a like grant. If, at the time of
the death of the testator, one or more of the executors was
unavailable, the remaining executor(s) would go to court and
receive a grant, which gave authority to the absentee execu-
tor(s) to come, at a later date, and receive a like grant. If, at
the time of the original application for a grant of probate, all
the executors were minors, the court would grant Letters of
Administration (with-Will-annexed) to a tutor or curator
(i.e., a guardian) of the executors with authority to administer
the estate during the minority of the executors, but with power
reserved to the minors, when they were of age, to receive a like
grant. A subsequent grant of probate (to remaining executors)
is designated, in some courts, as a Double Probate. If no
executor is named, or the executor(s) renounced (i.e., declined
to act) or had died, the next-of-kin (or in rare cases, the
principal creditor) applied for Letters of Administration, in
which case the documents are sometimes given the name of
Administration-with-Will-annexed.[1]

1. An examination of many such Wills (i.e., Admon.-with-Will-annexed) shows
that in some courts Wills of this class are *not* copied into the Registers of
Wills, but are classed and filed with Administrations (Admons.). Some
common abbreviations used to indicate them are: W/Admons.; Ad:w:T.;
A.T.; T.w.A.; Ad.cu-T.; Ad.-cum.T.

While most Wills are written on paper, some are written on parchment. The amount of information given in a Will varies. There are some that contain a great deal of genealogical information—others contain comparatively little. The following example can be considered typical of the genealogical contents of a Will.

Example. Will of Joane Browne of Denby, Derbyshire, widow.

The place (or parish), Denby, is described as ". . . a parish . . . county Derby . . . [in the] archdeaconry of Derby, and diocese of Lichfield and Coventry.'[2] According to the article for Derbyshire in Chapter 9, the county of Derby (i.e., Derbyshire) is in the jurisdiction of the Episcopal Consistory Court of Lichfield [and Coventry], and the probate records of that court are kept at the Public Library, Lichfield, Staffs.

The Calendar for the probate court records that on 29 March 1706 the Will of Joan Browne of Denby, was proved.

The original Will (and attached documents) is a folded document contained in a file or bundle of Wills for the year 1706. The following are the items of interest abstracted from the Will:

Abstract of the Will. In the name of God Amen the 19th day of January Anno Dom 1705/6 . . . Joane Browne of Denby in the County of Derby Wid: . . . do make this my Last Will and Testament . . . Viz, first I bequeath my Soul into the hands of Almighty God my maker . . . and as for my body to be buried in Christian burial at the discretion of my Executor . . . Item I give unto my son Thomas Browne five pounds over and above what was given him by his father's Will . . . [and] bedsted and bedding belonging to said bed which said bed he useth to Lye in the Chamber over the house, . . .
my son Henry Brown the sum of five pounds, . . .
my daughter Hannah wife of William Ouldknowle the sum of five pounds, . . .
my daughter Mary wife of William Challener the sum of five pounds, . . .
my son Ellis Browne five pounds, . . .
my son Daniel Browne the sum of five pounds to be paid unto him when he shall come to the age of one and Twenty years.

---

2. Samuel Lewis, *A Topographical Dictionary of England,* op.cit. [1831 & 1833 editions only].

All the rest . . . to my son John Browne and make him sole
Executor . . . paying the said Legacies . . . and also Paying my
debts and funeral Expenses . . . declared to be the Last will &
Testament . . . Revockeing all others . . .

Joan Browne
X
her marke

Signed & Sealed in the
presence of us

Samuel Walker
John Searson.

[Proved at Derby] 12 Aprilis 1706.   Joh: Husband, Sur[rogate].

Inventory. A true inventory . . . of Widow Browne of Denby . . .
5 February 1705/6. [Includes items such as household goods,
farm stock and implements of husbandry, etc.]. Total value
£93.16s 6d.

PROBATE PROCEDURE.

The general practice seems to have been for the execu-
tor(s), after the death of the testator, to take either the Will,
or a notarized copy of it, to the appropriate court. When the
officials of the probate court approved the Will (that is,
probate was granted) the court passed a Probate Act. Details
of this action were recorded either in a book generally known
as a Probate Act Book, or at the end of the Will, and in a few
courts, in both places. In some courts, Acts Books were not
kept and those of a number of courts have been lost.

Some courts required the executor(s) to make a Testamen-
tary Bond, obliging him "well and truly to execute" the Will.
This bond is evidence that a probate act or grant was made,
even though that act or grant may not be entered in the customary manner at the end of the Will or in an Act Book.
An example of a Will with a Testamentary Bond is that of
Mrs. Mildred Gale whose husband, George Gale, signed a
Testamentary Bond for payment of his wife's debts and legacies.
(See pages 80, 81.) It was not common for a married woman
to make a Will, and it was only with the consent of her
husband that she was empowered to make it.

After the Will was approved, the original Will (or copy of
it) would then be officially sealed and handed to the execu-
tor(s) as evidence of probate, and a copy (or the original)

". . . to my sonne John one bedstedde . . ."

retained in the Probate Court. The Will (including its Probate Act recorded at the end of the Will) might then be copied into a volume of Registered Wills, the registers being kept by the court for future reference. A fee usually was charged for the copying and registering of a Will. As some persons did not wish to pay any extra fees to have the Will registered, some Wills were unregistered. Such Wills, usually known as "Unregistered Wills" are equally as valid as registered Wills, and should not be confused with Unprobated (i.e., unproved) Wills.

All Wills, both those original Wills for which copies were made in the Registers and the Unregistered Wills, were filed in bundles or boxes. Some original Wills may be found bound in books. Sometimes, especially in the earlier periods, the registered copy of the Will is the only surviving record, the filed Will having been lost. In other instances, when Registers have been lost, the bundles of original Wills only remain. These bundles or boxes of original Wills sometimes contain Unprobated (i.e., unproved) Wills, that for some reason or other have been deposited with the court, but have not been proved.

The importance of reading all documents that might have been kept at the probate court in connection with Wills that are registered is emphasized. Even though the Will is recorded in a Register, any documents associated with the Will will not have been copied into the Registers. The original filed copy of the Will (if still existing) might be filed with such documents as Testamentary Bonds, Administration Bonds (with-Will-annexed), Inventories, Bonds of Tuition and Cura- tion (i.e., guardianship) and occasionally with Accounts, Re- nunciations, Deeds and Letters. These important papers may be attached to the Will, or they may have become separated from it, although present in the same bundle or box, or they may have been filed elsewhere or entirely lost.

Probate Searches.

When searching for record of a Will, it is usual to find reference to it in both a Calendar (or Index) and a Probate Act Book, as will be explained later. It is often easier, after finding such a reference, to locate the Registered copy of the Will in a volume rather than to find the original (loose) Will filed in a bundle or box. Where both the Registered copy of the Will and the original Will exist, however, it is un- doubtedly a wise plan not only to read the registered copy (and its probate act) but also to search the bundles or boxes of filed Wills (original documents, usually unbound) and finding not only the Will, but also important documents (if any) associated with it.[3] There are also many Registers of Copy Wills where the Calendar or Index references to a particular Will may be so inadequate that it is necessary to search the Register for that year page by page.

It is important to remember that searches may be made in vain in the Registers for a Will that was proved and listed in the Calendar (or Index) and in the Act Book, but being an Unregistered Will, might be found in the files of bundles or boxes of original Wills. If the court did not keep Registers covering the period in which the Will was proved, recourse has to be made to the files of original documents.

It should be noted that if the reference to a Will has been found, and it is planned to search the microfilm copy

---

3. Methods vary from court to court. Sometimes original Wills might be found bound into volumes. Usually a filed Will is found in a bundle, box, or file of loose documents, filed under the year of the grant of probate. Associated documents might be filed in the same bundle, but in some courts allied documents might be filed in entirely separate bundles.

of the Wills to find the document concerned, it will be necessary to find whether the probate court concerned maintained
either the files (bundles or boxes) or original Wills or the
Registers of Copy Wills, or both. If both were kept, it will
be necessary to determine whether or not the two categories
are available on microfilm.

All the records of a probate court might not have been
microfilmed, but only those that were available at the time
the microfilm was made. If all the Registers of Copy Wills
were microfilmed but *not* the bundles or boxes of original
Wills, Administrations, and associated documents for the
same period as the Registers, then important documents connected with the Wills, the Unregistered Wills, and the Administration Bonds including Admons.-with-Wills-annexed,
would not be available on microfilm.

TYPES OF WILLS.

Until 1838, a verbal Will could be made by an individual
in the presence of reliable witnesses. Either at that time or
after the death of the testator, his statement, known as a
Nuncupative Will, was reduced to writing and probated in
the usual manner. In some courts Nuncupative Wills were
treated as Administrations-with-Will-annexed because the
testator might not have named an executor, or for some valid
reason an administrator was appointed in place of the executor.
(See pages 59, 60 for examples of Nuncupative Wills).

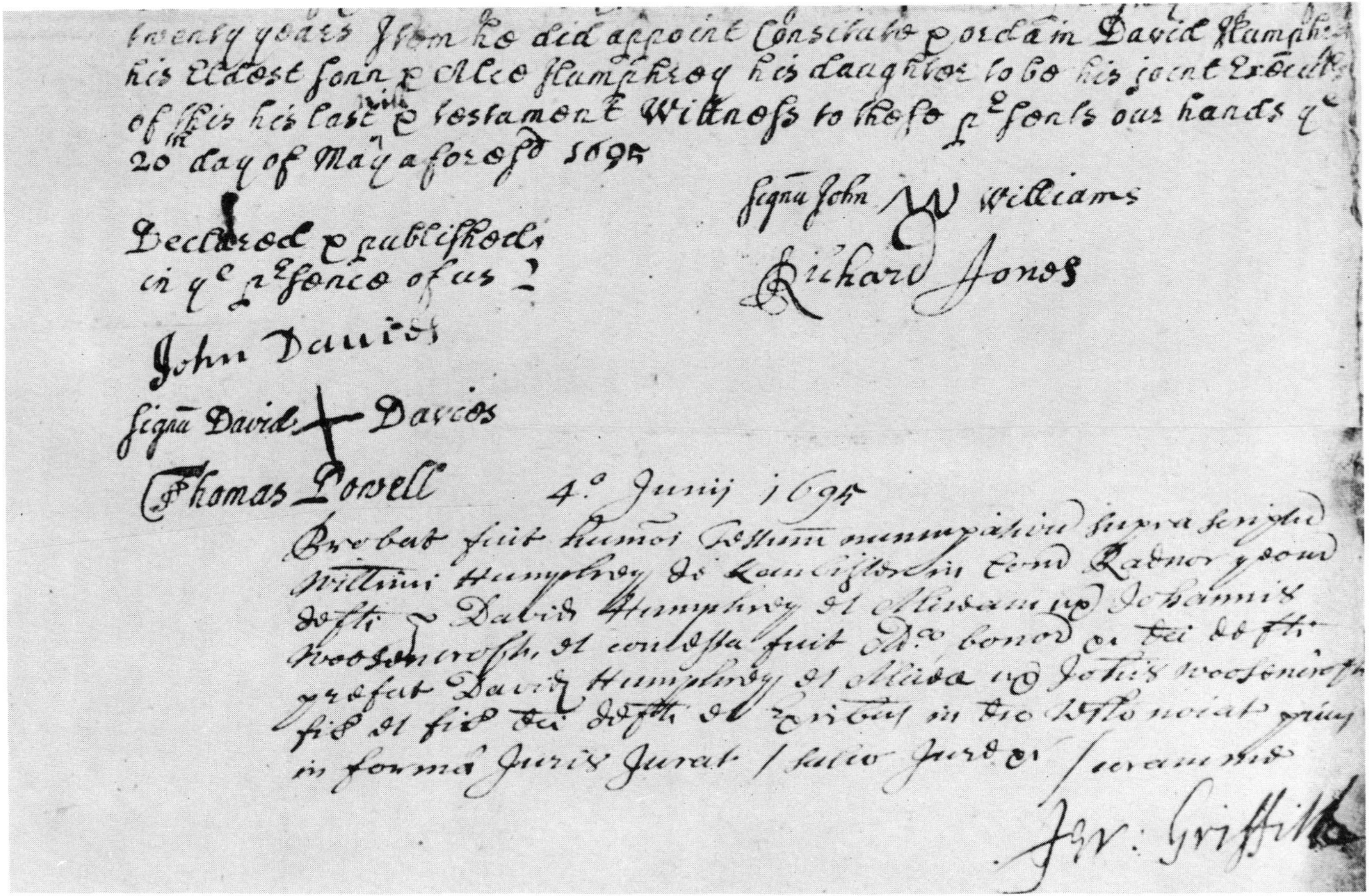

twenty yeares from he did appoint Constable ordain David Humphr̄
his Eldest sonn & Alce Humphrey his daughter to be his joint Exōut̄
of his last testament Wittness to those & Seals our hands &
20 day of May aforesd sayd

signe John W Williams

Richard Jones

Declared & published
in ye presence of us

John Davies

signe David + Davies

Thomas Powell

4.º Junii 1695

Probat̄ fuit hmōi testam̄ coram venerabili viro ——
Williō Humphrey & Ã Humphrey & Alce Humphrey fil̄ et ——
coram David Humphrey & coram ——
—— David Humphrey et Alica & Jotis executor̄ ——
—— in fid̄ ——

Joh. Griffith

The Latin Probate Act and its translation from the foot of the of the Nuncupative Will of William Humphrey of Llanbister, 1695.

Mention is made concerning record of such Probate Acts in Chapter 4 under "Act Books."

4° Junij 1695

Probat[um] fuit hu[jus]mo[d]i Test[ament]um nun-cupativu[m] supra scriptu[m] Willimi Humphrey de Llan-bister in Com[itatu] Radnor yeom[an] def[unc]ti p[er] David Humphrey et Aliceam ux [orem] Johannis Woosencroft, et concessa fuit Ad[ministra]cio bonor[um] &c. d[i]c[t]i def[unc]ti prefat[is] David Humphrey et Aliceae ux[ori] Johannis Woosencroft fil[io] et fil[iae] d[i]c[t]i def [unc]ti et Ex[ecuto]ribus in d[i]c[t]o Test[ament]o no [m]i[n]at[is] prius in forma Juris Jurat[is] salvo Jure &c.

Coram me

Jer: Griffith

4 June 1695.

The above-written nuncupative will of William Hum-phrey of Llanbister, co. Radnor, yeoman, deceased, was then proved by David Humphrey and Alice the wife of John Woosencroft, and administration of the goods, &c., of the said deceased was granted to the aforesaid David Humphrey and Alice the wife of John Woosencroft, son and daughter of the said deceased and executors named in the said will, they being first sworn in due form of law (saving the right [of all])

before me

Jer: Griffith.

Since the Act of 1837, no Nuncupative Will is considered valid unless made by "any soldier, being in actual military service; or of any mariner or seaman, being at sea."

A holograph Will is one written entirely in the hand-writing of the testator and is valid even though it might not bear the signature of the testator.

PROBATE PERIODS.

The earliest existing Wills in the Prerogative Court of Canterbury, London, date from around 1383, although there are a few earlier Wills, such as those at Lambeth Palace (London) and at Lincoln. In most courts there are few Wills dating earlier than 1540, and in some courts, Wills dating before 1660 are mutilated, fragile and often missing. A missing period in a series of probate records is described as a "chasm" or "a hiatus."

The Nuncupative Will of William Humphrey of Llanbister, County Radnor, yeoman, declared 17th May, written 20th May, and proved 4th June 1695.

This shows a portion of the document—the Will and the signatures of those to whom the declaration was made. On page 59 the rest of this document appears—showing the Latin Probate Act and its translation.

Under the heading "Examples," in chapter 6, there will be found information that demonstrates the tremendous value of Wills in the solving of genealogical problems.

2.   ADMINISTRATIONS.

When a person with property died without having made a valid Will he is designated as an intestate or as having "died intestate." Before distribution was made of an intestate's personal estate, some person applied to a probate court for a grant of *Letters of Administration*. In most cases, the applicant was a next-of-kin, but there are instances where some other person (perhaps a friend of the family or sometimes a principal creditor) has been granted Letters of Administration, probably because the next-of-kin was either unable to act, or being unwilling, had renounced the right to so act. The court appointed at least one administrator, who, together with one or two other persons, then entered into a bond before the court "well and truly to administer according to Law" the goods, chattels, credits, etc., of the deceased.[4] (See illustration on pages 64-65.)

When *the* Letters of Administration had been granted, details of this action usually were recorded in an Administration Act Book, a reference was entered in the Calendar or Index of the court, and the Administration Bond (often abbreviated to "Admon. Bond.") was filed.[5] The method of filing differed from court to court. In some courts where the Administration Bonds have been lost, the entry testifying to the Admon. Act will be found in the Admon. Act Book if such is still in existence. Some courts however, recorded both the acts or grants of probates of Wills and Letters of Administrations in the same book, often given the title "Probate Act Book." Where both the record of the Acts granting the Letters of Administration exist in an Act Book and the original Bonds in the files (of bundles or boxes, etc.), efforts should be made to examine the Admon. Bonds, as sometimes there are found attached or associated with them other important documents, such as Inventories, Bonds of Tuition and Curation (i.e., guardianship),

---

4. Prior to 1672 there was no law that governed the manner in which an administrator could distribute the property and possessions of an intestate. In 1672, however, a law was enacted making a fair and just distribution mandatory and under which an administrator could be made to submit an inventory.

5. A few courts have Registers of Admons. The Bonds (and attached or associated documents) are usually found in bundles or boxes under the year of the grant.

Renunciations, and Wills in those cases where the Will is annexed to another document. (See information on page 53). Other documents that may be attached, such as a deed of gift, are also of interest.[6]

These records, whether consisting of lists of names of the intestates entered in a Calendar (or Index), or entries of the official grant in an Act Book, or original Bonds (with other documents associated or attached to them), generally are known as Administrations, commonly abbreviated to Admons. or Adcons. Many record searchers, for this reason, refer to probate records as *Wills and Admons.* The information found in an Administration Bond identifying the deceased, the ad-ministrator, and bondsmen, does not yield as much genealogical information as is usually found in a Will.

In searching for an Administration Bond (such as shown on pages 64-65) the name of the deceased [George Lawrence] must first be located in the second part of the bond, i.e., "The Condition," that commences (in the illustra-tion) with the words "THE CONDICON" and it will be seen that his name appears in the 3rd line, reading: "and credits of *George Lawrence of ye parish of Pembrey* — deceased."

Not all bonds are exactly like those shown in the illustra-tions. Some courts used different methods of recording. In the Court of the Dean and Chapterof York, for instance, the 16th and 17th century bonds have a Latin portion of the bond written on the face of the document, with the "The Condition" that contains the name of the deceased written on the *dorse* (that is, on the back) of the bond. These paper or parchment documents are of various shapes and sizes.

The name of the court in which the record is filed generally must be known before a successful search can be made, but it is of interest to note that the particulars of the jurisdiction (i.e., the court) in which the grant was made usually is found mentioned in the bonds. In the Testamentary Bond and also in the Bond for the redelivery of the Will of Mildred Gale (see page 80) and in the Tuition (i.e., guardianship) Bond (see pages 125-126) entered into by George Gale, it will be noted that the court is disclosed as the Commissary for the

---

6. Attached to an Admon. Bond of a grant dated 1726 at Lichfield is a deed of gift whereby Thomas Lees, the intestate, deeded property for some con-sideration but held an interest in the property during his lifetime, but at death the property passed to the administrator.

Archdeaconry of Richmond (in the Diocese of Chester). In the Administration Bond relating to George Lawrence (see pages 64-65) the court is shown as that of the Bishop of St. David's.

Administration Bond relating to the goods
and chattels of George Lawrence of Pembrey,
Carmarthenshire, February 1720/1.
Amplified transcript of the Latin portion:

Noverint vniversi per p[re]sentes nos William' John et Morrice Jenkin de Kidwelly in Com[itatu] Carmarthen Yeom [en] teneri et firmiter obligari Reverendo in Christo Patri ac D[omi] no D[omi] no Georgio permissione Devina Menevensis Ep[iscop]o in Sexaginta libris bonae et legalis monetae Mag[nae] Brit[arniae] solvend[is] eid[em] Domino Episcopo aut suo certo Attornat[o] Executor[ibus] vel Administrator- [ibus] suis Ad quam quidem soluc[i]o[n] em bene et fid- eliter faciend[am] Obligamus nos et quemlibet n[ost]rum per se pro toto et in solid[o] Hered[e]s Executor[es] et Administrator[es] n[ost]ros et cujuslibet n[ost]rum firmiter per p[re]sentes. Sigillis nostris Sigillat[um] Dat[um] 25 die mensis Februarii Annoq[ue] Regni D[omi]ni n[ost]ri Georgii Dei gr[ati]a Magnae Britaniae Franciae et Hibernie Regis fidei defensor[is] &c. septimo Annoq[ue] D[omi]ni 1720.

Translation:

Know all men by these presents, that we William John and Morrice Jenkin of Kidwelly in the county of Carmarthen, yeomen, are held and firmly bound to the Reverend Father in Christ and Lord Lord George by divine permission Bishop of St. Davids in sixty pounds of good and lawful money of Great Britain to be paid to the said Lord Bishop or his certain attorney, his executors or administrators, To which payment well and truly to be made we bind ourselves and each of us by himself for the whole and in gross, our heirs, executors, and administrators and (those) of each of us, firmly by these presents. Sealed with our seals, dated the 25 day of the month of February in the seventh year of the reign of our sovereign Lord George, by the grace of God, of Great Britain, France, and Ireland, King, defender of the faith, &c., and in the year of our Lord 1720[/1].

Noverint universi per presentes nos Willᵐ iun̄ Iolie et Morꝰ Jenkin
de Kewelly in Com Carmarthen Yeo

tenori et firmiter obligari Reverendo in Christo Patri ac Dᵘᵒ Dᵒ
George permissione Divina Menevensis Epᵒ in Sexaginta
libᵘⁱˢ bonæ et legalis monetæ Mag Brit solvend dcᵒ Domino Episcopo — aut
suo certo Attornat Executor vel Administrator suis Ad quam quidem solvendam bene
et fideliter faciend Obligamus nos et quemlibet mᵘⁱ per se pro toto et in solid
Leceded Executor et Administrator nros et cujuslibet nrum firmiter per presentes.
Sigillis nris Sigillat dat 21 — die mensis februarii
Annoꝗ Regni Dñi nri Georgii
dei gra Magna Britannia ffrancia et Hibernia Regis — fidei defensor
&c Septimo — — Annoꝗ Dñi 1720

The Condicon of this Obligation is such that if ye above bounden Willᵐ & Iohn Morris
Jenkin Administrator of all and singular the goods chattells
and credits of George Lawrence of Cyff bogim of Kenden deceased
doe make or cause to be made a true and perfect Inventory of all and singular the goods
chattells and credits of the said deceased which have or shall come to the hands possion
or knowledge of them the said Willᵐ Iolie & Morris Jenkin or
into the hands and possession of any person or persons for them and the same soe
made doe exhibit or cause to be exhibited into the Registry of the Archdeaconry
of Carmthen at or before the first day of Aprill next
ensuing And the same goods chattells and credits and all other the goods chattells and credits
of the said deceased at the time of his death which at any time after shall come to the
hands or possession of the said William Iohn & Morris Jenkin or into the hands and
possession of any other person or persons for them doe well and truly administer
according to law And further doe make or cause to be made a true and just account
of his se Acon at or before the first day of June next ensuing
and all the rest and residue of the said goods chattells and credits which shall be found
remaining upon the said Administrators account the same being first examined and
allowed of by the Judge or Judges for the time being of the said Court shall deliver
and pay unto such person or persons respectively as the said Judge or Judges by his
or their decree or Sentence pursuant to the true intent and meaning of a late Act of
Parliament made in the two and twentieth and three and twentieth yeares of the raigne
of or late Soveraigne Lᵈ King Charles the second (Intituled An Act for the better
settling of Intestates estates) shall limit and appoint And if it shall hereafter
appeare that any last will and Testament was made by the said deceased and the
Executor or Executors therein named doe exhibit the same into the said Court making
request to have it allowed and approved accordingly if the said Willᵐ Iolie M Jenkin
above bounden being thereunto required doe render and deliver the said Lres of Acon
(approbation of such Testament being first had and made) in the said Court then this
Obligation to be void and of none effect or else to remaine in full force and vertue.

Sealed and delivered
in the presence of —

Woodford Rice
Mary Morgan
Tho Williams

Will John

Morries [mark] Jenkin

3. INVENTORIES.

Testamentary and Administration Bonds usually contain an obligation to produce an Inventory. Typical of these bonds are the examples given on pages 64, 65, 125, 126.

At the time of the probate of a Will or grant of Letters of Administration, several persons were appointed to take a "true and perfect" Inventory, that consisted of the listing of the personal estate, "goods, chattels, rights, credits" of the deceased and the rendering of an account to the probate court. If the will did not name those who were to perform the taking of the inventory, neighbors, friends of the family, or occasionally professional valuers performed this task.[7]

Inventories are not attached to or filed with the Registered Copies of Wills, nor filed in Act Books. If the record of a Will is taken from information in the Registers of Copy Wills or from an Act Book, then the presence of an Inventory might not be detected unless an attempt was made to find the *original* Will or Testamentary Bond in the files of boxes or bundles. The Inventory usually is attached to or associated with the *original* Will or Bond, but if separated, and not entirely lost, it might be filed in bundles of Inventories. Similarly, in cases of Letters of Administration, the Act Book might record that an Inventory was requested, but the document would be filed in the bundles of original documents, and often found attached to the Admon. Bond.

The system of requesting and preserving Inventories varied from court to court. In some courts they exist up to fairly recent times, but in the P.C.C. (London), there are very few Inventories from about 1480 to 1600, none between 1601 and 1660, and it seems that from about 1710 "it was not customary for them to be exhibited [in the P.C.C.] save when they were specially demanded."[8] For a long period at York, many references in the Calendars are marked "rpt." meaning "respited," indicating that when the Will was proved or Letters of Administration granted, no Inventory was submitted, no listing by Inventory therefore, was made, meaning that the value of the estate had not been ascertained by Inventory.

---

7. Those who took the Inventory were given various titles, such as supervisors, appraisers, praisers, valuers, etc.
8. *Wills in the P.C.C.*, 1383-1558, Vol. X, (1893), p. xxix. [ENG. PUB. AB., Vol. 10].

Authors of family and other histories will find to their great delight, that Inventories are a help in determining the social status and economic background of the family. Some Inventories give excellent descriptions of the rooms of a residence together with details of the household goods. Mr. Francis W. Steer, in his book *Farm and Cottage Inventories of Mid-Essex* has stated:

> The documents . . . help to create a picture of the homes of everyday men and women . . . and show that there was a story other than that of rich men . . .
> The varying degrees of personal well-being are perhaps shown more clearly in inventories than any other type of document, yet this source has been used but little. Sacks full of inventories lie at Somerset House [London] and at other probate registries waiting to be indexed and made available . . . This historical value of inventories cannot be too strongly emphasized, because these documents tell us precisely what goods a person had at the time of his death and what they were worth; they help, even more than manorial records, to determine the social positions of members of a community, and they supplement the evidence of past ages as shown in painting, literature, correspondence, and manuscripts.[9]

Genealogists should not overlook the value of these important documents as unexpected information may be contained in them. An inventory occasionally will disclose valuable genealogical information such as the occupation of the deceased not mentioned in the Will or in the Admon., or will indicate that the deceased had several business interests, the Will or Admon. naming one business interest, the others being indicated by the very nature of the goods and chattels listed in the Inventory. (See pages 68, 69).

---

9. Francis W. Steer, *Farm and Cottage Inventories of Mid-Essex, 1635-1749.* (Colchester: Essex Record Office Publications, 1950) No. 8. [ESSEX PUB. C. No. 8.]
For additional information see also:
B. C. Jones, "The Lancashire Probate Records," *Trans. Hist. Society of Lancashire and Cheshire,* CIV (1952) pp. 70-73. [LANCS. PUB. E. v. 104.]
F. G. Emmison, "Jacobean Household Inventories," 1617-1619, *Beds. Hist. Record Society,* (1938), XX. [BEDS. 6 v. 20]

A true and perfect Inventory of the Goods, Chattels and Credits of Athelustan Savage, of Caersws, in the parish of Llanwnog, in the County of Montgomery, Tawer — deceased.

	£	s	d
His Horse, Saddle, and Bridle, & Wearing Apparel	7	0	0
One old Mare and Colt, and 2 pairs of Gearing	6	10	0
Three Hill horses	3	0	0
Two Cows	18	0	0
Two pigs, and poultry	2	12	0
Implements in Husbandry, and Lumber	7	10	0
Four Bedsteads, and Bed-cloaths &c	20	0	0
Household Furniture in the Rooms	16	12	0
Household Furniture in the Kitchen	6	17	0
China, and Earthen-ware	2	5	0
Pewter plates	0	12	0
Pots and other Iron-ware	1	0	0
Two spinning Jennies	8	0	0
Stock in Trade	96	12	0
	196	10	0

Evan Evans
David Hamer } Appraisers

June the 20th 1814.

Inventory of the property of Athelustan Savage, Tawer. His occupation, tawer, indicates that he was engaged in preparing skins for the making of gloves. The list of property indicates that he was also engaged in husbandry. Both clues assist in determining whether or not references found in other records mentioning variously Athelustan Savage a husbandman and Athelustan Savage a tawer, relate to the same man or to two separate individuals.

A part of the Will of Athelustan Savage of Caersws, Llanwnog. No mention of his occupation is to be found in this Will, dated 12th June 1814, proved in the Episcopal Consistory Court of Bangor. Note that this original Will has a superscription at the end of it recording the Act of Probate. —

Chapter 4

PROBATE CALENDARS OR INDEXES AND ACT BOOKS

1. CALENDARS AND INDEXES.

After the court made a grant of probate or Letters of Administration, it was usual to list the name of the testator, or the intestate, as the case may be, with a varying amount of other identifying information, in a book so that reference to the Will or Admon. can be quickly and easily found. These lists are known in some courts as Calendars and in other courts as Indexes, and the methods of keeping them varied from court to court.

The titles, Calendars or Indexes, might be misleading. They are not indexes to all persons mentioned in the probate records, but are lists of the names of the testators (who left Wills) and intestates (for whom Letters of Administration had been granted). The entries were usually made on a day-by-day basis as the grants were made, with a reference to the year or date the probate or Admon. was granted with varying amounts of other information as will be described later.

These lists are not always arranged alphabetically, but a brief glance at the Calendars or Indexes of a particular court will soon determine the type of arrangement used in that particular list. Care should be taken to determine whether or not the Calendar or Index is a list of Wills *only* or of Admons. *only* or if it is a list of *both* Wills and Admons.

In seeking a record of probate, it is usual to search the Calendars or Indexes first, in an attempt to find references to the family or surname concerned. On the few occasions where no Calendar or Index exists, it is usually necessary to refer to the Probate and Administration Act Books.

When there is a *printed* Calendar or Index, it is usually more accurate than the original manuscript (or its microfilmed copy) from which it was taken because the societies printing them usually make careful checks to ensure their accuracy. Since it is much easier to search the printed copy of a Calendar or Index, care should be taken to ascertain if the particular Calendar or Index for *both* the Wills and Admons. for the relevant period has been printed before searching the original or microfilm copy. Details of Calendars and Indexes known to have been printed are listed for each probate court in Chapter 9 "The Counties of England and Wales."

Printed Calendars are usually the result of many years of effort, transcribing from old and faded manuscripts on to individual index slips and often checking these with the actual Wills and Admons.

> Moreover, these manuscript calendars have an omission factor of almost five per cent, so that to this date this Society has wrested little short of 10,000 Wills from oblivion as well as providing additional indexes of trades and conditions, places and ships, so important to the social and economic historian and to the topographer and at the same time of so much general interest . . . Since the records of this court [P.C.C.] relate to persons resident in all parts of England and Wales, and indeed, throughout the world, the importance of these indexes to all libraries and institutions affording facilities for research cannot be overestimated. [C. Harold Ridge in the *Preface* of Volume 77 of the publications of the British Record Society, London, (1958)]

Prefaces and Introductions to the printed Calendars and Indexes should be read carefully as editors usually give excellent information concerning the records and jurisdictions of the court concerned.

In searching publications and microfilms relating to records of probate, it is well to note carefully not only the name of the court, but also if the records belong to a certain subdivision of that court, such as a rural deanery. Unless careful note is taken, the *wrong* records could be searched. The place of deposit of the documents should also be taken into consideration although it is possible that the records may have been moved to some other repository since the book was published or the microfilm copy made.

Although a general title to certain original, printed and microfilmed records (including Calendars and Indexes) of a particular court states that "Wills and Admons." are included, a more careful scrutiny of the contents, sometimes given in a subtitle or a preface will indicate that the records relate to Wills *only* or to *Admons.* only.

The following examples illustrate some of the ways in which Calendars and Indexes are arranged:

i. *General notes on printed Calendars and Indexes.*

Each printed Calendar or Index usually consists of an alphabetical arrangement of the names of testators or intestates, or both. Many editors of printed Calendars or Indexes in addition to indexing the names of the testators and intestates, also produce additional indexes that are of great genealogical and historical value. These additional indexes include the following:

A. *Index to Places.* (Index Locorum) These are invaluable to the topographer and county and parish historians and are of similar value to genealogists. Genealogists sometimes find it necessary to consider Wills and Admons. of persons who were former residents of an ancestral parish but whose surnames are unknown. Indexes to places help to locate these records.

B. *Indexes to Names of Ships.* These are useful to historians of naval and merchant shipping, and to a lesser degree, genealogists.

C. *Indexes to Trades, Professions and Conditions.* The genealogist will find great value in these as will biographers, students of economics, and those interested in the histories of trades, crafts and professions.

D. *Indexes to Names, "Index Nominum," and "Stray Names."* These consist of the names of such persons who are mentioned incidentally in the printed Index or Calendar, and who bear surnames other than those of the testators or intestates. If the so-called "Stray Names" are listed from the original manuscript Calendars only, there will be few mentioned. When both the manuscript Calendars and the probate and administration Acts (described later) have been carefully compared, and the information combined, each printed Calendar (or Index) contains thousands of "Stray Names." These might be the names of executors, trustees, administrators, next-of-kin, guardians, minor children, etc., or others who had some part in the business of the grants. These indexes of "Stray Names," necessary to complete the utility of the printed calendars, provide clues on family relationships and connections unobtainable elsewhere.

E. *Lists of Corrections and Additions.* These are often called "Corrigenda and Addenda," and most printed books contain lists of them. Unavoidably many printed books contain errors and omissions. Sometimes these are never corrected. If they are, either a special notice will appear in the book, or details may appear in a later volume of the same series. For example, Volume 18 of the British Record Society is corrected in Volume 25 of the same series.

ii. *Example of a Fairly Common Type of Calendar or Index Entry.*

The Episcopal Consistory Court of Lichfield.

(from original manuscript calendar or Index.)

Date			Name of Testator or Intestate	Place	Notes
1780	Oct.	27	Sandford, Samuel	Hodnett	
1780	Dec.	26	Sandland, Ann	Whitchurch	adm.
1780	June	28	Sawyer, Edward	Birmingham	
1789	Feb.	5	Barker, William	*Quoad bona*	

iii. *Example of a Calendar without any alphabetical arrange-ments.*

Episcopal Consistories of St. David's and of Archdeaconry of St. David's and Archdeaconry of Cardigan, 1700-1747.

(from original manuscript calendar.)
1700.

Place	Document	Name of Testator, etc.	
St. Davids	Test.	Phillippi	Richard
Carew	....	William	David.
St. Davids	Ad.	Georgis	Davidi.
St. Ismaels	Ad. with Inventory.	Johannis	Allen.

This calendar from a Welsh court appears to be of entries made *de die in diem* or day-by-day without any attempt to alphabetize the surnames. Under each year, (such as 1700 above), without any day or month being entered, the record names the parish (but not the county), and then the name of the type of document, followed by the name of the deceased. Apart from an occasional reference to an Admon. the whole Calendar is for Wills. This is evident from the brief notice entered on the front fly-leaf of this manuscript Calendar — "Wills in St. David's and Cardigan Archdeaconries 1700-1747, 'Admons. not Calendared'."

There is no alphabetical arrangement in this type of Calen-dar, and it is necessary, therefore, to search the whole record for the relevant period to find mention of any particular name (whether surname or patronymic). The abbreviation "Test." (as shown above) together with such abbreviations as "T" and "Tment" means "Testament", another word for Will.

iv. *Example of Calendar or Index entries where patronymics are involved.*

Episcopal Consistory Court of St. Asaph, 1638-1648.

(from original manuscript calendar or index.)

Name	*Place*	*Name*	*Place*
Wills 1648.		Admons. 1648.	
John Griffith ap		Jane Jones.	Tryddyn
Edward.	Eastin	John Andrews.	Llandyssul
John Hughes.	Oswestry	Jane Salisbury.	Denbigh
Jane verch Hugh.	Berriew	etc.	etc.
John Powell.	Bodfari		
etc.	etc.		

This Calendar is from a Welsh court and illustrates pro-bates calendared alphabetically under the first letter of the *first given name* of the deceased, and *not* according to the last name. As few persons in Wales and in some of the English counties bordering Wales, possessed a surname at this period—the use of patronymics being common—the above system was the method to find the record of a person for whom the first given name was known. This method obviates searching for Thomas ap Hugh ap Evan under "H" for Hugh or under "E" for Evan. If a family had an established surname such as Butler or Salisbury, it would be necessary to search this type of Calen-dar from "A" to "Z" for each year to find all probates under such a family surname.

Note that this Calendar divides the page references into two categories—one column for Wills and the other for Admons.

v. *Examples of Calendars or Indexes for Courts where the Records are Divided and Subdivided.*

A. The Court of the Archdeaconry of Richmond, in the Diocese of Chester.

This court, also known as the Consistory Court of the Commissary of the Archdeaconry of Richmond in the Diocese of Chester, was controlled by a Commissary appointed by, and subject to, the Bishop of Chester. The probate records for this archdeaconry are from a district comprising Lancashire to the north of the River Ribble (which flows through Preston), and those portions of Cumberland, Westmorland and Yorkshire

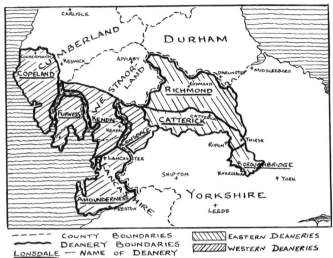

Map showing the Archdeaconry of Richmond and its five Western Deaneries and three Eastern Deaneries, comprising many parishes in the Counties of Cumberland, Westmorland, Lancashire and Yorkshire.

included within the archdeaconry. The records have been variously kept at Richmond (Yorks), Kendal, (Westmorland), and Lancaster, (Lancs.).

Searching the records of this court requires great care and understanding. The Richmond probate records are filed according to the deanery (of the archdeaconry) in which the deceased was domiciled, and there were eight deaneries within the archdeaconry. The records of the *five* Western Deaneries (known as Furness, Kendal, Lonsdale, Copeland and Amounderness) are now at the Lancashire Record Office in Preston. The records of the *three* Eastern Deaneries (known as Boroughbridge, Catterick, and Richmond) are kept at the Archives Department, Central Library, Leeds, Yorks.

Although there are in print Calendars and Indexes for the period 1457-1858, yet these cover a certain portion only of the records, and certainly by no means the records of the whole archdeaconry. All references to *Lancashire* probates in the Western Deaneries only are printed, but not to probates granted in the same deaneries for estates *outside* of Lancashire. Neither do references appear in these printed volumes to the Lancashire probates granted in the Eastern Deaneries nor to any references for probates for Lancashire estates granted elsewhere.

Prior to 1720, the manuscript Calendar (or Index) of the *five* Western Deaneries consists of several volumes having an alphabetical arrangement of surnames. Each volume is divided into parts, each part relating to one of the *five* deaneries, with' out any special headings of the pages indicating the names of the deaneries. In the following example, the volume or Calen' dar concerns surnames commencing with the letter "G". The seven references quoted are listed from *widely separated pages* within the same book, so as to show references from each of the *five* deaneries:

Manuscript Gazetteer and Calendar of Wills.
Surname "G" down to 1720.

Type of Documents	Date	Names	Residence	Code letter signifying deanery
a. Inv.				
Bd.	31 May 1666	Gardner, Jenetae,	de Pilling	A.
b. Inv.				
Bd.	30 Oct. 1662	Gardner, Nichol,	de Urswicke	F.
c. W.				
Inv.	27 Oct. 1681	Gardner, Francisci,	de Crowdubs	K.
Bds.			p. Heysham	
d. W.				
Bds.	7 May 1695	Gardner, Margaretta,	de Hornby Castle	L.
e. W.	25 Jan. 1706	Garner, Johis,	de Moorerow in	Co. Regd.
Inv.(2).			Guttber, p.	803
Bds.			Egermond.	Carr.
f. W.				
Bds.	18 Mar. 1700	Gale, Mildred,	de Whitehaven,	Co.
g. W.	1599	Goose, Johis,	de Salwick	Indexed in Cal. "W" and filed with Eastn.

The seven selected references indicate the type of docu' ments filed, such as *Inv* [Inventory]; *Bd* [Bonds, such as Testamentary, Admon., and Tuition Bonds]; *W* [Will]. Then are given the dates of probate, names and parishes of the deceased, and a special code or initial letter for the rural deanery under which the documents are filed. Additional notes, such as "Regd. 802 Carr," indicates a copy Will in a Register; and "filed with Eastn." indicates that the record is filed with the Eastern Deaneries. This latter item, however, is no indica' tion that all the records of the Eastern Deaneries are mentioned in this Calendar, as such references are rare. The code or initial letter indicates the rural deanery concerned, as follows:

A for Amounderness	F for Furness	K for Kendal
L for Lonsdale	Co for Copeland	

When searching in such an index, it is important to record details of the deanery — "A"(mounderness), etc. Without such deanery details, it is impossible to find the probate docu' ments in the bundles or files.

In searching for the probate record of Mildred Gale of Whitehaven, who died about 1700, it would be necessary to search the Calendar for the letter "G". The reference then should be copied in full. The indication from the reference (quoted above) is that the "W" (Will) and "Bds" (Bonds) are filed under Co., (that is, the Copeland Deanery). The reading of the actual documents would necessitate a search in the bundle of probate records for the letter "G" in the Cope' land Deanery records of the Archdeaconry of Richmond (Western Deaneries) for the year 1700. (See pages 78-81, 125, 126 for illustrations.)

To indicate the file containing the record concerned, the Calendars or Indexes of the *three* Eastern Deaneries employ initial letters:

B for Boroughbridge	Ca for Catterick	R for Richmond

Although the *three* Eastern Deaneries are entirely in York' shire, there are probate records filed therein relating to estates outside Yorkshire and situated in the *five* Western Deaneries. In the ten years, 1811-1820, there appear, under the letter "B," no less than six references to estates situated in the Western Deaneries but where probate was granted in the Eastern Deaneries. Most of these grants are by the Decree of Court (and usually at Richmond, Yorks.), but none appear in the Calendars or Indexes kept in the Western Deaneries.

In the name of God Amen. I Mildred Gale wife of Geo: Gale of Whitehaven in the County of Cumberland being doubtfull of the Recoverie of my Present Sickness but of Sound and Perfect mind & memory: praise be therefore given to Almightie God do make and ordain this my Present Last Will & Testament in Manner and Form following, Recomending my soul into the hands of Almightie God hopeing through the Merits Death & Passion of my Saviour Jesus Christ to have full and free pardon of all my Sins and to Inherit Everlasting life and my body I comitt to the Earth to be Decently buried at the Discretion of my Executor hereafter Nam'd, And as touching the Dispositions of all Such Temporal Estate as it hath pleased God to bestow on me wch by an Indenture of Marriage made & Executed by & between John Washington one of the Executors of my late husbands Will of the one part & My Present Husband Geo: Gale with my own consent and approbation thereof of the other Part bearing Date the Sixteenth day of May in this present year one thousand Seven hundred I am Inabled & impowered to demise by Will or other Instruments the Estate & Legacy of my Late Husband to the uses & purposes therin mention'd I give and dispose thereof as Followeth

First Wheras by the Late Will & Testament of my Late Husband (Lawrence Washington bearing Date the Eleventh day of March one thousand Six hundred Ninety Eight) I am Intrusted with the tuition of his Children & wth the proffitts of the Lands & Legacys left by the said Will of their Late father Lawrence Washington I do hereby Leave the Tuition & Guardian Ship of the Said Children with the proffitts of the Lands and Legacys, to my Present Husband Geo Gale he being accountable to them in the Same Manner as I am by the Tenure & purpose of the said Will obliged to perform.

Secondly that after the receipt of one thousand pounds Sterling by my husband Geo: Gale, what remains over & above the Said thousand pounds, shall be equally divided between my Said Husband & Children by Equal parts & portions. Lastly I do Ordain & apoynt my Loving Husband Geo. Gale my Full & Sole Executor of this my Last will & Testament. In witness whereof I the Said Milldred Gale to this my Last Will & Testament my hand & Seal have Set the twenty fourth day of January one thousand Seven hundred.

Sign'd Seal'd & Published
in the presence of
Fra: Yates
Matt: Gale
Joseph Sewell.

Mildred Gale

Collac[i]one f[a]c[t]a fideli concordat[a] haec Copia cum Testam[en]to
Or[igina]li q[uo]d Decretu[m] est Retradi in manus suprad[i]c[t]i Executoris
(Cauc[i]one p[ro] Redelib[er]ando praestita) & Examinat[a] decimo
Octavo die Marcii Anno D[omi]ni Millesimo Septingentesimo.
                        p[er] mee   Rich: Trotter
                                         Not[ar]ium Pub[li]cum.

John, Augustine, & Mildred Washington.

[Translation of the Latin subscription]. Comparison has been made and this copy truly agrees with the original Will which is resolved to be redelivered into the hands of the above said Executor (Provision for redelivery guaranteed) and examined on the eighteenth day of March in the year of our Lord one thousand and seven hundred.

By me Rich: Trotter.
Notary Public.

George Gale's testamentary bond for payment of his wife's debts and legacies, and for making a true inventory of her possessions, 18 March 1700/1.

[For amplified transcript of the Latin portion, see the abstract of the tuition bond made by George Gale, page 125]

Not all bonds are exactly the same as the one illustrated. Some have the Latin portion written on the front and the Condition written on the back of paper or parchment sheets of various shapes and sizes.

George Gale's bond for redelivery of original Will of Mildred,
late wife of George Gale, 18 March 1700/1.

[For amplified transcript of the Latin portion, see the abstract of the
tuition bond, page 125.]

B. Court of the Episcopal Consistory of Chester and the Rural Deaneries of the Archdeaconry of Chester.

The records of the above probate courts were derived from *two jurisdictions,* and the records of each jurisdiction are filed separately. The records of both these jurisdictions have been further divided according to the county of residence of the deceased, the divisions being Lancashire, Cheshire, and Wales.

In many courts there is one jurisdiction only, but in courts such as Chester, where concurrent jurisdictions exist, the records being recorded and filed separately, searches must be made in the Calendars (or Indexes) of all jurisdictions. It is essential that references listed from the Calendars (or Indexes) are clearly identified according to jurisdiction, such as "Supra," "Infra," or some other term or name of court. It will be noted that references in Calendars and Act Books (Act Books are dealt with later) record only the parish *and not the county.* It is necessary, therefore, to determine when the records of the court are divided, possibly on a county basis, the *name of the county* before a search can be made for the corresponding records to which references have been made in the Calendars. Unless such information is noted, it will be impractical, and often impossible, to find the correct records.

vi. *Example of a Calendar listing the Wills separate from the Administrations.*

The following example taken from the Calendars of the Episcopal Consistory Court of Chichester shows the necessity of searching the *two* Calendars that cover the same period before *all* references to Wills and Admons. can be found.

A. *Printed Calendar of Wills* 1482-1800.

Name	Place	Vol.	Page	Year
Dudman, Jhon	Sowthmundam	3	90	1554
" John	Farnhurst	27	243b	1681
" Nicholas	Boxgrove	36	104	1736

B. *Printed Calendar of Administrations* 1555-1800.

Name	Place	Vol.	Page	Year
Dudman, Catherine	Appledram	N	81	1728
[etc.]	[etc.]			
Fry, Richard	Stedham Adm. & Will	P	66	1744

The information in these two examples is taken from two different printed Calendars, that of the Wills only published in 1915, and that of the Administrations only published twenty-five years later in 1940. Failure to note that the earlier publication covered Wills *only* and the other Administrations *only* would be serious. A check of the printed Calendar of Wills would mean that an attempt to find the grant of Letters of Administration for Catherine Dudman would fail. Similarly, reference to the *Will* of Richard Fry would not be found, as record of it is Calendared in the printed volume of Administrations because a grant of Letters of Administration (with-the-Will-annexed) was involved.

For some courts, the Calendars of Wills *only* have been published, but *not* the Calendar for Administrations, in which cases, it is necessary to search the manuscript Calendar for Administrations after checking the printed Calendar of Wills. The date on which a printed Calendar ends should be noted so that if there are Calendars covering later dates, they also could be searched.

vii. *Example of a probate court having no Calendar.*

In some courts there may be probate records for which there is no separate Calendar or Index. In the Episcopal Consistory Court of Worcester there is a printed Calendar for the period 1451-1652, but no separate Calendar for 1661-1858. It is necessary, therefore, to search the indexes contained in each of the nineteen Act Books that cover the period 1661-1858. These indexes in each Act Book are arranged alphabetically under the *first letter of the surname*. A reference is given to the page or folio where the official grant is recorded. No indication is given as to the residence of the deceased or whether the document is a Will or Administration. The following entries are taken at random from the index in the manuscript Act Book 1730-1756:

Name	*Folio*	*Name*	*Folio*
Burt, John	83	Leager, Thomas	174
Long, Elizabeth	83	Mills oth: Hurst, Mary	226

viii. *Example of a Calendar listing persons with two surnames under only one of them.*

The manuscript Act Book described in item vii lists a number of persons having double surnames:

Name	Folio
Apley oth: Abbley oth; Moody, Elizabeth	84
Howton, Mary als. Parker	193

The first reference refers to the Will of Elizabeth Appley otherwise Moody, wife of Thomas Moody, formerly Elizabeth Appley, *spinster. As there is no reference in the index under the name of Moody* it would be impossible to find this Will if the searcher did not know the maiden surname of Mrs. Moody.

The reference, "Howton, Mary als. Parker," refers to a grant of Letters of Administration to George Parker, her lawful husband. No reference appears in the index under Parker, making it impossible to find the probate record under the married surname of Mrs. Parker.

ix. *Example of a Calendar that has a lengthy period missing, and where the Act Books are in Latin and not indexed.*

The Calendars or Indexes for the Prerogative Court and the Exchequer Court of York are printed as one Calendar for 1389-1688. From 1731 to 1858 there is one set of Indexes that consolidate or combine all references in *both* these courts. From 1688 to 1731, however, there is no complete Index, making it necessary to refer to the Act Books for references to the names of the testators and intestates. The Act Books are written in Latin for dates prior to 1733, and the Act Books for the Prerogative Court of York are separate from those of the various rural deaneries comprising the records for the Exchequer Court of York. These Act Books, which for the period 1688 to 1731 have to be used in the place of Calendars or Indexes, are as follows:

A. *The Prerogative Court of York.*

These Act Books are arranged chronologically, showing the Acts on a day-by-day basis, and they are not indexed. If it is thought that a Will or Admon. may be recorded, a page-by-page search must be made of the relevant period.

B. *The Exchequer Court of York.*

Within this jurisdiction there were sixteen different rural dean-eries, and a separate Act Book was kept for each. Before a successful search can be made in the appropriate deanery Act Book, it is necessary to determine in which deanery the parish or place where the deceased resided was situated. Among the original records at York is a manuscript entitled "Deanery Book" that lists parishes (and places) in the Diocese of York and stating the names of the rural deaneries concerned.[1] The Act Book for the appropriate deanery must then be searched for the relevant period, page-by-page.

x. *Example of a modern card index replacing the Calendar.*

In the court of the Archdeaconry of Bedford, the original manuscript Calendars or Indexes have been superseded by a master-index in the form of a card-index covering all Wills and Admons. The index references give the deceased's surname, given name(s), parish, occupation, and the year of the grant of probate or Letters of Administration. Modern indexes are extremely valuable and time-saving but, if it is thought to be of any advantage, the original manuscript Calendars or Indexes that were in use prior to the making of the master card-index can be checked.

xi. *Example of Calendars and Records for the Prerogative Court of Canterbury, London.*

The Prerogative Court of Canterbury (generally referred to as the "P.C.C.") claimed superior jurisdiction over probate matters in all of England and Wales. Many grants therefore are found in this court that are not recorded within the courts associated with the locality where the deceased left an estate. The P.C.C. claimed superior jurisdiction over the grant if any of the following situations arose:

    A. The deceased possessed *Bona Notabilia* situated in two or more dioceses or two or more Peculiars within the Province of Canterbury.

    B. The deceased possessed *Bona Notabilia* within both provinces—York and Canterbury.

    C. The deceased died in Ireland, Scotland or in foreign parts, that is, parts overseas, but possessed an estate in England or Wales.[2]

---

1. Deanery Book. [14430, F. Yorks., 9. Also Eng. 366].
2. Many grants were allowed in local or minor courts, although the deceased died overseas while possessing property solely within the jurisdiction of the minor court. See page 100 for mention of a man who died in the United States in 1801 and the grant was at Chester. Such cases are by no means uncommon.

D. The deceased was a person of means. B. G. Bouwens points out that "It has always . . . been a usual thing for men of substance and position to prove in this Court; probably for the greater prestige of its Acts and the great safety of its records."[3]

E. The probate was granted during the Civil Wars and Commonwealth periods. In the records of this court are many grants given in London during the Civil Wars (1642-1649) and the Commonwealth (1649-1660). The following are taken from the publications of the British Record Society "Index Library":

> "It is difficult to trace exactly what happened to the . . . courts of probate in the country at this juncture. The number of Wills proved in them begins to fall off from about 1645, and after 1650 they are rare." (Vol. 54, p. xv).
> ". . . on 8 April 1653, an Act was passed entitled 'An Act for the probate of Wills . . .' The entire probate jurisdiction of the country was united into one single whole. The local courts do not as a rule continue to exist after 1653 . . ." (Vol. 54, p. xvi).

For centuries the P.C.C. was situated in the City of London at Doctor's Commons in the parish of St. Benedict, Paul's Wharf. The court operated in five "Seats," each group of officials dealing with certain areas. The residence of the deceased decided the "Seat" at which the case was dealt. The names of these "Seats" are rather misleading in view of the wide areas covered by all except the London Seat.

Name of Seat.	*Area Covered.*
Registers Seat:	The Province of York and Parts Overseas (i.e., foreign parts). The latter often abbreviated to "Pts."
Surrey Seat:	Counties of Cornwall, Devon, Somerset, Dorset, Southampton (i.e., Hampshire or Hants.), Wilts., Surrey, and Sussex.
Welsh Seat:	Wales and Monmouthshire, and the counties of Salop (i.e., Shropshire), Stafford, Derby, Hereford, Worcester, Warwick, Leicester, Rutland, Northampton, Gloucester, Oxford, and Berks.
Middlesex Seat:	Counties of Bedford, Buckingham, Cambridge, Essex, Hertford, Huntingdon, Kent, Lincoln, Norfolk, Suffolk, and Middlesex including St. Paul, Covent Garden; St. Martin in the Fields; St. Dunstan, Stepney; St. Clement Dane; St. Paul, Shadwell; and other parishes in the outparts of Middlesex.
London Seat:	The City of London and its suburbs, but excluding any in the Middlesex Seat above.

---

3. *Wills and their whereabouts,* op cit., p. 48.

The existence of these "Seats" does not affect the use of the Calendars (Indexes) and the Registers of Wills. The Probate and Administration Act Books for each year, however, are divided into five "Seats," and the grants in each of the "Seats" are arranged together in the order given. In these Act Books only the "Registers Seat" division is usually so headed, the names of the other "Seats" not appearing. Instead, the divisions for these "Seats" are given names that were chosen and understood by the officials of the period concerned. In 1731, for instance, the five headings are "Registers," "Welham," "Searle," "Pennyman," and "London Walk," but fifty years later, in 1781, the headings are "Registers," "Marsh," "Farrant," "Torriano," and "Stubbs." The origin of these names seems to be unknown — perhaps the name chosen was the surname of the court official in charge of the "Seat" concerned.

If the executors or administrators were unable to visit the officials dealing with the area concerned, business was trans-acted before a local official commissioned by the P.C.C. The results of these transactions were forwarded to the P.C.C. for recording.

The Calendars (Indexes) for Wills and Administrations are as follows:

Periods		Brief Title and Publisher
A. WILLS:	i. 1383-1629	P.C.C. Wills, (Brit. Rec. Soc., Index Lib.), Vols. 10, 11, 18, 25, 43, 44. [Eng. Pub. AB., same Volumes].
	ii. 997-1559	Sede Vacante Wills (Kent Arch. Soc., 1914), Vol. 3. [Kent 8, Vol. 3].
	iii. 1620	Register "Soame," by J. H. Lea, covers folios 1-120 only. [Eng. Pub. ABc].
	iv. 1620-1624	Abstracts of Probates and Sentences, by J. & G. F. Matthews, "Year Books of Pro-bates," (1911) [Eng. Pub. ABh].
	v. 1630	Register "Scroope," by J. H. Morrison, cov-ers folios 1-117 only. [Eng. Pub. ABa].
	vi. 1630-1654	Abstracts of Probates, by J. & G. F. Mat-thews, "Year Books of Probates," (1902-1927), Vols. 1 to 8, and an "Extra" Vol-ume. [Eng. Pub. ABb. Vols. 1-8, & "Ex-tra"].
	vii. 1495-1695	Wills from Doctor's Commons, (Camden Soc., 1863), Old Series, Vol. 83. [Eng. Pub. E., O.S., Vol. 83].
	viii. 1653-1660	P.C.C. Wills, (Brit. Rec. Soc., Index Lib.), Vols. 54, 61. [Eng. Pub. AB., Vols. 54, 61].
	ix. 1658	Register "Wootton," by W. Brigg, covers folios 1-52 only. [Eng. Pub. ABf].

  x. 1661-1670.....P.C.C. *Wills, Sentences, Probate Acts*, by
     J. H. Morrison, [Eng. Pub. ABe].
  xi. 1671-1693.....P.C.C. *Wills*, (Brit. Rec. Soc., Index Lib.),
     Vols. 67, 71, 77. [Eng. Pub. AB., Vols.
     67, 71, 77].
  xii. 1694-1700.....In preparation of printing.
  xiii. 1694-1852.....Search the manuscript Indexes and Act
     Books.
  xiv. 1853-1857......*Calendar . . . Probate and . . . Admon.*,
     1853-1857, Vols. 1-16. [Kent 27].

B. ADMONS: **i.** 1559-1580.....*Admons. in the P.C.C.*, by R. M. Glencross,
     Vols. 1, 2. [Eng. Pub. ABg. Vols. 1 and
     2]. [Also in the "Supplement," *The Gene-*
     ealogist, Vols. 26-28. [Eng. Pub. AF., New
     Series, Vols. 26-28].
  ii. 1581-1595.....P.C.C. *Admons.*, (Brit. Rec. Soc., Index
     Lib.), Vol. 76. [Eng. Pub. AB. Vol. 76].
  iii. 1596-1619.....Search the manuscript indexes and Act
     Books. Omissions from the Calendars might
     be found in the Admon. Act Books.
  iv. 1620-1630.....P.C.C. *Admons.*, by J. H. Morrison. [Eng.
     Pub. ABd].
  v. 1631-1648.....Search the manuscript indexes and Act
     Books. Omissions from the Calendars might
     be found in the Admon. Act Books.
  vi. 1649-1660.....P.C.C. *Admons.*, (Brit. Rec. Soc., Index
     Lib.), Vols. 68, 72, 74, 75. [Eng. Pub. AB.,
     Vols. 68, 72, 74, 75].
  vii. 1661-1852.....Search the manuscript Indexes and Act
     Books.
  viii. 1853-1857.....*Calendar . . . Probate . . . and Admon.*,
     1853-1857, Vols. 1-16. [Kent 27].
C. MISCELLANEOUS................There are many printed books that contain
     abstracts of Wills and Admons. from the
     P.C.C.

Except for the publications mentioned above, there is a manuscript Calendar for each year in which the surnames are alphabetically arranged under the first letter of the sur-name. The entries are then in chronological order under that initial letter. These Calendars usually list the Wills separate from the Admons., and sometimes the entries are found either on the same page but in different columns, or there may be several pages of references to Wills followed by several pages of Admons. While searching these, it will be necessary to check the lists of *both* Wills and Admons., and it is imperative that the entries not only be copied in full, but that each reference is marked either "WILL" or "ADMON."

In the following references, taken at random from the manuscript Calendars, note the varying amount of informa-tion given. Each reference has a corresponding entry in either the Probate Act Book (in the case of Wills)or the Admon. Act Book. In addition, those marked "Wills" are usually copies, in the folio (page) number given, in the large Registers of Wills. The original Admon. Bonds (and attached documents, if any) are too fragile or decayed for public inspection, and therefore the concise, and usually somewhat disappointing information recorded in the Admon. Act Book is all that is available at present.

Year	Will or Admon.	Notes if any	Name of deceased with comments, if needed	Residence	Month	Folio if any
1758	Will		Skay, Beale	Middx	Apr	132
1772	Will		James, Peter (Admon with Will)	Guernsey	Nov	409
1772	Admon	Ser.	Jarvis, Samuel	Pts	Feb	
1772	Admon		Isaac, John (Admon of Goods, unadm. Former grant Aug. 1763)	Mid	Jan	
1772	Will	Esqr.	Jordan, John Morton (Limited Probate)	Pts	July	263
1772	Will	Esqr.	Knight, Henry (Admon with Will unad. Will Regd. 345 St. Eloy)	Bucks	May	
1772	Will		Ker, David (Double Probate. Will regd in April 1770)	Essex	Apr	
1772	Will	Pts.	McIntosh, John	Mid	July	266
1772	Will	By Int. Decree	Oram, Roger	Wilts	June	227
1772	Admon	By Decree	Ormsby, James	Surry	Aug	
1772	Admon		Phillipps, John	Pts	May	
1796	Admon		Barton, William (Limited Admon.)	Kent	Oct	
1796	Admon		Boyd, John (98th Regt.)	Pts	Oct	
1796	Admon		Broad, Joseph (M. S. "Jamaica")	Middx	May	
1796	Admon	Ser.	Bartram, Robert ("Galatea")	Pts	Apl	

In regard to these entries in the Calendars of the P.C.C., the following points are worthy of note:

A. Where the residence is in England and Wales, the county (such as "Kent") is entered. Occasionally, in lieu of the county, the name of the city (such as "Bath") is entered.

B. If the residence was in Scotland, the abbreviation "N.B." (meaning North Britain) is entered. Ireland is occasionally mentioned. If in the Channel Islands or the Isle of Man, the entry may be similar to the foregoing example showing "Guernsey."

C. If the residence was outside the British Isles or the deceased died "in foreign parts," the designation "Pts" is usually entered in lieu of the name of a place. This means the deceased had property within the jurisdiction of the court. Occasionally both the name of a place and the designation "Pts" are entered.

D. Entries for soldiers often include name of the regiment such as "98th Regt.," and for sailors the name of the ship, such as

"Galatea." When the designation "Ser" is given, this indicates a "Serviceman" who was usually in the British Navy. The entry "M.S. Jamaica" refers to a merchant ship. If "E.I.Co." appears, this refers to the East India Company. Until 1801 the references appear in the General Calendar, but from 1801 the names of non-commissioned officers and men appear at the end of the General Calendar.

E. If Administration-with-Will-annexed has been granted, it is noted in the Calendar. This type of grant is discussed on pages 53, 82 and 83.

F. Wills usually name two or more Executors. Occasions arise where not all the Executors were present and so probate was granted to those present "with power reserved to the remaining Executor(s)." Should the remaining Executor(s) later apply for inclusion in the grant, this is described as a "Double Probate" and is noted as such in the Calendar. A reference is usually given, such as "Will registered in April 1770," back to the original grant.

G. When the reference relates to a "Limited Probate" or a "Limited Administration," this is detailed in the Calendar. These types of probates are described later.

H. A notation such as "By Decree," "By Interlocutory Decree," or "Sentence," indicates that a judgment of a court has entered into the process of probate. Details of the litigation involved may be filed in the Public Record Office, London, or elsewhere, and not in the P.C.C. records. In the P.C.C. it seems that until the 18th century such Wills which eventually received probate were often calendared together (in the year concerned) under the letter "S" and not under each testator's surname. At a later date reference to the Will was entered under the name of the testator in the normal place, with a note "by decree" or "int. dec."

I. When the Calendar reference relates to a second or later grant, this is noted. If it is a further grant of Administration, the date of the former grant is usually given. If it is a further grant concerning a Will, the volume and folio of the Registered Will is usually given. Sometimes the date, such as "Will Registered April 1770," is given. More often, however, the *folio number and name of the Register* only is given, such as, "Will Registered, 345 St. Eloy." The reference, such as "St. Eloy," is of interest, and the explanation is as follows:

The Registers of Copy Wills of the P.C.C. from 1384-1840 have been identified by *names* (such as "St. Eloy") and not by numbers or dates. Each year may cover several volumes, but the same distinguishing name is applied to all the volumes in the same year. There are 1,938 volumes down to 1840, and by 1858 this number had increased to 2,263. In order to determine to which year "St. Eloy" refers, it is necessary to consult the list that shows the name of each register and its corresponding year.

Alphabetical List of Names of the P.C.C. Registers of Wills.

Abbott, 1729
Abercrombie, 1801
Adderley, 1800
Adeane, 1506
Alchin, 1654
Alen, 1546
Alenger, 1540
Alexander, 1775
Anstis, 1744
Arden, 1840
Arran, 1759
Arundell, 1580
Ash, 1704
Aston, 1714
Auber, 1730
Audley, 1632
Aylett, 1655
Ayloffe, 1517

Babington, 1568
Bakon, 1579
Bargrave, 1774
Barnes, 1712
Barrett, 1708
Barrington, 1628
Bath, 1680
Beard, 1830
Bedford, 1732
Bellas, 1776
Bence, 1676
Bennett, 1508
Berkley, 1656
Bettesworth, 1752
Bevor, 1791
Bishop, 1790
Blamyr, 1501
Bodfelde, 1523
Bogg, 1769
Bolein, 1603
Bolton, 1724
Bond, 1696
Bowyer, 1652
Box, 1694
Boycott, 1743
Brent, 1653
Bridport, 1814
Brodrepp, 1738
Brook, 1728
Browne, 1740
Browning, 1719
Bruce, 1664
Brudenell, 1585
Bucke, 1551
Buckingham, 1721
Bunce, 1674
Busby, 1751
Butts, 1583
Byrde, 1624

Caesar, 1763
Calvert, 1788
Cambell, 1642

Cann, 1685
Capell, 1613
Carew, 1576
Carr, 1667
Chaynay, 1559
Chayre, 1563
Cheslyn, 1761
Clarke, 1625
Cobham, 1597
Coke, 1669
Coker, 1693
Collier, 1777
Collingwood, 1810
Collins, 1780
Coode, 1550
Cope, 1616
Cornwallis, 1783
Cottle, 1682
Coventry, 1640
Crane, 1643
Cresswell, 1818
Crickitt, 1811
Crumwell, 1536
Crymes, 1565
Dale, 1621
Daper, 1572
Darcy, 1581
Daughtry, 1577
Degg, 1703
Derby, 1736
Dixy, 1594
Dodwell, 1793
Dogett, 1491
Dorset, 1609
Drake, 1596
Drax, 1683
Drury, 1590
Ducarel, 1785
Ducie, 1735
Duke, 1671
Dycer, 1675
Dyer, 1701
Dyke, 1690
Dyngeley, 1537

Edmunds, 1746
Eedes, 1706
Effingham, 1817
Ellenboro', 1819
Ely, 1808
Ent, 1689
Erskine, 1824
Essex, 1648
Eure, 1672
Evelyn, 1641
Exeter, 1797
Exton, 1688

Fagg, 1715
Fairfax, 1649
Fane, 1692
Farquhar, 1833

Farrant, 1727
Fenner, 1612
Fetiplace, 1511
Fines, 1647
Foot, 1687
Fountain, 1792
Fox, 1716

Gee, 1705
Glazier, 1756
Gloucester, 1835
Goare, 1637
Godyn, 1463
Gostling, 1782
Greenly, 1750
Grey, 1651

Hale, 1677
Hare, 1684
Harrington, 1592
Harris, 1796
Harte, 1604
Harvey, 1639
Hav, 1778
Hayes, 1605
Heathfield, 1813
Heber, 1827
Hele, 1626
Henchman, 1739
Hene, 1668
Herne, 1702
Herring, 1757
Herschell, 1822
Heseltine, 1804
Hogen, 1533
Holder, 1514
Holgrave, 1504
Holman, 1794
Holney, 1571
Horne, 1496
Howe, 1799
Hudleston, 1607
Hutton, 1758
Hyde, 1665

Irby, 1695
Isham, 1731
Jankyn, 1529
Jenner, 1770
Juxon, 1663

Kent, 1820
Kenyon, 1802
Ketchyn, 1556
Kidd, 1599
King, 1679

Lane, 1709
Langley, 1578
Laud, 1662
Lawe, 1614
Lee, 1638

Leeds, 1713
Legard, 1767
Leicester, 1588
Lewyn, 1597
Lisle, 1749
Liverpool, 1829
Lloyd, 1686
Loftes, 1561
Logge, 1479
Lort, 1698
Loveday, 1809
Luffenam, 1423
Lusnington, 1807
Lynch, 1760
Lyon, 1570

Macham, 1789
Major, 1787
Mansfield, 1821
Marche, 1401
Marlbro, 1722
Marriott, 1803
Martyn, 1574
May, 1661
Maynwaryng, 1520
Meade, 1618
Mellershe, 1559
Mico, 1666
Milles, 1487
Montague, 1602
Moone, 1500
More, 1554
Morrison &
   Crynies, 1565

Nabbs, 1660
Nelson, 1805
Nevell, 1593
Newcastle, 1795
Nicholl, 1838
Noel, 1700
Noodes, 1558
Norfolk, 1786
North, 1681
Norwich, 1837

Ockham, 1734
Oxford, 1812

Pakenham, 1815
Parker, 1619
Paul, 1755
Pell, 1659
Pembroke, 1650
Penn, 1670
Peter, 1573
Pett, 1699
Pile, 1636
Pinfold, 1754
Pitt, 1806
Plymouth, 1726
Poley, 1707

Populwell, 1548	Sadler, 1635	Stevenson, 1564	Vaughan, 1839
Porch, 1525	Sainberbe, 1591	Stokton, 1454	Vere, 1691
Potter, 1747	St. Albans, 1825	Stonard, 1567	Vox, 1493
Powell, 1552	St. Eloy, 1762	Stowell, 1836	
Price,1733	St. John, 1631	Strahan, 1748	Wake, 1737
Pyckering, 1575	Savile, 1622	Streat, 1562	Wallop, 1600
Pye, 1673	Scott, 1595	Sutton, 1828	Walpole, 1798
Pyne, 1697	Scroope, 1630	Sutton, 1828	Warburton, 1779
Pynnyng, 1544	Seager, 1634	Swabey, 1826	Watson, 1584
Reeve, 1678	Searle, 1753	Swann, 1623	Wattys, 1471
Richards, 1823	Secker, 1768		Webster, 1781
Richmond, 1723	Seymer, 1745	Tashe, 1553	Weldon, 1617
Ridley, 1629	Shaller, 1720	Taverner, 1772	Welles, 1558
Rivers, 1644	Sheffelde, 1569	Tebbs, 1831	Whitfield, 1717
Rockingham, 1784	Simpson, 1764	Teignmouth, 1834	Windebanck, 1608
Romney, 1725	Skinner, 1627	Tenterden, 1832	Windsor, 1586
Rous, 1384	Smith, 1710	Tenison, 1718	Wingfield, 1610
Rowe, 1583	Soame, 1620	Thower, 1531	Wood, 1611
Rudd, 1615	Spencer, 1587	Tirwhite, 1582	Woodhall, 1601
Rushworth, 1765	Spert, 1541	Trenley, 1742	Wootton, 1658
Russell, 1633	Spurway, 1741	Trevor, 1771	Wrastley, 1557
Ruthen, 1657	Stafford, 1606	Twisse, 1646	Wynne, 1816
Rutland, 1588	Stevens, 1773	Tyndall, 1766	Young, 1711

Commencing in 1841, the Registers of Wills are identified by the year, and not by name.

ADMINISTRATION CALENDARS. No. 1, 1559-90; No. 2, 1591-1600; No. 3, 1601-8; No. 4, 1609-14; No. 5, 1615-30; No. 19b, 1653-4; No. 23b, 1658.

ADMINISTRATION ACT BOOKS complete from 1559, except that 1662 is lost.

ORIGINAL WILLS begin 1484, but are very sparse to about 1524. Fairly complete from about 1600.

PROBATE ACT BOOKS begin November 1526. Wanting from October 1538 to October 1547, and the years 1650, 1653, 1654 and 1662.

COUNTIES are not indicated in Will Calendars previous to 1631.

DATES IN THIS LIST are given in "historical" or "new" style throughout.

J. Each folio number given in the Calendar references relates to a folio in the Register of Wills for the year concerned. The folio number is *not* strictly a page number, as a folio consists of a number of pages, often as many as sixteen. To locate the Registered Copy of the Will it is necessary to find the folio number in the Register and then to search forward from that point.

Pitfalls to avoid when using Calendars and Indexes.

Each of the following items taken from Calendars and Indexes illustrates a pitfall that may await the record searcher. There are many others.

i. *Overlooking second probates.*
References, such as "William Eastcott, A., 1740; d.b.n., 1742," indicate that in 1740 a grant of Letters of Administration was made, and that in 1742 a further grant, "D.B.N." was made. Reference to "d.b.n." found in the list of Abbreviations in Chapter 2, will disclose that these letters mean *de bonis non administratis,* a Latin phrase indicating that a further grant was

made "of goods not administered by" the previous administrators, who may have died or renounced before the estate was fully settled.

ii. *Assuming all Calendars are cross-referenced.*
References, such as "*Udy,* see *Eudy,*" are of interest. Some Calendars cross-reference different spellings of a surname, but it is unwise to expect this to occur in all Calendars. Further, some Calendars may contain some cross-references, but such listings may not be exhaustive. Surnames that have variations unknown to the compiler of the Calendar would not be cross-referenced. It is, therefore, difficult to determine whether or not an existing probate record is hidden under some uncommon spelling of a surname.

iii. *Being alert for possible spelling errors.*
References that contain spelling or other errors are hard to detect, as the two following examples indicate:

(i). In a manuscript Calendar or Index the Will of Thomas Seager is recorded under letter "L" (and spelled Leager), instead of under letter "S".

(ii). In 1776 the Will of *David* Jones was proved, but the Calendar for that year does not contain the name of *David* Jones. The name of *Daniel* Jones, however, does appear, and it is an error for *David* Jones.

2. ACT BOOKS

Probate Act Books usually relate to Wills, and *Administration Act Books* relate to Letters of Administration, although the Acts relating to both Wills and Admons. were often recorded in the same book. Entries in an Act Book recording Wills and Letters of Administration apparently are regarded as official or authoritative evidence of the issue of grants relating to them, as they briefly state the *action* (Act) of the court.

Endorsements of the Act on original Wills (see examples of endorsements on the Wills of William Humphrey [pages 59-61] and Robert Coundley [page 95]) and the existence of Testamentary and Administration Bonds, also indicates that the court has acted and issued official grants. As some courts have either lost or did not keep Act Books, endorsements on Wills, and Bonds are a clear indication of the Acts.

Act Book entries were made on a day-by-day basis as each event took place. These entries are often helpful and may supply important information that *cannot be found elsewhere.* The following items of genealogical interest may be found in Act Books:

i. The parish of residence of the testator or intestate.

ii. The previous place of residence of the testator or intestate.

iii. His marital status.

iv. His trade, profession or status.

v. Details of the appointed executor(s).

vi. Details of appointed administrators.

vii. Details of second or further grants.

viii. Mention of Registered or Unregistered Wills that may have been omitted in the Calendar.

ix. Details of tuitions, curations and guardianships.

x. Details of caveats and other testamentary business.

Act Books may supply details of a person (and family) where a Will or Admon. has been lost since the grant was made.

* * *

The Latin Probate Act and its translation from the foot to the Will of Robert Coundley, 1696. (Peculiar Court of the Chancellor of the Choir of the Cathedral [Church of Hereford] in the parishes of Little Hereford and Ashford Carbonell (Salop).

Probatum erat h[ujus]mo[d]i Test[ament]um apud Hereford[iam] p[ar]va[m] secundo die mens[is] Novembris A[nn]o d[omi]ni 1696° Cor[am] Reu[eren]do viro Joseph Harvey Art[ium] M[agist]ro Cancellario Chori &c., p[er] Eliz[abeth]am Coundley Relict[am] et Ex[ecutri]cem &c. Cui &c. primitus de bene &c. ac de pleno &c. Necnon de vero &c. Coram discreto viro Thoma Marston Art[ium] M[agist]ro Surr[ogat]o &c. Jurat[am] (salvo Jure cujuscu[n]que)

This will was proved at Little Hereford the second day of November in the year of our Lord 1696 before the Reverend Joseph Harvey, Master of Arts, Chancellor of the Choir [of the Cathedral Church of Hereford] &c., by Elizabeth Coundley relict and executrix &c. to whom [administration was granted] &c., she being first sworn well [and truly to administer the same and to exhibit an inventory of all and singular the goods chattels and credits of the said deceased] before Thomas Marston, Master of Arts, Surrogate &c. (saving the right of all)

2° Novem[bris] 1696°

Jur[ata] fuit Executrix in h[ujus]mo[d]i Test[ament]o
no[m]i[n]ata de p[er]implend[o] id[e]m Test(ament)um
ac de veritate In [venta] rij ex [hibi] ti

Cor[am] me
Tho: Marston Sur[rogato]

2 November 1696.

The Executrix named in this will was then sworn duly
to perform the same and to the truth of the Inventory
exhibited.

Before me
Tho: Marston Surrogate

* * *

If there are Calendars or Indexes for the court, they
should be used to determine the date or year of the grant
and then a check of the Act Books is practical. As Act Book
entries usually mention all Wills and Admons., including any
which may have been omitted from the Calendar, Unregistered
Wills not found in the Registers, and bonds, renunciations,
inventories, tuitions, curations, caveats, etc., there is an obvious
value in the searching of Act Books. A search of the files
of bundles or boxes of Original Wills and Admons. is necessary to locate the documents mentioned.

The following examples, only a few of the many that
could be cited, illustrate the different ways in which Act
Books are arranged. Some of these examples contain abbreviated forms of common probate terms, but usually such abbreviations are obvious in their meaning and it is not difficult
to make genealogical abstracts of the record. When the
abbreviated words are in Latin it is more difficult to determine
the correct meaning unless the searcher is familiar with Latin.
There is no standard list of abbreviations, often the shortened
version of a word or term being peculiar to one clerk.

i. *General Notes on Printed Abstracts from Act Books.*

Where Act Books have been used as one of the sources
for compiling indexes to Wills and Admons., much valuable
genealogical material is available in print. This has already
been discussed under "General Notes on Printed Calendars
and Indexes" (see page 72). It is of further interest to
note the following quotation from Volume 1 of *Abstracts of
Probate Acts in the P.C.C. 1630-1634:*

Probate Act Books of the P.C.C. exist in an almost unbroken series from the year 1526, and are of great value . . . because . . . they afford a means of obtaining a list of Wills . . . more complete even than the Official [manuscript] Calendars themselves . . . the probate Acts not only state where the Testator died, but often note changes of residence during his lifetime, and, in cases where a comparison of the Will with the Probate Act shows the Testator to have changed his place of residence in the interval between making of the Will and his death, the fact will be noted by the Editors. Also an index which gives the names of Executors as well as Testators will prove invaluable . . . The great advantage of such an index is illustrated by the [printed] Year Book [of Probate Acts] for 1630, *whose portion of the Index Nominum contains half as many references again as the Official Calendar for that year,* while *one one quarter of the "different" names occurring in the former are not to be found at all in the latter.*

ii. *Common Type of Act Book Entries.*

The illustrations on pages 98 and 99 are taken from the Act Books of the probate courts formerly at Chester. On page 82 mention is made of the "Infra" and "Supra" jurisdictions and the present division of the records on a county basis. By comparing the illustrations with the following transcripts the meaning of the contracted words used in these particular examples is apparent.

A. *Act Book of Chester — "Infra" Jurisdiction.*

JONES March 27, 1776, before Mr. Vanbrugh. Will of David[4] Jones, estate valued under £40, late of Little Neston in the Deanery of Wirral, Yeoman, deceased, was executed and Administration etc. granted to Hannah Jones the sole executrix.

SEDDON March 27, 1776, before Mr. Fishwick. Letters of Administration, dated 18th Instant [i.e., the same month], of Samuel Seddon, the estate valued under £40, late of Liverpool, Watchmaker, deceased, was granted to Elizabeth Seddon, Daughter and next of kin of the said deceased.

SWARBRICK April 2nd, 1776, before Mr. Fishwick. Letters of Administration, of William Swarbrick, late of Liverpool, mariner, deceased, *was* granted unto William Swarbrick the Grandfather and Tutor and Curator of Ellen Fisher Swarbrick, a Minor of the Age of two years or thereabouts, the Natural and lawful Daughter and next of kin of the said deceased, for the use and only during the minority of the said Minor. Estate valued under £20.

---

4. The name in above Act Book is David Jones. In the original Will it is David Jones. In the printed Calendar for Chester it is Daniel Jones.

Note that in the foregoing examples that the *county* of residence is not stated. Because this probate court covered more than one county and because the probate records have been divided among the record offices of those counties, the name of the county must be determined before a search in the corresponding original or microfilmed records can be made.

In the two examples that follow note that the *county* is included. In the case of John Woolrich note that a renuncia' tion occurred disclosing valuable genealogical detail.

B. *Act Books of Chester — "Supra" Jurisdiction.*

CLARKE 3rd January 1778. The last Will and Testament of George Clarke, late of Hyde . . . Chester, Esquire, deceased, . . . granted to Robert Crispin and William Sanford, the Executors . . .

WOOLRICH 8th January 1778. Letters of Administration . . . of John Woolrich, late of Wrenbury ffrith . . . Gentleman . . . granted to John Woolrich his Son, etc. . . . Mary Woolrich, Widow and Relict of the decedent and Thomas Woolrich, Henry Woolrich, and Elizabeth the Wife of Thomas Cooper, Sons and Daughter of the said deceased having . . . re' nounced . . .

The Third day of January 1711/12

Clarke.

The last Will and Testament of George Clarke late of Ryde in the County and Diocese of Chester Esquire deceased was intimated proved approved and sworn Valid and Execution thereof and Administration of the Goods Chattels and Credits of the Cedent were granted to Robert Beckman and Valliant Comford the Executors therein named being first sworn before the Reverend Charles Trenchman Clerk Surrogate the right of every Person and person allowed them to exhibit an Inventory.

8.

Woolrich.

Letters of Administration of the Goods Chattels and Credits of John Woolrich late of Wrexham within the County and Diocese of Chester Gentleman deceased were granted to John Woolrich the son to being first sworn to and the married Mr Mannering Surrogate Mary Woolrich Widow and Relict of the deceased and Thomas Woolrich Henry Woolrich and Eliza both the sons of Thomas above son and Daughter of the said deceased having first under the hand and seal renounced the right of Administration of the said Goods to the right of every Person being sworn as usual they being also such a time allowed him to exhibit an Inventory.

iii. *Act Book entry disclosing the name of the father of the testator when the Will fails to do so.*

It is of interest to note that The Calendar for Chester records the entry of Matthew *Neeld*, of Sutton, in 1776. In the original Will mention is made of the appointment of the testator's father and brother William as executors. The name of the father is *not* stated. The Act Book ("Infra" Jurisdiction) records:

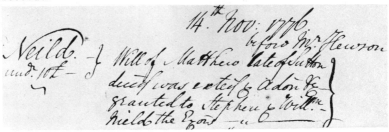

NEILD 14th Nov. 1776. Will of Matthew [Neild] late of Sutton
deceased was executed and administration etc. granted to
Stephen and William *Nield* the Executors.

iv. *Act Book entry recording a residence different from that stated in the Calendar.*

An Act Book entry might indicate that the address of the deceased was different from that mentioned in the Calendar. The probate record of John Davall is listed in the "Supra" Calendar for 1801 of the Episcopal Consistory Court of Chester, stating that he was of *Savannah in North America*. Such information would be misleading if a search was being made for the Davall family connected with Liverpool. The corresponding "Supra" Act Book entry is as follows:

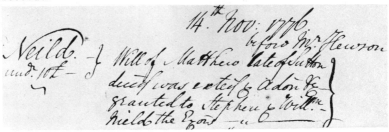

DAVALL Administration of John Davall late of Liverpool Master
and Mariner deceased was granted unto Priscilla Davall
Widow the Relict. Estate under £600. [3rd Sept. 1801.]

v. *Act Book Entry where Patronymics are involved.*

In the Episcopal Consistory Court of Saint Asaph the Act Book for 1787 to 1805 has an index of persons. Because of the use of patronymics in Wales, a search in the records of St. Asaph for a reference relating to Richard Edwards of

Garthbeibio would be made in the index under the letter "R" for Richard, the first given name of the individual concerned. The index reference appears as follows:

Type of Documents	Names	Residence	Folio No. in Act Book
A.T.	Richard Edwards,	Garthbeibio,	73.

The index reference to the letters "A. T." indicates that this type of document is an "Administration-with-Testament-annexed," which means that the grant was that of Letters of Administration-with-Will-annexed.

The following illustration shows the original entry on folio 73:

Note that the name of the parish or place appearing in large handwriting in the margin, while the name of the deceased is not so clearly discernible. This method of recording is of advantage to a record searcher interested only in the probate records relating to a particular place without concern to surname. Some courts follow the procedure of recording the name of the parish in large handwriting although others enter the name of the deceased in the same place.

vi. *Example of an Act Book entry written in Latin.*

Many Act Books, as well as other probate documents are written in Latin. It was not until 1733 that the law ordered that all legal documents be written in English. The following reproduction is taken from the original manuscript Act Book for 1693 of the Commissary Court of London (for Essex and Herts.):

Compare the illustration with the following transcript and translation:

TRANSCRIPT.

Probatum fuit Testamentum Richardi ffrogg nuper de Thaxted in Com Essex yeoman defuncti apud Dunmow—primo die Mensis Aprilis Anno Dni 1693 coram M[agist]ro Jacobo Carkesse Cler[ico] Surrogato ven[erabi]lis viri D[omi]ni Caroli Hedges Mil[iti] Legum Doctoris in partibus Essexiae et Hertfordiae Comissarii &c juram[en]to Thomae Franklin Executoris &c cui com[m]issa fuit Ad[ministra]tio &c de bene &c jurat salvo &c. ⸴ ⸴ ⸴

TRANSLATION.

The Will of Richard Frogg formerly of Thaxted in the County of Essex, yeoman, deceased, was proved at Dunmow the first day of the month of April in the year of our Lord 1693, before "master" James Carkesse, clerk, surrogate of the venerable "man" "lord" Charles Hedges, Knight, Doctor of Laws, Com-missary etc., "in partibus,"[5] for Essex and Hertfordshire, by the oath of Thomas Franklin, the executor, etc., to whom the administration was committed, etc., [being] sworn [to] well [and faithfully administer] etc., saving, etc. ⸴ ⸴ ⸴ [The estate being valued at £283 1s 4d].

The translation of Latin in probate records should not be attempted without a knowledge of Latin. Rather than guess at the translation of seemingly obvious words, the assistance of an expert should be obtained.

vii. *Example of Cross-References in Act Books.*

Additional notes, often added in the margin, appear oc-casionally in Calendars, Act Books, Registers and other probate records. These additional notes sometimes contain details of earlier grants or other business concerning the grant.

General Script Indexes for Wills and Admons., covering the Prer-ogative Court of York and Exchequer Court of York for 1779:

March: ARMSTRONG, Francis of Scampston, Gent., P'rog. T rpt.

---

5. "in partibus" a Latin term for "in those parts [of Essex and Herts. that came under the jurisdiction of the Commissary Court of London]."

This example indicates that a Testament or Will of Francis Armstrong of Scampston was proved in the Prerogative Court of York in March 1779. The abbreviation "rpt" means "re-spited" and indicates that when the Will was proved there was no inventory submitted, the actual value of the estate not having been determined.

In the Register of Wills (P.C.Y.) for 1779 is the copy of the Will of Francis Armstrong. At the end of this copy Will brief mention is made that the grant of probate was dated 4 March 1779. No marginal or other note is in this Register entry. *It would be unwise to disregard the possible Act Book entry.* Note the full entry as it appears in the P.C.Y. Act Book for 1779:

March 1779

ARMSTRONG. See another Grant 2nd October 1843.	The fourth day . . . The last Will and Testament of Ffrancis Armstrong late of Scampston . . . . County of York (having &c) Gentleman dece[ase]d passed the Seal of this Court . . . was granted to Robert Knowsley and George Telford Gentlemen joint Executors in the said Will.

The notation in the left-hand margin of the Act Book, "See another Grant 2nd October 1843," is mentioned neither in the 1779 Calendar reference nor in the Register of Wills, yet it gives a direct connection with a further grant of no less than *sixty-four years* later. This later grant found by reference to the P.C.Y. Act Book for 1843, contains the following information:

October 1843.

ARMSTRONG. Under £600. Former Grant 4th March 1779.	The second day . . . Administration (with the Will annexed) of the goods . . . of Francis Armstrong late of Scampston . . . granted to Mary Knowsley spinster his Granddaughter one of the next of kin and one of the reversionary residuary Legatees named in the said Will (left unadministered by Robert Knowsley the son in law and George Telford the Nephew . . . the said Robert Knowsley having survived the said George Telford and died intestate, George Knowsley, Eliza Chapman widow and Henrietta Thistlethwaite widow the grandson and granddaughters remaining next of kin . . . having renounced).

A *search that had been confined to the Calendar and the reading of a Will and that had ignored the Act Books would have failed to find important information relating to the family.*

In addition to the copy Will in the Register, there is the original Will in the bundles (or files) to which a Testamentary Bond is attached. This bond records *additional* information concerning the executors, stating that Robert Knowsley and George Telford were both of the City of York. A third bondsman, Thomas Brook of the same City, gentleman is also named. The Registered copy Will does not contain original signatures, but the original Will and Testamentary Bond have the autographs (i.e., original signatures) of all parties, including witnesses.

A search of the original Wills (in bundles and files) as well as the copy in the Register of Wills is, therefore, wise genealogical practice.

It is logical, when searching for a probate record to confine the search to the period in which a person is thought to have died, in this example, around 1779. Although there would be little or no reason to search up to as late as 1843, circumstances may occur where the reference to a second (or later) grant will be the *first* mention found of the deceased's probate record. Many second (or later) grants are given within a year or several years of the first grant, and the period of sixty-four years in the case of Francis Armstrong is rather unusual. The Script Indexes for the P.C.Y. has the following reference:

1843
October   ARMSTRONG, Francis of Scampston, Prog Ad.b.n.c.T. 600£.

This brief Calendar reference in 1843 *does not show that it relates to a Will* proved in 1779. The abbreviations, however, supply clues. *Prog* indicates the grant was in the Prerogative Court. *Ad.b.n.c.T.* 600£ means "*Administratio* [de] *bonis non administratis cum Testamentum* [value under] £600" and indicates that administration, of goods not administered by the previous executors or administrators, with Will-annexed, was granted.

A search of the Registers of Wills for 1843 would be fruitless, but the Act Book entry in 1843 discloses the earlier grant in 1779.

Note that the Will of Francis Armstrong was proved in 1779, entered in the Act Book and copied into the Register of Wills for that same year. The Register of Wills for 1843 would not disclose a copy. The Act Book entry recording the second grant dated 1843, cross-references back to the grant of 1779, the year in which the Will will be found registered and filed.

The previous example is straightforward — the Will was proved in 1779 and the second grant was made in 1843. References in the General Script Indexes indicated that both these grants were made in the same Court. References in the General Script Indexes of York, however, refer to *two* courts:

(a) *The Prerogative Court of York.*

Nearly all Wills, except in cases of litigation, were proved locally. Usually some neighboring clergyman received a special commission to prove Wills or make grants of Letters of Administration, and later he returned the documents into the court at York. The grants then were entered into the Prerogative Court Act Book, most Wills were registered, and the documents, as described below for the Exchequer Court, were filed in bundles.

(b) *The Exchequer Court of York.*

The practice in the Diocese of York was for the Will to be proved or Letters of Administration granted locally. The probate court for the diocese was The Exchequer Court. Each of the rural deans in the Diocese of York had a commission from the Commissary of the Exchequer Court to prove Wills and grant Letters of Administration within their own rural deanery. The rural dean, having made grants, periodically returned the documents into the court at York.

Entries were then made of the grants of probate and Letters of Administration in the Act Book of that particular deanery. Most Wills were copied into registers, although occasionally, some Wills were not registered. The original documents, Wills, Testamentary and Administration Bonds, Curations, Tuitions, Inventories, Renunciations, and other papers were then filed in the bundles.

The General Script Indexes (Calendars) of York for 1809 disclose:

1809
December   TAYLOR, Montague of Sheffield.   T.   800.

This indicates that a T(estament) or Will of Montague Taylor of Sheffield, (no county stated) was proved in December 1809, and that the value of the estate was under £800. The absence of the notation "P'rog," as in the example of Francis Armstrong, 1779 and 1843, is an implication that the Will was proved in the Exchequer Court of York. A search of the Registers of Wills for 1809 would disclose whether or not the Will was registered. As well as reading the Will, it is essential to check the Act Book entry, and as there were sixteen deaneries in the Diocese of York, it would be necessary to check the *Deanery Book* to find the name of the deanery in which Sheffield is situated. This reference book records that Sheffield was in the Deanery of Doncaster and the following abstract is taken from the Act Book for Doncaster Deanery for 1809:

[December 1809].

TAYLOR.
See another
Grant
2nd October
1843

The sixteenth day . . . the last Will . . . of Montague Taylor late of Sheffield . . . granted to Samuel Taylor his son and William Jessop his son in law the joint executors . . .

Note the marginal notation dated 1843 but added to this Act Book entry of 1809. This prompted a search of the Act Book for the same Doncaster Deanery under date 2nd October 1843, but no record of any such further grant was found, implying that the second Grant must have been made in *another* court and *not* in the Exchequer Court. A check of the General Script Indexes for 1843 lists the following reference:

1843
October   TAYLOR, Montague of Sheffield. Preog. A. 201.

This indicates that Letters of Administration were granted in October 1843 in the Prerogative Court. The Act Book for the Prerogative Court discloses the following abstract:

October 1843.

TAYLOR.
(*By Decree*)
Former Grant
16 Dec. 1809.

The same day [2nd October] Administration of . . . Montague Taylor late of Sheffield . . . bricklayer . . . was granted (by Decree of Court) to Joseph Woodcock . . . (left unadministered by William Jessop the surviving executor . . . deceased intestate . . .) *Limited* . . . to . . . the residue . . . of a certain Indenture of Demise [dated] . . . 15 July 1805 . . . etc.

A comparison of these records demonstrates the importance of studying each one and shows that cross-references found in second or later grants are useful in checking back to the first grant. The example of Montague Taylor is in the records of York where the Indexes and Registers for the Prerogative Court of York and the Exchequer Court are consolidated. If the original grant had been in some other diocesan or other minor court, and the later grant(s) made in yet another court, *there would be, except on rare occasions, no cross-references in the margins* of Act Books, Calendars and Registers of Wills.

There are some probate courts which did not take the trouble to give marginal cross-reference to the dates of the original and subsequent grants occurring in the same court. Some courts did not keep or have lost their Act Books. Some Wills mention a Will or grant of Letters of Administration of another individual, and the earlier record is not necessarily filed in the same probate court as the document in which it is mentioned. In some instances, it might be necessary to look far afield for the earlier record.

viii. *Example of Lack of Cross-references in Act Books.*

Not in all courts do the Act Books and Indexes cross-reference subsequent grants. There is the possibility that a testator appointed an executor or trustee to take care of all or a portion of the estate which eventually was held in the name of the executor or trustee who died, leaving a portion of the trust estate unadministered. If such a trustee's Will made no mention of the trust property, or if the trustee died *intestate* the next-of-kin of the first mentioned testator would apply for Letters of Administration of the estate of the trustee (*Limited* to the trust concerned) in order to gain possession of the property.

The references to the original grant in Act Books and Calendars may not have cross-references to those relating to the grant concerning the intestate trustee, and vice versa. Such grants conceivably could be in entirely different courts!

Note the following example:

(i). *The P.C.C. Calendar (Index) for 1758.*

WILL: Skay, Beale Middx. April [folio] 132.

(ii). *The P.C.C. Probate Act Book for 1758.*

APRIL.   On the 24th day, the Will of Beale Skay, late of . . . St.
Mary, Islington, Co. Middx., decd., was proved by the oath
of Frances Skay, widow the relict . . .

(iii). *P.C.C. Register of Wills "Hutton" for 1758, folio 132.*
Abstract of the Will of Beale Skay, of Bucklesbury,
London, victualler, dated 8 January 1756.

I bequeath to my brother, Edward Skay, of Petticoat Lane, County
Middlesex, Tallow Chandler, and William Barton, of Grays Inn
Lane, Holbourne, Brewer, £1,000, Three percent Annuities in
the Bank of England, in *TRUST*. That they . . . shall place the
said sum in their joint names and pay the interest to my wife,
Frances, for the rest of her life.

After the decease of my wife . . . that they pay the said interest
of Annuities to such child or children I may have . . . in equal
shares until they attain the age of twenty-one years, when the
said Annuities shall be assigned in equal proportions . . .
Should there be no child or children . . . or that they should
die before the age of twenty-one years, without issue, then . . .
to sell the said Annuities and share the proceeds amongst my
brothers and sisters [not named] and their representatives.
To my Mother and Father [not named] £20 each . . . also the
same amount . . . to my brothers and sisters . . .
To Mr. Richard Cox, a guinea for a ring, and £5 to each of my
trustees. I appoint the said brother, Edward Skay, and William
Barton, as Supervisors of my Will, and after the decease of my
wife, Guardians of such of my child or children until they reach
twenty-one years of age.
All the rest . . . to my wife, Frances Skay, whom I make sole
executrix.

Wits: John Wilson.
Jno. Savile.

[Will proved 24 April 1758 by executrix].

Note that there are no additional references or cross-
references in the probate Act Book, Calendar, and Registered
Will to any further business connected with the Will and
trust-estate of Beale Skay. It is likely, however, that in many
similar instances there would be no need of further action,
as the administration of the whole estate might have been
settled during the lifetime of the executor(s) and trustee(s),
and the trust ended.

There are cases where later mention of such property
occurs, but not cross-referenced, and a search for further reference would depend upon the circumstances. If a sole surviving
executor, administrator, or trustee died possessing in *his* name

an unadministered portion of an estate, he could have disposed of it to the rightful heirs by mentioning it in his Will. Failing such mention, or having died *intestate,* the next-of-kin (*of the earlier testator*) could apply for Letters of Administration Limited[6] to the unadministered portion which, at the time of death, was in the possession of such an executor, administrator, or trustee.

In the example of Beale Skay, the trustees appointed by him were survived by Mrs. Frances Skay, his widow and relict and sole executrix. The Calendar does not disclose, after 1758, any grants relating to his widow, Mrs. Frances Skay and his brother Edward Skay (one of the trustees). The name of William Barton, the other trustee, is a common one but there was no reference to a William Barton of London or Middlesex — the Will of 1758 having described him of Holborn, a locality in London and Middlesex — identifiable with the trustee. In the Calendar for 1796, how-ever, the following reference was noted:

(i). *The P.C.C. Calendar (or Index) 1796.*

ADMON: Barton, William   Kent   Oct.
          (Limited Admon.)

The above reference prompted a search in the Act Book for 1796, which disclosed the following information:

(ii). *The P.C.C. Admon. Act Book 1796.*

OCTOBER   Barton, William—"Limited Admon. entered at length."

The following is partial abstract of the record "entered at length" in the Act Book:

William Barton, formerly of St. Andrew Holborn, Middlesex, but late of Chatham, Kent.

Thomas Answell [applying for Letters of Admon.] alledged that William Barton died November 1767 *intestate,* leaving Elizabeth his widow and William and John his only children. That William Barton was whilst living the surviving trustee named in the Will of Beale Skay who died in 1756, and that Edward Skay, the other trustee died in 1760. Elizabeth Barton, the widow of William Barton, had died intestate, and the son William went to the East Indies thirty years ago and died intestate, a bachelor, neither

---

6. Limited Probates are explained later.

having taken upon them Letters of Administration of the said deceased William Barton. The other son, John, was now residing in Jamaica and had not appeared [to accept Letters of Admon.]. The said Beale Skay died without any issue, and his widow Frances Skay died 1795 [intestate] and the estate of £1,000 in trust was distributable amongst the brothers and sisters of Beale Skay. Thomas Answell was son and administrator of the goods, etc., of Mary Answell formerly Skay, widow, deceased, who was the sister and one of the next-of-kin of Beale Skay.

Therefore Thomas Answell was granted authority to Administer . . . limited as far only as concerns the said sum of £1,000. Dated 17 October 1796.

The Will of Beale Skay was proved in 1758 and the grant of Letters of Admon. for William Barton (the trustee) was in 1796, both in the same court. Nothing in the Calendars (Indexes) indicate that Beale Skay, his widow Mrs. Frances Skay, his brother Edward Skay, his sister Mrs. Mary Answell (formerly Skay), and his nephew Thomas Answell are in any way connected with the grant of Letters of Admon. of William Barton in 1796.[7]

It has already been pointed out (see page 107) that original and subsequent grants might not have been made from the same court. The determining from an original grant where (if any) a subsequent grant might be recorded, or from a later mention of a Will or Admon. where the original record is to be found consequently is made difficult.

It is unfortunate that, where an executor, trustee, or administrator died possessing in his name, property that rightfully should pass to the next-of-kin of the original owner, the Calendars (or Indexes) do not give the names of the original testator (or intestate) and the subsequent next-of-kin in conjunction with the final settlement of such a case, especially when the surnames of all parties concerned may be different. "Index Nominum" or "Indexes to Stray Names" might be essential before the clues of such records can be found by the record searcher.

ix. Non-testamentary Recordings in Act Books.

The ecclesiastical probate courts existing before 1858 also dealt with matters other than those connected with testamentary business. Many of the registers, journals, account books, diaries, act and bill books, minute books and other

---

7. See additional notes and comments on the Answell and Skay problem under "Limited and Special Probate Records," see page 122.

bound records of these courts contained the proceedings of both probate and the non-testamentary cases. After 1858, when ecclesiastical probate jurisdiction ceased, many of these records were turned over to the officials of the civil probate registries. These records contain valuable information con' nected with matters that came under the jurisdiction of the courts, such as marriage licenses, presentments for not attend' ing church, for not baptizing children, for bastardity, etc.; depositions and citations, etc. in ecclesiastical matters; faculties of court for Pews and other matters; parish church terriers; visitation records, etc.

x. *Examples of Litigation recorded in Act Books.*

Details of litigation arising out of probates occasionally are found recorded in the Act Books of some probate courts.

A.   In the Act Book of the Archdeaconry Court of Huntington [Herts. Division at Hitchin] appears recitation of the lawsuit concerning the estate of Thomas How of Berkhampstead St. Peters, [Herts.]. Details appear under various dates from July to November 1639 and are entered on folios (pages) 18, 20, 22, 24, 26, 28, and 30. These record the cause or James Lucas of Berkhampstead, St. Peters, (guard' ian of Elizabeth Lucas, his daughter by his late wife Elizabeth How *alias* Lucas, deceased, who was the daughter of the said Thomas How, and a legatee under his Will) against Isabel How *alias* Stevens, of Berkhampstead St. Peters, the executrix of the Will of the said Thomas How, "*in causa legati.*"

B.   Entry of the proceedings of a court in the Act Book occasionally discloses that the probate record, ordinarily ex' pected to be filed in that court, was actually proved elsewhere. In the Act Book it is recorded that on 23 May 1751, "the Office of the Judge" of the Archdeaconry Court of Huntingdon alledged that George Priest had taken the Will of his late Mother, Mrs. Catherine Priest of Willian, County Hertford, widow, to the Prerogative Court of Canterbury in London, although "it appearing that there was no foundation for prov' ing the Will . . . in the Prerogative" Court. Record of such proceedings is rarely found, but when they are located in Act Books, the clue is given where a Will of a family might be found. In the P.C.C. (London) Calendars appears a reference to the above Will:

WILL   Priest, Katherine,   Hertford.   December [1750] [folio] 397.

This indicates that the Will is to be found at folio 397 in the Registers of Wills for the P.C.C.

The recitation of litigation or other court business con' cerning probates often contains genealogical information not recorded elsewhere. If found in the Act Books, persons who are related to the deceased may be mentiond and often clearly identified. The process of law in connection with probates will be found under a variety of terms, such as "Limited" and "Special Probates," "Caveats," "Assignations," "Testamentary Suits," "Monitions," etc., all of which are dealt with in the chapter that follows.

Chapter 5

MISCELLANEOUS PROBATE RECORDS

1. CAVEATS.

When a creditor, widow, brother, sister, or other relative of the deceased, who might have an interest in the estate wished to prevent probate being granted without their knowl-edge, they would enter a *Caveat*, that is, a warning notice, at the court so that no action would be taken without their case being heard. Many notices concerning Caveats are entered in the Act Books, although some courts kept separate records, similar to the following example.

i. *Caveat Book 1727-1838, Deanery Courts of South Malling and Battle.*

> 29 Sept. 1810 In proving the will of William Payne, West-hoathly, yeoman. [Caveat] at instance [of] John Stone of Worth, son-in-law of the deceased.

If there is no Caveat Book or Register for the court, an entry might be found in the Act Book mentioning the fact that a Caveat had been entered. Such an entry would probably pre-date the Act Book entry recording a grant.

ii. *Archdeaconry of Bedford, Caveats 1660-1723.*

Bedford St. Peter.   31 May 1723.

> Cave That no prtended Will of John Mason of the same Maulster pass not under Seal of this Office . . . till Richard Mason of Bromley in the County of Kent ye nral & lawfull Brother of the said deceased be first called, who interposes this Caveat.

Caveat Books, as well as Act Books, also deal with other than Testamentary matters, as the following example taken from the Archdeaconry of Bedford, demonstrates:

Bletsoe.   6 June 1723.

> Let no Marriage Lycence be granted to Essex Archer Junr of the Parish of Bletsoe in the County of Bedd. and Elizabeth Webster spinster of the same unless Essex Archer Senr ffather of the sd Essex Archer Junr be first called who enters this Caveat.

2. ASSIGNATIONS.

An assignation might be the assignment to some persons, who, as sureties to a bond, are obliged well and truly to administer the estate of the deceased. In cases where a grant of probate or Letters of Administration has been made, but there is sufficient evidence to presume that the conditions of the Testamentary or Administration Bond have been broken, persons interested in the estate may summons the sureties of the bond to show causes why an order should not be made that the bond be assigned to some other person. This would entitle such an assignee, as trustee, to sue and recover the full amount concerned in respect of any breach in the conditions of the bond.[8]

i. The records of the Commissary Court of London for Essex and Herts. contain a series of assignation books numbered 1 to 15 and described as "Probate and Admon. Acts — Assignations, 1619-1668."

> These volumes are assumed to be the registrar's working copies, giving the whole process of probate administration, and record probate and administration acts in a different *form* from the acts in the Act Books for 1669-1858.

An assignation may be defined in ecclesiastical law as an interlocutory order (or decree), and the above Probate and Administration Act Books for prior to 1669 have many examples of such orders beginning "Caveat," for example, not to grant probate until the persons named have had their case heard, and have had an opportunity to put in their claim.

ii. There are Assignation Books among the records of the Court of Delegates that refer to court cases, some of which were testamentary.

The Court of Delegates of England.

The Court of Delegates was erected by an Act during the reign of Henry VIII in 1533. It was created to hear and determine all appeals that formerly were customarily made at Rome. Judges heard the cases of disputed probates and their interlocutory decree passed sentence and committed and granted probate.

---

8. For further information on the definition of assignation see Tristram and Coote, *Probate Practice* (London: Butterworth Modern Text Books, No. 4, 20th Ed., 1955).

The Court of Delegates was originally the Court of Appeal from the Prerogative Courts of Canterbury and York, and also from the Irish Probate Courts. It was so called because the Judges were delegated for each particular case . . . many of the Wills were actually not proved in the Delegates Court, though entered upon the Register Books. Many of the Wills are also entered in the Register Books of the P.C.C., and as in the case of Wills proved and Administrations granted in the various Diocesan Courts an appeal lay to the Court of Arches [London] and thence to the Court of Delegates, there will also be found . . . several Wills which originally were proved in a local court. . . . in most cases a search in the Muniment Books will disclose further particulars concerning the testators. Documents relating to Processes in the Court of Delegates are deposited at the Public Record Office [London], and can only be inspected by a special permit. There are also a series of Act Books, which are not at the [Principal] Probate Registry at Somerset House [London], and may perhaps be found among the Records of the Admiralty Court.

The Court of Delegates was abolished in 1832, when the Judicial Committee of the Privy Council was established.[9] (This latter body continued from 1832 and there was later established in 1858 the modern Court of Probate and H. M. High Court of Appeals).

The records consist of Assignation Books, Act Books, Repertory Books, Depositions, Processes, Sentences, etc.[10]

It seems that when searching the probate records filed among the records of this court, "There is nothing on the face of them to show in what suit they were required. . . This information can only be determined by reference to the Processes."

The Assignation Books give the dates the causes were assigned for Sentence, and the dates the cases were heard. The Muniment Books and Calendar of Original Wills, etc., are at the Principal Probate Registry, Somerset House, London, but the documents and other records are deposited at the Public Record Office, Chancery Lane, London.[10]

---

9. "Wills and Administrations in the Court of Delegates," *The Genealogist,* New Series, Vol. XI, (London: 1895), pp. 165 & 224. The article explains the purpose of the Court and gives an index listing all probate records found in the *Muniment Books* 1651-1859. The *Muniment Books* have been microfilmed. [ENG. PUB. AF., N.S., Vols. 11, 12 & 17].

10. "Records of the High Court of Delegates," *A Guide to the Manuscripts preserved in the Public Record Office* [London], Vol. 1 (London: 1923) pp. 292-293. Here will be found listed the Acts, Assignation Books, Case Books, Cause Papers, Examinations, Processes, Sentences, and Miscellanea, connected with this court, as deposited at the P.R.O. [ENG. 100, Vols. 1 and 2].

3. TESTAMENTARY SUITS.

The ecclesiastical courts not only acted as probate registries, but when disputes arose, concerning probates, they delivered judgement. The interrogatories and depositions sometimes were attached to the original Will or Administration Bond.

i. Among the records of the diocese of Chester was a series of documents from 1478 to 1800 now known as "Testamentary Suits." Because of some testamentary disputes, these became separated from the main group of Chester probate records and were kept in the Diocesan Registry when the main group was transferred to the District Probate Registry. These are:

> The Depositions in many cases are more useful to the antiquary than the original Wills, as various interesting points were fre-quently brought out in the evidence, and also sometimes the Will itself, or a large portion of it, is recited in the Depositions. Many of the documents are very incomplete, and consequently dis-appointing.[11]

After 1541, these disputes probably were heard in the Court of the Vicar-General or Chancellor of the Diocese in the Episcopal Consistory of Chester.

ii. The decisions of ecclesiastical courts arose out of litiga-tion on the estates of testators and intestates and any other matters that lay within their jurisdiction.[12] Testamentary cases might be tried locally, as in the case of Chester, but appeal lay to the Court of Arches of Canterbury, London, and by further appeal to the Court of Delegates of England.

iii. The records of the P. C. C. contain Testamentary Suits, but they are usually designated as "Sentences." etc. Sentences are the decisions as the result of litigation. A Sentence for the Validity of a Will, etc., might contain statements such as:

> "The matter and circumstances of a certain Testamentary Suit having been seen, heard and understood and fully and maturely discussed . . ."
> "We Pronounce, Decree, and Declare as thus We grant by these Presents and by this definitive Sentence, or final Decree . . ."

---

11. "An Index of the Wills, . . . in Testamentary Suits . . . 1487-1800," (Record Society of Lancs. and Chesh.), Vols. 33, 43, 52. [CHESH. 1, Vols. 33, 43, 52]. The Lancashire documents are at the Lancashire Record Office, the Cheshire at the Cheshire Record Office, and the Welsh at the National Library of Wales. See also B. C. Jones, "The Lancashire Probate Records," (Transactions of the Historic Society of Lancs. and Chesh.), Vol. 104, page 64. [LANCS. PUB. E., Vol. 104].
12. For an interesting list of "All Causes Belonging to the Ecclesiastical Court (of York)." See C.I.A. Ritchie, The Ecclesiastical Courts of York (Arbroath, Scotland: The Herald Press, 1956).

There seems to have been many kinds of disputes, some trivial but others of importance. Types of cases that were tried in these courts might include:

"For pronouncing the deceased intestate,"
"For confirming the Will and Codicil,"
"For the nullity of the Will," etc.

J. and G. F. Matthews, in their "Year Books of Probates," *Sentences and Complete Index Nominum (Probates and Sentences)*, 1630-1639 (London, 1907), "Extra Volume," list twenty-four forms of Sentences in Latin on page 4. [ENG. PUB. ABb. "Extra Volume"].

J. H. Morrison, in his publication *Register "Scroope"* (1630), (London, 1934), [ENG. PUB. ABa.], referring to the records of 1630, states:

Interspersed among the Wills [of the P.C.C.] are the records of the decisions of the Court in cases of testamentary disputes; and these *Sententiae diffinitivae* are, like the Probate Clauses, always in medieval Latin.

Many Wills, with the Sentences, were registered in the P. C. C., although the proceedings of the Court may be filed at the Public Record Office, London, or elsewhere. In the P. C. C. it appears, that until the 18th century, such Wills that eventually received probate were often calendared together in the year concerned under the letter "S" and not under the testator's surname. In the later periods, however, references to Wills accepted by the probate court "by Sentence" are entered in the Calendars under the names of the testators in the normal place, with a note "by decree," "by Sent." or "int. dec." in the margin of the calendar. The following example is based on the entry taken from the P. C. C. Calendar for 1772:

BY)
SENT) WALL, Susanna, [of] Hertford[shire] July [1772] [folio] 279.

The Registers of Wills for 1772 are known also by the name "Taverner," and consist of ten large volumes. The sixth volume contains folios 236 to 281. In folio 279 is the copy of the Will of Susanna Wall, and at the end of the Will are entered details of the Act or Grant of Probate, followed by the words:

"A Definitive Sentence having been pronounced."

Information concerning such a Sentence is usually found at the end of the last register of the particular year. As there are ten registers or volumes for 1772 it is necessary to search the end of the tenth or last volume where information on the "Sentence for the Validity of the Will of Susanna Wall, spinster, deceased," is detailed.

iv. In the various diocesan courts there may have been Wills entered after a Sentence had been pronounced, but no note of the Sentence made in the manuscript Calendars or Registers. Such cases, if properly recorded, might be found in the Bishops' or Archdeacons' Act Books, Court Books, and Registers, filed with the diocesan records.

v. The Probate and Administration Act Books recording the business of the probate court usually mention the decision of the court in contentious matters. The probate court often will accept a Will by Sentence and in other cases will pass the Will by Decree.

These records must not be confused with *Chancery Pro-ceedings,* a series of records that will receive attention in a later volume of this series.

4. LIMITED AND SPECIAL PROBATE RECORDS.

Limited Probate Records deal with grants *limited* to a certain portion of an estate. *Special* probates concern grants made in cases where *special problems* have arisen.

The P. C. C. has a series of *Limited Probate Books,* 1781, 1800, 1802, and 1806-1858, and *Limited Administration Books,* 1815-1858. There are Limited and Special Probate and Administration records for the years *not* registered in these books, the details being entered at length in the general series of Probate Act Books and Administration Act Books.

i. *Example of an American Will proved in England.*

Among these records, are cases where the deceased held property in Great Britain and elsewhere, such as Holland, Switzerland, Germany, India, Africa, Australia, New Zealand, Canada, and America, etc. The testator might have appointed executors of his property in England and Wales and other executors of his property overseas. Probate would then be granted *limited* to the property in England and Wales. Simi-larly, if the deceased was intestate, Letters of Administration would then be granted *limited* to the estate in England and Wales. The P. C. C. Calendar (Index) for 1772 discloses the following reference to a Will:

Esqr. JORDAN, John Morton.   Pts.   July 263
Limited Probate.

The Register of Wills for 1772 (named "Taverner") records at folio 263:

JOHN MORTON JORDAN, Esq.	This is the last Will . . . of . . . John Morton Jordan of Annopolis in Maryland and late of London, merchant . . . This Will was proved at London . . . 1772 . . . in respect of the deceased's estate in England . . . but no further or otherwise. [Mention is made in the Will of his wife Dorothy, property in Virginia, Maryland, and in Antigua (British West Indies), his son John Nisbett Jordan (under 21 years), half-brothers Joseph and George Morton, half-sister Frances Mereweather, half-sister Mrs. Mary Sydenham widow of Jonathan Sydenham, late of London, and others.

The Probate Act Book for 1772 records his name, stating that the proceedings concerning the *Limited Probate* are "entered at length." As there is no separate *Limited Probate Book* for 1772, these proceedings are entered in the beginning of the Probate Act Book, the details occupying three pages of the book.

ii. *Example of the Will of a Merchant in India.*

Considerable delay may occur between the death of a testator or intestate and the grant of probate in England if the deceased died outside of the British Isles. Henry Wadham Diggle died prior to 1812, but his name does not appear in the P.C.C. Calendars until 1827. The reference in the Calendars indicates that he died in "Foreign Parts," that his Will is registered at folio 579, and that it is a *Limited Probate*. The Probate Act Book for 1827 states that the details of the Limited Probate are "entered at length." There is a Limited Probate Book for 1827, and the details include:

> The Court of the Recorder of Bombay [India] had granted, 18 April 1811, probate for the last Will of Henry Wadham Diggle late a junior Merchant. This Will was now proved at London 17 October 1827 by one of the Executors for England to whom Admon. was granted *limited* to the deceased's effects in England.

iii. *Example of a married woman's Will.*

Not all Limited Probates and Administrations concern property of residents in "foreign parts." The P.C.C. Calendar for 1827 indicates that Charlotte Francis, of Glamorgan, has a Will registered in November, 1827, at folio 640, and that it is a *Limited Probate.*

The Register of Wills for 1827 (named "Heber") records at folio 640:

CHARLOTTE FRANCIS.

This is the last Will . . . of Charlotte Francis the wife of David Francis of the town of Swansea, Glamorgan, blockmaker, whereas by a certain indenture by way of Settlement made upon my marriage with my said husband . . . 20 April 1804 [etc.]. Proved at London 26 Nov. 1827 . . . by the oath of Harriet Gell (wife of Charles Gell) the sister . . . Admon. was granted *Limited* so far as concerns all that right, title, and interest [mentioned in the Settlement].

The entry in the Probate Act Book for 1827 states that the details of the Limited Probate are "entered at length." The Limited Probate Book for 1827 recites full details of the case. In this recitation appears information not mentioned in the Calendar, the Probate Act Book, and the Register of Wills. These additional details include:

Charlotte Francis (now deceased) by her then (i.e., in 1804) name of Charlotte Withey . . . of the same place widow and relict of Thomas Wythey deceased. [she] departed this life . . . May [1827] . . . leaving no issue of the said marriage [i.e., with David Francis].

iv. *Example of Limited Probates in courts different from that of an original grant.*

There are many records of cases where the grants of probate have been made in diocesan or other minor courts, but in which it later became necessary to obtain further grants in a higher court.

A. In the Will of Montague Taylor (see pages 105-106) probate was granted 16 December, 1809, in the *Exchequer Court* of the Diocese of York. On 2 October, 1843, a further grant, by Decree of Court, was made. Note the wording of the following partial abstract from the Probate Act Book of the *Prerogative Court* of York, clearly indicating that the second grant is a *Limited* Probate:

. . . Administration . . . was granted . . . to Joseph Woodcock . . . *Limited so far only as related to and concerns the residue and remainder of a certain term of One Thousand Years . . . by virtue of a certain Indenture of Demise* . . . [dated] 15 July 1805 . . .

In the above case, the deanery Act Book for the Exchequer Court cross-references the 1809 entry to the 1843 entry, as previously explained on pages 105 and 106.

B. There are cases where there may be no cross-references from an earlier grant to a later grant of *Limited* Probate or Administration. Note the following example:

> In 1842 a Will was proved in the Consistory Court of Lichfield, the grant covering property in that diocese only. Later, it was found that the deceased possessed additional property in other parts of England and outside of the diocese of Lichfield, and therefore which was not covered by the first grant.
>
> In 1858, a grant of probate was requested and allowed in the Prerogative Court of Canterbury, *Limited* to Administration of all the personal estate not covered by the diocesan grant of 1842. These latter proceedings are indexed under the name of the deceased testator in the P.C.C. Calendar for 1858, and the Probate Act Book contains a reference to the fact that the details are "entered at length" in the *Limited Probate Book* of the P.C.C.

The records of the Consistory of Lichfield for 1842 do not show a cross-reference stating that in 1858 further proceedings are to be found in the P. C. C.

v. *Do all courts keep separate Limited Probates and Limited Administration Books?*

As previously stated, the P. C. C. has Limited Probate and Admon. Books for certain years, but Limited records for years *not* recorded in special books are to be found in the general series of P. C. C. Act Books. The Episcopal Consistory Court of Chester has Limited Administration Books from 1824 to 1858. Other *Limited* grants in that court for dates prior to 1824, without doubt, would be mentioned in the Act Books. In the case of Montague Taylor, mentioned in item iv, the *Limited* grant of 1843 appears in the Prerogative Court of York Act Book and apparently is not "entered at length" elsewhere. In the records of the Commissary Court of London (for Essex and Herts.), some of the Act Books for Wills and Admons. contain details of the court business dealing with *Limited* Probates and Administrations.

Grants *Limited* to a portion of an estate undoubtedly are mentioned in the Acts of Probate or Administration when such cases have been considered and dealt with by the court.

vi. *Example of ancestral connections hidden in Limited Probate or Administration Records.*

The name under which a *Limited* grant is recorded and indexed might be unknown to the researcher. In the case of Beale Skay, (see pages 107-108), his Will is dated 1756, and proved in 1758 by his executrix and widow, Mrs. Frances Skay. In this Will is a bequest of £1,000 to be invested jointly in the names of two trustees — his brother Edward Skay, who died in 1760, and William Barton, who died intes- tate in 1767. Mrs. Frances Skay, the widow and executrix, lived until 1795, however, and died intestate. No grant of Letters of Administration was issued, probably indicating that she left no possessions in her name.

It appears that Beale Skay died without issue, and in 1796 his next-of-kin, a nephew named Thomas Answell, the son of Mrs. Mary Answell formerly Skay, deceased, desiring to gain possession of the £1,000, applied for Letters of Administration of the estate of the "surviving" Trustee, William Barton, now deceased, *Limited* to £1,000. The following items are of interest:

A. Generally, genealogists work from *known* information, attempt- ing to find unknown information, usually of an earlier period. If the searcher on the Answell family did not know that Thomas Answell was connected with the Skay family, the Will of Beale Skay would not have been read. The surname Skay and the name of the trustee, William Barton of Holborn [London and Middlesex], consequently would not enter into the research problem.

B. The Limited Admon., dated 1796, for William Barton, of Kent, is listed under that name in the Calendar and appears under that name in the Admon. Act Book and is entered at length in the record of the Limited Administration.

C. There is no cross-reference from the 1758 Calendar, Probate Act Book, and Register of Wills entries for Beale Skay to the 1796 entry of William Barton.

D. Beale Skay's name appears in the Calendar and Act Book references for 1758 only, there being no further entries to his name in later years.

E. The names of Thomas Answell and his mother, Mrs. Mary Answell formerly Skay, do not appear in the Calendars in connection with 1796 and the Limited Admon. of William Barton.

F. Unless the Will of Beale Skay appointing the Trustees was read, it would be impossible to know that a search for the record of a William Barton would be necessary.

G. Connections such as the above "are lost or unavailable to the searcher until adequate indexes of the 'Stray Names' (or Index Nominum) have been made . . . unlocking the treasure chest containing one of the richest stores of material." An index reference relating Thomas Answell to the Limited Admon. of William Barton would be invaluable!

5. CURATION, TUITION AND GUARDIANSHIP.

Curation is guardianship over minors (persons under twenty-one years), whose ages are generally over fourteen years for a male and twelve years for a female. Tuition is the protection or guardianship over minors who are younger than the ages of curation. The records of the appointment of the curators or tutors are usually found in the Probate and Administration Act Books and Tuition and Curation Bonds filed in the boxes or bundles of original Wills and Admon. Bonds.

A few courts maintained record of Curation and Tuition in separately labelled volumes or books, but generally mention of Curation and Tuition is found in the Act Books and Bonds. The Calendars of some courts indicate if curation or tuition took place. If the court did not maintain separately recorded Curation and Tuition books, a search should be made of the Act Books, after first locating the reference in the Calendar of the date of the grant relating to a testator or intestate. If there are no Act Books, a search will have to be made in the boxes or bundles of original Wills and Admons.

Few courts maintained separate Tuition and Curation records, and library catalogs for printed and microfilmed copies of probate Calendars, Indexes, and Records, will not necessarily have specific mention of Tuition and Curation (guardianship) records.

i. *Example of an Act Book entry.*

In the records of the Peculiar Court of Howdenshire (Yorkshire), the following information is recorded in the Act Book for 1600-1735:

15 Dec. 1733.

ELLIOTT.   Ffifteenth Day of December . . . administration . . . of Thomas Elliott of Walkington . . . Deceased Intestate . . .

was granted to Anne Elliott his widow . . . An Inventory was Exhibited and Bond is Entered.

Curation   Curation of the person and portion of William Elliott
ELLIOTT.   a minor aged seventeen years the Nrall and lawfull [son]
of Thomas Elliott . . . was granted to Anne Elliott his
Mother according to the Voluntary Election of the Said
Minor made.

Curation   Curation . . . of Elizabeth Elliott a minor aged ffifteen
ELLIOTT.   years . . . daughter of Thomas Elliott . . .

Tuition   Tuition . . . of Thomas Elliott and Mary Elliott minors
ELLIOTT.   the Naturall and Lawfull children of Thomas Elliott . . .

After finding the entry in the Act Book, a search could then be made in the bundles of original Wills and Admons. Bonds for the Admon. Bond, Inventory,—in this case, the value of the property is recorded as £565.10s0d,—and the Bonds of Cura-tion and Tuition. These documents, corresponding to the Act Book entries, are unbound and may be scattered through the bundle. In this example, the bonds were separated, and there were at least five other loose documents relating to quite differ-ent cases, between each of the guardianship bonds, as well as between them and the Admon. Bond and Inventory. In the case of a testator, an original Will and probably a Testamen-tary Bond would be found instead of an Admon. Bond.

ii. *Example where there is no Act Book.*

In the Calendar for the Archdeaconry of Richmond (Five Western Deaneries) (see pages 76-77) indication is given that in 1700, Mildred Gale's Will and associated Bonds were filed with the records of the Copeland Deanery. No mention is made in the Calendar of any guardianship records. There are no Act Books for 1700. A search through the bundles of original Wills and Admon. Bonds for Copeland Deanery disclosed the Will (see page 79) and several Bonds. One Bond relates to the Tuition of her children.

Comparision should be made of the Latin portion of the Bond (see page 125) with the amplified transcription and translation. The amount of useful information found in the Latin portion will then be apparent.

The important part of a Bond is usually the CONDITION, the portion ordinarily written in English, (see also page 63) The following abstract of the genealogical information should be compared with the illustration (page 126).[13]

---

13. Augustin Washington (1694-1743) was father of George Washington (1732-1799).

THE CONDITION . . . if . . . George Gale . . . educate . . . John, Augustin and Mildred Washington the natural and lawful children of Mildred Gale his late wife by a former husband deceased with sufficient meat drink clothes and all other necessaries . . . during their minority . . .

[Witnesses]

Matt. Gale.	Geo.: Gale
Fran: Yates.	John Gale
	Jo: Gale, Junr.

ABSTRACT OF THE TUITION BOND

George Gale's bond for the tuition of John, Augustin and Mildred Washington, children of Mildred Gale, his late wife, by a former husband. 18 March, 1700/1.

Amplified transcript of Latin portion:

NOVERINT universi per presentes nos Georgium Gale de Whitehaven Generosum et John Gale Senior et John Gale Junior of the same place. teneri et firmiter obligari Reverendo in Christo patri et domino domino Nicolao permicione divina Cestriensis Episcopo necnon Venerabili viro Edwardo Walker Legum Baccalario in et per totum Archidiaconatum Richmondie Cestriensis Diocesis Commissario legitime constituto in Mille Libris bone et legalis Monete Anglie Solvendis eisdem reverendo in Christo patri et domino Commissario ant eorum certo Attornato Executoribus Administratibus Successoribus Sive Assignatis Suis Ad quam quidem Solucionem bene et fideliter faciendum obligamus nos et quibuslibet nostrum Heredes Executores et Administratores nostros firmiter per presentes Sigillis nostris Sigillatum. Datum decimo octavo die Mensis Martii Anno Domini 1700.

Translation:

Know all men by these presents that we George Gale of Whitehaven, gentleman, and John Gale, senior, and John Gale, junior, of the same place are holden and firmly bound unto the Reverend father and lord in Christ, Nicholas by divine permission Lord Bishop of Chester and also to the Venerable Edward Walker, Bachelor of Laws, Commissary established by law in and for the whole Archdeaconry of Richmond in the diocese of Chester, in a thousand pounds of good and lawful money of England to be paid unto the same Reverend father and lord in Christ, his Commissary or their certain attorney, their executors, administrators, successors or assigns, to which payment well and truly to be made we bind ourselves and any one of us, our heirs executors and administrators firmly by these sealed with our seals. Dated the eighteenth day of the month of March in the year of our Lord 1700.

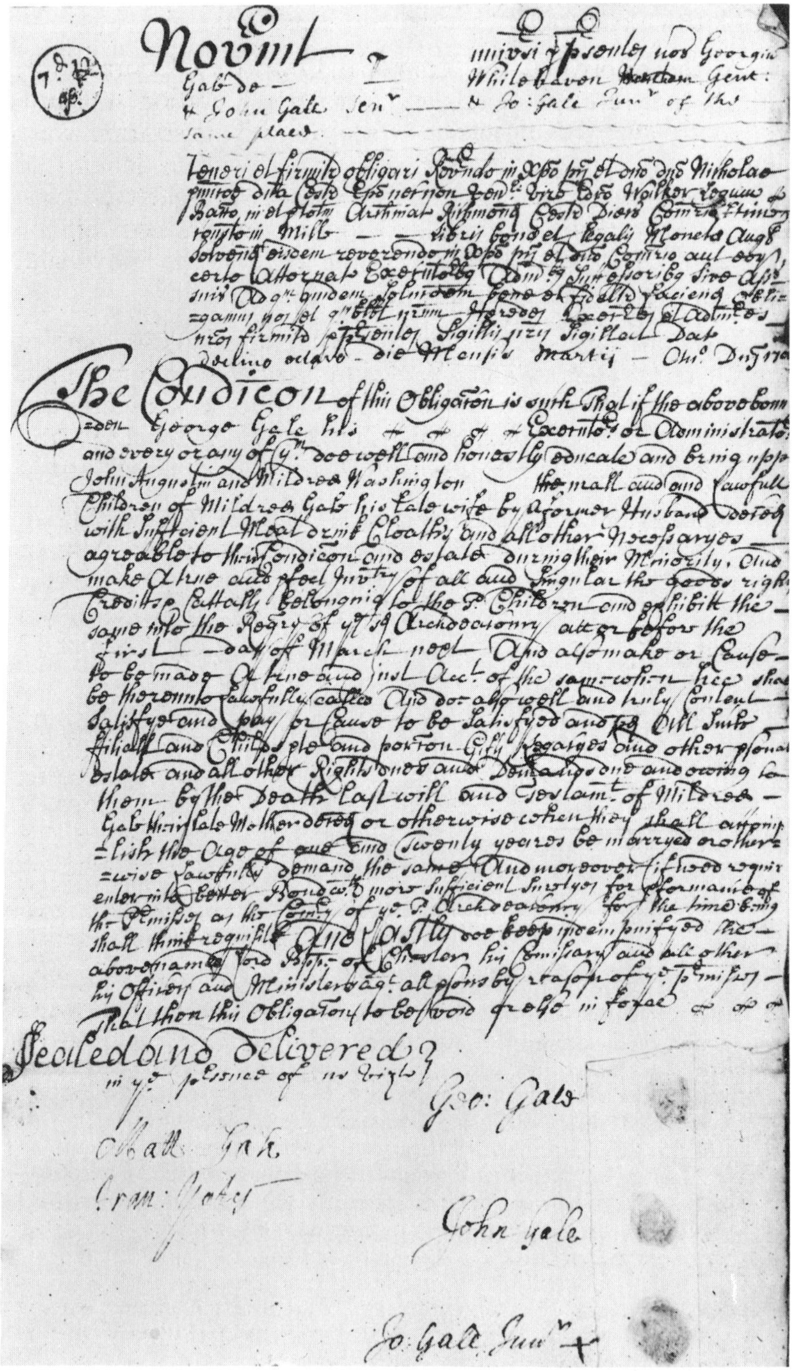

Noverint universi per presentes nos Georgium Gale de Whitehaven [illegible] Gent: & John Gale Senr & Jo: Gale Junr of the same place [illegible]

The Condicon of this Obligacon is such That if the above bounden George Gale his Executors or Administrators and every or any of them doe well and honestly educate and bring upp John Augustin and Mildred Washington the male and lawfull Children of Mildred Gale his late wife by a former Husband deceased with sufficient Meat drink Cloathes and all other Necessaryes agreable to their Condicon and estate during their Minority. And make A true and perfect Inventory of all and singular the goods rights Creditts & Cattells belonging to the said Children and exhibit the same into the Registry of the said Archdeaconry at or before the first day of March next And also make or Cause to be made A true and just Account of the same when hee shall be thereunto lawfully called And doe also well and truly Content satisfye and pay or Cause to be satisfyed and paid All such filiall and Childs part and porcon Gifts legacyes and other personall estate and all other Rights dues and Demands due and owing to them by the Death last will and testament of Mildred Gale their late Mother deceased or otherwise when they shall accomplish the Age of one and twenty yeares be marryed or otherwise lawfully demand the same And moreover if hee be required enter into better Bond with more sufficient Suretyes for performance of the Premisses as the Court of the said Archdeaconry for the time being shall think requisite And lastly doe keep indemnifyed the abovenamed Lord Bishop of Chester his Comissary and all other his Officers and Ministers against all persons by reason of the premisses That then this Obligacon to be void or else in force &c.

Sealed and delivered in ye presence of us [illegible]

Geo: Gale

Matt. [illegible]

[illegible] Yates

John Gale

Jo: Gale Junr

iii. *Example of a hidden Guardianship Record.*

In the records of the Episcopal Consistory Court of St. David's there are few Bonds of Tuition and Curation. According to the Act Book entry, Letters of Administration were granted 3 July 1835, for the estate of William Jenkins of Llandissiliogogo, Innkeeper, to his widow, Margaret Jenkins. At that date there was no need for the appointment of any guardianship, as the widow was the next-of-kin, and would take care of the needs of any minor children.

Later, in 1837, the widow, Mrs. Margaret Jenkins, married the Reverend David Williams, and in order to secure the rights of the minor children in their father's estate, it was necessary to elect and assign a guardian. The Act Book for 1835 and 1837 does not disclose any information that there was a guardianship record made in 1837.

This court has a record known as "Register of Acts of Court in Special Cases." The title of this Register gives no clue to its containing guardianship cases. The following is an abstract of the case relating to above persons, under date of 17 November, 1837:

> A Business of Electing and Assigning Margaret Williams the wife of David Williams of Cefenllwyndafidd . . . Llandissiliogogo . . . Cards . . . Minister of the Gospel . . . (formerly Margaret Jenkins, widow) to be Curator or Guardian . . . to . . . four of the . . . children of William Jenkins late of Cefenllwyndavidd aforesaid Deceased. Grace Jenkins of the age of Sixteen years . . . Eleanor . . . Fourteen years . . . Evan Jenkins . . . Eleven years and . . . Mary Jenkins . . . Nine years . . . made choice of their Mother . . . Margaret Williams to be their Curator or Guardian . . . at Llanarth Vicarage.

This example shows the importance of becoming acquainted with the business procedures of the court of probate where the records of the family concerned are to be found.

iv. *Example of Cities having Special Orphan Records.*

A. The City of London had a special court, The Court of Husting, London, which dealt with the estates of deceased Citizens of London. Connected with the City was a court of orphans. The following is of interest:

> If a freeman or freewoman [of the City of London] died leaving orphans under age and unmarried, the custody of their bodies as well as their goods became vested by custom in the Mayor and

Aldermen, who, following the practice in guardianship in socage, placed them under the care of those next friends to whom the inheritance could not descend.[14]

The Mayor and Aldermen exercised their equitable jurisdiction over matters relating to orphans in the character of a Court of Orphans . . . It was only, however, in the absence of a testamentary guardian that one was appointed by the Court to take charge of the persons and property of infants who had lost their father, and to see that their substance was not wasted either by their mother or by some scheming adventurer who sought by marrying the mother to get possession of her children's portions.[15]

The Court of Orphans had its origin in the Court of Aldermen, which had custody of the orphans of a Freeman and supervised the administration of the personal estate of the deceased.[16]

B. The City of Bristol has among its muniments, records known as the *Great Orphan Books*. These contain copies of Wills proved in various courts and involving the orphans of Citizens and Freemen of Bristol.[17]   This title, *Great Orphan Books,* seems to be confined to those records in Bristol.

C. It is not known how many cities, and boroughs (towns) may have similar records, but inquiry might disclose informa- tion of records of freemen (citizens and burgesses) and their orphaned families, although in the strictest sense, such records might not come under the heading of probate records. The records of ancient merchant guilds and livery companies might disclose information dealing with their members and families.

6. MONITIONS, COMMISSIONS, REQUISITIONS, etc.

In the bundles or boxes of filed original Wills and Admons., Monitions occasionally appear. There are usually summons or citations from a probate court of superior jurisdiction to the lower court admonishing the court to send certain documents to the higher court.

i. *Example of a Monition from the Prerogative to a Diocesan Court.*

---

14. *Calendar of Wills . . . Court of Husting, London, 1258-1688,* (London: 1889) p. xlvi. [LOND. 21].

15. ibid. p. xlvii.

16. *A Guide to the Records in the Corporation of London Records Office and the Guildhall Library Muniment Room,* (London: 1951). [LOND. 60].

17. T. P. Wadley, *The Great Orphan Book and Book of Wills . . . Bristol.* (Bristol: Bristol and Gloucs. Arch. Soc., 1886). [GLOUCS. PUB. A. Supp. 2] and [ENG. PUB. AB. Vol. 17].

In the Calendar of the Episcopal Consistory Court of Lichfield, reference is made in 1826 to the Will of Sarah Cater of Derby. The filed Will is a copy of the original that was proved at Derby, 11 April 1826. Attached to this copy Will is a *Monition,* dated 9 October 1826, from the "Official of the Court of the Prerogative Court of Canterbury, London," requesting the transmission of the original Will as follows:

> . . . to the Common Hall of Doctors Commons[18] situate within the Parish of Saint Benedict near Pauls Wharf [City of] London . . . [as the executor had] . . . incautiously and inadvisedly obtained a Probate in the Consistorial and Episcopal Court of Lichfield . . . [and as] . . . the deceased, Sarah Cater, late of Derby, left goods . . . in divers jurisdictions sufficient to found [that is, to have it proved] in the Jurisdiction of Our said Prerogative Court . . .

In response to this Monition, the Will was copied and the original transmitted to London on 24 October 1826. Reference is made in the Calendars of the P. C. C. to this Will.

ii. *Example of a Commission or Requisition.*

Filed with the original documents may be Commissions and Requisitions, dealing with a variety of out-of-the-ordinary probate matters. Prior to 1733, these papers are often written in Latin. The following is an abbreviated example of one of these:

> John Dale, Master of the merchant ship "Elizabeth and Sarah" from the Island of Barbadoes, died in St. John's parish, Wapping [London], but was formerly of the parish of Fylingdales, Yorkshire. The grant of probate was in the P.C.Y. in June 1724, but his widow and son John, a minor, resided in the parish of St. John's, Wapping. Attached to the original Will is a lengthy three page document, written in Latin, stating that in response to Letters of Commission and Requisition received from York, the widow, Mrs. Frances Dale, had been entrusted with the Tuition of John Dale, the son, a minor, as well as with Letters of Administration with the Will annexed. This document was issued from the office of the Vicar-General of the Bishop of London, and acted as a covering letter for transmittal of the original Will, Admon. Bond, and Tuition Bond from London to the Prerogative Court of York.

---

18. Doctors Commons. Until 1858 the P.C.C. proved Wills and granted Letters of Admon. This registry was situated at Doctors Commons in the City of London. The term "Doctors Commons," found in manuscripts and publications, usually refers to the P.C.C., although the probate records from that court are now at the Principal Probate Registry, Somerset House, London.

7. DIARIES, JOURNALS, MINUTE BOOKS.

Some courts have books named Diaries, containing details of the probates filed in the court. These are entered in chrono-logical order and, in fact, form a "Day-book" for the probate registry. (See also "Act Book" detailed in Chapter Four)

A few courts have a series of old journals, minute books, and other papers concerning the business of the court. In some of these records, the entries are of little genealogical value, but occasionally mention is made of persons and places concerned with grants, decrees, renunciations, etc. In instances where the actual documents have been lost, the journal entries, etc., contain the only record of the existence of such documents.

8. RENUNCIATIONS.

When a testator or intestate left property, and the execu-tors or next-of-kin did not wish to officiate as administrators, they could renounce all rights in the settling of the estate. Records detailing transfer of the right of administrator are known as Renunciations, and are found filed in the bundles or boxes of original Wills and Admons. The Act Book entry usually indicates the individual who had the original right of administration and who had renounced that right. The origi-nal Testamentary or Administration Bonds often have a notation stating that there had been a renunciation. The fol-lowing example is taken from the records of the Peculiar Court of the Dean of York:

    i. Know All Men By These Presents that I, Marie Widd, wid-dow and relict of John Widd late of Wilton of ye parish of Ellerburne, deceased, doe desire that Administration of all and singular the goods . . . of John Widd my late husband . . . may be granted to George Bower my Brother . . . 4 March 1681.

    ii. Know All Men . . . that I, Elizabeth Jackson of Moursome . . . York, widow and relict of Willm. Jackson late of Allerston . . . butcher . . . do hereby renounce all my right title interest claim and demand of in or unto the Administration of . . . goods . . . of . . . Willm. Jackson . . . [and] desire that Admcon . . . be granted to Willm. Calvert son-in-law . . . 17 January 1719.

On the Administration Bond, William Calvert is mentioned as the recipient of Letters of Administration "in right of Mary, his wife . . . Administrator . . . of Willm. Jackson, (father of the said Mary), late of Allerston."

9. NON-DEPOSITED PROBATE RECORDS.

There are a number of probate records that were not trans-ferred to the Probate Registries after the change of jurisdiction from ecclesiastical to civil, in 1858. There are various probate records among the muniments of several cities and boroughs (towns), in certain diocesan registries and archives, at Lambeth Palace Library, at the Public Record Office, London, at Eton College, among the records of the Universities of Oxford and Cambridge, and in libraries. It is also possible that some records, such as those of the old Manor Courts, still remain in private hands. Examples of these non-deposited probate records are:

i. The Registers of the Archbishops of York, being Consistory Wills and known as The Archbishops' Wills, from 1316 to 1822 remained at the Diocesan Registry, York, after the transfer of the bulk of the probate records. They are now in the Borth-wick Institute of Historical Research, York.

ii. Many Diocesan Registries undoubtedly contain testamentary records:

If desired a copy of the Will could be entered in the bishop's [Chester] register on payment of a fee. Prior to 1838 [at Chester] these registrations were made in enrollment books of the court, books containing a miscellaneous collection of docu-ments and not set apart for probate registrations. These remain in the custody of the diocesan authorities.[19]

iii. Some testamentary papers are in the Diocesan Registry, Salis-bury, Wiltshire.

iv. Records at the Guildhall, Exeter, Devonshire, include "Court of the Mayor" and "King's Customary Court," with records from about 1280 to 1600.

v. In the Shrewsbury, Shropshire, Public Library, is a bundle of Wills [Calendar No. 7731] proved in the Manorial Court of Ruyton-in-the-Eleven-Towns, Shropshire.[20] There are also two manuscript volumes of Wills and Admons. covering the period 1666-1816 and two manuscripts containing copies of Wills and Inventories 1765-1783.

vi. At one time there was a small register book, containing copies of early Wills proved in the St. Mary's (Shrewsbury) Peculiar Court, kept in the muniment room of St. Mary's Parish Church. In 1948 it had been mislaid and cannot at present be found.

---

19. *Transactions of the Hist. Soc. of Lancs. & Chesh.* Vol. 104 (1952), p. 65.

20. The Calendar for these is in print in the *Trans. of the Shrops. Arch. Soc.,* Vol. 52 (1948), pp. 116-118. [SHROPS. PUB. A. Vol. 52].

IMPORTANT NOTE.

It is essential that notes compiled from any of these sources are accurate. The titles and names of the courts must be recorded. If the court concerned has its records divided into deanery, county, or some other order, that must be mentioned. The name or names of the deceased, the period covered by the search, the name of the type of documents (such as Wills, Admons., etc.) involved, together with the date of the grant of probate or Letters of Admon. are all necessary.[21] If special code letters (perhaps peculiar to the court being searched) or other particulars connected with a reference appear, these must be included so that the Registers, Act Books, files, bundles, boxes, etc., might be found.

---

21. B. G. Bouwens in *Wills and their whereabouts*, *op. cit.*, pages 76-78 gives "A Few Hints on making Will Abstracts." This should be read carefully.

Chapter 6

THE VALUE OF PROBATE RECORDS

The value of any genealogical record is in its contents, and perhaps no other single type of record can contain such a wealth of information as the probate. It is true that the actual contents of probate records vary, and while some Wills are disappointing in the detail they give, others contain a veritable gold mine of information.

The main contribution of the probate record is perhaps the details of family relationship it gives.[1] There are, however, a number of specific points of value, and limitation, that can be found in probates, as the following items demonstrate.

1. *Not all living children mentioned in Wills.*

A testator often considered it unnecessary to detail in his Will provisions that had been made and understood by members of his family before his death. In many instances, children of a testator may have given their "portion" of the estate during the lifetime of the testator. This is true particularly in the cases of daughters, who may have received their share of the estate in the form of dowries at the time of marriage. Details of the portion allotted to the eldest son and heir often were arranged long before the making of a Will. Some children of a testator may not be mentioned in the Will simply because they had lost favor and had been "cut off" without even the proverbial shilling.

The following extract demonstrates an example of a daughter receiving the major part of her share or portion during the lifetime of the testator. There are undoubtedly many instances of children receiving their portion before the making of a Will who are not mentioned in that Will.

Archdeaconry Court of Sarum.

The nuncupative Will of Susannah Hinton of Codford St. Mary, Wilts, proved 22 February 1690:

. . . except one shilling, which she gave her daughter Mary Swetman to whom she had before given her part . . .

---

1. The evaluation of Probate Records and the genealogical validity of their contents is discussed in Chapters 2, 3, and 12, of Volume 2, *A Basic Course in Genealogy*, op. cit.

2. *Living children in the same family bearing identical given names.*

There is ample genealogical evidence to show that in some families children have been given identical names. It is often assumed that, merely because two sons or daughters have the same given name, the first child must have died before the second one was named. It is thought to be inconceivable that in the same family there should be two boys, both living, both bearing the same given name(s). While such a situation is unusual, (and was without doubt the cause of some consider' able confusion within that family!) it is not wholly uncommon.

The following example shows a family in which several boys were given the same given name.

> Will of William Kingdon of North Molton, Devon.
> Dated 20 October 1570.
>
> To be buried in church yard of North Molton or where it shall please God.
> To the church 2/-; to the poor mens chest 16d.
> To the poor of North Molton 5/8.
> To Phillip my son a silver spoon.
> To *John Kingdon of Molland* MY SON 6/8 a silver spoon and all my apparel except one cote; and all the debts he doth owe me.
> To *John Kingdon of Nympton* MY SON a silver spoon and all the debts he doth owe me.
> To *John Kingdon of Fledon* [? *Filsdon*] MY SON a silver spoon.
> To Austice Conebear my dau. a silver spoon; to Elizabeth Bale my daughter 20s, a grene covlet and a candlestick and a silver spoon.
> To Philip Kingdon son of John Kingdon, at home with me a yeo [ewe] and a lamb.
> To Johan Kingdon my daughter in law a heifer.
> To Thomas Kingdon my kinsman a coate.
> Residue to *John Kingdon* MY SON the which doth dwell with me called MYDDLE JOHN and him I do make my exr. and I do ordain and make Sir John Treed, vicar, Thomas Burge and John Thorne my ruler and overseer to se this my last will fulfilled . . .

It was not only the sons who were innocent participants in this rather surprising situation. The following example indicates that two daughters were given the name of Mary — both lived to maturity and married. The two Wills refer to the same family. The Will of William Hillier, was proved in the Consistory Court of the Bishop of Winchester, while that of Charles Hillier, the son of William, appears in the records of the Archdeaconry Court of Winchester. Note that in the Will of Charles Hillier the surname is spelt differently and that the parish of Faccombe appears as Fackham.

> Abstract of the Will of William Hiller of Faccombe, yeoman. The Will of my late brother John. My son William and my son-in-law John Sherman to be Trustees. My property to be divided into eight parts. One part to my son William. One part to my son James. One part to my son Robert. One part to my son Joseph. One part to my son George. One part to *my daughter Mary wife of William Smith*. One part to *my daughter Mary wife of John Sherman*. One part to the children of my son Thomas. Witnesses: Richard Townsend, Thomas Townsend, Philip Lockton. Dated 6 Nov. 1804. Codicil dated 10 Oct. 1805. Same witnesses. Probate granted 1808.

> Abstract of the Will of Charles Hillier of Fackham, labourer. My father William Hillier to have the residue of my estate for life, and then to my brothers and *sisters* equally—William Hillier, James Hillier, Robert Hillier, Joseph Hillier, George Hillier, *Mary wife of William Smith and Mary wife of John Sherman,* and my brother Thomas's issue to have one equal share when 21 years old. Dated 25 Sep. 1804. Witnesses: Thomas Lambden, John Shurman, George Bulpitt. Probate granted 3 June 1806 to William Hillier. Value under £200.

3. *Determining which of two likely connections is ancestral.*

Probate records are invaluable in the details they give of family relationship. Their use can often mean the difference between the acceptance of the right or the wrong pedigree connection.

Eleanor Barker married John Johnson at Weaverham, Cheshire, 29 October 1707. Searches in the parish registers of Weaverham disclosed the following christening entries:

> 4 Dec. 1679 Eleanor, daughter of John Barker.
> 24 Feb. 1682/3 Eleanor, daughter of Richard Barker.

Which if any, was the ancestral entry? Which Eleanor Barker married John Johnson? A search in the burial registers inferred that both had survived infancy. The parish registers then, while giving two possibilities, could not determine which of the two entries was ancestral.

Among the Wills proved in the Episcopal Consistory Court of Chester was one of Richard Barker, of Weaverham, proved 22 January, 1715/6. In it he mentions:

my son Richard Barker
my son John Barker
Mary Barker (no relationship given)
my grand daughter Mary Joynson
my grandchildren William and Mary Joynson
my son-in-law John Joynson and daughter Eleanor Joynson
my brother Henry Barker
my brother William Barker

The Will provides the required evidence. The ancestor is Eleanor, the daughter of *Richard* Barker. (Note the difference in the spellings of the married surname of Eleanor). The parish registers did not give this required evidence, but with the co-ordinated use of probate records, the problem was solved.

4. *Avoiding incorrect pedigree connections.*

The use of parish registers as the sole source on which to build a pedigree has many pitfalls. The type of circum-stantial evidence concerning family relationship given in parish registers should not be accepted without first making an attempt to substantiate the hypothesis suggested by the infor-mation they contain. It is emphasized again that probate records give not only invaluable evidence of family connections but also evidence of a high calibre. Consider the use of probate records in the following example.

John Rishton married Elizabeth Huddleston at Slaidburn, Yorkshire, in 1764. In an effort to extend the Huddleston ancestry, searches were made in the parish registers of Slaid-burn for the christening entry of Elizabeth Huddleston. The registers contained only one reference to an Elizabeth Huddles-ton, namely:

Christened 29 December 1748, Elizabeth, daughter of Thomas and Ann Huddleston.

This entry was accepted as ancestral and further searches continued at Slaidburn for the ancestry of Thomas and Ann Huddleston, the parents of the child christened in 1748. What was wrong with this research? Obviously, there was no direct evidence to substantiate the assumption that the child christen-ed in 1748 was the same individual who married in 1764.[2]

---

2. For the definitions of Direct and Circumstantial evidence and their use in genealogical procedure, see Chapter 3, Volume 2, *A Basic Course in Gene-alogy*, op. cit.

Probate records, genealogically famous for their details of family relationship, had not been considered and yet it was essential that further evidence be obtained before acceptance or rejection of the 1748 christening entry. The following Will was found in the Exchequer Court of the Diocese of York:

> The will of John Huddleston of Newton, Slaidburn, tailor made 15 August 1768 and passed 16 August 1769.
> Mentions:
> John Huddleston my eldest son
> Thomas Huddleston my second son
> Johun Huddleston my third son
> James Huddleston my youngest son
> *Elizabeth Rishton my daughter who married John Rishton* . . .

This newly-found evidence establishes that the ancestor was the daughter of a *John* Huddleston, not Thomas as origin' ally supposed. Once again, the use of probate records meant the difference between the right and wrong connection.

5. *Following probable connections for additional ancestral evidence.*

There is a great deal connected with genealogical procedure that comes with experience. The following examples demon' strate this point extremely well and serve to show that constant awareness and imagination is an essential attribute of a success' ful genealogist.

Catherine Geer, the ancestor, was married at Porstlade, Sussex, and several of her children were christened in that parish. The registers of Portslade were searched for her chris' tening, but the required entry was not found. In this search, however, it was noted that the registers, as well as the Bishop's Transcripts were missing for a number of years in the period when Catherine would have been born. It was possible, of course, that the required christening took place in one of the years missing from the registers and the transcripts and this asumption was strengthened by the fact that the required entry did not appear in any of the registers of surrounding parishes.

In the registers of Portslade, a marriage entry is recorded between Diones Geer and Catherine Stanns, about the time when the birth of Catherine Geer was thought to have taken place. The fact that the ancestor Catherine named a child Diones, a rather unusual name, added strength to the assump' tion that Diones and Catherine were the parents of the ancestor, Catherine. Without further evidence, however, the assumption was not strong enough to accept as fact.

Reference to Lewis' *Topographical Dictionary*, 1831 and
1833 Editions, gave the information that Portslade was in
the Archdeaconry of Lewes, Diocese of Chichester. No Will
was found in the Episcopal Consistory Court for the Archdeaconry of Chichester for Diones Geer, nor for his wife
Catherine, formerly Catherine Stanns. Searches under the
surname Stanns, however, showed that there was a phonetic
connection betwen this surname and the surname Stone and a
Will was found in the aforementioned probate Court for a
Thomas Stone, a butcher, of Portslade. The Will was dated
2 February, 1735, and proved 13 April, 1737 and mentions
in it "*my niece, Catherine Geer.*" Further searches at Portslade
showed that Thomas Stone, or Stanns, was the brother of
Catherine Stanns, the wife of Diones Geer.

The connection was effected, once again, by the use of
probate records, showing that, although the required christening was not found, the parentage of Catherine was, in fact,
Diones Geer and Catherine Stanns.

6. *Co-ordinating family tradition and probate records.*

The following example demonstrates how a genealogical
problem was solved by the use of probate records in the verification of family tradition. The following ancestral marriage
appears in the parish registers of St. Chad, Lichfield, Staffordshire:

16 November 1789   Thomas Heap and Jane Walton, widow.

Searches to find the previous marriage and maiden surname
of Mrs. Jane Walton were made in the three parishes in the
City of Lichfield, also in the registers of near-by parishes, but
the required information was not found.

Family tradition indicated that the maiden surname of
Mrs. Jane Walton was Sandland, but there was no actual
known foundation for this tradition. On the assumption that
Mrs. Jane Walton was of Lichfield, the next logical step was
the testing of this family tradition. Reference to Lewis' *Topographical Dictionary* showed that the city of Lichfield comprises
the three parishes of St. Mary, St. Chad, and St. Michael, all of

which are in the peculiar ecclesiastical jurisdiction of the Dean and Chapter of Lichfield. The records of this Court disclosed that the Will of an Elizabeth Sandland, dated 26 June, 1784, was proved there 5 October, 1792. The Will records that Elizabeth was a spinster and mentions:

> Her sister Mary Wright;
> Her nephew Jacob son of Mary Wright;
> Her nephews Henry, Richard, John and Joseph Wright, sons of Mary Wright;
> Her nephew William, son of her late brother John Sandland;
> Her nieces Jane Walton, Elizabeth Giles and Catherine Sandland, daughters of her late brother John Sandland;
> Sarah Gorton daughter of her niece Mary Young.

The Will not only added evidence to the assumption that Sandland was the maiden surname of Mrs. Jane Walton, but also gave the name of her father, brother, sisters and aunts. This new data proved of invaluable assistance in the further searches on these ancestral lines.

7. *The genealogical problems of widows.*   ....

The marriage registers of Tilehurst, Berkshire, contains the following entry:

> 26 April 1749 Richard Applebee, of Bucklebury, and Sarah Barefoot, of Tylehurst.

It would appear, in the absence of information to the contrary, that Sarah Barefoot was a spinster at the time of this marriage, although it should be remembered that few marriages prior to 1754 detail the marital status of the bride and groom.

Bucklebury and Tilehurst, according to the 1831 Edition of Lewis' *Topographical Dictionary,* are in the Archdeaconry of Berkshire and Diocese of Salisbury. A map illustrating this jurisdiction appears on page 36. In the probate records of the Archdeaconry Court of Berks., it was found that a Will of William Barfoot of Tilehurst, was proved 11 May, 1749. William Barfoot, in this Will, mentions his wife Sarah, and names her as the executrix. In granting the probate, the Court describes Sarah as *Sarah Barfoot, now Appleby.*

Searches at Tilehurst showed that William Barfoot was buried there 29 October,1748, strengthening the circumstantial evidence to the hypothesis that Sarah, the widow of William Barfoot, married Richard Applebee of Bucklebury, 26 April

1749, six months after the death of her first husband. Without the probate evidence, it would not have been evident that Sarah was a widow at the time of her marriage to Richard Applebee, and without doubt, searches would have been made for her christening under the wrong name of Sarah Barefoot.

The probate evidence prompts searches for the marriage entry of William Barfoot and Sarah, from which the maiden surname of Sarah will be learned.

8. *Supplying information on the direct ancestral surname not found in the parish registers.*[3]

The children of John Bailey and his wife, Mary, were christened at Helpringham, Lincolnshire, and John Bailey was buried in that parish at the age of 65 years in 1760. Searches were made at Helpringham for the christening of John Bailey, born about 1695, and although there were a number of Bailey families living in that parish at that time, the required entry was not found. There was a John Bailey who married in 1693 and who had children christened in the parish during the period 1696 and 1717. None of these children had been given the name of John, lending credulity to the possibility that the ancestor John was a child of the John Bailey married in 1693.

Following this possibility, it was learned from Lewis' *Topo-graphical Dictionary,* 1831 Edition, that the parish of Helpring-ham is in the Archdeaconry and Diocese of Lincoln. The probate records of the Episcopal Consistory Court of Lincoln included a Will of a John Bailey, dated 29 October, 1737, and proved 14 October, 1742. The Will mentions not only the names of the children born to John Bailey, whose christenings appear in the Helpringham registers, but refers to "my eldest son John." The first son of John Bailey recorded in the parish registers as being christened in 1696, was named James, showing that there was a son John born between 1693 and 1696.

Searches could have been made in the registers of surround-ing parishes and possibly christenings of other John Baileys would have been found, none of which would have been the ancestral entry. Once again, the "genealogical rescue" was made by the probate record.

3. The details of a "Surname Target" approach to the pedigree problem are dis-cussed in Chapter 7, Volume 2, *A Basic Course in Genealogy,* op. cit.

9. *Probates help to prove unusual circumstances.*

The parish registers of Abenhall, Gloucestershire, disclosed that a John Meeke married there to Elizabeth Lea 10 January, 1623/4. They had children named Eleanor, Thomas, John, Thomas, Elizabeth, William, Joseph, Walter and Joan or Jane, all christened between 1624 and 1641. Elizabeth, the wife of John Meeke, was buried 24 August, 1665.

A John Meeke married at Abenhall, 16 July, 1672, to Jane Howell, by license. Jane is described as aged 22 but no age is given for her husband. Neither the parish registers, the Bishop's Transcripts nor record of their marriage license disclosed their marital status. Children James, Richard and Elizabeth were born to them between 1674 and 1680. Is the John Meeke who married in 1672 the boy John who was christened in 1629, and is it possible that these two sets of children, one set born in the 1630's and 1640's and the other set born in the 1670's, belong to only one John Meeke? If these were all the children of the *same* John Meeke then he would have been about 74 years old when his last child was born. A very unlikely situation. It would be more reasonable to assume that the children born between 1674 and 1680 belonged to his son, John. A John Meeke was buried at Abenhall, 2 May, 1682, and his Will was proved in the Episcopal Consistory Court of Gloucester, 26 May, 1682. The Will reads:

> In the name of god Amen the last day of Aprill 1682, I, John Meeke, of the parish of Abinghall and County of Gloucester, yeo-man, sick in body but of sound and perfect memory, doe make and declare this my last Will and Testament.
> I give unto my now wife JANE the Measuadge or dwelling howse wherein I now live in the parish of Abinghall with all the outhouses belonging, during the terme of her widdowhood onely, and on her marriage or decease my two sonnes JAMES and RICHARD shall have the same.
> I give and bequeath unto my said wife all my livinge Cattle whatsoever.
> I give and bequeath unto my two sonnes JAMES & RICHARD and to my daughter ELIZABETH all my brasse and pewter, beddinge, lynninge, etc., to be equally divided betwixt them, but my will is that my wife shall have the benefitt & use of all the said goodes duringe her widdow hood and noe longer.
> I give and bequeath unto my daughter JANE twelve pence and to my sonnes JOHN MEEKE, THOMAS MEEKE, WILLIAM MEEKE and WALTER MEEKE, twelve pence a peece, within twelve months after my decease.

I doe hereby appoint my said wife JANE to be sole executrix of
this my last Will and Testament and I desire my lovinge friend
CHARLES MORGAN and my sonne JOHN MEEKE to be
overseers.

JOHN X MEEKE his marke.

Witnesses: - Thomas Meeke, William X Bradly, Patience X Davies
Charles Morgan
Proved 26th May 1682

This clearly shows that both families were by the same
John Meeke, one of them in his old age. Probate records are
invaluable in solving such unusual problems.

10. *The value of Admons.*

A study of the previous chapters will have shown that, on
the whole, Wills contain much more genealogical information
than Letters of Administration. It is *not* true however, that
Admons. are of *no* genealogical value, in fact, many problems
have been solved by the use of these documents.

The following two examples demonstrate their value and,
it is hoped, will prompt beginning genealogists to consider their
use in research programs.

i. Eleanor Woodhouse married Thomas Grumble at Alnwick, North-
thumberland, 18 November 1729, and four of their children were
christened in that parish. Searches were made for the christening
of Eleanor Woodhouse at Alnwick and in the registers of a number
of surrounding parishes, but the required entry was not found.
Searches were then made in the probate records of the Episcopal
Consistory Court of Durham and it was found that Letters of
Administration dated 1729, had been granted to Eleanor Woodhouse, giving her authority to administer the goods of her deceased
husband, George Woodhouse. The bondsmen to this application
were Roger Nesbitt and *Thomas Grumwell.*

The parish registers of Alnwick disclosed that George and Eleanor
Woodhouse had children christened there 1722, 1724, and 1727
and that George Woodhouse had been buried there 29 April 1728.
The combined use of the parish registers and Admon. gives strong
circumstantial evidence to the fact that Eleanor was the widow
of George Woodhouse at the time of her marriage in 1729, in spite
of the fact that the registers do not state so. It is interesting to
note that Thomas Grumwell, or Grumble, was a bondsman at
the time the Admon. was granted.

This example is not altogether an unusual one. There are
many instances of such happenings, where the bride is a widow
at the time of the recorded marriage, although the registers

are silent on this very important fact. There was little wonder that the registers of Alnwick and surrounding parishes failed to disclose the christening of Eleanor Woodhouse — her maiden surname was not Woodhouse. Most marriage entries before the passing of the Marriage Act in 1754 do not record the marital status of the bride and groom, and even after 1754, when this specific information was called for, many recorders failed to include these vital details.

ii. Thomas Wragg and his wife, Nancy Young, were married and had their children christened at Ashover, Derbyshire, but the christening entry of Nancy Young is not recorded in the registers of that parish. Among the Wills and Admons. of the Lichfield Consistory Court, the Admon. of Ann Younge was found:

> Administration of Ann Younge of Tansley in the parish of Crich, widow. Died intestate October 20, 1809. Administra-tion dated Lichfield November 11, 1809. Thomas Wragg of Berridge Lane in the parish of Ashover, farmer and George Pursglove of Ashover, laborer and William Milnes of Ashover, gentleman are bondsmen. *Nancy Wragg, wife of the above bounded Thomas Wragg was natural and lawful daughter of the deceased and was appointed Administratrix.*

Note the valuable information given in this document. Not only is the parish of residence of the Younge family mentioned, but also the name of Nancy's mother is given. Searches at Crich, the parish of residence of Ann Younge, disclosed the christening of Nancy Younge.

Chapter 7

NAVAL AND MILITARY RECORDS; MERCHANT SHIPPING RECORDS; CHURCHES ON FOREIGN SOIL

The records kept by the British Navy, the British Army, the Mercantile Marine and by parishes of the Church of England in foreign countries have a great value in providing items of genealogical and biographical value such as dates of birth, details of children of couples and their activities. These records are not used as much as they ought to be by the genealogist, simply because details of their value, contents and accessibility have never appeared in print. The impressive amount of information presented in this chapter is not considered to be exhaustive and encyclopedic. It is a great step forward, however, and the reader should become aware that these records can be of great genealogical value and should be considered as a source of value, even when it is not actually known that an ancestor was a military man.

There is a great deal still to be learned about these types of records and it is hoped that those who have personal access to them and who specialize in their use will attempt a more complete description of them. As the majority of these records are located in London, they are immediately accessible only to those who can visit London. Even then, there are certain records of a military nature that are not available to the public at all.

General Information on Naval and Military Records.

In searching through any type of genealogical record, a good deal of patience is necessary. This requisite is most essential in searching military records.

Generally speaking, records of the navy and the army are transferred from the Admiralty and the War Office to the Public Record Office in Chancery Lane, London, when they are one hundred years old. They are then available for public inspection.[1]

There is another series of records that are in the care of the Registrar General, Somerset House, London. Searches in these records is best done by correspondence.

The more recent army records, that is, those under one hundred years old, are kept at the Army Records Centre, Hayes, Middlesex. The more recent navy records are kept at the Admiralty, Whitehall, London. Records of the Military and Marine Forces of the East India Company and some records of the British Army in India up to 1947 are kept at the Military Records Section, Commonwealth Relations Office, King Charles Street, Whitehall, London.

Even with some search restrictions much can be accom- plished, preferably by employing an experienced and qualified researcher in London. It is still essential, however, for all genealogists to have a knowledge of the locality and contents of these records even though the searches themselves may have to be carried out by someone else. A clear and explicit request for searches in these records can then be made and reports from the person who made the searches can be understood more readily, and the problems connected with the searches better appreciated.

In chapter 8, "Historical Events related to Genealogical Research," the years of the main wars are listed and will indi- cate the possibility of major army and navy movements. For a detailed study of the military history of Great Britain there are a number of historical publications that will be of value.[2]

1. ARMY RECORDS.

In early days, Britain's only armed forces was the Fyrd, a fuedal levy organized on a county basis, developing later into the Militia. In addition to this "national force," the Sovereign's

---

1. A useful book, detailing the Military Records at the Public Record Office, although it does not describe their value is A Guide to the Manuscripts pre- served in the Public Record Office, by M. S. Giuseppi, F.S.A. (London: 1924). [Eng. 100. Vol. 2.]
2. Suggested is History of the British Army by J. Fortescue in thirteen volumes and six volumes of maps. Also A History of the Royal Navy by Clowes in seven volumes.

bodyguard, consisting of professional soldiers, also dates from early times.

The British standing army may be said to have originated in 1645 when Parliament established the New Model Army of Cromwellian fame which continued through the Restoration. This Regular Army expanded in size in proportion with the country's colonial development but it basically remained a collection of individual regiments rather than a coordinated force. Until 25 May, 1855, when they came under the jurisdiction of the War Office, the artillery and engineer arms were administered by the Board of Ordnance, the cavalry and infantry by the War Office and the Commissariat by the Treasury.

Although enlistment was normally for life, a soldier could be discharged at any time as national conditions dictated. A centralized system in which a regiment was a part of a National Army was not known until comparatively recent times and it should be remembered that such a lack of liaison means that these earlier military records were kept and filed by regiment.

It is always helpful, in fact it is often necessary, to know the name of the regiment or regiments in which an individual served before searches begin in army records. The names of such regiments may be given in genealogical records such as birth, marriage and death certificates, census returns, old letters, pension certificates, parish registers, etc. If it is known that a soldier was stationed in a specific town at a specific time it is often possible to learn the name of the regiment by finding what regiments were stationed in that town at that time. The regimental lists at the Public Record Office give this type of information. A military medal may indicate the campaign in which a soldier participated and help to locate details of his regiment.

i. *Records of Officers Only.*

Until about the last one hundred years, most commissions in both the infantry and cavalry were purchased. Some were, however, granted to sons of officers and to outstanding enlisted men. An officer, was therefore, usually of good education and a sergeant was required to be able to read and write.

A Cavalry Officer

Various British Army Lists and Commission Registers, Lists of Officers on Half-Pay, etc., have been printed and cover periods beginning as early as 1661. The printed *Official Army Lists* begin in 1740, after which there is a gap until 1754, since when they have been printed annually. Records of Officers list the name of the officer, his regiment and details of his commission. They, unfortunately do not detail the place of birth, but as they do give the name of the regiment, other records can be searched that usually give the required place of birth. Those Records of Officers not in print are at the Public Record Office.

A very valuable source of information is Commander in Chief's Memoranda (War Office Series 31). This series includes correspondence dealing with applications for commissions, promotions, exchanges, retirements, etc., and such information often discloses genealogical facts about that officer which may include details of his father's former service. These records do not contain name indexes and their searching consequently may take considerable time.

Applications for cadetships in the Royal Military Academies usually have the baptism certificates attached as proof of age, parentage and religious conformity. (The Navy kept similar records and an example of their value is shown under "Navy Records.")

ii. *Muster Rolls.*

Regular roll calls of officers and men in each regiment were made. Royal Artillery and Royal Sappers and Miners usually "mustered" every month while the infantry and cavalry regiments usually mustered every six months, sometimes even less frequently. Except for the more recent ones, the Muster Rolls are all available at the Public Record Office.[3]

3. Muster Rolls of Royal Artillery and Royal Engineers units serving in India after 1857 are not available.

Their great genealogical value lies in the fact that from about 1795 they usually disclose, at the time of the man's first muster, his place of birth, age on enlistment and often records his trade on enlistment.

The first muster sometimes took place at a depot before joining his regiment, in which case the muster rolls of that depot will have to be searched.

An exception to the information given in Muster Rolls is that of the Royal Artillery. To find the place of birth of persons in this branch of the army, the Description Books, Artillery Records of Service, and sometimes the Recruiting Returns, have to be searched.

The earliest Muster Rolls for the Royal Artillery commence in 1719 and extend to 1880. The great majority of these are intact and available. For the Royal Sappers and Miners, they commence in 1816 and extend to 1880. For the cavalry and infantry, the earliest roll is 1732, but as many of the early ones from 1732 are missing, the general series cover 1759-1880.

The Muster Rolls usually are arranged by rank — officers, sergeants, corporals, drummers, privates, casuals, etc. Within these listings, the names are listed in the order of joining the unit. Before 1790 men were mustered by companies, but after that time, the muster was by regiment, although even then, the names were still listed by companies. Prior to 1790 each company roll was recorded on loose papers, but from 1790 the Muster Rolls are generally in bound books. From about 1809 the Muster Rolls continued to be recorded by regiment and rank, but usually in alphabetical order within the rank rather than in the order of joining that particular unit.

If the name of the regiment in which an individual served is not known, and has not been disclosed by using other genealogical sources, the searching of Muster Rolls is a formidable task. Even if the name of the regiment is known, it may be necessary to examine the lists of eight or ten companies and in each company there may be as many as six sub-divisions. If the name of the regiment is *not* known, the fact that in 1815 there were about 140 infantry battalions, 110 artillery companies, about 30 engineers corps and about 30 cavalry regiments besides Fencibles, Militia, Local Militia and Volunteers shows the importance of making every effort to learn the name of the regiment in which an individual served, especially if the given name and surname of the individual is common.

Once the regiment has been determined, the Muster Rolls of that particular regiment can be searched and the name and rank of the individual determined. His whole career in that regiment and the movements of the regiment can then be learned by searching both backwards and forwards. The move' ments of the regiment are valuable as the soldier ancestor may have had children born and christened in the places in which he was stationed. In the tours of foreign duty, the family of the soldier accompanied him in many instances.

iii. Description Books.

Regiments of cavalry and infantry and battalions kept Description Books in which were entered particulars of each recruit. These particulars usually included such items as date and place of enlistment, age and trade on enlistment, height, color of eyes and hair, complexion and place (usually parish, town and county) of birth.

Many Description Books were lost during regimental cam' paigns and there are few that date earlier than about 1795. The main Army use of the Description Book was as a means of tracing and physically identifying deserters. Notes may have been entered to show a soldier's final fate, for example "d" (discharged dead) or "to pensions list," etc.

Examples of the value of Muster Rolls, Description Books and other military records.

1. The following example demonstrates the procedure taken in efforts to find the date and place of birth of a soldier and although the search was unsuccessful in this regard, it shows the great amount of biographical detail that may be included in these records.

William Hopewell was married in the parish church of St. Margaret's in the town of Leicester, 28 May 1787, and had several children born in that town. The research problem was to find details of his date and place of birth.

Family tradition stated that one of his children was born in Ireland about 1796. The Napoleonic Wars were being fought at that period of time and as many English soldiers were sent to Ireland to defend that country against an anticipated attack, it was thought possible that William Hopewell could have been a soldier at the time of the birth of one of his children in that country.

William died before 1851 and so the census of that year which would have given his parish of birth could not be used. The 1841 census indicated that he was born in the county of Leicester but neither the census nor his certificate of death gave any evidence of his connection with the army.

The Army Chaplains Returns and Regimental Registers (described later in this Chapter) having failed to find record of the birth of the child said to have been born in Ireland, a professional record searcher, skilled in the searching of these records, made searches in the hope of finding the place and date of birth for William Hopewell. After considerable search, a report was prepared that reads:

As the child was born in Ireland about 1796, the Muster Rolls of a group of regiments stationed there at that time were searched. After searching through the lists of men for nine regiments, William Hopewell was found recorded in the Muster Rolls of the 24th Light Dragoons.

This regiment of six Troops was raised in England early in the French Revolutionary War in 1794. The Regiment formed at Netley Camp; Netley being a small village in Hampshire on the eastern shore of Southampton Water. William Hopewell enlisted on 19 May 1794 as a private and joined the Regiment at Netley Camp.

In October 1794, 24th Light Dragoons moved from Netley to Blandford in Dorsetshire and was billeted in neighbouring villages such as Shaftesbury, Sturminster, Stalbridge, Hinton, Bryanstone, Milton Abbey and Bere Regis. There the Regiment remained until April 1795 when it moved to Bath in Somerset where it was on 1st of May, being under orders to march to Liverpool for embarkment to Ireland.

The Regiment landed in Ireland on 25 May 1795 and was at first stationed at Clonmel, though Hopewell was with a detached portion at Kells (eight miles south of Kilkenny). Later, the Regiment moved to Armagh (March 1796) and then to Dungannon. From this time on, William Hopewell was with the Major's Troop.

By September 1797, the Regiment was at Drumilly (5 miles north of Armagh) and when the French landed in Ireland in August of that year the 24th Light Dragoons remained at Dublin and were not actively engaged. The Regiment remained at Dublin for the rest of its service.

On 20 August 1800, William Hopewell was discharged with a month's pay in lieu of travelling money to take him to his home. No reason for discharge is given in the Muster Roll, but it seems probable that as others were discharged about the same time, it

Infantry Man

was merely a sign of the Government's anxiety to reduce military expenditure as quickly as possible in view of the probability of peace being made with France. It should be explained that though at that period a soldier enlisted for "unlimited service" (i.e. for life), Government had the right to discharge a man without compensation at any time. As soon as the Treaty of Amiens had been signed, both 23rd and 24th Light Dragoons were disbanded on relief in Ireland by 4th Dragoon Guards and 3rd Dragoons.

At this point of the search it was decided to examine the Description Books of 24th Light Dragoons in order to trace further particulars of William Hopewell, including his date and place of birth and trade on enlistment. Unfortunately this important document is missing. It must have existed at one time as it was a most important regimental document used for the identification of deserters. Unfortunately also, there is no file of Service Returns for this Regiment; this file might at least have provided some of the information being sought.

Though it is clear that William Hopewell had no claim to pension for length of service—he had only served six years—it seemed just possible that he might have claimed a pension on the grounds of ill-health or of physical injury. The Chelsea Hospital Admission Books were therefore searched up till 1802 inclusive without results. Nor was their any trace of his discharge on account of physical infirmities, wounds or long service.

It seems therefore that William Hopewell was discharged in 1800 and returned to his home a perfectly fit man, a trained soldier of six years service and evidently a man of good character, since the Muster Rolls show no evidence of any punishment having been inflicted on him. Under these conditions it would be reasonable to expect that he would have joined some military unit in 1802-3 when the whole country was expecting a French invasion. It was therefore decided to search the Muster Rolls of the Leicestershire Yeomanry, Militia and Volunteers as a "long shot." This proved successful and it was found that William Hopewell served six years in the Loyal Leicester Volunteer Infantry from 1802-1808.

The Loyal Leicester Volunteer Infantry had been formed in 1798 as a two-company corps which was automatically disbanded about November 1801 when peace was made with France. When war broke out again, the corps was at once reformed as an eight company battalion composed of local citizens.

The records of this battalion disclosed that William Hopewell joined the Light Company in 1803 and attended the compulsory drills each year until 1808. After the threat of invasion was ended the battalion disbanded. Records of these local volunteer regiments do not show places of birth.

Because of the missing Description Book, the all-important place of birth of William Hopewell was not found, although much valuable detail about his life was found, useful in the writing of his life history. It is stressed again that many of the married soldiers took their families with them from depot to depot and the children could have been christened in any of the parishes in which that soldier was stationed. The records used would serve as a guide to determine which parishes to search for the christenings of such children.

The sustained but unsuccessful effort to find the birthplace of William Hopewell had a happy ending. Based on the information given in the 1841 census returns, every parish in the county of Leicester was searched for his christening and the required entry was eventually found. The expense of searching the records of these many parishes would not have been necessary, however, if the missing Description Book had been available.

2. In this example the search of military records for the all-important place of birth was successful:

It was known that William Davidson had enlisted in the 42nd Regiment of Foot (later known as the Black Watch) on 27 January 1794. In the hope of learning of his place of birth, the Muster Rolls of this regiment were searched and his career in the army traced. Although it was learned that he was promoted temporary corporal, missed two musters because he was slightly wounded at the Battle of Waterloo, moved to Gibraltar and finally deserted his regiment when it was stationed in Scotland, the Description Book relating to his first mustering into the army could not be found.

Some time later, the same researcher while searching for something else, came across this loose piece of paper among other records relating to this regiment. It gave details of men transferred from the Marquis of Huntley's Independent Company. William Davidson was one of these men.

This led to a search of the Muster Rolls of this Company. William Davidson actually enlisted in 1792 and the following valuable information about him was recorded at that time:

Height 5ft. 4¾ inches; age 21; complexion fresh; visage round; eyes hazel; hair brown.

Born Parish of Killemuir, Perth, Scotland.

Because Muster Rolls and Description Books give the place of birth of soldiers and provide a calculated year of birth, they are among the most valuable of all military records. It should be remembered however, that many boys enlisted under age, giving false names and ages, and even false places of birth.

iv. *Chaplains Returns.*

These consist of registers kept by Army Chaplains, *generally from stations abroad* and contain record of births, marriages, deaths and burials of army personnel and their families. They exist for the period 1796-1880 and are kept at the General Register Office, Somerset House, London. They are available to the public for inspection but because of their complexity it is more satisfactory to have the searches made by the officials at Somerset House. A comprehensive index of these returns has been made and the fee for a search in the index for a particular entry irrespective of the period required, is three shillings and nine pence (55 cents).

It is not necessary, therefore, because of the existence of an index, to know the name or number of the regiment in which a soldier served before searches can be made in the Chaplains Returns. In fact, this source is useful in determining the regiment to which a soldier did belong so that searches can be made in the records of that regiment for record of the place of birth. The Chaplains Returns are valuable in finding details of the marriages of soldiers and in finding details of children born to them during military service. The following example shows the value of this type of record.

Example of the value of using Chaplains Returns and other military records.

The following example demonstrates the procedure taken in an effort to find details of the dates and places of birth of the children of a soldier, details of his marriage and his own date and place of birth. The tremendous scope of military records is well illustrated.

Elizabeth Websdale married at Norwich, Norfolk in 1864, at which time her father was stated to be John Websdale, a pensioner. As there were few types of pensioners in those days except military pensioners, here was a clue that John Websdale might have served in the British Army although family tradition made no mention of such a possibility. Additional evidence was added to this hypothesis when a search in the 1851 census returns disclosed that Elizabeth, daughter of John Websdale had been born in Ireland.

Application was made to the Registrar General at Somerset House, London for a search of the Army Chaplains Registers giving the known facts that John Websdale was probably a soldier and that one of his children was born about 1822 in Ireland.

Searches were made for a birth or baptism record of Elizabeth Websdale. This was not found but the search did disclose the details of the marriage of her father in *Devon* and details of two other children, previously unknown to the descendants, born in *France*. The information given on these certificates is detailed below to show the amount and type of genealogical information given in this type of genealogical source.

A. 5th Regiment of Foot. Registry of Marriages.

Rank, Christian and surname of soldier..John Webdale, Private
(Specifying whether bachelor or widower)..............Widower
Christian and surname of the woman..................Sarah Snell.
Place of marriage, specifying parish,
    county, etc. ---------------------------------------St. Thomas, Devon.
Date of marriage ....5th April 1815.
Signatures of the parties married......................John Webdale.
                                                                        Sarah Snell.
Signatures of two witnsses present
    at the ceremony ....John Wellacott,
                                                                        Harriet Milton.
Clergyman by whom the marriage was
    solemnized ....J. B. Copleston, Vicar.
I certify the above Registry to be correct.
Signature of the Adjutant, Thomas Canch, Adj, 5th Reg't.
[St. Thomas, Devon proved to be St. Thomas, Exeter, Devon.]

B. 5th Regiment of Foot. Registry of Baptisms.

Date of Childs Birth ....2nd Dec 1816.
Place of Baptism ....Valencienne, France.
Date of Baptism ....1st Jan 1817.
Christian name of the child ....John
Parents names ....John Webdale
                                                                        Sarah Webdale
Rank of the father ....Private

Name of the Chaplain or other Clergyman by
whom the ceremony was performed........W. G. Chantley,
Chaplain to the Forces
I certify the above Registry to be correct.
(Signature of the adjutant Thomas Canch.)

C. 5th Regiment of Foot.

Date ....30 Aug. 1819.
Place ....Camp near Cambrai.
Childs Christian name ....William.
Parents names ....John and Sarah Webdale
Rank ....Private Soldier 9th Reg't of Foot.

Note the slightly different form used for recording the two births. Note also that although the records are said to be of stations abroad, a marriage is recorded *that took place in England.*

Now that the name of the regiment was known, searches were made in the Muster Rolls. The following notes were made as the search proceeded in the records of the 5th Regiment of Foot:

> *Certificate of Age and Enlistment.* ". . . That John Webdale, Private, born in the parish of Market Deeping, in or near the town of Market Deeping in the county of Lincoln was enlisted for the aforesaid regiment at Sunderland in County of Northumber-land on the 24th April 1805 at the age of Twenty-one for un-limited service."

(Note that his place of birth is given. Sunderland is actually in Durham, not Northumberland).

> *Certificate of Service.* ". . . that he hath served in the Army for the space of Thirteen years and 299 days after the age of eighteen according to the subjoined."

Note: The age, eighteen years, does not necessarily mean that his army service commenced at the age of eighteen. It does mean that his army service recorded here took place after the age of eighteen years, irrespective of the age at which he may have joined the army.

> *Statement of Service* (Service Returns.)
> 5th Foot. Period of Service.....................from 24 April 1805 to
> 16 Feb. 1819
> Period of Service as a private.....................13 Years 299 days.
> Total Service ....13 years 299 days.

Certificate of cause of discharge. ". . . That in consequence of being undersize and the reduction of Establishment of the Regiment, he is hereby discharged."

Certificate of Character. ". . . That his general conduct as a soldier has been very good."

Acknowledgement of receipt of all demands. ". . . I, John Webdale do hereby acknowledge that I have rec'd all my pay to time of discharge."

Certificate of Description. ". . . He is about 35 years of age, is 5 feet 4¾ inches in height, Lt. Brown hair, hazle eyes and dark complexion and by trade a labourer." Given under my hand at Winchester Barracks this 15 day of Nov 1818.

Sign. Chas. Pratt. Col.

By the use of these military records, the family connections were taken from Norwich to Ireland, France, Devon and Lincolnshire, a task that would have been virtually impossible without the use of this source.

v. *Regimental Registers*.

These are available at the General Register Office, Somerset House, London. They are available for public inspection, but the officials prefer to make the searches themselves because of the complexity of these records. They cover the period 1790-1924 for the births, baptisms, marriages and deaths. They are the original registers kept by various regiments of H. M. Land Forces (officers, soldiers and their families) and include details of regiments stationed at home and abroad.

An index has been prepared for the *births and baptisms* and this index can be searched without knowing the name of a regiment in which a soldier served. As no index has been prepared for records relating to *marriages, deaths and burials,* it is necessary to know the name of the regiment to which a soldier belonged before this section of the Regimental Registers can be searched. The fee for searches for a particular entry in these registers is three shillings and nine pence (55 cents) for a period of five years. A certified copy of any entry costs an additional three shillings and nine pence (55 cents).

vi. *Artillery Records of Service*.

These cover the period 1756-1917 and are available at the Public Record Office, Chancery Lane, London. They include details of both officers and men, giving names, descriptions, places of birth, trade, lengths of service, details of promotion, marriages and discharges or deaths.

For some regiments of artillery there are Description Books 1776-1874, registers of marriages and baptisms 1817-1883, registers of deceased soldiers 1821-1873 and other miscellaneous records.

vii. Pension Records.

In the period under review, many soldiers died or were permanently disabled due to wounds that today would be termed only minor. Those who became unfit for further service, and those who had served a sufficient number of years were able to apply for a pension. Widows of former pensioners and widows of serving men, also applied for pensions. Widows of such men were required to furnish proof of marriage to the deceased soldier, and pension records consequently, often contain affidavits of date and place of birth and marriage of the applicant.

At the Public Record Office there are various types of pension records including those of Widow's Pensions 1735-1912; Pensions for Wounds and Superannuation 1814-1913; Pension Returns 1842-1883; Miscellaneous Pensions 1795-1856; and others.

A soldier of long and meritorious service could apply for a pension, and if his application was granted by the Chelsea Board of Pensions, he became a Chelsea Pensioner. Apparently there were Chelsea Pensioners who were granted permission to reside in Chelsea Army Hospital, Chelsea, London, in which case they were known as "In-pensioners." Others, known as "out-pensioners," resided in their own homes or wherever they might choose to settle. Chelsea Pension Records, kept at the Chelsea Hospital, may be searched providing the regiment and regimental number of the soldiers are known. The records often disclose the date and place of birth.

Incidentally, the Chelsea Hospital kept registers of baptisms 1691-1812; marriages 1691-1765; and burials 1692-1856, relating to the families of both Pensioners and Hospital staff. These registers are not indexed, and are deposited at the General Register Office, Somerset House, London.

Great *Britain.*

INSTRUCTIONS

For the Guidance of SOLDIERS Pensioned FROM THE MILITARY CORPS UNDER THE ORDNANCE, DISCHARGED IN GREAT BRITAIN.

CERTIFICATE.

THIS IS TO CERTIFY, That *Richard Brough* the Bearer hereof, was examined on the *Six teenth* Day of *December 1822* before ~~the Lieutenant General~~ of the Ordnance, and that he is a Pensioner of the Honorable Board of Ordnance, at *one Shilling* per Day, BRITISH, having served *upwards of Seventeen* Years, in the *Royal Regiment* of *Artillery,* Commanded by *Field marshal His Grace The Duke of Wellington* and in other Corps, according to the following Statement:

Regiment or Corps.	Serjeant Major	Q^r Master Serjeant	Serjeant	Corporal	Trumpeter	Drummer	Private	East or West India Service	Total Service	Other Service not allowed to reckon for Pension.
Royal Artillery							*17 Years 10 days*		*17 Years 10 days*	

And to prevent any improper use being made of this Certificate, he is *Thirty Seven* Years of Age, *five* Feet *11* Inches in Height, *Brown* Hair *grey* Eyes, *Brown* Complexion, by Trade a *Labourer,* was born in the Parish of *Trentham* in or near the Town of *Trentham* in the County of *Stafford*
State whether unfit for Service or otherwise. *and was discharged, being Unfit for Service,* and that he is to reside in *Newcastle under Line*

Dated at Woolwich, this *Thirty first* Day of *December* 18*22*

To be signed by the Commanding Officer of Battalion or Corps.

N B. The Pensioner is particularly ordered not to part with this Paper, it being no Security for a Debt, and will only be replaced under very special Circumstances, with the sanction of the Master General and Board. In the event of the Death of the Pensioner, these Instructions are forthwith to be returned under Cover to the Secretary to the Honorable Board of Ordnance, London, by such Person or Persons into whose Possession they may come.

Part of pension record illustrating the value of this type of document. Richard Brough is stated to have been born at Trentham, Staffordshire, about 1785.

It may be possible to find the record of a soldier in the various Muster Rolls of his regiment and search until the date of his discharge is found, although such an approach is undoubt'edly the "long way round." Searches could then be made in the Chelsea Hospitals Registers using the regiment and regimental number found by the searches in the Muster Rolls.

Example of the value of pension records.

> When Robert Fish married Elizabeth Hill, 28 July 1799, the parish registers describe him as a private soldier in the 5th Regi'ment of Foot.
>
> Robert Fish was found recorded in the Muster Rolls of this regiment for 1798 and from that time until 1819 he was noted as being at various stations with this regiment. In 1819 he was at Chatham Depot where it was noted that he passed the Chelsea Board of Pensions.
>
> Contact was then made with the Secretary of the Royal Chelsea Hospital stating the information already discovered. The pension records at the Hospital disclosed the following:
>
> > Robert Fish born in the parish of Lincoln, county of Lincoln. Enlisted at Lincoln 8 March 1798 for the 5th Regiment of Infantry aged 23 years. Trade, laborer.
> >
> > Discharged 24 February 1819 aged 45 years. Total service 20 years 254 days. Character very good. Awarded a life pension of one shilling per day.

Note the all'important place of birth and a calculated year of birth. Incidentally the death certificate for Robert Fish was also found. He died in 1845 aged 67 and the registrar des'cribes him as a "laborer and pensioner in the 5th Regiment of Foot at 1/' (one shilling) per day." Death certificates are not usually so descriptive.

viii. *Casualty Returns.*

These give the name, rank, place of birth, trade on enlist'ment, details of the casualty and next'of'kin. They also include copies of Wills of deceased soldiers, inventories of effects and letters from relatives.

These cover the period 1809'1857 and are at the Public Record Office.

ix. *Garrison Registers.*

Forts and other types of defences both inland and around the coasts of the British Isles, were manned continuously and some events of genealogical importance took place in these garrisons.

The registers kept by these garrisons are at the General Register Office, London, the earliest being those of Landguard Fort, Suffolk, beginning in 1761. An index of births taking place in these garrisons has been prepared and has been combined with the index for births and baptisms recorded in Regimental Registers (see item v).

x. *Courts Martial.*

Reports of courts martial give valuable genealogical details. For the period 1684-1847 they are at the Public Record Office, London.

xi. *Registration abroad after 1880.*

On and after 1 January, 1881, when the Registration of Births, Deaths and Marriages (Army) Act, 1879, came into force, registers of births, marriages and deaths *occurring out of the United Kingdom* among army personnel and their families were compiled by the headquarters of the various commands.

For these records, to which were added in 1920 records of births, marriages and deaths among personnel and members of families of the Royal Air Force, there are separate alphabetical indexes for each approximate period of five years for births, deaths and marriages. These records are at the General Register Office, Somerset House, London, and the fees for searching are three shillings and nine pence (55 cents) for a five year search of the index for a particular entry. A charge of the same amount is made for a certified copy of any entry supplied.

* * *

The following publications are available at the Genealogical Society, Salt Lake City, Utah:

  i. *English Army Lists and Commission Registers, 1661-1714* by Charles Dalton, (London), Vols. 1 and 2. [R3A6].
 ii. *Army List* (A list of Officers in the Army and Marines), for various dates from 1785 to 1915 [R3A1].
iii. *List of the Officers who died in the Great War, 1914-1919,* [R3A5].
 iv. *List of Soldiers who died in the Great War, 1914-1919,* [R3A4, parts 1-80].
  v. *List of the Officers of the Bengal Army, 1758-1834,* by V. C. P. Hodson, Vols. 1-4. [R3A3].

2. THE BRITISH EAST INDIA COMPANY.

The British East India Company (not to be confused with East India Companies formed by France, Holland and other countries) was a name given to what were originally several private companies formed for trade with India and South East Asia. It is also called the Honourable East India Company often abbreviated to H. E. I. C.

This Company was first given a charter in 1600 by Queen Elizabeth I and, against competition from and conflict with other rival countries, set up trading posts and factories in India, opening that vast country to trade. It is credited with making India part of the British Empire.

The British East India Company maintained its own military forces to protect its property. In 1757 these forces, led by Sir Robert Clive, won a great victory at Plassey and this date is considered the beginning of British power in India. The Company continued to rule India until it was abolished by Parliament in 1858, the governing of India passing to the British Crown.

Although records of the Company[4] still exist back to as early as 1600, some of the earlier ones have been neglected and even destroyed. In 1771 an official was placed in charge of the records and they have been better preserved since that time. Following is a brief description of those records most valuable to the genealogist, although there are others of a biographical and historical nature. These records are preserved at the Military Records Section, Commonwealth Relations Office, King Charles Street, London S. W. 1.

It would seem that most families in the upper and upper-middle classes had some connection with the Company during its existence. There is a reasonable chance of finding valuable information about these families in the records of the East India Company.

Clues to connections with the Company can be obtained from old letters, birth, marriage and death certificates, census

4. See also *Guide to the India Office Records* by William Foster, (Eyre and Spottiswoode, London), and "India Office Records," *The Genealogist's Magazine,* Vol. 6. p. 198.

returns, etc. For example, the following enumeration from the 1851 census returns of Birmingham, Warwickshire clearly shows such a connection:

John Carter	Head	Mar	46	East India Pensioner	Worcester. Worcs.
Mary A. "	Wife	Mar	38		East Indies
Edward "	son		16	shoemaker	" "
Ann "	dau		6		
Rosanna "	dau		2		Birmingham, Warws.
Eliza "	dau		11 mos		" "

The Civil Service.[5]

This title was introduced in 1750 to describe those employ-ed in responsible Company positions. These individuals were known as Factors in earlier periods of the history of the Company. Among the particulars each applicant for a position in the East India Civil Service had to provide was a copy of his birth or baptismal certificate.

Military Officers.

1. Applications for cadetships 1790-1816 are accompanied by birth or baptismal certificates.
2. Embarkation Lists 1753-1860 give the place of origin of officers.
3. Lord Clive's Fund records sometimes give details of the widows of deceased officers and occasionally gives details of their issue.

Medical Services.[6]

Cadet papers 1804-1854 are accompanied by birth or baptismal certificates.

Veterinary Services.

Birth and baptismal certificates are available 1826-1859.

Marine Services and Shipping.

1. Baptismal certificates for some officers are available 1780-1830.
2. Ships' Logs 1605-1833 contain a list of officers, crew and passengers. A record of deaths occurring on each voyage is also kept.

---

5. See also A *Register of Civil Servants* 1790-1842 by H. T. Princep, and *Record of Services of Madras Civilians* 1741-1858 by C. C. Princep and three volumes edited by Dodwell and Miles dealing with Bengal, Madras and Bombay.
6. See also *History of the I.M.S.* (2 vols.) and *Rolls of the I.M.S.* 1615-1930 by Lt. Col. D. G. Crawford (Thacker and Co. London).

Ecclesiastical Returns.
1. Registers of births, marriages and deaths occurring in the following three Presidencies are available:
   i. Bengal 1713 onwards.
   ii. Madras 1698 onwards.
   iii. Bombay 1709 onwards.
2. Many tombstone inscriptions have been printed.
3. Probate records for varying years from all three Presidencies are also available.

Company's Dependencies.

The East India Company administered several dependencies and factories in various parts of the East. Some of these were Penang (Prince of Wales Island), Singapore, Malacca, Sumatra (Fort Marlboro), Java, Persia, Persian Gulf, and also at Macao and Whampoa in China and also on the Isle of St. Helena in the Atlantic Ocean. Births, marriages and deaths registers relating to these dependencies are available for varying periods.

Indian Periodicals.

Various publications such as the *Asiatic Journal, Allens Indian Mail, Allen's Overland Mail, Asiatic Annual Register* and *East India Register and Army List,* contain valuable domestic information about East India Company families. Of the periodicals listed, the last mentioned is the most valuable since it contains details of births, marriages and deaths for the period 1808-1844 and lists of Europeans not in the Company's service 1803-1837.

East India Docks, London.

Valuable genealogical information may also be found in the parish registers of churches situated near the East India Docks in London. Of particular mention is All Saints Poplar, (now St. Matthias, Poplar), that was built on ground given by the Company in 1654. The East India Hospital, demolished in 1866, was established here for the maintenance of the widows of officers and seamen in the Company's service. Some records relating to the hospital and also to the chapel are in Central Library, Poplar, London, E.14 while others relating to the hospital are at the Commonwealth Relations Office, London.

3.   MILITIA RECORDS.

Prior to the establishing of a regular standing army, fighting men were supplied from the local county militia. The organizing of militia men dates back to Anglo-Saxon times and was based on the idea that the duty of every free able bodied citizen was to be prepared to defend his home and country.

Under the Militia Act of 1662, all owners of property, under the orders of the Lord Lieutenant of the County who had complete control of the County Militia, were charged with the responsibility of maintaining in readiness horses, arms and men. The number of such men maintained by each land owner depended on the number of men he employed and the amount of property he owned. A yeoman farmer, for example, was expected not only to supply men, but also to provide much of the equipment used in times of emergency and u n r e s t . These yeomen of England achieved fame in battle and although at one time it usually referred to England's farmers the term "yeomen" is now widely used in military circles.

In 1757, responsibility for raising fighting men was shifted from the property owner to the parish, each county being assessed a number of men. This assessment was divided among the parishes in the county according to their population. By 1761 the raising of the necessary quota was enforced by threat of a penalty of fine. Certain men in each parish were chosen to serve in the militia for three years or to provide a sum of money to pay for a substitute. The maintaining of the parish's contribution in men and equipment was one of the many duties of the parish constable.

The officers of Militia and Local Militia were commissioned through the Lord Lieutenant of the County and the Militia units came under the jurisdiction of the Home Office (a department of the Government). Home Office records conse-quently contain much information regarding the appointment of officers, their promotion, retirement, etc. Information of a genealogical value often is given as well as details of service in other military units.

The Fencibles (regulars for home service only), Yeomanry and Volunteers as well as the Militia kept Muster Rolls. Unlike the Muster Rolls of the regular army, however, they do not usually give the place of birth of the individual. The Public Record Office, London, has records of disbanded Militia regiments covering the period 1778-1919. These include En-rollment Books, Description Books and other types of military records.

Although the Militia Muster Rolls do not give a place of birth they do help to determine the residence of certain persons at a specific time. In some instances they form a complete census of the able-bodied adult population. A few of these records have been printed. Others are at the Public Record Office, while still others are in County Record Offices or in private hands.

An example of a printed book is *Able Men of Suf-folk, 1638*, by Charles E. Banks, published in 1831. This lists all the able bodied men in most parishes in the county of Suffolk for the year 1638. The men listed are all between the ages of 16 and 60 and are listed under their parish of residence. They number about 24,000 individuals.

If searches were being made for a particular person and the surname of the individual was not too common, such a list could be of considerable help since it represents a census of the able-bodied men of that area.

Here is an example of how that book was used to good effect:

> Records in the United States disclosed that Joseph Calfe, born about 1672 "of London" emigrated to America with his parents Robert Calfe and Mary Trace Calfe. Robert Calfe died in 1719

aged 71 years, born therefore about 1648. As the surname Calfe was uncommon, Boyd's partial marriage index, available for some English counties was searched. The surname was found to occur occasionally in Suffolk and the following marriage was found entered in the index for that county:

1670 Robert Calfe to Maria Trace at Bacton.

The parish registers of Bacton were searched and the full entry of this marriage obtained. The christening records of two children of this couple were also found in these registers but that of Robert Calfe was not. It appeared from a careful search of Bacton registers that the Calfes came into that parish a few years prior to the marriage of Robert Calfe in 1670.

Searches for the christening record of Robert Calfe were made in nearby parishes without success and probate records failed to disclose any likely clue. A search in the book, *Able Men of Suffolk* 1638 listed men of this surname in two parishes in the county:

Parish of Stanstead: Robert Calfe, Joseph Calfe, Jerom Calfe. Parish of Alpheton: William Calfe.

A search was made of the registers of both parishes and those for Stanstead disclosed that Robert Calfe was christened there in 1648. From this new discovery it was possible to trace the ancestry for several more generations back, in fact, to the beginning of the registers.

Even though they do not record places of birth, copies of lists of local militia can be used to good advantage as the following example demonstrates:

Underwood Mails and his wife had children born and chris-tened at Codicote, Hertfordshire from 1779 to 1789. They were married at Clothall, a parish a few miles distant. The christening of Underwood Mails himself was not at either place. In the Militia Lists for Rushden (a parish not far away) now preserved at the County Record Office, Hertford, valuable information was found:

The lists begin 'A *trew list of all persons yousaly and at this time dwelling within the parish of Rushden between the ages of 18 and 45.*'

For 26 June 1775 is listed:
Underwood Mails, a servant.
For 14 December 1778 is listed:
Underwood Mails, a farmer.

Underwood Mails does not appear in later lists, although they continue to 1786. It seems he resided in Rushden prior to his marriage and for one year afterwards. Then he moved to Codicote, Such records, therefore, help to fill in the movements of ancestors and provide clues to new localities the records of which could then be searched.

4. NAVAL RECORDS.

In its earliest days the Royal Navy was practically a private service of the Sovereign. With the consolidation of the power of Parliament after the Civil War, the office of Lord High Admiral was created and the Service administered by a committee (the Board of Admiralty) under the direct jurisdiction of the Secretary of State.

From about 1700, the Navy to some extent was subject to political influence. So vital was the Navy to Britain's survival that even in that liberty loving land, the government recognized the necessity of manning the fleet in time of emer-gency by "pressing" seamen.

Until the mid-nineteenth century the lower deck (non-commissioned ratings) was manned by seamen engaged either by voluntary recruitment or by impressment for the duration of a ship's commission. The officers and warrant officers

alone had the security of permanent "employment" in the Navy. Since the sailors were merely hired merchant sea-men, the Royal Marines was established as a disciplined enlisted force to preserve order on board the Fleet.

The records available for officers and men of the Royal Navy are similar in many respects to those kept by the Army. *The Records of Naval Men*[7] and *Naval Records*[8] give a general idea of the types of records available and the information likely to be found in them.

i. *Records of Officers only.*

(i)   The following books are helpful. Many of them give details of birth and parentage of officers:

Memoirs of the Officers of the Navy from 1600, published in four volumes in 1794.

Lives of British Admirals, published in four volumes in 1794.

Naval Biography of Great Britain, published in 1828.

Royal Naval Biography in twelve volumes.

Naval Biographical Dictionary published 1849 and 1859-1862.

Navy Lists, dating from 1772.

Sea Officers Lists, published by the Admiralty begin 1st January 1717/8. This is an official list of officers by name only.

7. *The Records of Naval Men* by Gerald Fothergill, 1910.
8. "Naval Records" by Commander R. D. Merriman, D.S.C., R.I.N., Ret'd., in *The Genealogists' Magazine,* Vol. 10, No. 4. [Eng. Pub. V. Vol. 10.]

The publication *Sea Officers, A List of . . . officers . . . of . . . the Fleet,* for 1818, 1825, and 1833 only, is available at the Genealogical Society, Salt Lake City [R3A2].

Earlier official and unofficial lists consist of:

a. *Pepys's Flag Officer List 1666-1668.*
b. *Pepys's Sea Officer List 1666-1668.*
c. *House of Commons Journal* 2 July 1698.
d. *Sergison's Entitlement to Half-Pay Lists* 18 April 1700 and 27 May 1700.

Commissioned Sea Officers of the Royal Navy, 1660-1815 recently published in thirteen volumes by the National Maritime Museum at Greenwich, England, is the newest and most helpful addition to the series of books relating to naval officers.

(ii)   *Applications for Cadetships* in the Royal Navy usually have the baptismal certificates of each candidate attached to the application as proof of age.

(iii)   *Lieutenant's Passing Certificates* are available at the Public Record Office for the period 1691-1832. Those dating from 1789 usually have baptismal certificates attached. Another group of certificates of lieutenants, pursers, boatswains and gunners are at the same office for the period 1731-1820.

Example of the value of passing certificates.

Robert Delap died in 1849 in Lancashire. According to his death certificate he was aged 65 and was described as a lieutenant in the Royal Navy.

When his daughter married in 1838 she is described on her marriage certificate as the daughter of Robert Delap, Naval Officer.

In the 1841 census of his place of residence Robert Delap's place of birth is given as Ireland.

The Lieutenant's Passing Certificates were searched and a certificate was found dated 15 April 1811, showing that Robert Delap had passed the examination for Lieutenant at Plymouth. Attached to this certificate was a copy of his baptismal certificate showing that *he was born 2 June 1788 and baptized 6 June 1788 at Fahan, County Londonderry, Ireland, the son of Henry and Jane Delap.*

(iv)   *Lieutenants Records of Examinations* are available at the Public Record Office for the period 1795-1832. They give the age of each individual being examined.

(v)   *Entry Books of Lieutenants Certificates of Service,* are available at the Public Record Office for the period 1802-1848. They show the place of birth and the age of each person listed.

(vi) *Midshipmans Papers* exist for the period 1799-1854 and are at the Public Record Office. They give the date of birth and baptism, the place of birth and the names of the parents.

ii. *Records of All Ranks.*

(i) *Ships Musters.*

Regular roll calls were made of the officers and men aboard each commissioned warship and hired "armed ship." Each ship kept a muster book showing the name, rank, dates of entry and discharge, age and birthplace of all members of the ship's company and also the names and dates of entry and discharge and rating of all supernumaries (including soldiers and passengers). The Ships Musters date from about 1680 but very few of the early ones exist. They are fairly regular, however, from about 1696 and are more or less complete from 1740. Names on the Ships Musters are not arranged alphabetically but as follows:

a. The ship's company arranged in the order of joining, irrespective of rating or rank.
b. Royal Marines.
c. Boys 1st Class.
d. Boys 2nd Class.
e. Boys 3rd Class.
f. Supernumaries books for wages and victuals.
g. Supernumaries books for victuals only.
h. Supernumaries books for victuals less spirits.

The Ships Musters extend until the year 1872 and are at the Public Record Office. After that year Ships Ledgers carry a similar amount of information but these, for the years 1878-1909 were destroyed by enemy action in World War II.

(ii) *Description Books.* These are at the Public Record Office and date from around 1790. They give the same type of information as the Description Books for the Army. The description of every recruit includes valuable details of date as well as parish and county of birth.

(iii)   *Certificates of Service*. These exist for the period 1802-1894 and are at the Public Record Office. They are registers of Certificates of Servitude and Records of Service of warrant officers, gunners, boatswains, carpenters, cooks, artificers and seamen. These registers help to determine the ships on which service was given. Once the names of the ships are known the Muster Rolls of those ships can be searched to learn the vital dates and places of birth.

Example of the value of Ships Musters and Certificates of Servitude.

The death certificate of James Marchbanks who died 12 November 1850 indicated that he was aged 74 and had been a naval gunner. He married at Plymouth 29 March 1800 and his children were born there. Searches were made in the Ships Musters of ships sailing out of Plymouth and finally, the following was found from the muster of the ship Modeste:

"Date of entry to ship 3 October 1806
Age on entry to ship—32 years
Place of birth—Worcester"

The Index to Certificates of Servitude was then searched and it was discovered that James Marchbanks had served on about thirty ships. In each instance the Ships Muster indicated his place of birth as Worcester. The Gunners Service Records gave the date of his superannuation as 14 November 1835.

(iv)   *Royal Marines*. Apart from the Muster Rolls mentioned in item (ii) other Muster Rolls and other Royal Marine records have not been available for public inspection in the past. They are now being calendared and will be made available in the Public Office, London in 1959/60.

It is assumed that the types of records kept by the Royal Marines will be very similar to those kept by other branches of the services.

(v)   *Bounty Papers*. The Bounty Papers covering the period 1675-1822 give the names and addresses of those to whom bounty was paid. If it was paid to a relative of the officer or seaman, baptismal and marriage certificates were required as proof of relationship and many of these certificates are still attached to the official Bounty Papers which are at the Public Record Office, London.

(vi) *Courts Martial.* Papers relating to courts martial are at the Public Record Office and often provide valuable genealogical information about the persons involved.

(vii) *Pension Records.* Applications and approvals of pensions give details of service, and place of birth. When widows of naval men applied for pensions, proof of relationship had to be provided. Such proof usually consisted of affidavits or a marriage certificate. The various types of pension records range from 1734-1885 and are at the Public Record Office.

Example of the use of pension records and ships musters.

Amelia Ann Laddick was born 4 April 1840 at 5, Duffs Court, Hanover Street, Portsea, Hampshire, the daughter of George Laddick, a seaman and his wife Ruth Laddick formerly Backaller. In the 1841 census returns of Portsea the enumeration of the same family is shown as:

Brittania Street, Portsea, 1841.

Ruth Laddick   age 25 sailors widow Not born in county.
Amelia A. Laddick age 1   Born in county.

It appeared that George Laddick died between 1840 and 1841 and since George was a sailor, it appeared possible that his widow may have applied for a pension. A search of the pension records disclosed the following:

"George Laddick, deceased, a seaman, Royal Navy. H.M.S. *Larne.* The deceased died 5 January 1840 and the claim of his lawful widow, Mrs. Ruth Laddick, to receive the Naval Assets due to his estate for the purposes of administration was admitted 13 January 1842.

At the time of the investigation Mrs. Laddick was living at 2, Colton's Court, Catherine Row, Portsea, Hampshire and the marriage certificate produced by her showed that:
George Laddick, late of H. M. S. *Warspite* a bachelor and Ruth Backaller were married 29 March 1833 in the parish church of Portsea.

A search in the Ships Musters of H.M.S. *Warspite* indicated that he was received on the ship 10 December 1828 from H.M.S. *Talbot,* that he had been in the Service 8 years, that he volunteered at Plymouth and that he was born at Falmouth.

By the use of naval records, details of the birthplace and marriage date and place of George Laddick were found, items which would have been difficult if not impossible to find from other genealogical sources.

(viii) *Greenwich Hospital Registers*. The naval counter- part of the army's hospital at Chelsea is Greenwich Hospital near London. Some of the records of Greenwich Hospital are at the General Register Office, Somerset House, London and cover the periods 1720-1856 for baptisms, 1724-1754 for marriages and 1705-1857 for burials. These registers record details of the baptisms of pensioners' children, marriages and burials of pensioners and their close relatives. Similar details of the families of the Hospital Staff may also be recorded.

Greenwich from the River Thames. Lining the river front are the buildings of the Royal Naval College. In the center is the National Maritime Museum.

At the Public Record Office, London, is a group of records known as the Greenwich Hospital Registers covering the period 1694-1856. Their contents include:

a. Records of apprenticeship of children of Greenwich Pensioners.

b. Details of assistance given to junior officers and seamen of good service, who, through old age or disability were in need of help.

c. The Rough Entry Book of Pensioners 1704-1869 gives the date of entry into the hospital, date of discharge, date of death, place of birth, where last resided, name of last ship, years of service and if married.

d. The Greenwich Hospital Book of Wills covering the period 1732-1767.

e. The Hospital Registers for 1825-1865 give much valuable genealogical detail including births, marriages, number of chil- dren, ages of children and the parish of marriage of the children.

f. Greenwich School Admission Papers contain a record of the birth or baptism of children of pensioners as well as the marriage certificates of their parents, the naval service of their fathers, etc.

None of the hospital registers are indexed.

Greenwich Hospital was not used for pensioners after 1865. Some of the more recent Pension Rolls for the period 1860-1870 were destroyed by enemy action during World War II.

(ix) *Widows Marriages and Register.* These records are at the Public Record Office and give details of widows who re-married and whose pensions ceased as a result.

(x) *Seamen's Wills.* The group of records under this heading are also at the Public Record Office and cover the period 1786-1882. This is only one group of Wills originally filed at the Admiralty and may be copies of Wills proved in local courts. It must not be assumed that this series covered Wills of *all* seamen. Many others were also proved locally or in one of the Prerogative Courts.[9]

(xi) *Dockyard Records.* The dockyards at Devonport, Chatham, Sheerness, etc., and some overseas yards kept records of some genealogical value. Names and other details of artificers are listed and the records often indicate the marital status of these employees and give details of their families. These records cover the period 1748-1830 and are part of the Admiralty Records at the Public Record office. The only section of these records that has been indexed is "Standing Orders for Dock-yards 1748-1792."

(xii) *Births and Deaths on H.M. Ships.* Record of births and deaths on H.M. Ships are at the General Register Office, Somerset House, London from 1 July 1837. Prior to 1875 such events were also noted briefly in the Ships' Logs. The fees for searching are those normally charged for searches at Somerset House, three shillings and nine pence (55 cents) for the search and the same amount for preparation of a certificate.

---

9. See Chapters 2-6 dealing with Probate Records.

On the 3rd May, 1800, John Hill, a mariner of H.M.S. Regulus, obtained a marriage license to marry Sarah Dowling, a spinster, residing *on board the same ship*. They were married at Portsmouth the same day.

(xiii) *Marriages on H.M. Ships*. These marriage records are at the General Register Office, Somerset House, London. They consist of record of marriages of British Subjects performed on board H. M. Ships by Captains or Chaplains. They cover the period 1842-1879. The fees for searching are the same as those described in item xii.

Example of the Use of Naval Records.

The following example shows the successful use of naval records combined with the use of other genealogical sources.

John Shapcote Leaver married at Tardebigge, Worcestershire, 7 January 1839, at which time his father's name was given as William Henry Leaver, a Lieutenant in the Royal Navy. This connection wth the Royal Navy led to a search in the Ships Musters until the name of William Henry Leaver was found listed in the records of a particular ship. From this lead the naval career of William Henry Leaver was found. He entered the navy as an Ordinary Seaman in June 1801 at the age of 18 at which time his place of birth was recorded as Gosport, Hampshire. He served in nine ships before being made a Lieutenant 22 February 1815. His naval record ends in 1844 and from this information his death certificate was searched for and found. He died 6 June 1844 at Kennington, Surrey aged "about 64 years."

According to the Register of Widows Pensions at the Public Record Office (Adm 23/55) Sarah Elizabeth Leaver, his widow, was granted a pension, payment to commence 1 July 1844. Another Pension Record (L-Z 1867-1869) gave similar details and stated that payment of the pension ceased because Sarah Elizabeth, the widow of William Henry Leaver died 9 September 1867. With the date of death known, it was possible to obtain a copy of her death certificate.

The place of birth of William Henry Leaver had been given as Gosport, a large naval base, and so a search was made of the registers of that particular parish. Gosport is a sea-port on the south coast of England and although it has its own registers it is classed as a daughter church to Alverstoke. The registers neverthe-less are very large, filled with events relating to the many naval families stationed in that area. The registers of Gosport showed that William Henry Leaver was born there 27 September 1782 the son of Robert and Mary Leaver. His sister, Martha Brown Leaver was also born there in 1780, both children being christened at Gosport in September 1783.

There were no further details of this family in the Gosport registers but a search of the Alverstoke parish registers disclosed that Robert Leaver married there by license 5 October 1769. The registers of Alverstoke also record the christening of another of their children, Charles Tovey Leaver.[10]

As the marriage took place by license and as Alverstoke is a Peculiar in the Diocese of Winchester, searches were made for documents relating to this marriage at the Diocesan Registry, Winchester, Hampshire.

The allegation was found and read:

5 Oct. 1769. Robert Leaver of Alverstoke and of H.M.S. Rippon, midshipman, aged 26, bachelor and Mary Brown of the same place, aged 24, spinster.

The allegation disclosed valuable information, namely that Robert Leaver was serving in H.M.S. Rippon. The Ships Musters of this ship were searched and under the year 1768 the following entry was found:

10. The *Commissioned Sea Officers of the Royal Navy* 1660-1815 recently pub-lished in thirteen volumes by the National Maritime Museum list this boy as a Lieutenant 13 March 1797 as well as his brother William Henry Leaver, Lieutenant 22 February 1815. Their father is also listed as a Lieutenant 16 December 1776.

Robert Leaver. Entry 16 Aug. 1768.

Appearance ....(not entered)
Whence and whether prest or not........Hound sloop pay list
Qualities ....Midshipman
Place where born ....(not entered)
Age ....(not entered)

From 1 November 1768 to 31 October 1769 there are seven returns similar to the above but a fuller return follows:

Robert Leaver. Entry 1 Nov. 1769.

Appearance ....(not entered)
Whence and whether prest or not........Hound sloop pay list.
Place and county where born...................................Oxford
Qualities ....midshipman to 22 Aug. 1769, then master mariner to 19 Sept. 1769 then midshipman.

Note that the place of birth is given as Oxford which could refer either to the town or the county of that name. The Ships Musters for H. M. Sloop Hound were searched and the following information was found:

Robert Leaver.

Entry 22 Nov. 1766.
Appearance 22 Nov. 1766.
Whence and whether prest or not ....Sheerness.
Place and county where born.................Kidlington, Oxford.
Age at time of entry to ship..27.

The all-important *parish* of birth is listed in this Ships Muster. (The Will of this Robert Leaver was proved in the Prerogative Court of Canterbury, London, dated 5 September 1797. At the time he was a Lieutenant on board H.M.S. Centaur and he makes his wife Mary sole executrix. The Probate Act Book describes him as "late of Gosport on half-pay in H.M.'s Navy.)

The Leaver example again demonstrates what can be accomplished when military and naval records are used in conjunction with other genealogical record sources.

5.   CHURCHES ON FOREIGN SOIL.

There are a number of "parishes" of the Church of England in foreign lands and these were attended by the families of military personnel stationed in these foreign lands. Records of the christenings of children of soldiers, sailors and marines, burials and marriages connected with these families are also found in the registers of these churches and provide, therefore, items of great genealogical value.

In 1952, the Registrar General, Somerset House, London, published *Abstract of Arrangements Respecting Registration of Births, Marriages and Deaths in the United Kingdom and other countries of the British Commonwealth of Nations and in the Irish Republic.*[11] [R6A 95]. This valuable reference book gives details of registration and the cost of searching for and supplying certificates of registered entries in all countries connected with the British Commonwealth of Nations. In the appendix is a list of Church of England churches or chapels on foreign soil whose early registers are now preserved in some London repository. There may be records other than those listed in this reference book belonging to these churches, particularly for later periods.

Those kept in London and listed in this publication are housed in three repositories namely:

1. The Bishop of London's Registry.
2. The Office of the Vicar-General.
3. The Commonwealth Relations Office.
4. Office of the Registrar General, Somerest House.

Among those kept at the Bishop of London's Registry, No. 1, Dean's Court, Doctor's Commons, London, E.C. is the register of the church at the Cape of Good Hope, South Africa, for the period 1796-1803.

Among those kept at the Office of the Vicar-General No. 1, The Sanctuary, Westminster, London S. W. 1, is the register of the English church at Lisbon, Portugal, for the period 1721-1794. In this particular church in the year 1798, over twenty children of soldiers of the 12th Light Dragoons and several children of the men of the First Regiment of Foot were baptised. Many military marriages are also recorded.

Among the records housed at the Commonwealth Relations Office, King Charles Street, London S.W.1, is the register of St. Helena for the period 1746-1835.

Among those kept at the General Register Office, Somerset House, London, is the register of the English church as Leghorn, Italy for the period 1707-1824.

---

11. Obtainable from Her Majesty's Stationery Office, Kingsway, London, price six shillings. $1.10 should be sent from the United States to cover cost and postage.

The registers of a number of these "foreign" churches, particularly those in Africa, often record the christenings of children of negro slaves. In such cases the registers indicate this fact.

Example of the value of using these records.

The 1851 census of Oldham Road, Newton, Manchester, showed the following family:

James Stansfield Head Age 62 silk winder born Rochdale, Lancs.
Sarah   "   Wife   57   "   Plymouth, Devon.
Sarah   "   Single dau. 38 silk winder " on ship Lisbon.
                                                    British Subject

Using the book described earlier it is noted that there is a Church of England at Lisbon. Registers of marriages 1822-1859 are at the General Register Office, Somerset House; registers of baptisms 1830-1848 and marriages 1812-1890 are at the Bishop of London's Registry whilst at the Office of the Vicar-General there are registers for Lisbon as follows:

Vol. 1. Marriages, births, baptisms and burials 1721-1794
Vol. 2. Marriages 1765-1783.
Vol. 3. Marriages 1764-1799.
Vol. 4. Marriages, baptisms and burials in the British Factory at Lisbon 1794-1807.

The majority of the marriages recorded in Volumes 2 and 3 are also recorded in Volume 1.

According to the 1851 Census Returns, Sarah Stansfield was born between 30 March 1812 and 30 March 1813. None of the registers listed above cover this period but they do show evidence that there was a Church of England church there and that registers were kept.

The minister at Lisbon was contacted by mail and he verified that Sarah, daughter of James and Sarah Stansfield was christened there 28 November 1812.

Thus is was possible to obtain a date of christening which could not have been found by any other means.

6. MERCHANT SHIPPING.

Births, deaths and marriages occurring on board British merchant vessels and certified by the Captains, Commanding Officers or Masters of those vessels, are at the General Register

Office, Somerset House, London and cover the period 1 July 1837 to 31 December 1874. After that date they are in the care of the Registrar General for Shipping and Seamen, Llandaff, Cardiff, Wales. These records relate mainly to the crews of British ships that terminated their voyages in the United Kingdom. Prior to 1 July 1837 such events were recorded in the ship's log and the majority of these logs were destroyed by enemy action during World War II.

The Registrar General for Shipping and Seamen also holds a record of certificated officers from as early as 1850. These documents normally give the date of birth and place of birth of those officers as well as some record of their service.

No individual records were kept of other members of crews of merchant ships until 1913, although crew lists exist from 1835. The name of the ship and the approximate dates of service must be supplied in order to find any details of an individual.

Examples of the use of these records.

 1. Family tradition indicated that John Taylor was an officer on board a merchant ship and was drowned at sea in 1884. Application for a certificate of his death was made to the Registrar General of Shipping and Seamen because that office had charge of records made after 1874. The death certificate was supplied and indicated the following:

 John Taylor, Master Mariner, age 45
 Cause of death—supposed drowned
 Date of death—26.1.1884 Vessel stranded 28.1.1884.
 Name of ship—Victoria Nyanza
 Last place of abode—11, St. Helens Crescent, Swansea.

 Having learned the name of the ship and the fact that he served as an officer after 1850 it was possible for the Registrar General of Shipping and Seamen to supply the following details:

CAPTAIN JOHN TAYLOR

Born 5.3.1839. at Port Eynon,
Glamorgan, South Wales

Held Certificate No. 35218 as Second Mate from 11.11.1864 when his address was 18 Kent Square, Liverpool.

Held Certificate No. 35218 as Only Mate from 22.8.1865 when his address was 18 Kent Square, Liverpool.

Held Certificate No. 35218 as Master on 19.11.1867 when his address was 49 Kent Street, Liverpool.

When this Officer applied for his Certificates of Competency, he claimed the following service:—

Name of Ship	Port of Registry	Rank or Rating	Period of Service From	To
GAWERIAN	Swansea	App.	24. 5.1854	30. 6.1854
GAWERIAN	Swansea	App.	1. 7.1854	31.12.1854
GAWERIAN	Swansea	App.	5. 2.1855	30. 6.1855
HANNAH	Swansea	A.B.	29. 5.1860	7.10.1860
LEWES	Newhaven	O.S.	10.10.1860	26. 4.1861
DEER SLAYER	Swansea	A.B.	16. 6.1861	16. 4.1862
DEER SLAYER	Swansea	A.B.	15. 5.1862	2. 1.1863
STAR OF THE WEST	Bristol	A.B.	7. 1.1863	12.10.1863
JANE ANN & ELIZABETH	Swansea	Mate	1. 1.1864	30. 6.1864
JANE ANN & ELIZABETH	Swansea	Mate	30. 6.1864	30.10.1864
PEMBROKE CASTLE	Swansea	2nd Mate	23.11.1864	8. 8.1865
PEMBROKE CASTLE	Swansea	1st Mate	3. 9.1865	20. 7.1866
PEMBROKE CASTLE	Swansea	1st Mate	21. 7.1866	20.11.1866
ADVENTURE	Valparaiso	Master	29.11.1866	24. 6.1867

It has also been ascertained that Captain Taylor was in command of the **VICTORIA NYANZA** during the following periods:—

*VICTORIA NYANZA	Liverpool	Master	4. 9.1880	1. 8.1881
VICTORIA NYANZA	Liverpool	Master	31. 8.1881	10.10.1882
VICTORIA NYANZA	Liverpool	Master	24.11.1882	26. 1.1884

(Supposed drowned at sea)

* Captain Taylor gave his previous ship as the "GLADLYS" of Swansea, but it has not been possible to trace this vessel.

Note that the date and place of birth of John Taylor is given which is extremely valuable. The biographical information given in this record is valuable material that can be used in the writing of the life story of John Taylor.

2. It was known that John Hall, a ship's officer died at sea in 1874 off the coast of Spain. As the records of deaths occurring on merchant ships are kept by the Registrar General at Somerset House, London, application was made and the following information was supplied:

John Hall, ship's master died 14 August 1874 on board the barque Emilia in the bay of Aquilas, Spain.

Knowing that John Hall was a ship's officer and that he served as an officer after 1850, the Registrar General for Shipping and Seamen was able to supply details of John Halls' place of birth, date of birth and service up to the time he received his Masters Certificate as follows:

John Hall

Born 15. 12. 1811 at South Shields, Durham.
Master's Certificate of Service No. 40631 issued at Shields — 20. 3. 1851.
The following service was recorded in his application form:—

Name of Ship	Port of Registry	Tonnage	Rank or Rating	Period of Service	Trade
DIANA	Newcastle	250	Carpenter	3/1830 - 12/1832	Amer. & Cstg. trades
MARY	-do-	130	-do-	12/1832 - 1/1837	Coasting
HENRY & HERIETE	-do-	200	-do-	2/1837 - 11/1838	Coasting
AMFERTRITE	-do-	266	-do-	11/1838 - 4/1840	Coasting
THENSTON	-do-	110	Mate	4/1840 - 2/1841	Baltic & coasting trades
GRACESIS	-do-	190	-do-	3/1841 - 11/1843	Coasting
LESTER	London	195	-do-	12/1843 - 12/1844	Coasting
LORD JOHN RUSSEL	-do-	267	Master	4/1845 - 3/1846	Amer. trades
LESTER	-do-	195	-do-	3/1846 - 12/1846	Baltic trade
THERON	Shields	292	-do-	3/1849 - Continuing	American and Meditn. trades

7. TRINITY HOUSE.

Trinity House was founded about 1529 in Deptford, Kent, and it developed into a corporation for the encouragement of navigation, and the supervision of lighthouses, buoys, and, indeed, all naval matters not under the express jurisdiction of the Admiralty. They enrolled apprentices to the sea and examined and gave certificates to masters and pilots for the Royal Navy and the merchant service. Trinity House expended funds in the maintaining of poor disabled seamen and their widows and orphans.

There is a group of records, known as Trinity House Petitions, that record applications for pensions or grants-in-aid by seamen and their families. The two examples that follow are taken at random from these records:

i. 12 Sept. 1811, petition of John Bean of Phillip Street, Parish of St. George in East, London, aged 66 years. Mentions his wife, Mary Bean, aged 62 years, and four children—John aged 38, Ester aged 30, Mary aged 26, and Charlotte aged 18.

ii. 6 April 1790, petition of Margaret Bean, of 59, Great Hermitage Street, widow of Captain Alexander Bean, late of the ship Douglas of London, and who was lost overboard recently. She was aged 76 years.

Particulars of the Trinity House Corporation's Manuscripts will be found in the *Eighth Report of The Historical Manuscript Commission*, 1881. Owing to the destruction of the Trinity House by enemy action in 1940, the Corporation had to build temporary offices and their records were not available for research purposes.

There are 102 volumes of Trinity House Petitions, covering approximately 1778 to 1850, at the Society of Genealogists, London.

*   *   *

The value of any genealogical record lies in the information it contains. It is obvious then that there is a great deal of genealogical value in the various types of records discussed in this chapter. Their use, of course, is dictated by the period of time of the genealogical problem, making necessary a knowledge of the periods of time for which the various types of documents discussed are available.

This particular field can produce a rich harvest.

Chapter 8.

HISTORICAL EVENTS RELATED TO GENEALOGICAL RESEARCH

History is the study of events, and, as both local and national events are likely to have an effect on people, both the local and national aspect of history should be considered. The many items of genealogical value that can be contributed by local and national histories have an important bearing on the lives and customs of the inhabitants of any locality.[1]

Here are a few examples of local and national events that may have some influence on genealogical research procedure.

Local Events.

i. Many of the registers of parishes situated on the southwest coast of Wales are missing. It is thought that because of the threat of invasion during the Napoleonic Wars ministers may either have buried or otherwise hid their parish registers, many of them never being recovered.

ii. A vigorous nonconformist preacher may have appeared in the neighborhood and attracted many followers from a number of parishes in that area to his congregation. Such a situation would cause a decrease in the number of entries appearing in the registers of the parish churches.[2]

iii. The opening of a coal mine, the erection of an iron works or the building of a cotton mill in or near a small village might result in the increase in population in one village and in the decrease of the population in another.[3]

---

1. Harland. *A Basic Course in Genealogy,* Vol. 2. p. 139. (Bookcraft, Salt Lake City, 1958.)

2. An example of this is the Nonconformist chapel at Ripley, Derbyshire. At the height of the popularity of a particular Nonconformist preacher there are more christening entries in the Nonconformist register than there are in the parish registers of Pentrich yet Ripley was part of the parish of Pentrich and the christenings, marriages and burials of Ripley people are normally recorded in Pentrich parish registers.

3. In 1801 the population of Ripley was 1091. By 1851 it had increased to 3071 due to the opening of iron and coal mines. During the same period, the population of Pentrich village had decreased from 670 to 486.

    In 1831 the population of Middlesboro, Yorkshire was 383. By 1841, it had increased to 5,000 and to 7,893 in 1851. This was due to the establishment of iron works and the introduction of the railway.

    Because of increased industrial activity the population of Merthyr Tydfil, Glamorgan rose from 7,705 to 1801 to 46,378 in 1851.

National Events.

i. The Civil Wars (1642-1649) and the establishment of the Commonwealth, (1649-1660) are classical examples of national events affecting genealogical research in English and Welsh parish registers. Many ministers fled their parishes and although other persons were placed in charge, the registers were either badly kept or not kept at all. In some instances the earlier registers, prior to 1660, are lost.

Due to the unsettled state of the country, the local probate courts were closed in 1653 and until 1660, the Prerogative Court of Canterbury was the only court allowed to grant probate.[4]

ii. The eighteenth century witnessed the Industrial Revolution in England and Wales, resulting in the tremendous growth of small towns into great industrial centers. The movement of workers from the rural and agricultural areas to the industrial towns had an obvious effect on the tracing of families in genealogical records.

International Events.

While national and international histories rarely give detailed accounts of specific areas, they do contain items that can affect the whole approach to the research campaign and by their contents suggest research in certain types of record sources.

Details of wars, epidemics, revolutions, etc., are recorded within the pages of national histories . . . the Napoleonic Wars in Europe, affecting as they did, the movements of soldiers to foreign lands and the records resulting from such movements . . . all such records are of great importance and have a direct bearing on the study of and the approach to a genealogical problem coinciding with the time and the locale of such historical happenings.[5]

The table that follows lists the main historical events that occurred between 1500 and 1900.

---

4. See Chapters 2-6, which deal with Probate Records.
5. Harland, A Basic Course in Genealogy, Vol. 2, p. 143. (Bookcraft, Salt Lake City, 1958.)

THE SIXTEENTH CENTURY

Historical	Religious, Social, Economical	Record Keeping
1509 HENRY THE EIGHTH (1509-1547)	c.1510 Early years of the English Renaissance or New Learning.	
1512 War with France.		
1513 Battles of the Spurs and of Flodden Field.		
1520 Field of the Cloth of Gold.	c.1521 Early years of the English Reformation.	
1522 War with France.	1523 Tyndale's English version of the Bible secretly distributed.	
1534/5 Henry VIII assumed the title of Supreme Head of the Church of England.	1534 English renunciation of Papal supremacy.	1536 First attempts to initiate the keeping of parish registers fail.
1536-1538 Rebellions in the northern counties against the suppression of the monasteries.	1535-1538 Suppression of first the lesser and then the greater monasteries.	1538 Parish registers ordered to be kept and successfully initiated.[1]
1544 War with France.		
1547 EDWARD THE SIXTH (1547-1553)	c.1550 Walloon Protestants arrive as refugees from the Low Countries.[2]	1547 The injunction to keep parish registers reiterated.
1553 QUEEN MARY (1553-1558)	1553-1558 Protestants persecuted and many burnt at the stake.	1553 Many parish ministers replaced by those favoring the Queen.
1557 War with France, loss of Calais.		1558 Injunction re-enforcing the keeping of parish registers.
1558 ELIZABETH THE FIRST (1558-1603)	1559 Reorganization of the Church of England settled moderately.	
1560 War with Scotland.	1560 Calvinism the national religion of Scotland.	
1562 African slave trade commenced.	1563 Papal recusants heavily fined for non-attendance at Church. The Test Act excluded Roman Catholics from governmental office.	1567 Earliest date in the French Protestant and Walloon registers.[3]

1. See Vol. 1 Chapter 10 "The Parish Registers."
2. See S. Minet, "Huguenot Records" The Genealogists' Magazine. (London, March 1956) commencing at page 149.
3. French Protestant Chapel at Southampton, Hampshire.

Historical	Religious, Social, Economical	Record Keeping
1579 Act of Uniformity in matters of religion enforced.	1571-2 Presbyterianism introduced into England by Thomas Cartwright.	1578 Earliest date in the Quaker (or Society of Friends) Records.[4]
	1580-1 Robert Browne, an early Separatist from the Church of England. His followers "Brownists," later known as Independents or Congregationalists.	
1584 Virginia first colonized.		
1588 Defeat of the Spanish Armada.	1592 A Congregational (or Independent) Church formed in London.	
1599 Revolt in Ireland.	1593 The Conventicle Act aimed against the preaching and worship of nonconformists.	1597 All parish registers ordered to be copied on parchment. A copy to be sent to the Bishop's office annually.[5]

THE SEVENTEENTH CENTURY

Historical	Religious, Social, Economical	Record Keeping
1603 JAMES THE FIRST (1603-1625)	1606 Groups of Separatists fled to Holland.	1603 Further reiteration of previous acts concerning the keeping of parish registers.[6]
1607 Jamestown, Virginia founded by Captain John Smith.	1611 King James or Authorized Version of the Bible published.	
	1614 Some Separatists returned to London and established a church which later became known as the General Baptists.	
1618 Beginning of the Thirty Years War with Germany.	1620 Congregationalists sailed on the Mayflower and founded Plymouth Colony in Massachusetts Bay.	
1621 New York settled by the Dutch.		

4. The date is that indicated for the records in the custody of the Registrar General, Somerset House, London. Although the Quaker meetings did not commence until after 1650, many of their birth records go back much earlier.
5. See Vol. 1 Chapter 13 "Bishop's Transcripts and Their Value."
6. See Vol. 1 Chapter 11 "Laws Relating to the Keeping of Parish Registers."

Historical	Religious, Social, Economical	Record Keeping
1625 CHARLES THE FIRST (1625-1649)		
1626 Charles and Parliament struggle for power. War with France and Spain.		
1629 Parliament dissolved by the King and did not meet for another eleven years.		
1642 Beginning of the Civil Wars. Battle of Edgehill.		1642 From the commencement of the Civil Wars some parish registers ill-kept and earlier records lost or destroyed.
1643 Battle of Roundaway Hill and seige of Gloucester.	1643 England and Scotland sign a covenant to bring about changes in religion and government and to extirpate Popery.	1644 Earliest known date in known Presbyterian registers.[7]
1644 Battles of Cropredy Bridge, Marston Moor, Newbury and Tippermuir.		1644 Earliest date in known Independent (Congregational) registers.[8]
1645 Battles of Naseby and Philliphaugh.	1647 Presbyterians in power in both church and government.	1647 Earliest date in known Baptist registers.[9]
1648 Battle of Preston.	1648 The Westminster (Presbyterian) Confession of Faith.	
1649 Charles I executed. The Commonwealth established and the monarchy abolished.	1649 George Fox, founder of the Society of Friends (or Quakers) commenced his preaching. First Welsh Baptist Church founded at Swansea, Glamorgan.	
1650 Battle of Dunbar, Scotland.		
1651/2 Battle of Worcester, Union with Scotland and War with Holland.		
1653 OLIVER CROMWELL became Lord Protector.	1653 The meetings of the various Nonconformist groups begin to increase in number.	1653 Provincial probate courts abolished and all probates granted in London only 1653-1660.[10]

7. Presbyterian Chapel, Hindley, Lancashire
8. Bull Lane Chapel, Stepney, London
9. Chapel at Coate, parish of Bampton, Oxfordshire.
10. See Chapters 2-6.

Historical	Religious, Social, Economical	Record Keeping
		1653 Justices of the Peace alone empowered to solemnize marriages. The parish clerk to record births, marriages and deaths. Some parish registers not kept at all. This condition lasted until 1660.[11]
1654 War with Spain. England mistress of the seas. Capture of Jamaica.	1657 A few Jews permitted to settle in England.	
1658 Battle of the Dunes. Capture of Dunkirk. Death of OLIVER CROMWELL.		1654-1661 Many Quaker records commence about this time.[12]
1658-1660 RICHARD CROMWELL (son of Oliver) Lord Protector.		
1660 CHARLES THE SECOND (1660-1685)	1660 The ejected ministers return to their livings.	1660 Provincial probate courts reopened.[13] All parishes again recording events in normal manner
1662 Act of Uniformity.	1662 About 2000 vicars and rectors driven from their parishes as nonformists (Presbyterians and Independents). Persecution of all nonconformists. Presbyterianism disestablished. Episcopalian Church of England restored. New system of Poor Law administration. Lasted until 1834.[15]	
1665 Plague of London. War with Holland.		1663 Earliest date in known Roman Catholic registers.[14]
1666 Fire of London.		1667 Burials in woollen enforced by law to help support the declining wool trade.[16]

11. See Vol. 1, Chapter 11, "Laws relating to the keeping of parish registers."
12. See footnote 4.
13. See footnote 10.
14. Chapel at Danby on Yure, Yorkshire.
15. See Vol. 1, Chapter 9, "The Parish and its Administration."
16. See Vol. 1, Chapter 10, "The Parish Registers."

Historical	Religious, Social, Economical	Record Keeping
1672 War with Holland. British Army increased to 10,000 men.	1671/2 Declaration of Indulgence freed nonconformists from prison and permitted their free worship.	1669 Earliest date in known German Lutheran registers.[17]
1679 The Habeas Corpus Act.	1672 The Test Act excluded Roman Catholics from public office.	
1682 Pennsylvania founded by William Penn.		1679 Burials in woollen more strictly enforced.
1685 JAMES THE SECOND (1685-1689) died 1701. Monmouth rebellion and battle of Sedgemoor. British Army raised to 20,000 men.	1685 Revocation of the Edict of Nantes drove thousands of Protestants (Huguenots) out of France many of whom settled in England.[19]	1684 Huguenot French Protestant registers commence in London.[18]
1688 Army raised to 40,000. William of Orange landed in England. Bill of Rights.	1689 The Presbyterian Church established by law in Scotland. The Toleration Act permitted freedom of worship for protestant nonconformists. Bill of Rights passed.	1689 Earliest known Royal Dutch Chapel registers commence.[20]
1689 WILLIAM (1689-1702) MARY died 1694. Siege of Londonderry.		
1690 Battle of the Boyne.	1693/4 Bank of England established. Board of Trade formed.	1695 Commencement of lists in parish registers of "Dissenters" children born but not christened in the parish church. Some were named "Papist" and others "Protestants."[22]
1692 French intention to invade England came to naught.	1695 Act of Parliament imposing a fine upon all who failed to inform the parish minister of the birth of a child. This Act repealed in 1706.[21]	1698 Duties (taxes) on entries in parish registers. Repealed after five years.

17. German Lutheran Church, City of London.
18. At LaSavoy, Strand, London.
19. See footnote 2.
20. Royal Dutch Chapel, St. James Palace, Westminster, London.
21. See Vol. 1, Chapter 17, "The Roman Catholics and Their Records," page 261.
22. Ibid.

THE EIGHTEENTH CENTURY

Historical	Religious, Social, Economical	Record Keeping
1702 QUEEN ANNE (1702-1714)		
1704 Battle of Blenheim.		
	1711) An Occasional Conformity Law,	1711 Order to keep parish registers with ruled and numbered pages given, but generally not observed.
1707 United Kingdom of Great Britain formed by Union with Scotland.	1715) aimed against the Nonconformists.	
1713 Spain ceded Gibraltar to England.	1714 Landholders compelled to take the Oath of Allegiance and renounce Roman Catholicism.	1714 *Quarter Sessions Records*[22] from this date often mention protestant dissenters and Roman Catholic recusants.
1714 GEORGE THE FIRST (1714-1727)		
1715 The Jacobite rebellion during which the Roman Catholic Pretender attempted to seize the throne.	1717 Roman Catholics forced by law to register their estates.	
	1720 Manufacturing towns commence to increase in population. Rise of new wealth.	
1727 War with Austria and Spain.		
1727 GEORGE THE SECOND (1727-1760)	1730 The first Moravian (later also called the United Brethren) congregations first established in England.	1733 Law forbidding the use of Latin in parish registers generally obeyed, although some continued in Latin for a few years.
1733 Proceedings in courts of justice to be in English instead of Latin.	1738 Howel Harris' sermons in Wales laid foundations for Welsh Calvinistic Methodism.	1738 Earliest date in known Calvinistic Methodist registers.[23]
1733 War in Europe (Polish war).	1739 Wesley and Whitefield commence great Methodist revival.	
1739 War with Spain and France.	1740 John Wesley separates himself from the Moravians.	1741 Earliest date in known Moravian church registers.[24]
	1741 Benjamin Ingham founded the Moravian Methodists or Inghamites.	

22. A chapter dealing with "Quarter Sessions Records" is planned for a later volume.
23. Calvinistic Methodist Chapel, Shoreditch (London).
24. Moravian Chapel, Fetter Lane, London.

Historical	Religious, Social, Economical	Record Keeping
1743 40,000 English and Hanovarian soldiers fighting in Europe.	1741 George Whitefield preaching in London and founder of English Calvinistic Methodist Church.	1741 Earliest date in known Scotch Church registers in England.[25]
1745 Battle of Fontenoy.	1744 First Wesleyan Conference held.	
1745 The Young Pretender, Bonnie Prince Charlie, and the Jacobites land in Britain in unsuccessful attempt to seize the throne.		1752 New style calendar inaugurated. Year to commence on 1 January instead of 25 March.[26]
1746 Battle of Culloden.	1748- Countess of Huntington's (Calvinistic) Methodist Connexion founded 1756	1752 Earliest date in known Lady Huntingdon's New Connexion registers.[27]
		1753 Earliest date in known Inghamite Register.[28]
1755 The Seven Years War—in Europe, India and America, known also as the French and Indian Wars.		1754 Marriage Act (Lord Hardwicke's) to prevent clandestine marriages, and ordering marriages to take place in parish of residence.[29]
1757 Black Hole of Calcutta, and the Battle of Plassey and the foundation laid for the Empire of India.		
1759 Fort Duquesne (Pittsburg) conquered by forces under George Washington.		
1760 First English navigation canals.		
1760 French surrender Heights of Abraham, in Canada.		

25. Scotch Church, Stepney, Mile End and St. George in East, London.
26. Vol. 1, Chapter 11, "Laws relating to the keeping of parish registers," pages 159-160.
27. Lady Huntingdon's Connexion Chapel, Norwich, Norfolk.
28. Inghamite Chapel, Colne, Lancashire.
29. Vol. 1, see Pp 146-149 and 160-161.

Historical	Religious, Social, Economical	Record Keeping
1760 GEORGE THE THIRD (1760-1820).		
1762 French surrender Canada and Florida.		1762 Earliest date in known Unitarian registers.[30]
		1762 Earliest date in known Swiss Church registers.[31]
1764- Early years of the Industrial Revolution — Watt improved his steam engine.	1765 Universalism preached in England.	
1765 Invention of the spinning jenny.	1770 New Connexion of General Baptists organized in London.	
	1773 First organized beginnings of Unitarianism in England.	
1776 American Declaration of Independence and the Revolutionary War.	1778 Penal Laws against Roman Catholics mitigated.	1779 Earliest date in known New Connexion Methodist registers.[32]
		1780 Earliest date in known Wesleyan Methodist registers.[33]
1788 Settlement and colonization of New South Wales and Australia.	1781 Sunday Schools founded by Robert Raikes.	1783 Duty (tax) of threepence imposed upon each entry made in the parish registers causing some imperfect recordings.
1789 The French Revolution.	1788 First congregations of New Jerusalemites or Swedenborgians.	
1793 War with France — 10,000 English soldiers in Flanders.	1791 Penal laws abolished.	1787 Earliest date in known Swedenborgian (Church of the New Jerusalem or Jerusalemite) registers.[34]
1798 Naval victories at Cape St. Vincent, and Battle of the Nile.	1793 Napoleonic War stopped reforms.	1794 The Duty (tax) on parish register entries repealed.
	1797 Methodist New Connexion organized.	

30. Unitarian Chapel, Liverpool, Lancs.
31. Swiss Church, Soho Square, London.
32. New Connexion Methodist Chapel, Ovenden, Yorkshire.
33. Wesleyan Methodist Chapel, Ilminster, Somerset.
34. New Jeruselamite (Swedenborgian) Chapel, Friar Street, Blackfriars (London).

THE NINETEENTH CENTURY

Historical	Religious, Social, Economical	Record Keeping
1803 Napoleon plans to conquer Europe and invade England.	1801 First population census taken, but not of any genealogical value.	1800 Earliest date in known Bible Christian registers.[35]
1805 Naval victory at Trafalgar.	1802 Act concerning health and morals of apprentices.	
1808 British Army in Portugal.	1807 Abolition of the slave trade.	1806 Earliest date in known Primitive Methodist registers.[36]
1809 British Army at Antwerp (Belgium)	1810 Bible Christians denomination formed by schism in Wesleyan Methodists.	
1812 French armies driven out of Spain,		
1813 Portugal and Germany.		
1812 American "War of 1812" against England and Canada.	1810-1812 Primitive Methodists formed after expulsion from Wesleyan Connexion.	1813 New type of parish register books introduced consisting of ruled and numbered pages.[37]
1814 Great distress through depression of trade due to war.		1814 Act of burial in woollen repealed.
1815 Battle of Waterloo and Napoleon defeated. Corn laws enacted which impoverished the poor.		1823 New laws concerning marriage by license.
1819 Riots in connection with social reforms.	1829 Catholic Emancipation Act; triumph of religious toleration.	1829 Earliest known registers of the Irvingite or Catholic Apostolic registers.[39]
1820 GEORGE THE FOURTH (1820-1830)		1831 A list of all parish registers dating prior to 1813 compiled.[40]
1830 WILLIAM THE FOURTH (1830-1837) Opening of first railways.		1835 Earliest known date in Universalist church registers.[41]
		1837 New law concerning the civil registration of births, marriages and deaths enforced from 1 July.[42]

35. Bible Christian Chapel, Salford, Lancashire.
36. Primitive Methodist Chapel, Newington Butts, Surrey (London).
37. See Vol. 1, pp 145, 153, 161, and 181.
39. Irvingite Chapel, Bishopsgate, London.
40. Parish Register Abstract, 1831. See Vol. 1 pp 141, 142 & 165.
41. Universalist Chapel, Liverpool, Lancs.
42. See Vol. 1, Chapters 4 & 5.

Historical	Religious, Social, Economical	Record Keeping
1837 QUEEN VICTORIA (1837-1902)	1837 First missionaries of the Church of Jesus Christ of Latter-day Saints preach in England.	1841 The first population census of value to genealogists.[43]
1846 Irish potato famine. Corn Laws repealed.		1851 The population census improved and the information of great value to genealogists.[44]
1854 The Crimean War.		1858 Probate courts taken out of ecclesiastical jurisdiction.[45]
1879 Zulu War.	1870-1874 Married Women's Property. Acts protecting her use of and disposal of her own property.	1872 Penalties enforced for failing to register births, marriages or deaths.
1899 South Africa (Boer) War.		

43. See Vol. 1, Chapters 6, 7, 8.
44. Ibid.
45. See Chapters 2-6 for complete details.

Chapter 9

THE COUNTIES OF ENGLAND AND WALES

There are four major items to be considered in the use of genealogical records:

i. The type of records that are of genealogical value.
ii. The amount of information they give.
iii. The specific periods of time they cover.
iv. Their places of deposit.

Once the value of genealogical records has been understood, their availability is of prime importance. The purpose of this chapter is to provide information regarding the location of and the period covered by certain of such records.

There are forty ancient and historic counties (or shires) in England, including Monmouthshire. With the twelve ancient counties of Wales, the total is fifty-two, the same number as there are weeks in the year.

Generally speaking, the term county and the term shire mean the same. The names of the counties that have the suffix, *shire, like* Nottingham*shire,* are also known as County Nottingham. In more recent times some counties have been divided or new counties created for judicial and administrative purposes. Examples of those that have been divided are Yorkshire (where the three ridings,—East Riding, North Riding, and West Riding — are now administrative counties), and Lincolnshire (where the divisions of Holland, Kesteven, and Lindsey are now administrative counties). Examples of those that have been created are the Isle of Wight (from Hampshire) and London (from parts of Kent, Middlesex, and Surrey). While such division of the historic counties has little affect on actual research work, it does influence the location of county record offices.

County boundaries are certainly worth consideration, as most changes in the boundaries of parishes and the ancient counties have taken place principally in the past 130 years.

This affects not only a few border parishes, but also parishes that were in a small *detached* part of one county, but geographically surrounded by another county. For examples of detached portions of counties, see the map of Wiltshire (shown later in this chapter) and compare the detached parts of that county with the map of Berkshire. Similarly, prior to 1844, considerable parts of the present county of Northumberland were detached parts of County Durham.

Such irregularities might be found in most counties, but these have been cleared up by changes in boundaries. This means that descriptions of such parishes found in modern gazetteers, directories, text books, and library catalogues, will place them in their *present* and not their *former* counties. Bartholomew's *A Survey Gezatteer of the British Isles* [R.10 A17], available in most libraries, indicates the county in which parishes are *now* situated. Information on the standard abbreviations of the counties, and details of the standardized recording of places in England and Wales, as used by the Genealogical Society, Salt Lake City, is to be found in *A Basic Course in Genealogy,* (An Introduction to Record Keeping and Research), Vol. 1, pages 167-172.

The borders of counties are merely imaginary lines, not insurmountable barriers, but there is a tendency for some to confine their searches to places within one county. Research problems that involve places near to a county border should take into consideration the adjoining counties, as people were free to move from county to county without border restrictions.

This Chapter lists alphabetically each one of the historic counties, and under "London" includes information relating to the Metropolis. The details listed under the name of each county are grouped into categories, of which the following is an explanation:

AREA: The areas of the counties given are the areas as in 1831, and in most counties the areas have varied little since then. This information will allow comparison to be made with the size of other counties, and perhaps with areas with which the genealogist is familiar.

POPULATION: The population figures are those given in the Lewis' *Topographical Dictionary of England* (1831 and 1833 editions) and *Topographical Dictionary of Wales* (1833 edition). These figures will represent the population of each county at a time before the building of the railroads and better highways and at a time when some of our ancestors lived, and consequently are better than up-to-date figures. Compared with the area, these figures will assist the researcher to deter-mine the density of the population. Lancashire, for example, had a population of about 741 per square mile, whereas Cumberland had a population of only 116 per square mile. This type of information when compared with the number of parishes within a county, indicates that parish registers in the more heavily populated counties will likely contain many more entries than those with a smaller population and, conse-quently, the searching of the former will take considerable time. The *Municipal Year Book,* published annually by Muni-cipal Journal, 3 Clement's Inn, Strand, London, W. C. 2, England, lists the present population, extent of the counties, cities, towns and various administrative districts of the British Isles, together with the names of the officials of the local government offices, including archivists and librarians. [R6A-100].

ANCIENT PARISHES: An ancient parish is any place (either a parish or a parochial chapelry) that had parish registers *prior to January,* 1813. The number of ancient parishes is taken from the *Parish Register Abstract,* 1831: "Abstract of An-swers."[1] Information on the names of ancient parishes will also be found in Burke's *Key to the Ancient Parish Registers of England and Wales.*[2]

It will be noted that many towns and cities have more than one ancient parish. Additional parish churches may have been built after 1813. Prior to 1813, many towns, particularly those in industrial areas, had only one parish church, the registers of which are very large. Bradford, Yorkshire, for ex-ample, with a population in 1831 of over 76,000, had only one parish church. On the other hand, Norwich, Norfolk, had thirty-nine ancient parish churches, but in 1831, its population was, by contrast, only a little over 61,000. Such information is of paramount importance. A research problem in Norwich should involve the searching of the registers of each of the thirty-nine parishes, whereas a search in Bradford would, prior to the building of additional churches after 1813, be confined to the one set of registers of that town's only parish, although these registers are voluminous.

COUNTY TOWN: The County Town is usually the center of civil administration of a county, and also the town in which

1. See Vol. 1, Chapters 9-12.
2. See Vol. 1, Chapter 10, page 141.

the County Record Office is situated. In counties where there is no County Record Office, the county town is the most likely place for the future establishment of such an office. Under the name of each county, mention is made of the location of its County Record Office, if it has one.

The Clerk of the County Council is the chief legal adviser to that council, and usually his office is divided into sections, one being the County Record Office, with the County Archivist in charge. The County Archivist is responsible for the safe custody of the records. Generally, County Record Offices have facilities for students to personally visit and use the records, but prior to doing so, students should find whether or not there is a printed guide, or other published list, detailing the nature and type of available records. However, since such a printed list or guide was made, there may have been further accessions.

Inquiries by mail should be kept to a minimum. It is stressed that the main duties of the staff of a record office is the care of the deposited records and the collecting, sorting, and cataloguing of new accessions, and making all records available to the officials of the county and to students. Although the staff may do short searches requested by mail, it must be realized that lengthy searches cannot be undertaken, but the County Archivist, in accordance with county regulations, may permit searches by students and responsible persons.

Main Occupations: Listed under this heading are some of the occupations mentioned by Lewis in his Topographical Dictionaries of England and Wales (1831 and 1833 editions). They refer, therefore, to the *main* occupations of more than one hundred years ago. The occupations in that county may have changed considerably since then.

Principal Rivers: Prior to 1830, when the first railroads were introduced, water transport was economical and therefore common. A study of the rivers and canals can be helpful in considering the possible movements of an ancestor.

Lewis, in his *Topographical Dictionary of England,* states for example, that at Thorne, Yorkshire, vessels for the coasting trade were built, then conveyed down the River Don to Hull to be rigged and otherwise completed. It is not surprising, therefore, to find families having connections with both places, although they are about forty miles apart.

Ecclesiastical Divisions of the County: Counties are *civil* divisions. The Church of England has always had its own *ecclesiastical* divisions of administration that in some instances follow county boundaries, but in others they do not.

As the keeping of records such as Bishop's Transcripts, Marriage Licences, and Probate Records was, in the main, a function of the ecclesiastical courts, it is essential to know the ecclesiastical divisions. The areas of ecclesiastical jurisdiction, already enlarged upon in more detail in Chapter 2 are as follows:

Provinces:
  i. Province of Canterbury, covering the midland and southern counties of England, the Channel Islands, and, until 1920, Wales.
  ii. The Province of York, comprising the northern counties of England and Wales, and the Isle of Man. See the map on page 38 illustrating the division between the provinces.
  iii. The Province of Wales, created in 1920 from the Province of Canterbury, comprising all of Wales and Monmouthshire.

Dioceses:
  Each province is divided into several areas known as dioceses, each headed by a bishop of the Church of England. The principal office and record repository of each diocese is known as the Diocesan Office or Registry, which is usually situated in the Cathedral City—the chief city of that diocese.

Archdeaconries:
  Each diocese is divided into one or more archdeaconry, each headed by an archdeacon, who, if he has an office, conducts his business in the Archdeacon's Registry, where the records may be deposited.

Rural Deaneries:
  Each archdeaconry is divided into rural deaneries, and each is an area consisting of a number of ecclesiastical parishes. One of the parish ministers within each rural deanery is appointed Rural Dean to supervise the parishes within that rural deanery. Usually it is not necessary to know how the name of the rural deanery unless the records of marriage licences, Bishop's Transcripts, and probates, are arranged in order of rural deanery. Sometimes a rural deanery may be referred to as a "deanery."

Parishes:
  An ecclesiastical parish is a district served by a clergyman of the Church of England, and for genealogical purposes, it is the smallest unit of ecclesiastical jurisdiction.

The ecclesiastical divisions shown for each county are confined to stating the names of the archdeaconries, dioceses, and province involved.

PARISH REGISTERS:[3] This category deals mainly with their availability on a broad scale only. It is obvious that details of more than 11,000 parishes cannot be given here. However, the authors plan to make such information available in later publications.

Many people go to great expense in searching an *original* register, overlooking the fact that it has been transcribed, printed, or microfilmed, and therefore more economically available. The Genealogical Society, Salt Lake City, Utah, has a copy of almost all the parish registers that have been *printed,* as well as a number of transcript copies of other parish registers. That Society has also microfilm copies of a number of other parish registers. However, the total number of all copied registers is small when compared with the number that have not been copied in any form whatsoever.

The Society of Genealogists, 37 Harrington Gardens, London, S. W. 7, has an excellent collection of printed and transcribed registers. The British Museum and the College of Arms, both in London, also have valuable collections of parish register copies.

The details given here about parish registers concern those parishes that had registers *prior to* 1813. That year saw the commencement of new-style registers composed of printed and ruled forms on which specific items were to be recorded. For this reason, many transcribers and publishers of parish registers have used 1812 as the logical year at which to stop their transcription of the registers of parishes. The original parish registers are, in large measure, in the care of the local clergy.

As the population of the country increased, it became necessary to build additional parish churches. There is no complete list of these new parishes showing the year of the commencement of their registers, but a study of Lewis' *Topographical Dictionaries,* the 1851 *Census* "Population Tables of England and Wales," and county *Directories,* will, between them, usually provide the desired information.

Reference is made in this category to Boyd's *Marriage Indexes.* There are several series of this important genealogical source, as follows:

---

3. See also Vol. 1, Chapter 10.

Boyd's Marriage Index.

i. The first series was prepared by Percival Boyd on a *county* basis. Marriage references in this series were usually obtained from printed, transcribed and otherwise easily accessible parish registers. This is an alphabetical index to the names of bridegrooms and brides, and is limited to the period 1538-1837. It does *not* contain references to *all* marriages that took place in the county, as it covers *certain parishes* in the county for *certain periods only,* that is, only such periods that were available to the compiler. In many instances, therefore, the Index does not cover the period 1538-1837 for all the parishes involved.

Each county index is divided into sections roughly covering, in the main, twenty-five years—for example, 1538-1600, 1601-1625, 1626-1650, and so on, concluding with 1801-1837. In some instances, because of the large number of references, the index is divided—one section or index for bridegrooms, and a separate one for brides.

Details of the counties involved in this first series, together with the names of the parishes and periods covered, are contained in the booklet, *A Marriage Index on a New Plan,* issued by the Society of Genealogists, London. The listings in this booklet are believed to be incomplete.

ii. The second series prepared by Percival Boyd is known as the *Miscellaneous Marriage Index, 1538-1837.* It is arranged in a way similar to the first series, but it is an index *involving many counties.*

The marriage references are other than those in the first series, and it provides a consolidated index to marriages taken from *certain* parishes for *certain* periods only, irrespective of the county from which the entry was taken.

iii. At the time of Percival Boyd's death in 1955, details of over one million marriages had been entered on small index slips. These are in *addition* to those marriages covered by the first and second series above. These additional marriage references have now been arranged and typed in a way similar to the first series by the Genealogical Society, Salt Lake City, Utah.

Between these three indexes it is possible that Percival Boyd covered the majority of printed and transcribed marriage registers, marriage license records, and certain miscellaneous sources. It should be remembered, however, that since these indexes were made there have been additional marriage records printed and transcribed that were not available to Percival Boyd. Copies of all three indexes are available at the Society of Genealogists, London, and at the Genealogical Society, Salt Lake City, Utah. It is hoped that a list of the parishes and periods covered by these indexes will be made available.

While these indexes are of tremendous help, they are still *only indexes,* and should only be used as such.[4] Complete details of any marriage reference listed in them must be found by using the original parish registers, or their verbatim copy.

Each marriage reference consists of a one-line entry. The following example is from *Derbyshire Marriage Index,* and the portion for "Grooms" for 1800-1837 for letter W:

			Where
Year.	*Male.*	*Female.*	*Married.*
1810.	WHYSALL Robert [married to]	Mary STANLEY	Pentrich

In the appropriate volume for "Brides" the same marriage is found indexed under "S" and STANLEY, Mary. The entry of this marriage appears in the printed marriage registers of Pentrich, Derbyshire, as follows:

12 April 1810. Robert Whysall, age 18 years to Mary Stanley, age 21.

As has been pointed out in Volume 1, page 183, in the case of William Udy and Isabella Varcoe, sometimes the printed copy of a parish register does not disclose all details that are to be found in the original. In the printed parish register, the entry for Isabella Varcoe did not disclose, as did the original, that she was a widow. Therefore, in many instances, the original parish register gives details of marital status and sometimes residential connections with other parishes. It is emphasized again, that to use any marriage index as the *sole* source is dangerous. Their use as short cuts in research—providing leads and clues—is of obvious value.

Each volume of these marriage indexes should be carefully examined, as there may be divisions within each volume:

Examples:

1. *The Marriage Index for Devonshire, Vol.* 21, *for* A-Z, 1751-1775.

    i. Pages 1 to 125 comprises an index A to Z for "grooms" (i.e., males). Then follows a dividing page, and this is followed by:

    ii. Pages 1 to 124 comprising an index A to Z for "brides" (i.e., females).

---

4. For important basic research standards, see *A Basic Course in Genealogy (An Introduction to Record Keeping and Research)*, Vol. 1, Chapter 15, "Basic Research Standards," by Gardner, Harland and Smith, (Bookcraft, Inc., Salt Lake City: 1958).

When searching for the surname "Tucker," it is easy to turn to the end of the Volume, and under "T" search for that surname. Although entries (if any) found actually relate to females, yet it is easy to overlook the other "Tucker" entries entered nearer the front of the book under the "grooms" portion of the Volume.

2. *The Marriage Index for Yorkshire, Vol. 8, for A-Z, 1776-1800.*

   i. Pages 1 to 512 comprise an index A to Z, combining "grooms" and "brides." Then page 512 is follows by:

   ii. Pages 1 to 60 comprising an index A to Z combining "grooms" and "brides." Note that pages 1 to 512 in "i" and pages 1 to 60 in "ii" are separate indexes referring to different marriages.

3. *The Marriage Index for Devonshire, Volumes 21, 22, and 23,* 1751-1775.

   i. Volume 21 contains an index A to Z, 1751-1775, within which there are separate divisions for "grooms" and "brides."

   ii. Volume 22 contains an index A to K, 1751-1775, within which there is an index *combining* "grooms and "brides."

   iii. Volume 23 is a continuation of Volume 22, and contains an index L to Z, 1751-1775, within which there is an index *combining* "grooms and "brides."

   The parishes included in Volume 21, are *not* the same as the parishes included in Volumes 22 and 23, although all cover the same period. Therefore the period covered has two *separate* indexes, each of which covers separate places and persons.

It is stressed that care must be taken to note whether or not there are divisions within volumes, or whether or not there are more volumes than one for the same period.

BISHOP'S TRANSCRIPTS:[5] Bishop's Transcripts are one of the most important and widely used of all genealogical records. While parish registers usually are in the custody of the incumbent of the parish, Bishop's Transcripts are found in central record repositories, usually Diocesan Registries or County Record Offices. Not all parishes have Bishop's Transcripts; in some counties they extend to 1812; in others up to 1841 and in rare instances they extend to around 1900. In many counties, searching in these transcripts is no sinecure, as the condition of many of the repositories leaves a great deal to be desired—unheated, damp, and without artificial light.

---

5. See Chapter 13 of Volume 1 for a complete explanation of their origin, contents and value.

It is emphasized again that County Archivists and Diocesan Registrars cannot be expected to undertake lengthy searches in these records. Lengthy searches should be made by a competent record searcher or professional genealogist.

All the Bishop's Transcripts for Wales and Monmouthshire that were available in 1947 at the National Library of Wales have been microfilmed by the Genealogical Society, Salt Lake City, Utah. The situation regarding each county in England is detailed under its respective heading.

MARRIAGE LICENCES:[6] In most areas, the documents connected with marriage by *licence* are deposited in the registry of the appropriate diocese, emphasizing once again, the importance of being acquainted with the areas of ecclesiastical jurisdiction. These documents provide a very valuable source and for some areas, abstracts have been printed from them. Where no printed or transcribed abstracts are available, searching of the original documents can be long and tiresome. For these areas the licences of which are printed, details of the periods covered are given under each county heading, together with details of the book or publications in which they appear. The Call Number of these publications at the Library of the Genealogical Society, Salt Lake City, is given in square brackets. The records of the marriage licences for Wales and Monmouthshire that were available at the National Library of Wales in 1947, have been microfilmed for the Genealogical Society, Salt Lake City.

PROBATE RECORDS: Chapters Two to Six of this Volume describe in detail the probate records as a genealogical source. The category, "Probate Records," as listed under each county, deals with the disposition of the pre-1858 probate records, showing the probate jurisdictions within each county. As it is not practical to indicate here the probate court applicable to each parish, the authors hope, in later publications, to make available information on the ecclesiastical jurisdictions for each parish in England and Wales. Meanwhile it is necessary to use reference books that detail these former jurisdictions. The most helpful is the out-of-print Lewis' *Topographical Dictionary of England* (1831 and 1833 editions only) and *Topographical Dictionary of Wales* (1833 edition only).

---

6. See Chapter 14 of Volume 1 for a complete explanation of their origin, contents and value.

Printed Calendars (or Indexes) and printed abstracts of Wills and Admons., are noted under each probate court respectively, together with the name of the relevant book or series of publications. The Call Number of such publications that are in the Library of the Genealogical Society, Salt Lake City, are shown in square brackets.

It is unfortunate that various societies that have been transcribing and printing the Calendars of Wills and Admons., parish registers, marriage licences, etc., have been forced to curtail their efforts because of a lack of financial support. It has been suggested that, if all persons whose ancestry came from a given area were to financially support the societies established in that area, much more could be accomplished. A microfilm copy of an original record is of obvious value, but an accurate, well-indexed printed copy is time-saving and far easier to use.

NONCONFORMIST REGISTERS:[7] The number of Nonconformist chapels listed for each county is based on information in the Lists of Non-parochial Registers printed by H. M. Stationery Office, London, in 1841. This states the names of the chapels and periods prior to 1838 covered by their registers that are on deposit with the Registrar General, Somerset House, London.

Nonconformist chapels, other than those whose registers are deposited at the General Register Office, Somerset House, did exist, and their registers may be in the Nonconformist chapels, in libraries, or they might have been destroyed. The figures given for each county do not include the records of the Society of Friends (Quakers), the Jewish Synagogues, the Foreign Churches, or the majority of the Roman Catholic chapels. A complete list of all known Nonconformist chapel registers will be made available by the authors in later publications.

PUBLICATIONS: A few of the more important publications of a genealogical value have been listed for each county. There are other valuable publications, such as parish histories, directories, etc. It is hoped that a thorough study of the county will be made by those who have ancestry in that county, and that such a study will include a survey of all the printed material available, no matter how insignificant it may at first appear.

---

7. See Volume 1, Chapter 15, for a complete explanation of their origin, contents, and value.

This list is not meant to be an exhaustive bibliography on the county.

Some of the more outstanding publications, not included in the listings, but relating to a county or the country as a whole, are as follows:

i. Samuel Lewis, *Topographical Dictionary of England* and *Topographical Dictionary of Wales*, already mentioned previously.

ii. *The Victoria History Of The Counties Of England.* From the general advertisement of this series the following is taken: "The Victoria History of the Counties of England is a National Historic Survey which, under the direction of a large staff comprising the foremost students in science, history and archaeology, is designed to record the history of every county of England in detail." Histories for some counties have been completed, but others are still in progress. Articles of ecclesiastical history and topography are helpful in the study of parishes and their records. Some detail is included of the genealogies of many of the principal families of the county. The work is being carried out by various committees, and the volumes are published by the Institute of Historical Research of the University of London.

iii. County Directories are valuable reference books. They usually give a brief history of each parish, sometimes the date the parish registers commence, and the names and addresses of residents, tradesmen, etc.

iv. *Crockford's Clerical Directory,* published every two years by Geoffrey Cumberlege and the Oxford University Press, is a reference book of the clergy and to the ancient and modern parishes of the Church of England. From this book the correct address of the present parish minister can be ascertained. The other information in this publication is too modern to be of genealogical value on an ancestral research problem.

v. The following are of general interest to those with Welsh pedigree problems:

(i.) The National Library of Wales *Journal and Supplements,* including *Handlists of Manuscripts in the National Library of Wales.*

(ii.) *Transactions* of the West Wales Historic Society.

(iii.) The publications and journals of the Cambrian Archaeol. Soc.; Chester and North Wales Archaeol. Soc.; the Hon. Soc. of Cymmrodorion, and their magazine, Y Cymmrodor; *Archaeologia Cambrensis; Bibliotheca Celtica;* and the Welsh Bibliographical Society.

(iv.) There are many Welsh publications issued by various religious denominations, such as the Calvinistic Method-

ists; Welsh Baptists; Welsh Independents or Congrega-
tionalists; and The Church of England in Wales.

It is not possible to detail in this chapter the vast and
highly important genealogical collections that are to be found
in the county record offices and other repositories throughout
the country. Every county, and some cities and towns, have
collections of Quarter Sessions Records and other related
records relating to the legal administrations of towns, cities,
and counties. There are also records of apprentices and freemen
(citizens and burgesses of cities and towns), and many other
records. For an example of records generally found in the
care of counties, see F. G. Emmison's *Guide to the Essex Record
Office,* Numbers 1 and 2, issued in 1946 and 1948. [ESSEX
PUB. C. Nos. 1 and 2]. Details of the value and use of these
county collections will be included in a later volume of this
series.

TOPOGRAPHY AND GEOGRAPHY IN RELATION TO GENEALOGICAL RESEARCH PROBLEMS.[8]

The topographical features of a region or locality play an
important part in genealogical research. A study of the locality
and its people should precede actual research. The best county
maps for genealogical purposes are those printed about the
time in which the ancestor lived, or those at least one hundred
years old. Those incorporated in Lewis' *Topographical Dictionaries* are ideal for genealogical use, and are reproduced in
this volume for each county. They have been supplemented
by hand-drawn maps for those counties the maps of which
were more complicated than the others. Some of these hand-
drawn maps show the parish boundaries and where possible,
the date of the first entry appearing in the parish registers
of that parish.

It will be noted that the printed maps show the Unions and
Union boundaries as they existed at that time. A Union is a
civil division and its only genealogical value is in the fact Union
boundaries were used as the boundaries of the registration
districts when civil registration was commenced in 1837. Since
that time most of the registration district boundaries have
changed. It should not be assumed that each place marked
with a cross on these printed maps is an ancient parish.

Roads, mountains, rivers and other features have a distinct
bearing on the movements and habits of a people. The farmers
took their produce to the market town most easily accessible

---

8. This is the section promised in Vol. 1, page 188, footnote 40.

along the existing roads. Here, his son, his husbandman, or his carter may have met their future wives, who themselves may have travelled to the market town from some nearby town or village *situated in the opposite direction.*

Many counties like Brecon and Caernarvon in Wales, and Westmorland in England are partly wild and mountainous. In such counties, the roads follow the valleys and it is likely that the records of the next parish along the valley may hold the desired genealogical clue rather than the records of a parish that is much nearer in miles but across a range of mountains. The maps used in this volume show the high ground by shading.

What happened to the children of farmers and shepherds who wrested a living from countryside like this? In wintertime it would be almost impossible to take their children to be christened in the parish church many miles away. In the spring were they too busy with their many farm duties to take the children to be christened by the parish minister or were they attracted to a local Quaker group or some Nonconformist meeting place that was more convenient.

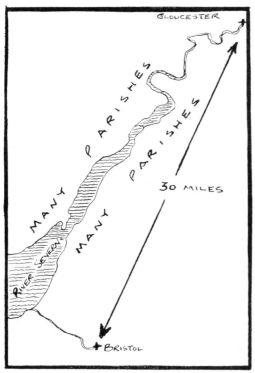

Rivers such as the Severn and the Thames, as well as inland canals, can also present difficult problems. A man may be employed on a barge ply-ing between Bristol and Gloucester City through the Bristol Channel, the River Severn and the Bristol to Gloucester Ca-nal. He could have met his future bride at any stopping place on the way. When he married and made the barge his home, he could have had his children christened at any church along the route. If the family were alive when the 1851 cen-sus was taken and if it is important to locate them in order to learn their place of birth, where does the search for them commence? Where were they on the night the census was taken?

The young man employed on a collier (i.e., a ship transport-ing coal) from Newcastle-upon-Tyne, Northumberland, to London may have met his future wife in London. The fisherman from Whitby on the Yorkshire coast trawling for fish in the North Sea may have sold his catch at Hull, Grimsby, or in some other sea-coast town. He may have met his bride at any one of the places he visited, and may have eventually settled in one of those towns.

Each county differs is some respect from all others. A glance at the map of Norfolk, for example, shows hundreds of small villages, each with its own parish church and parish registers. Such a situation will indicate to the experienced researcher that a research problem in such an area will require the searching of the registers of a large number of these small parishes before a correct analysis can be made. On the other hand, in some parts of the country a parish covers a wide area. Rothwell, for example, a parish in Yorkshire, comprises the townships of Carlton, Lofthouse, Middleton, Oulton, Rhodes-Green, Rothwell, Haigh, Thorp and Woodlesford. As could be expected under these circumstances, the parish registers of Rothwell are very large since that parish covers a large area and includes a number of towns and villages.

To demonstrate the value of maps, consider the following problem which involved the locating of the christening of Thomas Green, who it was known, died 10 March, 1874, in Portage, Utah. His first marriage, to Sarah Pierce, took place in England, and after her death he married Margaret Connoley, 7 March, 1836, at the Cathedral, Manchester, Lancashire. After the death of his second wife, Thomas Green married Mary Ann Gibson, 12 October, 1837, at Manchester Cathe-dral. It was possible to obtain a copy of this marriage certificate and because it took place after the commencement of civil registration, it stated that Thomas Green was the son of Edward Green.

The L. D. S. Church Membership Records of the Man-chester Branch of the British Mission showed that Thomas Green was baptized into that Church 16 March, 1839. He emigrated to the United States soon afterwards, and, in a record made at Nauvoo, Illinois, in 1843, his date of birth is given as

27 January, 1803 and his place of birth as Lower Walton, Cheshire. Family records gave the names of his two sisters, Ellen and Mary, and stated that his mother's name was Jane Green, formerly Savage.

According to Lewis' *Topographical Dictionary,* Lower Walton, or Walton Inferior as it is also called, is a township in the parish of Runcorn. A search of Runcorn parish registers, however, failed to disclose the christening or birth record of Thomas, Ellen, or Mary Green. A marriage recorded in the Runcorn registers showed that Edward Green and Jane Savage were married in that parish, 14 July, 1800. Why were the children of this couple not christened in this parish since Lower Walton in part of the parish?

Runcorn is an extensive parish, having chapelries of Aston-by-Sutton, Daresbury and Thelwall as well as twenty townships, one of them being Lower Walton. The nearest parishes *in the same county* are Latchford and Grappenhall, but a search of the registers of these parishes did not disclose the required christening entries.

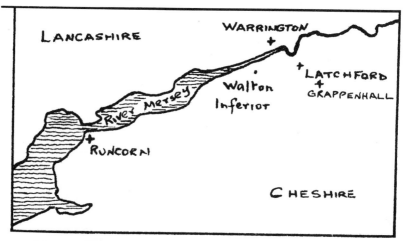

The beginning genealogist may consider the next step to be the searching of nearby parish registers in the county of Cheshire, failing to take into consideration that these places are close to the border separating Cheshire from Lancashire. A study of the map of this locality shows that part of the boundary between the two counties is the River Mersey, but communication was made possible by a bridge between Warrington and Latchford joining the two counties. Runcorn is nine miles west-south-west from Warrington, a large town in Lancashire. Lower Walton is seven miles from Runcorn *but only two miles from Warrington.* Based on these geographical findings, a search was made in the christening registers of Warrington and the christening entries of all three children of Edward and Jane were found:

chr. 11 Apr.. 1801   Mary daughter of Edward and Jane Green, weaver.

chr. 22 Jan. 1803   Ellen daughter of *Edmund* and Jane Green, weaver

chr. 24 Feb. 1805   Thomas son of Edward and Jane Green, laborer

In addition to demonstrating the value of using maps, the following items of interest can be noted in this particular example:

i. Thomas Green stated that he was born in 1803, whereas he seems more likely to have been born in January 1805. Such discrepancies occur often and can usually be solved by a careful evaluation of the two conflicting records.[9]

ii. Edward Green is called Edmund Green in one christening entry, but the synonymous use of these two given names cannot *always* be assumed in all cases.

iii. Edward Green changed his occupation between January 1803 at which time his occupation is listed as a weaver and February 1805 when he is described as a laborer.

ANGLESEY   **ANGLESEY**

(Ynysmon or Sir Fon)—an island county in North Wales.

(*For map, see page* 310)

Area: 270 square miles.   *Population:* 48,325.

Ancient Parishes: 72

County Town: Beaumaris, but the Shire Hall is at Llangefni.

Main Occupations: Agriculture, fishing, mining of coal, copper and lead, quarrying of stone and marble.

Principal Rivers: Cevin, Alan, Fraw, Dulas.

Ecclesiastically the county forms the Archdeaconry of Anglesey in the Diocese of Bangor, Province of Canterbury. In 1920 it became part of the Province of Wales.

Parish Registers: None have been transcribed or printed.

Bishop's Transcripts: These are at the National Library of Wales, Aberystwyth, and range from around 1660-1870 but contain many missing periods.

---

9. For a thorough treatment of conflicting record evidence, see D. Harland, *A Basic Course in Genealogy (Research Procedure and Evaluation of Evidence),* Vol. 2, (Bookcraft, Inc., Salt Lake City: 1958).

Marriage Licenses: These are at the National Library of Wales for 1757-1900 for the Diocese of Bangor.

Probate Records: The whole county was covered by the Episcopal Consistory Court of Bangor, the records of which are at the National Library of Wales.

Printed indexes to some Anglesey Wills appear in Transactions of the Anglesey Antiquarian Society for 1928 for the period 1635-1789. See National Library of Wales Manuscript No. 3617. [F. WALES 8, Part 110.]

Nonconformist Registers: There are records of fifty-nine Nonconformist chapels at the General Register Office, Somerset House, London.

Publications: The following publications are of interest:

1. *The First Report of the County Records Committee, July, 1935,* lists civil records in the custody of the County Council and local civil authorities in the county. [ANGLESEY 2]

2. *A List of Anglesey Manuscripts . . . in the National Library of Wales* (1938).

3. *Transactions* of the Anglesey Antiquarian Society and Field Club.

BEDFORDSHIRE   BEDFORDSHIRE

an inland county in the south midlands of England.

(For map, see page 312-3)

Area: 463 square miles.   *Population:* 95,400

Ancient Parishes:[10]   127, five of which are in Bedford town.

County Town: Bedford, where the County Record Office is situated in the Shire Hall.

Main Occupations: Agriculture, hatmaking and small manufactories.

Principal Rivers: Ouse and Ivel.

Ecclesiastically the county forms the Archdeaconry of Bedford that belonged to the Diocese of Lincoln from 1075 to 1837, to Ely 1837-1914 and since then to St. Albans. There were also two Peculiars— Biggleswade and Leighton Buzzard. The parish of Everton was in the Archdeaconry of Huntingdon. The county is in the Province of Canterbury.

Parish Registers: The Bedford County Council has published the registers of ninety-one parishes from the earliest dates to 1812.[11] Most of these copied registers were compared carefully with the Bishop's Transcripts that were available at the time of publication. The registers of a few parishes have been copied by private individuals.

10. For changes in the parish and county boundaries see *Guide to the Bedfordshire Record Office,* (Bedford: 1957) pp 27-30. [Beds. 14]
11. *Bedfordshire Parish Registers* (Bedford: 1931-1953). Details of the registers of the 91 parishes involved appears in Volume 44, p. ii. At page 88 there is a map showing all the parishes in the county. [Beds. 2. Vol. 44]

Bishop's Transcripts: The transcripts for the period 1602-1849 are arranged in parish order. Those for the period 1850-1871 are arranged chronologically for the whole county. The Bishop's Transcripts are at the Bedfordshire Record Office.

Marriage Licenses: The following documents relating to marriages by license, are located at the County Record Office as follows:

1. Archdeaconry of Bedford: Act book entries 1578; 1610-1611; 1616-1618; bonds and allegations 1747-1822: allegations only 1823-1879.

   1578-1618; 1747-1812, Pub. Beds. County Record Office Vols. 14. 15. [Beds 2. Vols. 14, 15]

2. Leighton Buzzard Peculiar: Bonds and Allegations 1792-1822.
   Ibid. Vol. 15. [Ibid. Vol. 15.]

3. Biggleswade Peculiar: bonds only 1714-1747; bonds and allegations 1750-1800, allegations only 1828-1860.
   Ibid. Vol. 15. [Ibid. Vol. 15.]

Probate Records: The following courts were in use:

1. The Archdeaconry Court of Bedford covered most parishes in the county. The records are at the County Record Office.

2. The Peculiar of Leighton Buzzard covered six places in the county. The records are mainly at the County Record Office, 1537-1846, although there are Wills and Admons. for this Peculiar among the Berks. Bucks. and Oxon. Peculiars kept at the Bodleian Library, Oxford. A photocopy of the latter records is at the County Record Office, Bedford.

3. The Peculiar of Biggleswade covered that parish. The records exist for the periods 1540-1559; 1639-1857. They are at the County Record Office.
   Calendar 1639-1740, Index Library, British Rec. Soc. Vol. 57. [Eng. Pub. AB Vol. 57.]

4. The Archdeaconry Court of Huntingdon covered the parish of Everton, Beds., which was in the Archdeaconry of Huntingdon, Diocese of Lincoln. See under Huntingdonshire for details on the probate courts.

The original indexes (manuscript calendars) have been superceded by a card index covering all Wills and Admons. of the above Archdeaconry and Peculiar courts. This index gives the surname, given name, parish, occupation and page reference.

There were early Wills proved at Lincoln and at Lambeth Palace.

"Abstracts of Beds. Wills and Admons proved at Lambeth Palace, London, 1379-1607 and 1307-1570; Archdeaconry of Huntingdon 1525-1627 and Lincoln 1319-1533." Pub. Beds. Hist. Record Society, Vols. 2, 14. [Beds. 6. Vols. 2, 14.]

"Abstracts of Beds, Wills at Lincoln 1601-1652." Bedfordshire Wills. [Beds. 10.]

Nonconformist Registers: There are records of twenty-eight Nonconformist chapels at the General Register Office, Somerset House, London.[12]

Publications: The following publications are of interest:

1. *Publications* of the Bedfordshire Historical Record Society. [Beds. 6. vols. 1 to 37 for 1913 to 1957.]

2. *Guide to the Bedfordshire Record Office* (1957) [Beds. 14.][13]

3. *Genealogia Bedfordiensis*, 1538-1700, by F. A. Blades. (London 1890). [Beds. 3].

4. *The Victoria History of the County of Bedford* (1904-1912) 3 Vols. and Index, (1914). [Beds. 8 Vols. 1,2,3, and Index].

5. *Bedfordshire Notes and Queries* (Bedford: 1886-1893), vols. 1, 2,3. [Beds 1. vols. 1-3].

BERKSHIRE   BERKSHIRE

(often pronounced "Barkshire") — an inland county in the south of England.

(For map, see page 314-5)

Area: 726 square miles.   *Population*: 145,200.

Ancient Parishes: 162, three of which are in Reading, two in Abingdon, two in Windsor, and three in Wallingford.

County Town: Reading, in which the Berkshire Record Office is situated.

Principal Rivers: Thames, Kennet, Loddon, Ock, Lambourn.

Ecclesiastically, the county has formed, since 1220, the Archdeaconry of Berkshire, and it was in the Diocese of Salisbury until 1836, at which time it was transferred to the Diocese of Oxford. The *Guide to the Berkshire Record Office*, page 37, states that "a few Berkshire parishes near Oxford are in the Archdeaconry of Oxford." The county is wholly in the Province of Canterbury.

Parish Registers: Very few have been printed. Many parish registers and other records of genealogical value, such as Poor Law documents, have been deposited at the Berkshire Record Office, Reading. Much of this collection, including some parish registers, have been microfilmed by the Genealogical Society, Salt Lake City, Utah.

---

12. See "Recusancy and Nonconformity in Bedfordshire . . . 1622-1842." in the publications of the Beds. Hist. Rec. Soc., 1938, Vol. 20. [Beds. 6 vol 20] At the Bedfordshire Record Office there are many certificates of registration of Dissenters' Meeting-houses 1740-1852, and these indicate many places of worship not represented in the official list of registers kept by the Registrar General, Somerset House.
The register for the Baptist Meeting-house, Little Staughton, 1772-1849 is deposited at the Bedfordshire Record Office.

13. Additional information concerning Bedfordshire County Records will be found: Joyce Godber: "Bedfordshire County Records" *Genealogists' Magazine*, (London: 1952-53) Vol. 11, pp. 269-273 and 303-306. [ENG. PUB. V. vol. 11.]

Bishop's Transcripts: These are at the Diocesan Registry, Salisbury, Wiltshire, and extend to as late as 1840. The series is in average condition. There are also a few miscellaneous transcripts at the Bodleian Library, Oxford.

Marriage Licenses: Most of these are at the Diocesan Registry, Salisbury, Wilts.

> 1. Those granted from Salisbury, 1615-1682, The Genealogist, Vols. 24-38. [Eng. Pub. AF. Vols. 24-38.] and 1682-1700, in typescript form [Wilts S2.]
> 2. Those granted by the Peculiar of the Dean and Chapter of Salisbury, 1629-1690, Wilts. Notes and Queries, Vols. 6-8. [Wilts. Pub. C., Vols. 6-8.] and 1739-1742, in typescript form. [Wilts. S2.]

Others are kept at Reading[14] and others at the Bodleian Library, Oxford. Those at Oxford cover 1616-1846. See under "Oxford" for their availability.

Probate Records: The following courts were in use:

1. The Archdeaconry Court of Berks. covered most of the county. The records are at the Bodleian Library, Oxford, Oxfordshire.

   > 1508-1652, Cal. of Wills and Admons. Index Library, British Rec. Soc., Vol. 8. [Eng. Pub. AB. Vol. 8].

2. The Episcopal Consistory Court of Sarum (Salisbury), had jurisdiction of the whole Diocese of Salisbury. The records are at the Wilts. Record Office, Trowbridge, Wiltshire.

3. The Berks., Bucks., and Oxon Peculiars of Great Farringdon with Little Coxwell, Church Langford with Grafton and Little Farringdon. The records are at the Bodleian Library, Oxford.

4. The Peculiar Court of the Dean of Sarum (Salisbury) covered nine parishes. The records are at the Wilts. Record Office above.

5. The Sarum Peculiar Court of the Dean and Chapter of Windsor covered four parishes. The records are at the Wilts. Record Office above.

   There are testamentary papers among the Diocesan Records at Salisbury, Wilts., in addition to those kept in the probate court records.

   > "Cal. of Wills and Admons." 1500-1700, The Genealogists' Magazine Vol. 5. [Eng. Pub. V., Vol. 5.]
   > "Abstracts of Berks. Wills proved P.C.C. prior to 1558," Berks. Arch. Soc. Journal for 1893, 1895 and Vols. 1, 3-7. [Berks. Pub. A., 1893, 1895, and Vols. 1, 3-7.]
   > Calendar 1540-1809, "Wilts. Wills, etc.," Wilts. Magazine, Vol. 45, pp 36-67. [Wilts. Pub. A., Vol. 45.] Includes a few Wokingham, Berks., Wills.

Nonconformist Registers: There are records of thirty-two Nonconformist registers at the General Register Office, Somerset House, London.

---

14. An Index to Berkshire Marriage Bonds may be inspected at the offices of A. H. Franklin & Sons, Solicitors, King Edward Street, Oxford.

Publications: The following publications are of interest:

1. *The Berks. Archaeological Journal.*
2. *Guide to the Berks. Record Office* (Berks. County Council, 1952). [Berks. 13]

BRECONSHIRE or BRECKNOCKSHIRE

(Bryncheiniog or Sir Fryncheiniog) — an inland county, created in 1536, in South Wales.

(For map, see page 311)

Area: 800 square miles.   *Population*: 47,763.

Ancient Parishes: 75.

County Town: Brecon also known as Brecknock.

Main Occupations: Agriculture, limestone quarrying, mining of coal and iron and manufacturing of iron and steel products.

Principal Rivers: Usk, Wye, Irvon, Taf, Nedd (Neath), Tawe.

Ecclesiastically, the county formed the Archdeaconry of Brecon, Diocese of St. David's, Province of Canterbury. In 1923 the Diocese of Swan-sea and Brecon was created, and includes Breconshire. Since 1920 the county has been part of the Province of Wales.

Parish Registers: None have been transcribed or printed.

Bishop's Transcripts: These are at the National Library of Wales, Aberystwyth, and range from around 1660-1870 but have many gaps.

Marriage Licenses: These are at the National Library of Wales for 1661-1867 for the "old" St. David's Diocese. There is a separate series for St. John and St. Mary, Brecon, 1666-1867.

Probate Records: The county was covered by the Archdeaconry Court of Brecon and the Episcopal Consistory Court of St. David's. All these records are at the National Library of Wales.

Nonconformist Registers: There are records of forty Nonconformist chapels at The General Register Office, Somerset House, London, but there may be others in local custody, libraries, etc.

Publications: The following publications are of interest:

1. *A List of Breconshire Manuscripts . . . in the National Library of Wales,* (1935). [Wales 26. Part 2.]
2. *Wesleyan Methodism in the Brecon Circuit 1750-1888.* (Brecon: 1888).
3. Theophilus Jones, *A History of the County of Brecon.* [Brecons 1.]

BUCKINGHAMSHIRE BUCKINGHAMSHIRE

an inland county in the south of England.

(For map, see page 316-7)

Area: 740 square miles. Population: 146,000.

Ancient Parishes: 206.

County Town: The historic county town is Buckingham, but the county seat for administrative purposes is Aylesbury, where there is a County Record Office, County Hall and Museum.

Main Occupations: Agriculture.

Principal Rivers: Thames, Thame, Ouse, Ouzel, Colne.

Ecclesiastically, the county formed the Archdeaconry of Buckingham, Diocese of Lincoln, until 1837, when it was transferred to the Diocese of Oxford, but the annexation did not take place until 1845. Four parishes, Winslow, Grandborough, Aston Abbots, and Little Horwood, were in the Archdeaconry of St. Albans, Diocese of London, until 1837 when they were transferred to the Archdeaconry of Bucks., Diocese of Oxford. The county is wholly in the Province of Canterbury.

Parish Registers: A few have been printed, usually for periods prior to 1813. There are a few original registers and a few transcript copies belonging to the Buckinghamshire Archaeological Society, on deposit at the Aylesbury Museum.

Bishop's Transcripts: These are at the Bodleian Library, Oxford, arranged in parish order. Some have been microfilmed for the Genealogical Society, Salt Lake City, Utah. It is likely that some seventeenth century transcripts are among the diocesan records at Lincoln.

Marriage Licenses: These are contained in fifty-three volumes at the Bodleian Library, Oxford. They exist for approximately 1600-1840.

Probate Records: The following courts were in use:

1. The Archdeaconry Court of Buckingham covered most of the county. The records are at the Principal Probate Registry, Somerset House, London, but plans are being considered for their transfer to the Bucks. Record Office, Aylesbury.

2. Episcopal Consistory Court of Lincoln, the records are kept at the Lincolnshire Archives Committee, Exchequer Gate, Lincoln, Lincs. (See under "Lincoln" for details).

   1601-1652, Abstracts of Bucks. Wills [Bucks. 16.]

3. The Archdeaconry Court of St. Albans (Diocese of London) covers parishes of Winslow, Grandboro, Aston Abbotts, and Little Horwood. In 1837 these parishes were transferred to the Archdeaconry of Bucks., but the transfer did not take effect until 1845. The records of the Archdeaconry of St. Albans are at the Hertfordshire Record Office, Hertford, Herts.

4. The Episcopal Consistory Court of London, having jurisdiction over places in the Archdeaconry of St. Albans. The records are at the London County Council Record Office, Westminster Bridge, London, S.E.

5. The Peculiar Court of the Archbishop of Canterbury in the Dean-ery of Monks Risboro, covered two Bucks. parishes. The records are at the Bodleian Library, Oxford.

6. The Peculiar Court of Bierton of the Dean and Chapter of Lin-coln covered Bierton, Buckland, Stoke Mandeville and Quarren-don, and the records are at the Bodleian Library.

7. The Peculiar Court of Buckingham of the Peculiar of Lincoln covered Buckingham, Bourton, Bourton-hold, Gawcott, Leathen-boro, and Prebend-end. The records are at the Bodleian Library.

8. Eton College, Bucks., used principally by persons connected with the college and the town of Eton. The records are kept at the Eton College Muniment Room, Windsor, and cover from about 1440 to 1784.

> "Notes Concerning Records of Eton College," Genealogists' Magazine, Vol. 5, p. 38. [Eng. Pub. V, Vol. 5.]
> There are about 1500 Bucks. probates for 1600-1875 in the custody of the County Record Office, Aylesbury, Bucks. These have been indexed as to names and parishes. There are also some original Wills kept in the Muniment Room, County Museum, Aylesbury.
> There are two volumes of miscellaneous Wills and Admons., 1526-1846, at the Bodleian Library, Oxford.

Nonconformist Registers: There are records of thirty-three Nonconform-ist chapels kept by the Registrar General, Somerset House, London.

Publications: The following publications are of interest:

1. The *Publications* of the Bucks. Archaeological Society.
2. The *Publications* of the Bucks. Record Society.
3. *Bucks. Sessions Records* (Bucks. County Council).

CAERNARVONSHIRE

(Caernarfon or Sir Arfon) — a maritime county in North Wales

(*For map, see page 320*)

Area: 500 square miles.   *Population*: 66,818.

Ancient Parishes: 68.

County Town: Caernarvon where the County Records Office is situated.

Main Occupations: Agriculture, weaving and slate quarrying.

Principal Rivers: Conway, Seiont.

Ecclesiastically, the county was mostly in the Archdeaconries of Merion-eth and Bangor, Diocese of Bangor, with three parishes in the Arch-deaconry and Diocese of St. Asaph, all in the Province of Canterbury. Since 1920, the county has been part of the Province of Wales.

Parish Registers: A few have been transcribed.

Bishop's Transcripts: These are at the National Library of Wales, Aberystwyth, and range from around 1660 to 1870 but have many gaps.

Marriage Licenses: These are at the National Library of Wales, 1757-1900 for the Diocese of Bangor and 1616-1900 for the Diocese of St. Asaph.

Probate Records: The following courts covered the county, the records of which are at the National Library of Wales:
1. The Episcopal Consistory Court of Bangor.
2. The Episcopal Consistory Court of St. Asaph.

Nonconformist Registers: There are records of seventy-five Nonconformist chapels at The General Register Office, Somerset House, London, but there may be others in local custody, libraries, etc.

Publications: The following publications are of interest:
1. *A Guide to the Caernarvonshire Record Office* (1952). [CARNARVS. 2.]

2. *Publications of the Caernarvonshire Historical Society,* (the *Transactions* from 1939 and the *Record Series* from 1951).

3. E. H. Hall, *Description of Caernarvonshire* (1952).

4. J. Lloyd Jones, *Enwau Lleodd Sir Gaernarfon* [Caernarvonshire Place Names] (1928).

5. *A List of Caernarvonshire Manuscripts . . . in the National Library of Wales* (1938).

CAMBRIDGESHIRE   CAMBRIDGESHIRE

a county in the east of England.

(For map, see page 318-9)

Area: 858 square miles.   *Population*: 143,200.

Ancient Parishes: 171, fourteen of which are in the town of Cambridge, two in Wisbech and three in Ely.

County Towns:
1. Cambridge in which the Shire Hall is situated.
2. March is the county seat for the Isle of Ely. This part of the county of Cambridge has been treated as a separate county for administrative purposes for hundreds of years.

Main Occupation: Agriculture.

Principal Rivers: Ouse, Cam and Nene.

Ecclesiastically, the county consisted of the Archdeaconry of Cambridge with its various deaneries in the Diocese of Ely; also fifteen parishes

within the deaneries of the Archdeaconry of Sudbury and Diocese of Norwich; and the parish of Isleham which was a Peculiar of the Bishop in the Diocese of Rochester. Changes were made in 1837 when certain parishes in the deanery of Fordham and Archdeaconry of Sudbury (Diocese of Norwich) were transferred to the Diocese of Ely. At the same time the parishes in the Deanery of Camps and Archdeaconry and Diocese of Ely were transferred to the Archdeaconry of Sudbury in the Diocese of Norwich. Since that date there have been several changes and today Cambridgeshire is now entirely within the Diocese of Ely. It has always been in the Province of Canterbury.

Parish Registers: A few have been printed. Many marriage registers covering periods prior to 1837 have been copied and are available at the Society of Genealogists, London. *Boyd's Cambridgeshire Marriage Index* covers parts of 170 parishes.

Bishop's Transcripts. These are the Diocesan Registry at Ely. Some of them stop at 1780 others go on to 1812 and later. It is possible that transcripts for those few Cambridgeshire parishes which were in the Diocese of Norwich may be still in that county or in the care of the Archdeacon of Sudbury, Suffolk. See the sections in this chapter for Norfolk and Suffolk, for details of their disposition.

Marriage Licenses: Those for the Diocese of Ely, 1562-1878 are kept at the Muniment Room, 4 Lynn Road, Ely. The very early marriage licenses were entered in the Bishop's Registers.

> 1562-1582 A Calendar . . of the Episcopal Records . . . at Ely. [Cambs 1a.]
> 1582-1891 The Northern Genealogist, Vol. 1. [Eng. Pub. R., Vol. 1]

Those for the Archdeaconry of Sudbury are at the Bury St. Edmunds and West Suffolk Record Office, 8 Angel Hill, Bury St. Edmunds, Suffolk, for the period 1684-1839.

> 1684-1839 Pub. Harleian Society, Vols. 69-72. [Eng. Pub. AC. Vols. 69-72.]

Those for the Diocese of Norwich are at the Diocesan Registry, Norwich, Norfolk.

Probate Records. The following probate courts were in use:

1. The Episcopal Consistory Court of Norwich covered twelve parishes in this county. The records are at the Central Library, Norwich, Norfolk. (See also Norfolk.)

   > Calendar of Wills 1370-1603, Index Library, British Rec. Soc. Vols., 69, 73. [Eng. Pub. AB Vols. 69, 73.]

2. The Episcopal Consistory Court of Ely covered most of the county, especially when other probate courts were inhibited. The records are at the University Archives, Cambridge.

    "Cal. of Admons" 1562-1582 A Calendar . . . of the Episcopal Records . . . at Ely. [Cambs Ela.]

3. The Archdeaconry of Ely having jurisdiction within fifty-three parishes and including the town of Cambridge. The records are at the University Archives, Cambridge.

4. The Court of the Chancellor of the University of Cambridge proved Wills of matriculated students, officers and tenants of the University. The records 1501-1765 are at Cambridge as above.

    Wills Proved in the Vice-Chancellor's Court, Cambridge, 1501-1765, (Cambridge: 1907).

5. The Peculiar of Thorney having jurisdiction over that parish and lordship. The records are at Cambridge as above.

6. The Peculiar of Isleham, a peculiar of the Bishop of Rochester. The records are at the West Suffolk Record Office, Bury St. Edmunds, Suffolk.

7. The Archdeaconry of Sudbury with the Episcopal Consistory Court for Bury St. Edmunds covered a few parishes in this county. The records are at Bury St. Edmunds as above.

    Wills and Inventories 1354-1535 Camden Society, Vol. 49. [Eng. Pub. E. Old Series Vol. 49.]

8. King's College, Cambridge, a peculiar jurisdiction within the precincts of the College. The records are at King's College.

    "The Muniments of King's College," in Proceedings of Camb. Antiqu. Soc., 1933, Vol. 33, p. 94. [Cambs. Pub. C. Vol. 33.]

There are bundles of Wills, Administrations, Inventories, Caveats, etc., in the Muniment Room, 4 Lynn Road, Ely in the custody of the Cathedral Librarian. These are diocesan records.

Abstracts of Admons at Ely Diocesan Registry 1592-1600; 1604-1620. [Cambs E2 Vols. 1-3.]

There are Administrators' Accounts mentioned in A Calendar . . of the Episcopal Records . . . at Ely referring to a most informative set of records sometimes providing the clue to a person dying intestate where no Letters of Administration were granted.

Nonconformists: There are records of thirty-five Nonconformist chapels at the General Register Office, Somerset House, London.

Publications: The following publications are of interest:

1. Transactions of the Cambridgeshire and Huntingdonshire Archaeological Society.

2. Alumni Cantabrigienses for the University of Cambridge, being a biographical list of students and officers down to the year 1900, containing about 136,000 names.

3. A Calendar and Concise View of the Episcopal Records Preserved in the Muniment Room of the Palace at Ely.

4. *Publications* of the Camden Society.

5. *Publications* of the Camden Series of the Royal Historical Society.

6. *Proceedings* and *Publications* of the Cambridge Antiquarian Society.

CARDIGANSHIRE   CARDIGANSHIRE

(Aberteifi) — a maritime county in South Wales.

(For map, see page 321)

Area: 590 square miles.   *Population:* 64,780.

Ancient Parishes: 70.

County Town: Cardigan, but the County Office is at Aberystwyth.

Main Occuptions: Agriculture, fisheries, mining of silver and lead, and the manufacture of stockings and flannel.

Principal Rivers: Teify, Ystwith, Rheidiol.

Ecclesiastically, the county was in the Archdeaconry of Cardigan, Diocese of St. David's, Province in Canterbury. Since 1920 it has been in the Province of Wales.

Parish Registers: None have been printed or transcribed.

Bishop's Transcripts: These are at the National Library of Wales, Aberystwyth, and there are a few prior to 1799 but generally range from 1799 to about 1870 but have occasional gaps.

Marriage Licenses: These are at the National Library of Wales for 1615-1900 for the Consistory Court of St. David's and 1661-1867 for the "old" St. David's Diocese. Some marriage bonds have been printed 1612-1799 in *West Wales Historical Records,* Vols. 3 to 12.

Probate Records: The county was covered by the Archdeaconry of Cardigan and Episcopal Consistory Court of St. David's. All the records are at the National Library of Wales.

Nonconformist Registers: There are records of fifty-eight Nonconformist chapels at The General Register Office, Somerset House, London. There may be others in local custody, libraries, etc.

Publications: The following publications are of interest:

1. *Publications* of the Cardiganshire Antiquarian Society.

2. *Transactions* and *West Wales Historical Records.*

3. *A List of Cardiganshire Manuscripts . . . in the National Library of Wales,* (1933).

CARMARTHENSHIRE CARMARTHENSHIRE

(Caerfyrddin) — a maritime county in South Wales.

(*For map, see page 322*)

Area: 974 square miles. Population: 100,740.

Ancient Parishes: 80.

County Town: Carmarthen, where the County Record Office is situ-ated.

Main Occupations: Agriculture, fishing, mining and production of coal, iron, tin, and lead goods.

Principal Rivers: Towy, Taf, Lloughor, Teify.

Ecclesiastically, the county was in the Archdeaconry of Carmarthen, with four parishes in the Archdeaconry of Cardigan, all in the Diocese of St. David's, Province of Canterbury. Since 1920 it has been in the Province of Wales.

Parish Registers: A few have been transcribed.

Bishop's Transcripts: These are at the National Library of Wales, Aber-stwyth, and range from around 1660 to 1870 but have many gaps.

Marriage Licenses: These are at the National Library of Wales for 1615-1900 for the Consistory Court of St. David's and 1661-1867 for the "old" St. David's Diocese. Many of the marriage bonds and fiats have been printed 1612-1799, in *West Wales Historical Records,* Volumes 3-12.

Probate Records: The county was covered by the Archdeaconry of Carmarthen, with four parishes in the Archdeaconry of Cardigan, all in the Episcopal Consistory Court of St. David's. The records are at the National Library of Wales.

Nonconformist Registers: There are records of sixty-seven Nonconform-ist chapels at The General Register Office, Somerset House, London. There may be others in local custody, libraries, etc.

Publications: The following publications are of interest:
1. *Transactions* of the Carmarthenshire Antiquarian Society.
2. *The Carmarthen Antiquary.*
3. *Transactions of the West Wales Historical Records.*

CHESHIRE CHESHIRE

(also known as County Chester) — a maritime and inland county in the north-west of England. The maritime section forms the Wirral Peninsu-lar that reaches out to the Irish Sea.

(*For maps, see page 324-7*)

Area: 1052 square miles. Population: 334,314.

Ancient Parishes: 130 ten of which are in the City of Chester.

County Town: Chester. The County Record Office is situated at The Castle, Chester.

Main Occupations: Agriculture, dairy farming, salt and coal mining, shipbuilding, cotton and silk manufacturing and seafaring.

Principal Rivers: Mersey, Dee, Weaver. The River Mersey, forming the northern boundary of the county gives its name to Merseyside, an important industrial and shipping area.

Ecclesiastically, the county forms the Archdeaconry of Chester in the Diocese of Chester, Province of York. It was in the Diocese of Lich-field and Province of Canterbury until 1541.

Parish Registers: A few have been published, mainly for periods prior to 1813. A few others have been transcribed.

Bishop's Transcripts: These are at the Diocesan Registry, Chester and are in average condition with some years missing. They cover the period 1660 to approximately 1850.

Marriage Licenses: There are kept at the Diocesan Registry, Chester. They exist from 1600 onwards.

> Abstracts, 1606-1632; 1639-1644; 1661-1719, Lancs. and Chesh. Rec. Soc. Vols. 53, 56, 57, 61, 65, 69, 73, 77, 82, 85, 97, 101. [Chesh. 1. Vols. as above.]

Probate Records: The following courts were in use:

1. The Episcopal Consistory Court of Chester covered the whole county, and functioned in two divisions as follows:

   a. If the estate was valued at more than forty pounds sterling, the grant was in the Bishop's court, and the records are known as "SUPRA."

      > Index Wills and Inv., 1545-1650, and 1660-1820, Lancs. & Chesh. Rec. Soc., Vols. 2, 4, 15, 18, 20, 22, 25, 37, 38, 44, 45, 62, 63, 78, 79. [Chesh. 1, Vols. as above.]
      > Index of P.C.C. Wills, 1650-1660, ibid, Vol. 4. [Chesh. 1, Vol. 4.]
      > Abstracts of some Wills and Inv., 1572-1696, Pub. Chetham Soc., New Series, Vol. 3. [Lancs. Pub B., N.S. Vol. 3.]
      > Wills and Inv. (early dates, abstracts), ibid, First Series, Vols. 33, 51, 54.
      > Abstracts of some Wills and Inv., 1477-1746, and appendix of ab-stracts of Wills now lost, ibid, New Series, Vol. 3. [Lancs. Pub. B., N.S., Vol. 3.]
      > Abstracts of some Wills not now found in any registry, 1301-1752, Lancs. and Chesh Rec. Soc., Vol. 30. [Chesh. 1, Vol. 30.]

   b. If the estate was valued at less than forty pounds sterling, the grant was made by the local rural dean in the deanery con-cerned, the records were then sent to Chester, and are known as "INFRA."

      > Index Wills and Inv., 1590-1650, 1660-1756, 1777-1820, Lancs. & Chesh. Rec. Soc., Vols. 15, 18, 20, 22, 33, 44, 45, 52, 62, 63, 78, 79. [Chesh. 1, Vols. as above.]

The Wills, Admons., etc. relating to Cheshire in items (a) and (b), have been separated from the main series, and are at the County Record Office, The Castle, Chester.

In addition, to the probate records for the above courts, the following should be noted:

1. A miscellaneous collection, known as "Wills, Inventories, Admon. Bonds, and Depositions in Testamentary Suits, 1487-1800," being records formerly kept at the Diocesan Registry, Chester. They were probably concerned with some testamentary disputes, and became disconnected with the probate records of the Episcopal Consistory Court of Chester (item 1 above). The Cheshire portion of these documents have been transferred to the County Record Office, The Castle, Chester.

    Index . . . Testamentary Suits, 1487-1800, Lancs. & Chesh. Rec. Soc., Vols. 33, 43, 52. [Chesh. 1, Vols. 33, 43, 52.]

2. Cheshire was part of the Diocese of Lichfield, Province of Canterbury until 1541, therefore probates earlier than 1541 might be found among the records of the Episcopal Consistory Court of Lichfield as well as in the Prerogative Court of Canterbury.

    Cal. of Wills and Admons., 1516-1652, Index Library, British Rec. Soc., Vol. 7. [Eng. Pub AB., Vol 7.]

3. Records of probates dated later than 1541 have been found at Lichfield relating to persons resident in Cheshire. The Will of Thomas Slack, for instance, was proved at Lichfield 5 December 1857. His estate was in the Diocese of Lichfield, but he resided at, and died in, Macclesfield, Cheshire.[15]

4. There were some probate records at Richmond, in the Court of the Archdeaconry of Richmond for some Cheshire families.

    Abstracts of some Cheshire Wills and Inventories, proved at Richmond, 1542-1649, Pub. Chetham Soc., New Series, Vol. 28. [Lancs. Pub. B., N.S., Vol. 28.]

The introductions and prefaces found in the published Calendars and Indexes relating to Wills at Chester should be studied carefully.

Nonconformist registers: There are records of eighty Nonconformist chapels kept at the office of the Registrar General, Somerset House, London.

Publications: The following publications are of interest:

1. *Transactions* of the Historic Society of Lancashire and Cheshire.

2. The Record Society for the publishing of Original Documents relating to Lancashire and Cheshire.

3. *Transactions* of the Lancashire and Cheshire Antiquarian Society.

4. *Publications* of the Chester and North Wales Archaeological and Historical Society.

5. The *Publications* of the Chetham Society.

---

15. The reference in the Calendar for the Episcopal Consistory Court of Lichfield states that William Slack's Will was proved *quoad bona*, a term meaning, in this court, "goods of a person residing outside of this jurisdiction."

6. A map showing the parishes and deaneries in the Archdeaconry of Chester is available at the Lancashire Record Office, Preston and also at the Library of the Genealogical Society, Salt Lake City, Utah. It is entitled *A Map of the Diocess of Chester Divided into Deaneries,* and published about the year 1750.

7. *The Historical Atlas of Cheshire* (Chester: Cheshire Community Council, 1958) contains important historical information including on page 37 a map of the Ancient Parishes and Townships, showing boundaries.

CORNWALL   **CORNWALL**

a maritime county in the extreme south-west of England

(including the Scilly Isles)

(*For map, see page* 323)

Area: 1327 square miles.   *Population*: 301,000

Ancient parishes: 204.

County Town: Truro is the administrative capital of the county. There is a County Record Office at Truro, although Bodmin is the historic county town and also the assize town.

Main Occupations: Agriculture and horticulture; copper and tin mining; fishing and seafaring; and there are china clay pits which are worked.

Principal Rivers: Tamar, Lynes, Tide, Seaton, East Looe, Duloe, Fawy, Fal, Hel, Heyl and Camel.

Ecclesiastically the county forms the Archdeaconry of Cornwall. Until 1876 it was in the Diocese of Exeter, when the Diocese of Truro was created. It is in the Province of Canterbury.

Parish Registers: A few registers, mainly for the period prior to 1838 have been published. The registers of many other parishes have been transcribed for the same periods and are in the Library of the Devon and Cornwall Record Society, Exeter, Devon. The marriage registers for most parishes in the county have been printed for the periods prior to 1813 or 1838. Percival Boyd compiled his *Cornwall Marriage Index* from these available copies and it includes 200 parishes.

Bishop's Transcripts: Those for the periods 1670-1736 and 1741-1772 are at the County Record Office, Truro. This series is also available on microfilm at the Genealogical Society, Salt Lake City, Utah.

Those for the periods 1737-1740 and 1773-1812 are at the Devon County Record Office, Exeter. The transcripts have annoying gaps, especially in the early periods. It is possible that transcripts for periods after 1812 may be found when material at the Bishop's Registry in Exeter is sorted.

Marriage Licenses: These are at the County Record Office, Exeter, Devon, and consist of Registers of Act Books 1734-1842 and bonds and allegations 1664-1842.

J. L. Vivian, The Marriage Licenses of the Diocese of Exeter from the Bishop's Registers, 1523-1631. (Exeter: 1887) [DEVON 14] This publication contains references to Cornwall.

A large collection of material relating to marriage allegations and licenses 1523-1747 is available among the records kept by the Devon and Cornwall Record Society.

Probate Records: The following courts were in use:

1. The Consistorial Court of the Archdeacon of Cornwall covered the greater part of the county. The records are at the County Record Office, Truro.

   Cal. of Wills and Admons, 1569-1799, Index Library, British Rec. Soc. [Eng. Pub. AB Vols. 56, 59.]

2. The Royal Peculiar of the Deanery of St. Burian with the parishes of St. Leven and St. Sennen. The records are at the County Record Office, Truro.

   Ibid.

3. The Episcopal Consistory Court of the Bishop of Exeter covered twenty-three parishes in Cornwall.

   Cal. Wills and Admons, 1532-1800, Pub. Devonshire Assoc. [Devon 20 Vol. 2.]

4. The Episcopal Principal Registry of the Diocese of Exeter covered the whole Diocese.

   Cal. Wills and Admons, 1532-1800, Pub. Devonshire Assoc. [Devon 20 Vol 1] also Index Library, British Rec. Soc. Vol. 35. [Eng. Pub. AB Vol. 35.]

5. The Consistorial Court of the Dean and Chapter of Exeter covered six parishes in Cornwall.

All the original records listed in items 3, 4, and 5, were destroyed by enemy action during World War II.

   Abstracts Cornish Wills proved P.C.C. 1383-1583. Cornish P.C.C. Wills [Corn. 13 Vols. 1-3.]

Nonconformist Registers: There are records of sixty-four Nonconformist chapels at the General Register Office, Somerset House, London.

Publications: The following publications are of interest:

1. *Publications of the Devon and Cornwall Record Society.*

2. *Parochial History of the County of Cornwall.*

CUMBERLAND CUMBERLAND

a maritime county in the extreme north-west of England on the borders of Scotland.

(*For map, see page 328-330*)

Area: 1478 square miles.   *Population*: 171,700

Ancient Parishes: 143, two of which are in Carlisle and three in White-haven.

County Town: Carlisle. The County Offices are situated here.

Main Occupations: Fishing and seafaring; agriculture; tanning; textile manufacturing; coal, lead, copper and iron mining and smelting.

Principal Rivers: The Eden and Derwent, and the estuary known as the Solway Firth on the borders of this county and Scotland.

Ecclesiastically the county was divided as follows:

1. The Archdeaconry of Cumberland in the Diocese of Carlisle.
2. The Deanery of Copeland in the Archdeaconry of Richmond which, until 1541, was in the Diocese of York and from 1541 to 1856 in the Diocese of Chester. In 1856 the Deanery of Copeland was transferred to the Diocese of Carlisle. Cumberland was always in the Province of York.

Parish Registers: The registers of a few parishes have been printed for the period prior to 1813. The *Cumberland Marriage Index* by Percival Boyd is based on some of these printed copies.

Bishop's Transcripts: These range from 1660 to about 1870 and comprise one of the best collections in the country. Arranged in parish order, they are kept at the County Record Office, The Courts, Carlisle and have been mircofilmed for the Genealogical Society, Salt Lake City, Utah.

Marriage Licenses: Those for the Diocese of Carlisle are kept at the County Record Office and have been microfilmed for the Genealogical Society, Salt Lake City. The marriage licenses for the Archdeaconry of Richmond, which includes the Deanery of Copeland in Cumberland, are kept at the Lancashire Record Office, Preston, Lancs. They have been microfilmed for the Genealogical Society, Salt Lake City, Utah, from 1745-1799.

> 1648-1745 Lancs. and Chesh. Rec. Soc. Vols. 74, 75, 80, 81, 83, 100. [Chesh. 1 Vols as above.]

Probate Records: The following courts were in use:

1. The Episcopal Consistory of Carlisle covered most of the county. The records are at the County Record Office, Carlisle.
2. The Archdeaconry of Richmond covered all Cumberland parishes in the Deanery of Copeland prior to 1856 and the records are at the Lancashire Record Office, Preston, Lancs.

> Abstracts of Some Wills 1458-1579, Pub. Surtees Soc. [Eng. Pub. F Vol. 26.]

3. The Palatine and Episcopal Consistory Court of Durham covered the parish of Alston. It also covered the parish of Over Denton prior to 1703. The records are at Durham University.

> Abstracts of most Wills kept at Somerset House and Lambeth Palace 1383-1604, Pub. Surtees Soc. Vols. 116, 121. [Eng. Pub. F Vols 116, 121.]
> Abstracts of some Wills 1609-1794. The Northern Genealogist, Vol. 1, 3. [Eng. Pub. R Vols 1, 3.]

In addition to the above, the following should be noted:

1. The records of Cumberland Wills and Admons. that received grants in the Western Deaneries (the deanery of Copeland covering Cumberland parishes) of the Archdeaconry of Richmond, prior

to 1856, are at the Lancashire Record Office, Preston, Lancashire. The printed Calendar *The Lancashire Wills proved within the Archdeaconry of Richmond*, 1457-1858, [Record Society . . . Lancashire and Cheshire, Vols. 10, 13, 23, 66, 99, 105] does *NOT* include references to the deanery of Copeland and Cumberland.

2. The records of Cumberland Wills and Admons. that received grants in the Eastern Deaneries of the Archdeaconry of Richmond, are at the Archives Department, Central Library, Leeds, Yorkshire.

Nonconformist registers: There are records of twenty-six Nonconformist chapels kept at the Office of the Registrar General, Somerset House, London.

Publications: The following publications are of interest:

1. *Publications* of the Westmorland and Cumberland Antiquarian and Archaeological Society.
2. *Publications* of the Surtees Society.
3. *The Northern Genealogist.*

The following two maps will be of value in determining some of the problems of ecclesiatical jurisdiction:

1. *A Map to Illustrate the Annals of Carlisle* which indicates the boundaries of the Diocese of Carlisle before and after 1856 as well as the parishes in that Diocese.
2. *A Map of the Diocess of Chester Divided into Deanries* (1750) showing the area covered by the Archdeaconry of Richmond.

Both maps can be found at the County Record Office, Preston, Lancs., and at the Library of the Genealogical Society, Salt Lake City, Utah.

DENBIGHSHIRE   DENBIGHSHIRE

(Dinbych)—a maritime county, created in 1536, in North Wales.

(For map, see page 334)

Area: 606 square miles.   *Population*: 83,027

Ancient Parishes: 58.

County Town: Denbigh, but the County Offices are at Ruthin.

Main Occupations: Agriculture, mining of coal, iron, and lead, quarrying of limestone and slate, manufacture of leather and woolen goods.

Principal Rivers: Dee, Clwyd, Conway .

Ecclesiastically, the county was mostly in the Archdeaconry and Diocese of St. Asaph, with fourteen parishes in the Rural Deanery of Dyfryn Clwyd (not in any archdeaconry) in the Diocese of Bangor. The whole county was in the Province of Canterbury until 1920 when the Province of Wales was created.

Parish Registers: A few have been transcribed.

Bishop's Transcripts: These are at the National Library of Wales, Aberystwyth. and range from around 1660 to 1870 but have many gaps.

Marriage Licenses: These are at the National Library of Wales for 1616-1900 for the Diocese of St. Asaph and 1757-1900 for the Diocese of Bangor. There may be a few among the marriage licences issued for the Diocese of Chester now kept at Diocesan Registry, Chester.

Probate Records: The following courts covered the county, the records of which are at the National Library of Wales.

1. Episcopal Consistory Court of St. Asaph.

2. Episcopal Consistory Court of Bangor.

3. Episcopal Consistory Court of Chester (for a very few records). See under "Cheshire," for full details of Wills at Chester.

Any Welsh probate records found among the records at Chester were transferred to the National Library of Wales. The printed Calendars, for Chester only, are as follows:

> Cal. of Wills, Admons., and Inv., 1545-1820, (Lancs. and Chesh. Rec. Soc.), Vols. 2, 4, 15, 18, 20, 22, 25, 30, 33, 37, 38, 43, 44, 45, 52, 62, 63, 78, 79. [CHES. 1. Vols, as above.]

Nonconformist Registers: There are records of ninety-eight Nonconformist chapels at The General Register Office, Somerset House, London. There may be others in local custody, libraries, etc.

Publications: The following publications are of interest:

1. *A List of Denbighshire Manuscripts . . . in the National Library of Wales* (1936).

DERBYSHIRE DERBYSHIRE

(sometimes pronounced Darbyshire)—an inland county in the north-midlands of England.

(For maps, see page 331-3)

Area: 1026 square miles.   *Population*: 236,900.

Ancient Parishes: 184, five of which are in the City of Derby.

County Town: The historic county town is Derby but the County Offices are at Matlock.

Main Occupations: Agriculture; coal, lead, copper and zinc mining; and textile manufacturing.

Principal Rivers: Trent, Derwent, Wye, Dove, Erwash, Rother.

Ecclesiastically, the county formed the Archdeaconry of Derby in the Diocese of Lichfield, Province of Canterbury, until 1884 when the Diocese of Southwell, consisting of Derbyshire and Nottinghamshire, was established. In 1927 Derbyshire was formed into the Diocese of Derby in the Province of Canterbury.

Parish Registers: A few of these, for periods prior to 1813, have been printed, and marriage registers of a number of other parishes have been printed, mainly for periods prior to 1813 with a few printed down to 1837. These printed registers were used by Percival Boyd in compiling the *Derbyshire Marriage Index* which includes about sixty parishes.

Bishop's Transcripts: These are arranged in parish order and are in an average condition. They extend from 1660-1837, and some a little later, and they are at the Diocesan Registry, Lichfield, Staffordshire. Information regarding the Bishop's Transcripts of Derbyshire parishes within Peculiars can be found in the *Publications of the William Salt Archaeological Society*, Volume VI, Part II, pages 82-85.

Marriages Licenses: These are at the Diocesan Registry, Lichfield, Staffordshire.

Probate Records: The following courts were in use:

1. The Episcopal Consistory Court of the Bishop of Lichfield and Coventry covered most of the county.

   Cal. Wills and Admons, 1516-1652. Index Library, British Rec. Soc. Vol. 7. [Eng. Pub. AB., Vol. 7.]

2. The Court of the Dean and Chapter of Lichfield covered seventeen parishes in the county.

3. The various Lichfield Peculiar Courts covered eight Derbyshire parishes.

   Cal. Wills and Admons, 1529-1652. Index Library, British Rec. Soc. Vol. 7. [Eng. Pub. AB Vol. 7.]

All the records listed above are in the care of the County Archivist, Lichfield City Library and Museum, Lichfield, Staffordshire.

4. The Manor of Dale Abbey covered that parish. The records are at the County Record Office, Nottingham.

   Cal. Wills, 1753-1790. Index Library, British Record Society, Vol. 7. [Eng. Pub. AB Vol. 7.]

In addition to the above there are a few Wills of very early date at York; at Lincoln; and among the probate records of the Diocese of Worcester at the Worcestershire Record Office.

Nonconformist Registers: There are records of sixty-three Nonconformist chapels at the General Register Office, Somerset House, London.

Publications: The following are of interest:

1. *Publications* of the Derbyshire Archaeological and Natural History Society.

2. The Harleian Society's *Familiae Minorum Gentium* found in volumes 37-40 and 88.

3. *Nottinghamshire and Derbyshire Notes and Queries.*

4. *The Old Halls, Manors and Families of Derbyshire*, by Joseph Tilley 1892-1902.

DEVONSHIRE   DEVONSHIRE

(also called Devon)—a maritime county in the south-west of England.

(For map, see page 338-9)

Area: 2579 square miles.   *Population:* 494,400.

Ancient Parishes: 472, twenty-one of which are in Exeter and two in Plymouth.

County Town: Exeter. The Devon Record Office[16] is situated here.

Main Occupations: Agriculture; cider making; cloth making; the mining of tin and lead, as well as considerable seafaring.

Principal Rivers: Axe, Otter, Exe, Teign, Tamor, Tavy, Torridge, Taw, and Okement.

Ecclesiastically the county was wholly in the Diocese of Exeter and Province of Canterbury and mainly divided into three archdeaconries:
1. The Archdeaconry of Barnstaple.
2. The Archdeaconry of Exeter.
3. The Archdeaconry of Totnes.

The Archdeaconry of Cornwall appears to contain several Devonshire parishes and there were some others that were of Peculiar jurisdiction. The Archdeaconry of Cornwall became part of the Diocese of Truro when the latter diocese was created in 1876.

In 1836 the parish of Stockland and the township or chapelry of Dalwood, both part of Dorset were united with Devonshire, and were transferred from the Archdeaconry of Dorset and Diocese of Bristol to the Archdeaconry and Diocese of Exeter. In the same year the parish of Thorncombe and places named Burhall Downs and Easthay (part of the parish of Axminster) that were part of Devonshire were made part of Dorset, and were transferred from the Achdeaconry and Diocese of Exeter to the Archdeaconry of Dorset and Diocese of *Salisbury*.

Parish Registers: A few, mainly for periods prior to 1813, have been printed but many others have been transcribed for periods prior to 1837. These transcripts are among the excellent genealogical collection of the Devon and Cornwall Record Society kept at the City Library, Exeter, Devon. It was from this series that Boyd's *Devonshire Marriage Index* was compiled which covers 170 parishes in Devonshire for varying periods.

Bishop's Transcripts: These exist from varying dates in the seventeenth century to about 1837, but the period 1813-1837 is being sorted and cleaned and may not be available for several years. They are housed at the Devon Record Office, The Castle, Exeter, and are in average condition with a number of missing years.

---

16. The county record office, officially known as the Devon Record Office, was formed in 1952 and is recognized as a Manorial Depository and is also the Exeter Diocesan Record Office. An annual report is to be found in the *Transactions of the Devonshire Association. See* Vol. 87 pp. 385-6 and Vol. 88 p. 291. [DEVON PUB D. Vols. 87 and 88.]

Abstracts of the existing Transcripts . . . Devon, 1596-1644, (1908), by Roger Granville. [Devon 9.] Covers a few parishes.

Marriage Licenses: Registes or Act Books 1734-1842 and bonds and allegations 1664-1842 are kept at the Record Office at Exeter.

J. L. Vivian, The Marriage Licences of the Diocese of Exeter from the Bishop's Registers, 1523-1631. [Devon 14.]

There is a collection of material from marriage allegations and licenses 1523-1747 among the collections of the Devon and Cornwall Record Society.[17]

Probate Records: The majority of the probate records for this county were destroyed by enemy action in 1942. The records of the following courts were destroyed:

1. The Principal Registry of the Bishop of Exeter which had juris-diction over the whole Diocese.

   Cal. of Wills and Admons, Principal Registry 1559-1799, Archdeacon-ry of Exeter (Devon only) 1540-1799-Index Library, British Rec. Soc. Vol. 35. Cal. Wills and Admons, Consistory Court of Bishop of Exeter. 1532-1800. Index Library, British Rec. Soc. Vol. 35. [Eng. Pub. AB Vol. 35.] All these are also recorded in Transactions of the Devonshire Association. [Devon 20 Vols. 1-3.]

2. The Consistory Court of the Bishop of Exeter which had juris-diction in fourteen parishes that were Peculiars of the Bishop, and in certain cases over the whole Diocese.

   Ibid.

3. The Consistory Court of the Dean and Chapter of Exeter, which had jurisdiction in twenty-three parishes that were Peculiars of the Dean and Chapter.

4. The Peculiar Court of the Dean, with jurisdiction of the Close of the Cathedral Church of Exeter and in the parish of Braunton, Devon.

5. The Peculiar Court of the Custos and College of Vicars Choral of the Cathedral having jurisdiction in the parish of Woodbury, Devon.

6. The Consistorial Court of the Archdeacon of Exeter, with juris-diction throughout the archdeaconry excluding the Peculiars.

   Ibid.

7. The Consistorial Court of the Archdeacon of Barnstaple,[18] with jurisdiction throughout the Archdeaconry except the Peculiars.

8. The Consistorial Court of the Archdeacon of Totnes, with juris-diction throughout the archdeaconry excluding the Peculiars.

The records are extant of the following courts and parishes for dates prior to 1858:

1. The Consistorial Court of the Archdeacon of Cornwall had juris-diction in Broadwood-Widger, St. Giles-on-the-Heath, North Petherwin, Virginstow, and Werrington; also in Northcott (De-vonshire) in parish of Boyton (Cornwall). The records are at the County Record Office, Truro, Cornwall.

   Cal. Wills and Admons. 1569-1799 Index Library, British Rec. Soc. Vols. 56, 59 [Eng. Pub. AB Vols. 56, 59.]

17. Marriage Licenses 1664-1734 have been transcribed and indexed by this Society but have not yet been published.

18. A manuscript Index of Wills relating to this Archdeaconry, covering 1683-1858, was made by J. J. Beckerlegge. One copy is at Exeter and another copy in New York Public Library.

2. The Prebendal Court of Uffculme. The main series of records 1623-1799 are contained in the Sarum Peculiar Courts now at the Wiltshire Record Office, Trowbridge. A few records are among the diocesan records at Salisbury, Wiltshire.

"Testamentary Papers at Sarum," 1550-1810 The Genealogists' Magazine Vol. 5. [Eng. Pub. V, Vol. 5.]

3. Thorncombe parish was transferred from Devon to Dorset in October 1836. Prior to that time it was in the Archdeaconry of Exeter but from 1836 to 1858 the probate records would be in the Archdeaconry of Dorset and Diocese of Salisbury, kept at the Dorset County Record Office, Dorchester.

4. Stockland and Dalwood were transferred from Dorset to Devon in October 1836 and prior to that time the records would be in the Achdeaconry of Dorset and Diocese of Bristol but from 1836 to 1858 the records would be in the Archdeaconry and Diocese of Exeter.

At the City Library, Exeter, Devonshire, there are many copies of Devonshire probate records in the Oswyn Murray Collection.

Abstacts of some Devonshire Wills have been printed.

Devonshire Wills. [Devon 10.]

Nonconformist Registers: There are records of 110 Nonconformist chapels at the General Register Office, Somerset House, London.

Publications: The following publications are of interest:

1. *Publications* of the Devon and Cornwall Record Society.
2. *Publications* of the Devonshire Association for the Advancement of Science, Literature and Art.
3. *Devon and Cornwall Notes and Gleanings.*
4. *Devon Notes and Queries.*

DORSET   DORSET

(also called Dorsetshire)—a maritime county on the south coast of England.

(*For map, see page 340-1*)

Area: 1005 square miles.   *Population*: 159,400.

Ancient Parishes: 260, three of which are in Dorchester, three in Shaftesbury and two in Weymouth.

County Town: Dorchester. The County Record Office is situated here.

Main Occupations: Agriculture and the manufacture of hemp.

Principal Rivers: Frome, Stour, Piddle and Ivel.

Ecclesiastically the County of Dorset was in the Diocese of Salisbury from 1075 until 1542, when this county, forming the Archdeaconry of Dorset, was made part of the Diocese of Bristol. In the year 1836 it was taken from the Diocese of Bristol and again united with the Diocese of Salisbury.

In 1836 the parish of Stockland and the township of Dalwood, both part of Dorset were united with Devonshire. In the same year the parish of Thorncombe and places named Burhall Downs and Easthay (part of the parish of Axminster) which were part of Devonshire were made part of Dorset. The parish of Holwell including the tithing of Buckshaw also became part of Dorset; whereas prior to 1836 they had been part of Somersetshire.

Parish Registers: The marriage registers of a few of the parishes for periods prior to 1813 have been printed.

Bishop's Transcripts: The main group was destroyed by fire at Blandford in 1731. From 1731 to about 1841, the transcripts are at the Diocesan Registry, Salisbury, Wiltshire, but there are many gaps in them. The Bishop's Transcripts of thirty-six parishes that were Peculiars were at Salisbury when the fire at Blandford took place and so are available back to about 1660 with a few that extend to even earlier dates.

Marriage Licenses:
1. Those for the Diocese of Salisbury.
   1615-1682, The Genealogist, New Series, Vols. 24-38. [Eng. Pub. AF., N.S., Vols. 24-38.][19]
2. Those for the Peculiar of the Dean and Chapter of Salisbury.
   1629-1690, Wilts. Notes and Queries Vols. 6-8. [Wilts. Pub. C Vols. 6-8.][19]
3. Those for the Royal Peculiar of Corfe Castle.
   1602-1800, Index Library, British Rec. Soc. Vol. 22. [Eng. Pub. AB Vol. 22.]

These documents are at the Diocesan Registry, Salisbury, Wiltshire.

Probate Records: The following courts were in use:
1. The Dorsetshire Division of the Episcopal Consistory of the former Diocese of Bristol, had jurisdiction over the estates of clergy. It also handled other probate business when the Court of the Archdeacon was closed.
   Cal. of Wills and Admons, 1681-1792. Index Library, British Rec. Soc. Vol. 22. [Eng. Pub. AB Vol. 22.]
2. The Court of the Archdeacon of Dorset covered most parishes in the county.
   Cal. of Wills and Admons. 1568-1792. Ibid.
3. The Peculiar Courts of Canford, Poole, Corfe Castle, Milton Abbas, Sturminster Marshall, Wimborne Minster and others.
   Cal. of Wills and Admons 1660-1799. Index Library, British Rec. Soc. Vols. 22, 53. [Eng. Pub. AB Vols. 22, 53.]
   A few additional Wills-Dorset Natural History [Dorset Pub. A Vol. 63.]

All of the above documents are at the County Record Office, Dorchester.

---

19. The period 1682-1700 has been transcribed and a copy is available at the Society of Genealogists, London, and at the Genealogical Society, Salt Lake City, Utah. This typescript also contains those for the Peculiar Court of the Dean and Chapter of Salisbury 1739-1743. [Wilts. S.2.]

4. The Peculiar Court of the Dean of Sarum (Latin for Salisbury), covered about forty places in this county.

> Cal. of Wills and Admons, 1500-1801. Index Library, British Rec. Soc. Vol. 53. [Eng. Pub. AB Vol. 53.]
> This volume gives a list of the Dorset parishes covered by this court. See also item 3.

5. The Sarum Peculiar Courts were several in number—the Prebend of Chardstock, including Wambrook 1639-1799; the Prebend of Fordington including Writhlington 1660-1799, the Royal Peculiar of Gillingham including Bourton, Motcombe and East and West Stour 1658-1799; Prebend of Lyme Regis including Halstock, Leigh and Colway 1664-1799; the Prebend of Netherbury in Ecclesia including Beaminster and Mangerton 1608-1799; the Prebend of Preston including Sutton Pointz 1761-1799; the Prebend of Yetminster including Chetnole, Grimston and Leigh 1654-1799 and the Peculiar of the Dean and Chapter of Sarum relating to Stour Paine and Durweston 1604-1799.

> Cal. to all these Peculiars, Index Library, British Rec Soc. Vol. 53. [Eng. Pub. AB Vol. 53.]

All of the documents listed in items 4 and 5 above are at the Wilts. County Record Office at Trowbridge.

The Archdeaconry Court of Sarum, the Episcopal Consistory of Sarum and the Archdeaconry Court of Wiltshire also have Dorset probates. See under Wiltshire for details of these courts. There are also some testamentary papers relating to Dorset among the Diocesan records at Salisbury.

> Genealogists' Magazine Vol. 5 p. 140. 1500-1700 "Cal. of Wills and Admons." [Eng. Pub. V., Vol. 5.]

Nonconformist Registers: There are records of thirty-eight Nonconformist chapels at Somerset House, London.

Publications: The following publications are of interest:

1. *Publications* of the Dorset Natural History and Archaelogical Society. One volume, *Index to the County Records at Dorchester* is of particular interest.

2. *Publications* of the Dorset Natural History and Antiquarian Field Club.

3. *Somerset and Dorset Notes and Queries.*

4. Robert Douch, *A Handbook of Local History, Dorset.* (University of Bristol: 1952).

DURHAM   DURHAM

(also known as County Durham)—a maritime county on the north-east coast of England.

(*For map, see page* 335-7)

Area: 1061 square miles.   *Population*: 253,700.

Ancient Parishes: 93, seven of which are in the City of Durham.

County Town: Durham.

Main Occupations: Agriculture; seafaring; coal mining; and there are industries connected with the production of iron goods; building of ships and the manufacture of carpets, worsteds, glass and paper products.

Principal Rivers: The River Tyne, forming most of the northern boundary of the county gives its name to one of England's important industrial areas, *Tyneside,* and the areas around the other two chief rivers, the Tees and Wear, are also of industrial importance.

Ecclesiastically the county forms the Archdeaconry of Durham in the Diocese of Durham and Province of York. Small districts formerly part of County Durham were annexed to Northumberland in 1844, and they were named:

1. Bedlingtonshire (parish of Bedlington with seven townships)
2. Norhamshire   (parish of Norham with twelve townships)
3. Islandshire   (comprising parishes of Kyloe [with five townships] Holy Island [with three townships] and Ancroft [with four townships]).

However these changes made little difference ecclesiastically as the county of Northumberland was in the Diocese of Durham until 1882.

Parish Registers: A few of the registers for periods prior to 1813 have been printed. The majority of the other parishes have had their registers transcribed for periods prior to 1813 and these are available in the Newcastle-upon-Tyne, Public Library, Northumberland. A microfilm copy of this collection is available at the Genealogical Society, Salt Lake City, Utah. The *Durham Marriage Index* compiled by Percival Boyd covers certain periods in seventy-two parishes.

Bishop's Transcripts: A few exist between 1760 and 1790. From 1790 onwards they are reasonably complete. They are kept at the University, Durham, in yearly bundles not arranged by parishes. They extend to at least 1850.

Marriage Licenses: These are at the Diocesan Registry, Durham. Series of marriage bonds 1664-1674 and 1590-1815 are available at the Public Library, Newcastle-upon-Tyne, Northumberland and were also microfilmed for the Genealogical Society, Salt Lake City. Some marriage bonds are filed with the probate records around 1700-1709 and 1734-1735. These have also been microfilmed as above.

Probate Records: The following courts were in use:

1. The Episcopal Consistory Court of Durham covered most of the county. The records are at Durham University.

   Cal. of Wills and Admons, 1540-1599. Pub. of Newcastle on Tyne Records Committee Vol. 8. [Northu. Pub. C., Vol. 8.]
   Abstracts of some Wills 1311-1599, Pub. Surtees Soc. Vols. 2, 38, 112, 116, 121, 142. [Eng. Pub. F Vols. as above.]

2. The Peculiar Court of Craike covered that parish. The records are at the Borthwick Institute, St. Anthony's Hall, York.

Nonconformist Registers: There are records of fifty-two Nonconformist chapels at the General Register office, Somerset House, London.

Publications: The following publications are of interest:

1. *Publications* of the Newcastle-upon-Tyne Records Committee.
2. The *Transactions* of the Architectural and Archaeological Society of Durham and Northumberland.
3. *Archaeologia Aeliana.*
4. *Publications* of the Society of Antiquaries of Newcastle-upon-Tyne.
5. The Newcastle Public Library possesses a large collection of manuscript notes on families, many of which have been microfilmed by the Genealogical Society, Salt Lake City.
6. The *Publications* of the Surtees Society.

See also the article on Northumberland as these two counties were operated jointly in many ecclesiastical matters.

ESSEX   ESSEX

a maritime county in the east of England.

(For map, see page 342-3)

Area: 1532 square miles.   *Population:* 317,200.

Ancient Parishes: 405, of which twelve are in the town of Colchester and three in Maldon.

County Town: Chelmsford in which the County Hall and the Essex Record Office are situated.

Main Occupations: Agriculture, seafaring and fishing.

Principal Rivers: Thames, Coln, Crouch, Chelmer, Blackwater, Lea, Stort.

Ecclesiastically, the county of Essex was divided into three archdeaconries, all within the Diocese of London, Province of Canterbury. These archdeaconries held jurisdiction over all parishes within their deaneries except Peculiars and those parishes subject to the Bishop of London's Commissary.

1. The Archdeaconry of Essex that held jurisdiction in the south part of the county and those parts nearest London.
2. The Archdeaconry of Colchester that held jurisdiction in the north part of the county.
3. The Archdeaconry of Middlesex, that exercised jurisdiction roughly across the center of the county and partly up to its northern boundary, intervening between the Archdeaconries of Essex and Colchester. In 1845 it ceased to have any control in Essex and its three Essex rural deaneries were transferred—Hedingham Deanery to the Archdeaconry of Colchester; Dunmow and Harlow Deaneries to the Archdeaconry of Essex.
4. Peculiar Jurisdictions. These were many peculiars within Essex, the most important of these being mentioned in *The Victoria History of the County of Essex,* Volume 2, pages 81 to 83.

5. Diocese of Rochester. On the 1st January 1846 the whole of the county, with the exception of nine parishes,[20] was transferred to the Diocese of Rochester. The nine parishes remained in the Diocese of London until 1863 when they were then transferred to the Diocese of Rochester.

6. In 1877 the whole of the county was transferred to the Diocese of Saint Albans.

7. The county now forms part of the modern Diocese of Chelmsford.

Parish Registers:[21] A number of the original parish registers have been placed in the care of the Essex Record Office, Chelmsford. Transcript copies of other parish registers have been made for periods prior to 1838. Some of these transcript copies are at the Essex Record Office, others are in private possession. The *Essex Marriage Index,* by Percival Boyd, covers certain periods taken from 170 parishes.

Bishop's Transcripts: Unfortunately, these are almost non-existent for Essex. There are a few for twenty-seven parishes 1860-1880 at the Essex Record Office. Those that exist for earlier preiods are at the Guildhall Library, London, E.C. 2.

Marriage Licenses: The following records are at the Essex Record Office, Chelmsford, and are indexed, and all have been microfilmed[22] for the Genealogical Society, Salt Lake City, Utah.

1. The Bishop of London's Consistory Court, covering Essex and East Hertfordshire, 1665-1853.

2. The Bishop of London's Commissary in Essex and Herts., 1681-1731.

3. The Archdeacon of Essex, 1693-1849.

4. The Archdeacon of Colchester, 1699-1851.

5. The Archdeacon of Middlesex in Essex and Herts., 1687-1851.

6. The Bishop of London's Peculiar of Good Easter, 1750-1808.

7. The Peculiar of Writtle with Roxwell, 1700-1847.

8. The Peculiar of the Sokens (Thorpe, Walton, Kirby), 1756-1861. These are also at the Essex Record Office, but have not been microfilmed.

The possibility that Essex residents used the London registries should be noted. See under "London" for details.

See under "London" for details.

---

20. The nine parishes are Barking, Chingford, East Ham, West Ham, Little Ilford, Low Leyton (Leytonstone), Walthamstow, Wanstead, St. Mary Woodford.

21. *Essex Parish Records, 1240-1894,* lists all parish registers and records, and contains a map of Essex showing the boundary of each parish. [Essex Pub. C, No. 7.]

22. The Index, arranged alphabetically by bridegrooms (by initial letter only) has the library call number at the Genealogical Society, Salt Lake City, 14006, F.Essex, 13. It should be noted that the marriage licenses issued in the Bishop of London's Commissary Court cease in 1731. From 1731, marriage licenses were dealt with and issued from the Bishop of London's Consistory Court.

Probate Records: The following courts were in use:

1. Court of the Archdeacon of Colchester, covered 107 parishes in N.E. and N.W. Essex.
2. Court of the Archdeacon of Essex, covered 140 parishes in South Essex.
3. Court of the Archdeacon of Middlesex (Essex and Herts. jurisdiction), covered 39 parishes in the W. and N. of Essex.
4. Court of the Bishop of London's Commissary (Essex and Herts. jurisdiction), extended in theory to 101 parishes in Essex, but in practice the court was used for grants in almost every Essex parish, not excepting the Peculiars.
5. Court of the Peculiar of Writtle with Roxwell covered those places.
6. Court of the Peculiar of Good Easter, covered that place.
7. Court of the Peculiar of the Deanery of Bocking, covered six places in Essex.
8. Court of the Peculiar of the Liberty of the Sokens, covered three places in Essex.

The records listed above are at the Essex Record Office, Chelmsford.

> 1400-1619, Wills at Chelmsford (for Essex and East Herts.) Index Library, Brit. Rec. Soc., Vol. 78. Covers courts in 1, 2, 3, 4, 5, and 6 above. The period 1620-1720 is in process of being printed. [Eng. Pub. AB., V. 78.]
>
> 1635-1749 Farm and Cottage Inventories of Mid-Essex, (Essex Rec. Office, 1950) list many Inventories and Admons for the Pec. Court of Writtle with Roxwell. [Essex Pub. C., No 8.]

9. The Episcopal Consistory Court of London, that had concurrent jurisdiction with the Archdeacon's Courts over the whole Diocese (except the Peculiars) as well as with the Court of the Bishop of London's Commissary (Essex and Herts.) and the Commissary Court of the Bishop of London (London Division). These records are at the London County Council Record Office, Westminster Bridge, London, S.E.1.
10. The Commissary Court of the Bishop of London (London Division), covered eight parishes in Essex. These records are at the Guildhall Library, London, E.C.
11. Court of the Peculiar of the Dean and Chapter of Westminster, covered one parish in Essex. These records are at the Westminster Public Library, Buckingham Palace Road, Westminster, London, S.W.1. See "London" for details.
12. Court of the Peculiar of the Dean and Chapter of St. Paul's Cathedral, covered six parishes in Essex. These records are at the Principal Probate Registry, Somerset House, London. Plans to transfer them are under consideration.
13. Probate records for residents of Essex are also to be found in the Prerogative Court of Canterbury, London, the Calendars of which are listed on page 87.

14. Some Essex Wills are to be found at Canterbury among "Vacan-cy" Wills.

> 1293-1559, Essex Wills at Canterbury, Trans. Essex Arch. Soc., Vol. 21. This covers about forty Wills. [Essex Pub. B., N.S., Vol. 21.]

Nonconformists: There are records of seventy-eight Nonconformist Chapels at the General Register Office, Somerset House, London.

Publications: The following publications are of interest:

1. *The Essex Review.*

2. *Transactions* of the Essex Archaeological Society.

3. *Guide to the Essex Record Office,* (1946-1948), Nos. 1 and 2. [Essex Pub. C., Nos. 1 and 2.]

4. *Essex Parish Records* 1240-1894, ibid. No. 7. [Essex Pub. C. No. 7.]

FLINTSHIRE   FLINTSHIRE

(Fflint or Sir Flynt) — a maritime county in North Wales formed in 1536.

(*For map, see page* 344)

Area: 270 square miles.   *Population*: 60,244.

Ancient Parishes: 30.

County Town: Flint, but the County Offices and the Flintshire Record Office are at Mold.

Main Occupations: Agriculture, mining of coal, iron, zinc, the manu-facture of metals and rope.

Principal Rivers: Dee, Clwyd, Alyn.

Ecclesiastically, the county was mostly in the Archdeaconry and Diocese of St. Asaph, Province of Canterbury, but a few parishes were in the Archdeaconry and Diocese of Chester in the Province of York. Since 1921 it has wholly been in the Province of Wales.

Parish Registers: A few have been transcribed.

Bishop's Transcripts: Those for the Diocese of St. Asaph range from around 1660 to 1870 but have many gaps, and are at the National Library of Wales. Those for the Diocese of Chester are at the Dio-cesan Registry, Chester.

Marriage Licenses: Those for the Diocese of St. Asaph cover 1616-1900 and are at the National Library of Wales. Those for the Diocese of Chester are at the Diocesan Registry, Chester. The printed abstracts of those, at Chester only, are as follows:

> Abstracts, 1606-1632, 1639-1644, 1661-1719, (Lancs. and Chesh. Rec. Soc.), Vols. 53, 56, 57, 61, 65, 69, 73, 77, 82, 85, 97, 101. [CHES. 1. Vols. as above.]

Probate Records: The following courts covered the county, the records of which are at the National Library of Wales:

1. Episcopal Consistory Court of St. Asaph.

2. The Peculiar Court of Hawarden, Flintshire, (in Diocese of Chester).

> Index of Wills . . . Hawarden, 1554-1800, in Flints Hist. Soc. Pubs., Vol. 4, part 2, (1914), pages 41-110. [FLINTS. PUB. B, Vol. 4, pt. 2.]

3. Episcopal Consistory Court of Chester. See under "Cheshire," for full details of this court.

> Cal. of Wills, Admons., and Inv., 1545-1820, (Lancs. and Chesh. Rec. Soc.), Vols. 2, 4, 15, 18, 20, 22, 25, 30, 33, 37, 38, 43, 44, 45, 52, 62, 63, 78, 79. [CHES. 1, Vols as above.]

Any Welsh probate records found among the records at Chester were transferred to the National Library of Wales. Those transferred are for dates prior to 1838.

Nonconformist Registers: There are records of thirty-seven Noncon- formist chapels at The General Register Office, Somerset House, London. There may be others in local custody, libraries, etc.

Publications: The following publications are of interest:

1. The *Journal* and *Record Series* of the Flintshire Historical Society.

2. *Guide to the Flintshire Record Office* (1955). [FLINTS. 3.]

3. Rev. D. R. Thomas, *History of the Diocese of St. Asaph* (1870), 2 Vols.

4. E. R. Harries, *Bibliography of County Flint* (1953).

GLAMORGANSHIRE   GLAMORGANSHIRE

(Morgannwg) — a maritime county in South Wales formed in 1536.

(For map, see page 345)

Area: 660 square miles.   *Population:* 126,612.

Ancient Parishes: 123.

County Town: Cardiff, where the County Record Office is situated.

Main Occupations: Agriculture, fishing, mining of coal, iron, and lead, and the manufacturing of copper, iron, and woollen goods.

Principal Rivers: Taf, Tawe, Nedd, Loughor, Rhymni.

Ecclesiastically, the county was in the Archdeaconry and Diocese of Llandaff, except for twenty-three parishes in Gower which were in the Archdeaconry of Carmarthen and Diocese of St. David's. In 1835- 1836 the whole of the county was placed in the Archdeaconry and Diocese of Llandaff. Until 1920 it was in the Province of Canterbury when it became part of the Province of Wales. In 1923 the localities around Swansea and Gower were taken out of the Diocese of Llan- daff to form the Diocese of Swansea and Brecon.

Parish Registers: A few have been transcribed. A few others have been printed.

Bishop's Transcripts: These are at the National Library of Wales, Aber-ystwyth, and range from 1660-1870 but have many gaps.

Marriage Licenses: These are at the National Library of Wales for 1665-1900 for the Diocese of Llandaff; for 1661-1867 for the "old" St. David's Diocese; and 1615-1900 for the Consistory Court of St. David's. Some marriages bonds from the St. David's Diocese have been printed 1612-1799 in *West Wales Historical Records,* Vols. 3-12.

Probate Records: The following courts covered the county, the records of which are at the National Library of Wales:

1. The Episcopal Consistory Court of Llandaff.
2. Archdeaconry of Carmarthen (for Gower) in the Episcopal Con-sistory Court of St. David's.

Nonconformist Registers: There are records of fifty-two Nonconform-ist chapels at The General Register Office, Somerset House, London. There may be others in local custody, libraries, etc.

Publications: The following publications are of interest:

1. *Publications of the S. Wales and Monmouth Record Society.*
2. *A List of Glamorgan Manuscripts . . . in the National Library of Wales.*

GLOUCESTERSHIRE   GLOUCESTERSHIRE

(pronounced Glostershire) — a maritime county in the west of England.

(For map, see page 346-7)

Area: 1256 square miles.   *Population*: 376,700.

Ancient Parishes: 347, nine of which are in the City of Gloucester and nineteen in the City of Bristol.

County Town: Gloucester.

Main Occupations: Seafaring, agriculture, coal mining and the manu-facture of fine cloth. Bristol is a large manufacturing area, forming with Avonmouth, one of the principal seaports in the country.

Principal Rivers: Severn, Upper Avon, Wye and Isis. The Bristol Channel is an important waterway.

Ecclesiastically, the county was divided as follows:

1. From 1291 to about 1541, the county was divided between the Archdeaconry of Gloucester in the Diocese of Worcester and the Archdeaconry of Hereford in the Diocese of Hereford.
2. In 1541 the Diocese of Gloucester was formed, consisting of the Archdeaconry of Gloucester and the Archdeaconry of Hereford in the Diocese of Gloucester, and in all containing over 300 parishes.
3. In 1542 the Diocese of Bristol was formed, and the City and rural deanery of Bristol, consisting of the parishes in the City of Bristol and about sixteen parishes adjacent thereto, was taken out of the Diocese of Gloucester.

4. In 1836 the Diocese of Gloucester and Bristol was formed by
uniting the above two dioceses, but in 1897 the Diocese of Bristol
was created. (For additional information see the *Victoria History
of Gloucester,* Vol. 2.)

The County has always been in the Province of Canterbury.

Parish Registers:[23] A good proportion of the marriage registers have been
printed for periods prior to 1813, with a few down to 1837. A master
index to these marriages, compiled by Mr. Eric Roe, is available at the
Society of Genealogists, London and the Genealogical Society, Salt
Lake City, Utah.

A few parish registers are available on microfilm at the Genealogical Society, Salt Lake City. Many others have been privately
microfilmed and stored at the City Library, Gloucester.

Bishop's Transcripts: Those for the Diocese of Gloucester (the larger
portion of the county) are a comparatively good collection and extend
from 1598 to around 1840. They are in parish order except for the
period 1813-1840 when they are arranged in bound volumes year by
year. All are at the City Library, Gloucester.

The Bishop's Transcripts for those parishes in the Diocese of
Bristol are, for periods prior to 1813, kept at the Council House,
Bristol. This collection is not as complete as the one at Gloucester.
For 1813-1840, they are at the City Library Gloucester, bound with
those for the Diocese of Gloucester.

Marriage Licenses: Those for the Diocese of Gloucester are at the City
Library, Gloucester.

> Marr. Allegations 1637-1680 and Surrogate Allegations to 1694—
> Bristol & Gloucester Arch. Soc. Records Section Vol. 2. [Gloucs. Pub.
> C Vol. 2.]

Those for the Diocese of Bristol are at the Council House, Bristol.

> Marr. Bonds 1637-1700 excluding Archdeaconry of Dorset—Bristol &
> Gloucester Arch. Soc. Records Section Vol. 1. [Gloucs. Pub. C Vol 1.]
> Bonds and Allegations Consistory Court of Bishop of Bristol 1660-
> 1686, Gloucs. Notes and Queries Vol. 10. [Gloucs., Pub. B Vol. 10.]

Probate Records: The following courts were in use:

1. The Episcopal Consistory Court of Gloucester covered most of the
parishes in the county outside of the jurisdiction of the Bishop of
Bristol. The records are at the Gloucester City Library.

> Cal. of Wills 1541-1650; 1660-1800, Index Library, British Rec. Soc.
> Vols 12, 34. [Eng. Pub. AB Vols. 12, 34.]

2. The Peculiar Courts of Bibury and Bishops Cleeve cover six
parishes. The record are at the Gloucester City Library.

> Ibid.
> There are also records for this Peculiar prior to 1649 among the
> Oxford, Berks. and Bucks. Peculiars kept at the Bodleian Library
> Oxford.

---

23. The volumes entitled *Historical, Monumental and Genealogical Collections
of Gloucester* by Ralph Bigland, printed in 1791 and 1792 are a very
valuable source for monumental inscriptions especially since many of the
stones copied then are now unreadable. These volumes are available at the
Gloucester Public Library and at the Genealogical Society, Salt Lake City,
Utah.

3. The Consistory Court of the Bishop of Bristol (in the Deanery of Bristol) having jurisdiction in the nineteen parishes in the City of Bristol and sixteen adjacent parishes. The records are at the Council House, Bristol.

> Cal. of Wills 1572-1792, Index Library, British Rec. Soc. Vol. 17. [Eng. Pub. AB Vol. 17.]

There are a few other ancient wills in the City Library and among the municipal records of the Guidhall, Gloucester.

The City of Bristol has among its muniments records known as the Great Orphan Books. These contain Wills proved in various courts and involving Citizens and Freemen of Bristol.

> The Great Orphan Book and Book of Wills, (Bristol and Glouc. Arch. Soc., 1886) [Gloucs Pub. A. Supp. 2.] also [Eng. Pub. AB. Vol 17.]
> Cal. of Wills, 1379-1792, (Index Library, British Rec. Soc.), Vol. 17.

There are a few other Wills at the Council House, Bristol. Before the bishoprics of Gloucester and Bristol were created in 1541 and 1542 respectively, Wills were supposed to have been proved at Worcester but they may be very few.

> Cal. of Worcs. Wills 1492-1563, Index to Worcester Wills. [Worcs. 24 Vols 1 & 2.]

Nonconformist Registers: There are records of sixty-three Nonconformist chapels at The General Register Office, Somerset House, London. A check should also be made under Somersetshire as the City of Bristol is included in that list.

Publications: The following publications are of interest:

1. *Transactions* of the Bristol and Gloucestershire Archaeological Society.

2. *Gloucester Notes and Queries.*

3. *Publications* of the Bristol Record Society.

4. *Catalogue of the Gloucestershire Collection in the Gloucester Public Library* (1928).

The Bristol and Gloucestershire Archaeological Society is in process of compiling information on the parish records of the county, to be published under the title *A Guide to the Parish Records of Gloucestershire*.

HAMPSHIRE   HAMPSHIRE

(abbreviated to Hamps. or Hants., but is also called the County of Southampton) a maritime county on the south coast of England. Hampshire included the Isle of Wight until 1889 when that island was taken from Hampshire and formed into an administrative county.

(For map, see page 348-9)

Area: 1628 square miles.   *Population*: 314,700.

Ancient Parishes: 307, of which Winchester has ten and Southampton five.

County Towns:
1. Winchester, where there is a County Record Office.
2. Newport, Isle of Wight, where there is a County Hall.

Main Occupations: Agricultural and maritime.

Principal Rivers: Test, Anton, Itchen, Ave, Boldre and Exe.

Ecclesiastically, the county formed the Archdeaconry of Winchester, Diocese of Winchester, Province of Canterbury. Incidentally, this Diocese includes the Channel Islands where there are two deans who exercise jurisdiction within those islands. When the modern Diocese of Guilford was created, a portion of Hampshire was transferred to it, and when the Diocese of Portsmouth was created, localities in and around Portsmouth and the whole of the Isle of Wight were transferred to it.

Parish Registers: The marriage registers of a few of the parishes for periods prior to 1813 have been printed. Transcripts of the registers of some parishes are at the Cathedral Library, Winchester.

Bishop's Transcripts: These are at the Diocesan Registry, Winchester, and they are practically non-existent prior to 1780 but extend to 1858. They are arranged by parish from 1780 to about 1820. The remainder are being sorted.

Marriage Licenses: These are at the Diocesan Registry, Winchester.
Granted by Bishop of Winchester 1680-1837 Pub. Harl. Soc. Vols. 35, 36. [Eng. Pub. AC Vols. 35, 36.]
Granted at Salisbury, Wilts. 1615-1682 The Genealogist Vols. 24-38. [Eng. Pub. AF Vols. 24-38.]
Additional Allegations 1607-1640 (not in above printed series) by G. W. Willis.

Probate Records: The following courts were in use:

Godshill, Isle of Wight

1. The Episcopal Consistory and Archdeaconry Court of Winton covered the whole of the county except for parishes with peculiar jurisdiction.
2. The Hampshire Peculiar Courts covered 23 parishes.
3. Certain Wills between 1448 and 1515 were copied into the Bishops Registers.
4. Returns of Papists Estates, 1717-1775, survive at the Hampshire Record Office.

Items 1 and 2 are at the County Record Office, Winchester and item 3 is at the Diocesan Registry, Winchester.

Nonconformist Registers: There are records of sixty-one Nonconformist chapels at the General Register Office, Somerset House, London.

Publications: The following publications are of interest:
1. *Publications* of the Southampton Record Society.
2. *Publications* of the Hampshire Record Society.
3. *The Parish Registers . . . Archdeaconry . . . Winchester*, (Faron and Williams, 1909) lists all parish registers down to 1812 and other documents to 1800.

HEREFORD   HEREFORD

an inland county on the border of Wales.

(*For map, see page* 350-1)

Area: 860 square miles.   *Population*: 110,300.

Ancient Parishes: 223, six of which are in the City of Hereford.

County Town: Hereford.

Main Occupation: Agriculture.

Principal Rivers: Wye, Lug, Munnow, Arrow, Frome, Teme, Leddon.

Ecclesiastically, the county formed the Archdeaconry of Hereford in the Diocese of Hereford, Province of Canterbury except for eight parishes near the border of Wales which were in the Archdeaconry of Brecon and Diocese of St. Davids.

Parish Registers: Very few have been printed, although a number of transcript copies and some original registers have been placed in the care of the Public Library, Hereford.

Bishop's Transcripts: These are at the Diocesan Registry at Hereford but do not extend later than 1812 although there is a possibility that when all the material in the Registry has been sorted, later transcripts may be disclosed. There are no facilities for searching these records at present due to lack of space at the Registry.

Marriage Licenses: The records of the Diocese of Hereford are at the Diocesan Registry, Hereford. Those for the Surrogates of the Bishop of Hereford, 1674-1784, and for the Deanery of Hereford, 1609-1761, have been microfilmed by the Genealogical Society, Salt Lake City. For those parishes in the Archdeaconry of Brecon and Diocese of St. Davids, the records are at the National Library of Wales. These include 1661-1867 for the "old" St. David's Diocese, and a separate series for St. John and St. Mary, Brecon, 1666-1867, that might include Herefordshire references. All these have been microfilmed as above.

Probate Records: The following courts were in use:
1. The Episcopal Consistory Court of Hereford covered most of the county.
2. The Consistory Court of the Dean of Hereford covered 32 parishes.

3. Three Peculiar Courts covered five parishes.

4. The Consistory Court of the Archdeaconry of Brecon and Epis-copal Consistory Court of St. David's covered eight border parishes.

All of the original records are at the National Library of Wales.

Nonconformist Registers: There are records of eighteen Nonconformist chapels at the General Register Office, Somerset House, London.

HERTFORDSHIRE   HERTFORDSHIRE

(sometimes pronounced Hartfordshire)—an inland county of England.

(For map, see page 352)

Area: 528 square miles.   *Population*: 143,300.

Ancient Parishes: 132, of which two are in the Town of Hertford and three in the City of St. Albans.

County Town: Hertford, where the County Record Office is situated.

Main Occupations: Agriculture.

Principal Rivers: Lea, Colne.

Ecclesiastically, the county formed:

1. The Deanery of Braugham in the Archdeaconry of Middlesex comprising 34 parishes.

2. The Archdeaconry of St. Albans comprising 24 parishes.

3. The Archdeaconry of Huntingdon (Hitchin, Herts. Division), comprising about 80 parishes.

  The Archdeaconry of Middlesex was in the Diocese of London, and the Archdeaconry of St. Albans was in the Diocese of Lincoln, but in 1845 both archdeaconries were transferred to the Diocese of Rochester. The Archdeaconry of Huntingdon was transferred to the Diocese of Ely in 1837, but in 1845, the Hertfordshire parishes were transferred to the Archdeaconry of St. Albans, Diocese of Rochester. The whole of the county remained in the jurisdiction of the Bishop of Rochester until 1877 when the new Diocese of St. Albans was formed and which embraces the whole county. It is in the Province of Canter-bury.

Parish Registers: The marriage registers of a few parishes have been printed. A few others have been transcribed and are at the Society of Genealogists, London. A number of the original parish registers have been deposited at the County Record Office, County Hall, Hertford.

Bishop's Transcripts: These, for both the Archdeaconry of St. Albans, and the Archdeaconry of Huntingdon, (Herts. Division), are at the County Record Office, Hertford. They are in average condition but have many gaps.

    The Herts. Genealogist & Antiquary, Vols 1-3, contains many printed abstracts of the Bishop's Transcripts for fourteen parishes in Herts. [Herts. 1, Vols. 1-3.]

The Bishop's Transcripts of those parishes which came directly under the Bishop of London are almost non-existent. The few that remain are at the Guildhall Library of the City of London, London, E.C.2.

Marriage Licenses: The following are the jurisdictions covering Hert- fordshire:

1. The Bishop of London's Consistory Court covering Essex and east Hertfordshire, 1665-1853.
2. The Bishop of London's Commissary in Essex and Herts., 1681- 1731. After 1731, marriage licenses were dealt with and issued from the Bishop of London's Consistory Court, as in item 1 above.
3. The Archdeacon of Middlesex in Essex and Herts., 1687-1851.

All records in items 1, 2, and 3, are at the Essex Record Office, Chelmsford, and have been microfilmed for the Genealogical Society, Salt Lake City, Utah. [14006, F. Essex 13, is the call number for the index.]

4. The Archdeaconry of St. Albans, 1611-1883, and the records are at the County Record Office, Hertford.

> 1582/3-1715, Herts. Genealogist & Antiquary, Vols. 1-3. [Herts. 1, Vols. 1-3.] (The list is continued, 1715-1830, in a manuscript at the County Record Office.) The printed list was made from Admon. Act Books.

5. The Archdeaconry of Huntingdon (Herts. Division at Hitchin, Herts.), 1682-1685; 1757-1860, and the records are at the County Record Office, Hertford.

> 1610-1649, Herts. Genealogist & Antiquary, Vol. 2. The list was taken from Probate Act Books. [Herts. 1, Vol. 2.]

6. The Archdeaconry of Huntingdon, (Huntingdon Division). The records are at the Archdeacon's Registry, Huntingdon, Hunts.

> 1517, 1610-1614, Index Library, Brit. Rec. Soc., Vol. 42. [Eng. Pub. AB., Vol. 42.]

Because of the unusual ecclesiastical arrangements of this county, residents may have used the London registries to obtain marriage licenses. See under "London" for details.

Probate Records: The following courts were in use:

1. The Archdeaconry Court of Huntingdon (Herts. Division at Hitchin), covered about 77 parishes in Herts. from about 1557- 1858.

> Abstracts of some Wills, 1579-1614, Herts. Genealogist, Vols. 2-3. [Herts. 1, Vols. 2-3.]

2. The Archdeaconry Court of St. Albans, covered most of the rest of the county.

> Abstracts of some Wills, 1415-1451, ibid., Vols. 1-3. [Ibid. Vols. 1-3.]

The records in items 1 and 2 are at the County Record Office, Hertford.

3. The Commissary of the Bishop of Lincoln and the Archdeacon in the Archdeaconry of Huntingdon (Huntingdon or Peterborough Division). These records, for dates prior to 1573, covered about 77 parishes in Herts.

> 1479-1652, Wills, and 1559-1614, Admons., Index Library, Brit. Rec. Soc., Vol. 42. [Eng. Pub. AB., Vol. 42.]

The records in item 3 are at the Huntingdon County Record Office, Huntingdon.

4. Court of the Archdeacon of Middlesex (Essex and Herts. jurisdiction), covered 25 parishes in east Hertfordshire.

Abstracts of some Wills, 1564-1598, Herts. Genealogist, Vols. 1, 2. [Herts. 1, Vols. 1, 2.]

5. Court of the Bishop of London's Commissary (Essex and Herts. jurisdiction), covered six parishes in east Hertfordshire, but in practice this court also covered all of Herts. that was within the Diocese of London.

The records in items 4 and 5 are at the Essex Record Office, Chelmsford.

1400-1619, Wills at Chelmsford (Essex and E. Herts.), Index Library, Brit. Rec. Soc., Vol. 78. [Eng. Pub. AB., Vol. 78.] Covers items 4 and 5 above. The period 1620-1720 is in process of being printed.

6. The Peculiar Court of the Dean and Chapter of St. Paul's Cathedral. The records are at Principal Probate Registry, Somerset House, London. Plans to transfer them are under consideration.

7. The Episcopal Consistory Court of London, having jurisdiction over the whole Diocese of London. The records are at the London County Council Record Office, Westminster Bridge, London, S.E.

Abstracts of some Wills, 1592-1628 Herts Genealogist, Vols. 2, 3. [Herts 1, Vols 2, 3.]

8. The Episcopal Consistory Court of Lincoln has some Wills for early years. See under "Lincolnshire" for details of records.

Abstracts of Wills . . . Lincoln, 1601-1652, "Abstracts of Herts. Wills," [Herts. 13, a typescript.]

There are some other early Wills, originally at Peterborough, but now at the County Record Office.

Nonconformist Registers: There are records of forty-one Nonconformist chapels at The General Register Office, Somerset House, London.

Publications: The following publications are of interest:

1. East Herts. Archaeological Society's *Transactions*.
2. *The Herts. Genealogist and Antiquary* by William Brigg, Vols. 1-3.
3. A guide to the County Record Office is in preparation, but will not be available for several years (1959).

HUNTINGDONSHIRE   HUNTINGDONSHIRE

an inland county of England.

(*For map, see page 354-5*)

Area: 370 square miles.   *Population*: 53,100.

Ancient Parishes: 93, two of which are in the town of Huntingdon.

County Town: Huntingdon. The County Record Office is in this town.

Main Occupation: Agriculture.

Principal Rivers: Ouse and Nene.

Ecclesiastically, the county forms the Archdeaconry of Huntingdon that was in the Diocese of Lincoln until 1837 when it was transferred to the Diocese of Ely. It is in the Province of Canterbury.

Parish Registers: Very few have been copied.

Bishop's Transcripts: There are two series of these as follows:

1. 1663-1812 and 1824-1860. These are in fairly good condition and are kept at the Archdeaconry Library, Huntingdon. A list of those still extant appears in the *Transactions of the Cambs. & Hunts. Archael. Soc.,* Vol. 4.

2. 1602-1632 and 1813-1826. These are at the Huntingdonshire Record Office, Huntingdon.

Marriage Licenses: Those at the Archdeacon's Registry are bonds and allegations, 1662-1883.

> 1517, 1610-1614, Index Library, British Rec. Soc. Vol. 42. [Eng. Pub. AB Vol. 42.]

Probate Records: The following courts were in use:

1. Commissary of the Bishop of Lincoln and of the Archdeacon in the Archdeaconry of Huntingdon, covered most of the parishes in the county.

> Cal. Wills, 1479-1652, and Admons., 1559-1614 Index Library, British Rec. Soc., Vol. 42. [Eng. Pub. AB Vol. 42]

The above court should not be confused with the Archdeaconry Court of Huntingdon (Hertfordshire Division at Hitchin, Herts.), this latter court covering certain parishes within Hertfordshire only, and the records are kept at the Hertford County Record Office.

2. The Peculiar Courts of Brampton, Buckden, Long Stow and Leighton Bromswold covered nine parishes.

> Cal. of Wills. 1549-1857, Index Library, British Rec. Soc. Vol. 42. [Eng. Pub. AB Vol. 42.] also recorded in Trans. Cambs and Hunts. Arch. Soc. Pub. Vol. 6. [Cambs. Pub. B Vol. 6.]

The above records are at the County Record Office, Huntingdon. There are also a few Wills at Lincoln relating to people of this county.

> Abstracts 1601-1652, Abstracts of Huntingdonshire Wills. [Hunts. 5.]

It should be noted that probate records for some of the residents of the parishes of Thurning and Winwick may be found in the Consistory Court of Peterboro, and for the parish of Stanground the records may be in either the Consistory Court or the Archdeaconry Court of Ely. After 1837 there may be some grants in the Consistory Court of Ely relating to this county.

Nonconformists: Only ten Nonconformist chapels are listed among the registers kept at the General Register Office, Somerset House, London.

Publications: The following publications are of interest:

1. *Transactions* of the Cambridgeshire and Huntingdonshire Archaeological Society.
2. *Guide to the Huntingdonshire Record Office*, (Huntingdon: 1958).

ISLE OF MAN
ISLE OF MAN

A self-governing island belonging to the British Commonwealth. It is situated in the Irish Sea off the north-west coast of England, about sixty miles from Liverpool, Lancs., forty-two miles from Whitehaven, Cumberland, sixty miles from Dublin, Ireland and twenty-one miles from Scotland. The people are known as Manx.

(For map, see page 353)

Area: 221 square miles.   *Population*: 41,000.

Ancient parishes: 17.

Capital: The ancient capital was in Rushen at Castletown, but the modern capital is Douglas. The Rolls Office and the Manx Museum and Library are in Douglas.

Main Occupations: Agriculture, mining of lead and copper, fishing, and considerable import and export trade by sea.

Principal Rivers: Ramsey, Douglas, Peel, Laxey.

Ecclesiastically, the island comprises the Diocese of Sodor and Man, which has, since 1536, been annexed to the Province of York.

Parish Registers: The originals are in the care of the local clergy, and the earliest is dated 1598, and none of them have been printed. The Manx Government has copied all the parish registers down to 1883, the copy being in the Rolls Office, Douglas. Generally the information is superior to that found in the average English parish register. These copy parish registers have been microfilmed down to 1883 by the Genealogical Society, Salt Lake City, Utah.

Bishop's Transcripts: These are at the Manx Museum and Library, Douglas, and are a series in average condition with several gaps. They generally cover 1734-1799 and have been microfilmed as above.

Marriage Licenses: The whereabouts of the marriage bonds, allegations, etc., (if kept) is unknown.

Probate Records: The following courts were in use:
1. The Episcopal Consistory Court of Sodor and Man, the records from 1659-1916 having been microfilmed as above.
2. The Court of the Archdeacon, the records 1629-1884 having been microfilmed as above.
3. As the Diocese is in the Province of York, there may be probate records for Manx families at York. As the Manx had business connections with the "mainland" it is probable that probate records of some could be filed among the records of the courts of Carlisle,

Richmond, Chester, and the P.C.C., all in England, and also in Scottish and Irish probate courts.

Nonconformist Records: There are none at the General Register Office, Somerset House, London, England. There are a few at the Rolls Office, Douglas, and these have been microfilmed as above. In 1841 there were over forty dissenting (i.e., Nonconformist chapels) on the Island.

Other Records:

1. The 1841 and 1851 census records are at the Public Record Office, Chancery Lane, London, England. The 1851 census has been microfilmed for the Genealogical Society above. The 1861 and later census records are kept by the Registrar General, Somerset House, London, England. A transcript copy of the census records 1821-1871, *but believed to be very incomplete,* was microfilmed at the Rolls Office, Douglas, and this copy is at the Genealogical Society above.

2. The various courts records of the Island, such as the Chancery, Exchequer, and allied courts, and the Enquest Records, and other miscellaneous court records were kept at the Rolls Office, Douglas. There were also many records of Deeds, Manorial Records, Mortgage entries, Bills of Sales, Land Records and Tithes, Military Records, copies of tombstone inscriptions, genealogical collections of various families, microfilmed at the Rolls Office and the Manx Museum Library for the Genealogical Society above. These records are of immense genealogical value, and no pedigree can be said to be complete unless these court and miscellaneous records have been examined. It is important to note that the laws of the Isle of Man retained much of the ancient peculiarity of character, especially concerning estates and inheritances, making the searching of the court records necessary.

Publications: The following publications are of interest:

1. *A New Atlas and Gazetteer* (1867). [ISLE OF MAN 13.]
2. A. W. Moore, *The Surnames and Place Names.* (1890 and 1906.) [ISLE OF MAN 2.]

KENT   KENT

a martime county on the south-east coast of England.

(For map, see page 356-7)

Area: 1537 square miles.   *Population:* 479,500.

Ancient Parishes: 400, seventeen of which are in Canterbury, three in Rochester, three in Sandwich, two in Deptford and two in Dover.

County Towns: Canterbury is generally regarded as the capital of the shire. It is also the county town for the eastern division of the county. There is a City Archives in the town. Maidstone is the capital of the western division of the county where the County Record Office is situated.

Main Occupations: Agriculture and occupations connected with a maritime area. There were important military and naval establishments at Greenwich, Woolwich, Chatham and Sheerness.

Principal Rivers: Thames and Medway.

Ecclesiastically, the county contains the following divisions:

1. The Archdeaconry of Canterbury, Diocese of Canterbury. In 1841 the Archdeaconry of Maidstone was formed from part of the Archdeaconry of Canterbury.
2. The Archdeaconry of Rochester, Diocese of Rochester. In 1845 some parts of the Archdeaconry of Rochester were transferred to the Archdeaconry of Maidstone and Diocese of Canterbury. There were other changes in 1867 and 1904, as listed in *The Victoria County History of Kent,* Vol. 2, p. 110.
3. The Peculiar of the Archbishop of Canterbury in the Peculiar Deanery of Shoreham.

The whole of the county is in the Province of Canterbury. The ecclesiastical establishments in Kent include the seat of the Primate of the Church of England at Canterbury,[24] Christianity having been first introduced into England in this county.

Parish Registers: Very few have been printed. A good proportion of those in north-west Kent have been transcribed for periods prior to 1837 and are available at the Society of Genealogists, London.

Bishop's Transcripts:

1. Diocese of Rochester — these are at the Diocesan Registry at Rochester and cover the northern part of the county. The transcripts are in fairly good condition.
3. Diocese of Canterbury—these are at the Diocesan Registry at Canterbury and cover the southern half of the county. This particular series, extending to as late as 1870 and commencing in 1558 is the most complete in the country. As transcripts were prepared by ministers each year for both the Archdeacon and the Bishop, a year missing in one series can usually be found in the other series.
3. Those for the Peculiars of Arches (London), Shoreham (Kent) and Croydon (Surrey), covering around 1750-1800, are at Lambeth Palace Library, London, S.E. 1, but they cover only a few parishes in the three peculiars, and are not available for inspection.

Marriage Licenses:

1. Diocese of Canterbury—these are at the Cathedral Library, Canterbury.
   Canterbury Marriage Licences, 1568, 1574-1646, 1660-1750, Vols. 1-6, by J. M. Cowper. [Kent C2b, Vols. 1s to 4s only covering down to 1700 only.] Vol. 1 lists parishes having Bishop's Transcripts at Canterbury.
2. Diocese of Rochester—these are at the Diocesan Registry, Rochester.
3. Peculiar of the Archbishop of Canterbury. Those for the Peculiars of Arches (London), Shoreham (Kent), and Croydon (Sur-

---

24. The Archbishop of Canterbury has his official archives at Lambeth Palace, London, and his ecclesiastical courts for the *Province* have always been held in London. He is, however, also Bishop of Canterbury, with *Diocesan* Offices at Canterbury, Kent.

rey) covering Allegations 1707-1804 and Bonds 1684-1804, are at Lambeth Palace Library, London, S.E.1.

Because part of County Kent adjoins London, many persons are likely to have been granted a marriage license from the Archbishop of Canterbury's Faculty Office, Vicar-General's Office, and the Bishop of London's Registry. These records are detailed under "London."

Probate Records: The following courts were in use:

1. The Episcopal Consistory Court of Canterbury that covered 52 parishes in the south of the county.

> Notes from some wills, 1451-1731, Misc. Geneal. et Heraldica, New Series, Vol. 3 and 5th Series, Vols. 2-5. [Eng. Pub. AE New Series, Vol. 3, 5th Series Vols. 2-5.]
> Cal. of Wills and Admons. 1396-1558; 1640-1650, Index Library, British Rec. Soc. Vols. 50, 65. [Eng. Pub. AB Vols. 50, 65.]
> Abstracts of some 16th century wills, Kentish Wills. [Kent 12.]

2. The Archdeaconry Court of Canterbury that covered 216 parishes in the southern part of the county.

> Cal. of Wills and Admons. 1396-1558; 1640-1650 Index Library, British Rec. Soc. Vols. 50, 65. [Eng. Pub. AB Vols. 50, 65.]

3. The Peculiar Court of the Archbishop of Canterbury in the Deanery of Shoreham that covered 35 parishes in that Deanery.

4. The Peculiar of the Rector of Cliffe in the Diocese of Rochester, covered the parish of Cliffe only.

5. The Episcopal Consistory and Archdeaconry Court of Rochester that covered the parishes in that Archdeaconry.

> Cal. of Wills, 1440-1561 Kent Arch. Soc. Vol. 9. [Kent 8 Vol. 9]

6. The Peculiar Court of Wingham existed 1471-1546 and covered five parishes.

All the above records are at the County Record Office, Maidstone. Many of the contents of this office are listed in *Archaeologica Cantiana*, Vols. 66, 68. [Kent Pub. A Vols. 66, 68.]

> Sede Vacante Wills, 997-1559. Kent Arch. Soc., Vol. 3. [Kent. 8. Vol. 3.]
> Some early 13th-15th century Wills, Arch. Cant. Vols. 11, 46. [Kent Pub. A Vols. 11, 46.]
> Notes from some 15th-16th century Wills Arch. Cant. Vols. 28, 30-32, 34-47, 49-51. [Kent Pub. A Vols. as above.]

Nonconformists: There are registers of one hundred and fourteen Nonconformist Chapels at the General Register Office, Somerset House, London. Consideration should also be given to the London list of Nonconformist chapels which lists some of the County Kent chapels as being in the metropolis of London.

Publications: The following publications are of interest:

1. *Archaeologia Cantiana* being Transactions of the Kent Archaeological Society.

2. The same Society has also published *Kent Records.* Vol. 2 of this series gives accurate details of many of the records of the county as at that date.

3. *Guide to the Kent County Archives Offices, Maidstone, 1958.* [KENT. 20.]

Cathedral Archives: There are at Canterbury, about 300 volumes of records of Church Courts with a card index 1590-1620. Most of the volumes from about 1580 onwards contain an index to the names of parties involved in matters which come under the jurisdiction of the ecclesiastical authorities.

LANCASHIRE   LANCASHIRE

a maritime and industrial county in the north-west of England.

(For maps, see pages 358-361)

Area: 1831 square miles.   *Population:* 1,355,800.

Ancient Parishes: 211, nine of which are in Manchester, thirteen in Liverpool, three in Lancaster, three in Bolton-le-Moors, two in Salford, and two in Oldham.

County Town: The historic county town is Lancaster, but the administrative county town is Preston where the Lancashire County Record Office is situated.

Main Occupations: Agriculture, spinning, weaving, production of cotton goods, coal-mining, production of steel, iron, etc., seafaring, shipbuilding, fishing, imports and exports.

Prncipal Rivers: Mersey, Ribble, Irwell, Douglas, Line, Wyer, Leven, Crake and Dudden. The River Mersey gives its name to Merseyside, an important industrial and shipping area.

Ecclesiastically, the county was anciently divided between two large areas known as the Archdeaconry of Richmond and the Archdeaconry of Chester, with the River Ribble as a natural boundary between them.

1. The Archdeaconry of Richmond contained Lancashire north of the River Ribble. It was in the Diocese of York, Province of York until 1541 when it became part of the Diocese of Chester which was almost immediately transferred to the Province of York.

2. The Archdeaconry of Chester contained that part of Lancashire south of the River Ribble, and it was in the Diocese of Lichfield, Province of Canterbury until 1541. In that year the new Diocese of Chester was created by uniting the Archdeaconries of Chester and Richmond. In the same year, the Diocese of Chester was transferred to the Province of York. Thus, since 1541, the Archdeaconry of Chester has been in the Diocese of Chester, Povince of York.

In 1847 the parishes of Little Mitton, Hurst Green and Thornton-in-Lonsdale were transferred to the Diocese of Ripon, and in 1856

nine parishes in the north of Lancashire were transferred to the Diocese of Carlisle. For additional information see the *Victoria History
of the County of Lancaster*, Vol. 2. The county was further divided
by the creation of the Diocese of Manchester in 1847, the Diocese
of Liverpool in 1880, and the Diocese of Blackburn in the early
1900s.

Parish Registers: Over one hundred volumes of parish registers have
been printed. Others are available in manuscript form in the libraries
at Manchester, Liverpool and Rochdale. A number of original parish
registers are at the Lancashire Record Office, Preston. The Genealogical Society, Salt Lake City, Utah, has additional microfilm and manuscript copies of a number of other parish registers from this county.

Boyd's *Lancashire Marriage Index* includes 170 parishes and
chapelries for varying periods.

Bishop's Transcripts: All Bishop's Transcripts, both for the Lancashire
parishes in the Archdeaconry of Richmond (Western Deaneries)
and the Archdeaconry of Chester, are kept at the Lancashire Record
Office, Preston. They extend from about 1600 to 1840, and are a
fairly good series. Those for the Archdeaconry of Chester usually
being more complete than those for the Archdeaconry of Richmond.
The Bishop's Transcripts for the Peculiar of the Dean and Chapter of
York are at the Borthwick Institute, St. Anthony's Hall, York.

Marriage Licenses: Those for the Archdeaconry of Chester are at the
Diocesan Registry, Chester. Act Books commence 1606, but the
bonds do not commence until 1661.

> 1606-1632, 1639-1644, 1661-1719, Lancs. & Chesh. Rec. Soc., Vols.
> 53, 56, 57, 61, 65, 69, 73, 77, 82, 85, 97, 101. [Chesh. 1, Vols. as
> above.]

Those for the Archdeaconry of Richmond (Western Deaneries)
are at the Lancashire Record Office, Preston, and have been microfilmed 1745-1799.

> 1648-1745, Lancs. & Chesh. Rec. Soc., Vols. 74, 75, 80, 81, 83, 100.
> [Chesh. 1, Vols. as above.]

There is a separate series of marriage license records 1613-1822,
relating to the Archdeaconry of Richmond (Eastern Deaneries) at the
Archives Department, Central Library, Leeds, 1, Yorks. These may
contain references to Lancashire residents. Those for the Dean and
Chapter of York are at the Borthwick Institute, St. Anthony's Hall,
York.

Probate Records: The following courts were in use:

1. The Episcopal Consistory Court of Chester, in theory covered the
   whole diocese, but in practice it covered those parishes south of
   the River Ribble and within the Archdeaconry of Chester. The
   court functioned through two divisions as follows:
   (a) If the estate was valued at more than forty pounds sterling,
   the grant was in the Bishop's court, and the records are
   known as "SUPRA."
   > Index Wills and Inv., 1545-1650, and 1660-1820, Lancs. & Chesh.
   > Rec. Soc., Vol.s 2, 4, 15, 18, 20, 22, 25, 37, 38, 44, 45, 62
   > 63, 78, 79. [Chesh. 1, Vols. as above.]

Index of P.C.C. Wills, 1650-1660, ibid, Vol. 4. [Chesh. 1, Vol. 4.] Abstracts of some Wills and Inv. 1572-1696, Pub. Chetham Soc., New Series, Vol. 3. [Lancs. Pub. B., N.S., Vol. 3.] Wills and Inv. (early dates, abstracts), Pub. Chetham Soc., 1st Series, Vols. 33, 51, and 54. Abstracts of some Wills and Inv. 1477-1746, and appendix of abstracts of Wills now lost. Pub. Chetham Soc., New Series, Vol. 3. [Lancs. Pub. B,, N.S., Vol. 3.] Abstracts of some Wills not now found in any registry, 1301-1752. Lancs. & Chesh. Rec. Soc., Vol. 30. [Chesh. 1, Vol. 30.]

(b) If the estate was valued at less than forty pounds sterling, the grant was made by the local rural dean in the deanery concerned, the records were then sent to Chester, and are known as "INFRA."

Index Wills and Inv., 1590-1650, 1660-1756, 1777-1820, Lancs. & Chesh. Rec. Soc., Vols. 15, 18, 20, 22, 25, 38, 44, 45, 52, 62, 63, 78, 79. [Chesh. 1, Vols. as above.]

The Lancashire Wills, Admons., and Inventories in items (a) and (b), and for which grants were made at Chester, have been separated from the main series and are now at the Lancashire Record Office, Preston.

2. The Commissary Court of the Archdeaconry of Richmond (Western Deaneries), covered most parishes north of the River Ribble. The Lancashire rural deaneries within the archdeaconry were Lonsdale, Kendal, Furness and Amounderness.

Index to Wills, etc. proved in the Lancashire Deaneries only, 1457-1858, Lancs. & Chesh. Rec. Soc., Vols. 10, 13, 23, 66, 99, 105. [Chesh. 1, Vols. as above.] Lists of Abstracts, at British Museum, 1531-1652, ibid., Vols., 10, 13. [Chesh. 1, Vols. 10, 13.] Abstracts of some Wills, proved at Richmond and York, 1542-1649, Pub. Chetham Soc., New Series, Vol. 28. [Lancs. Pub. B., N.S. Vol. 28.] Abstracts of some Wills and Inv., 1458-1579, Pub. Surtees Soc., Vol. 26. [Eng. Pub. F., Vol. 26.]

3. The Court of the Manor of Halton, covered that parish.

List of Wills, 1615-1812, Lancs. & Chesh. Rec. Soc., Vols., 23, 66. [Chesh. 1, Vols. 23, 66.] ،

4. The Court of the Manor of Nether Kellett, and the Court of the Manor of Slyne-with-Hart, covered those places. The records of Nether-Kellett were destroyed, and the whereabouts of the records of Slyne-with-Hart is unknown.

The records mentioned in items 2 and 3 above are at the Lancashire Record Office, Preston.

5. The Peculiar Court of the Dean and Chapter of York covered the parish of Kirkby-Ireleth, and included the places named Broughton-in-Furness, Dunnerdale, Seathwaite, and Woodland-with-Heathwaite. These records are at the Borthwick Institute, St. Anthony's Hall, York.

List of Wills, 1321-1724, Yorks. Arch. & Topo. Assoc., Vols. 38, 60. [Yorks. 7, Vols. 38, 60.]

6. The Commissary Court of the Archdeaconry of Richmond (Eastern Deaneries), had a registry at Richmond, Yorkshire, and in special cases, grants were made for estates in the Western Dean-

eries mentioned in item 2 above. Records of all Lancashire Wills and Admons., that received grants at Richmond (in the Eastern Deaneries) are at the Archives Department, Central Library, Leeds, 1, Yorkshire.

In addition to the above courts, the following records are also available:

1. A miscellaneous collection, known as "Wills, Inventories, Admon. Bonds, and Depositions in Testamentary Suits, 1487-1800," being records formerly kept at the Diocesan Registry, Chester. They were probably concerned with some testamentary disputes, and became disconnected with the probate records of the Episcopal Consistory Court of Chester (item 1 above). The Lancashire portion of these documents has been transferred to the Lancashire Record Office, Preston.

   Index . . . Testamentary Suits, 1487-1800, Lancs. and Ches. Rec. Soc., Vols. 33, 43, 52. [Chesh. 1, Vols. 33, 43, 52.]

2. A list of Wills, 1359-1858, relating to Lancashire which are not recorded in the printed indexes of either the Wills at Chester or the Wills at Richmond, and which are now found among records deposited in the Lancashire Record Office, is found in the Publications of the Record Society of Lancs. & Chesh., Vol. 105. [Chesh. 1, Vol. 105.] These are drawn from three sources:

   (a) Deposited Collections of private and family muniments.
   (b) Wills of Roman Catholics enrolled in the county records since 1717.
   (c) Wills found in recent years proved at Chester but not included in the printed calendars.

3. A typescript at Rochdale Public Library gives abstracts from about 2,400 Wills and Admons. relating to persons with Rochdale connections.

When the Diocese of Manchester was formed in 1847 there was no change in that area in the probate jurisdictions. When several parishes were transferred in 1847 to the Diocese of Ripon, probate records for those parishes since then might be found among the records of the Archdeaconry of Richmond (Eastern Deaneries). In the case of the several parishes transferred in 1856 from the Archdeaconry of Richmond to the Diocese of Carlisle, it is possible some estates might have been proved after that time at Carlisle, Cumberland.

Nonconformist Registers: Records of two hundred and fifty-three Nonconformist chapels are at the General Register Office, Somerset House, London. See also *The Genealogists' Atlas of Lancashire.*

Publications: The following publications are of interest:

1. *Guide to the Lancashire Record Office* (1948) [Lancs. Pub. D. No. 2.]
2. *Transactions* of the Historic Society of Lancashire and Cheshire.
3. *Publications* of the Record Society for the Publishing of Original Documents relating to Lancashire and Cheshire.
4. *Transactions* of the Lancashire and Cheshire Antiquarian Society.
5. *Publications* of the Chetham Society.

6. *Reference Library, Subject Catalogue,* (Genealogy), Manchester Public Libraries, Parts 1-3. [Lancs. Mli., Parts 1,2,3.]

Attention is drawn to Volume 76 of the *Publications* of the Record Society of Lancashire and Cheshire which carries an index of the names of persons mentioned on tombstones in 430 *printed* books in the Liverpool and Birkenhead libraries. A manuscript collection known as "Liverpool Epitaphs" is to be found in the Public Library at Liver-pool. A microfilm copy of this valuable collection is also available at the Genealogical Society, Salt Lake City, Utah.

The following manuscript collections of pedigrees, parish register extracts, etc. in the Manchester Public Library have been microfilmed for the Genealogical Society, Salt Lake City:

1. The John Owen Manuscripts. There are printed lists describing this collection at the Manchester Public Library and the Library of the Genealogical Society, Salt Lake City, Utah.
2. The Giles Shaw Manuscripts.
3. The H. T. Crofton Manuscripts.
4. The William Farrer Manuscripts.

Maps:

1. The publication *Genealogists Atlas of Lancashire* by J. P. Smith, (Liverpool: 1930), is an excellent guide as it shows the limits of the townships, chapelries and parishes and is an easy reference to trace the proximity of surrounding parishes and places. The book also contains a list of all pre-1813 Non-parochial registers and a fairly comprehensive list of seventy Roman Catholic chapels which have registers. This book, unfortunately, does not indicate the boundaries of the deaneries within the archdeaconries situated in Lancashire. [Lancs. 10.]
2. The *Map of the Diocese of Chester Divided into Deanries, etc.,* published in the year 1750, shows the parishes and rural deaneries in both Archdeaconries and the whole of the Diocese of Chester. The original is at the County Record Office and a copy is available at the Genealogical Society in Salt Lake City, Utah.
3. The maps accompanying this chapter show (a) a simplified ver-sion of the county showing parish boundaries and only those places with parish registers, and (b) the county as it appears in Lewis' *Topographical Dictionaries* in the 1840's.

LEICESTERSHIRE   LEICESTERSHIRE

(pronounced "Lestershire") — an inland county of England.

(*For map, see pages 362-3*)

Area: 804 square miles.   *Population*: 197,000.

Ancient Parishes: 256, six of which are in the town of Leicester.

County Town: Leicester. The County Record Office is at New Walk, Leicester, but the city of Leicester Archives Dept. is at the Leicester Museum, New Walk.

Main Occupations: Agriculture, coal-mining and the manufacture of hosiery and lace.

Principal Rivers: Soar, Wreke.

Ecclesiastically, the county formed the Archdeaconry of Leicester in the Diocese of Lincoln from the twelfth century until 1837 when it was transferred to the Diocese of Peterboro. It has been included in the Diocese of Leicester since the latter was formed in 1926.

Parish Registers: A number of the marriage registers of certain parishes have been printed for periods prior to 1813. Very few have been printed completely to include christenings, marriages and burials. The original registers of a few parishes have been deposited in the County Record Office.

Bishop's Transcripts: These are at the Archives Dept., Leicester Museum, New Walk, and cover periods from 1558 up to the 1840's and occasionally to as late as 1870. Many years are missing in these transcripts, particularly for periods prior to 1700. A full printed list of the years extant has been prepared by the Archives Department of the Leicester Museum, *Handlist of Leicestershire Parish Register Transcripts*, (1953).

Marriage Licenses: These are at the City of Leicester Archives Dept. for 1570-1891.

> 1570-1729. Index Library, British Rec. Soc. [Eng. Pub. AB Vol. 38.]

Probate Records: The following courts were in use:

1. The Archdeaconry Court of Leicester covered most of the parishes in the county.

   > Cal. of Wills and Admons. 1495-1750. Index Library, British Rec. Soc. Vols. 27, 51. [Eng. Pub. AB Vols. 27, 51.]
   > Unproved Wills and Admons to 1801. Index Library, British Rec. Soc. Vol. 27. [Eng. Pub. AB Vol. 27.]
   > List of uncalendared Wills 1489-1538. Pub. Leics. Arch. Soc. [Leics. 13.]

2. The Prebendal Court of St. Margaret's, Leicester, covered part of that town, and the chapelry of Knighton.

3. The Court of the Manor of Rothley covered that parish.

4. The Court of the Manor of Evington covered that parish.

5. The Court of the Peculiar of Groby covered that parish.

   > (for items 2, 3, 4 and 5), Cal. of Wills and Admons 1495-1750. Index Library, British Rec. Soc. Vols. 27, 51. [Eng. Pub. AB Vols. 27, 51.]

   All the probate records mentioned above are at the County Record Office, New Walk, Leicester.

6. The Episcopal Consistory Court of Lincoln that covered the whole diocese contains some early Wills and Admons. for estates in Leicestershire. See under "Lincolnshire" for details.

   There are forty-seven volumes of Wills and Admons. containing genealogical abstracts of probate records formerly kept at the Leicester District Probate Registry, 1563-1591, 1605-1649, and 1660-1800. These cover some 50,000 documents, and are at the City Archives Department, Leicester Museum.

Nonconformists: There are records of fifty-five Nonconformist chapels at the General Register Office, London.

Publications: The following publications are of interest:

1. *Handlist of Records of Leicester Archdeaconry.* (1954)
2. *Publications* of the Leicestershire Architectural and Archaeological Society.
3. *Leicester and Rutland Notes and Queries.*
4. *Records of the Borough of Leicester.*

LINCOLNSHIRE   LINCOLNSHIRE

a maritime county on the east coast of England.

(For map, see pages 364-5)

Area: 2,748 square miles.   *Population:* 317,400.

Ancient Parishes: 627, fifteen of which are in the City of Lincoln and five in the town of Stamford.

County Town: For administrative purposes Lincolnshire is divided into three separate civil jurisdictions:

1. Parts of Holland with the County Hall at Boston.
2. Parts of Kesteven with County Offices at Sleaford.
3. Parts of Lindsey with the County Offices at Lincoln.

Lincoln is the ancient and historic county town. The record office of the Lincolnshire Archives Committee, for both the County of Lincoln and the Diocese of Lincoln, is at Exchequer Gate, Lincoln.

Main Occupations: Agriculture and fishing.

Principal Rivers: Humber, Trent, Wellard, Witham, Archolme.

Ecclesiastically, the county formed the Archdeaconries of Lincoln and Stow, both in the Diocese of Lincoln, Province of Canterbury. The Diocese of Lincoln is one of the *ancient* ecclesiastical areas of England, at one time covering a much greater part of the country than it does at present.

Parish Registers: Very few have been printed but a number of the original parish registers are now in the care of the Lincolnshire Archives Committee at the Foster Library, Lincoln.

Bishop's Transcripts: The Bishop's Transcripts are a good series and are kept at the Library of the Lincolnshire Archives Committee in Lincoln. They range from 1598 to around 1840 but there are some gaps.

Marriage Licenses: These are in the care of the Lincolnshire Archives Committee, Lincoln.

> Abstracts of Marr. Allegation Books of Bishop of Lincoln, 1598-1628, A. Gibbons, Lincoln Marriage Licenses. [Lincs. L le.] and 1569-1670 The Northern Genealogist. [Eng. Pub. R Vols. 1-6.]

Probate Records: The following courts were in use:

1. The Episcopal Consistory Court and the Episcopal Commissary Court for the Archdeaconry of Lincoln and the Court of the Archdeacon covered about 520 parishes in that Archdeaconry. These were three separate courts having concurrent jurisdiction.

Cal. of Wills and Admons. of the Episcopal Registry of the old Diocese of Lincoln, 1320-1588 and the Consistory Court 1506-1652. Index Library, British Rec. Soc. Vols. 28, 41, 52, 57. [Eng. Pub. AB Vols. as above.]

Abstracts of all Wills and Admons. proved in the old Diocese of Lincoln 1280-1547. Early Lincoln Wills. [Lincs. 16.]

Abstracts of some Lincs. Wills 1500-1617 Lincolnshire Wills. [Lincs. 4.]

2. The Archdeaconry Court of Stow (merged with the Consistory Court in 1834) covered all but about fourteen parishes in that Archdeaconry.

Cal. of Wills and Admons. 1530-1699, Index Library, British Rec. Soc. Vols. 28, 41, 52, 57. [Eng. Pub. AB Vols. as above.]

3. Court of the Dean and Chapter of Lincoln covered 25 parishes. It was merged with the Consistory Court in 1834.

Cal. of Wills and Admons. 1534-1834, Index Library, British Rec. Soc. Vols. 28, 41, 52, 57. [Eng. Pub. AB Vols. as above.]

4. Courts of the Prebends of Lincoln covered ten parishes, not all of them in the county.

Cal. of Wills and Admons. of the Prebendaries of Biggleswade 1639-1740; Buckden 1691-1749; Caistor 1636-1833, Corringham 1632-1833; Empingham 1669-1744; Gretton 1657-1832; Heydour 1669-1810; Ketton 1666-1677; Kirton in Lindsey 1566-1834; Liddington 1668-1810; Louth 1612-1879; Nassington 1702-1744; Bishop Norton 1613-1814; Sleaford 1610-1834; Stow in Lindsey 1610-1833; Long Stow 1736-1744. Index Library, British Rec. Soc. [Eng. Pub. AB Vols. 28, 41, 52, 57.]

5. Peculiar Courts of Kirton in Lindsey and the Manor of Kirkstead covered seven parishes.

Cal. of Wills and Admons. 1636-1857 The Northern Genealogist. [Eng. Pub. R Vols. 1, 2.]

All the above records are in the care of the Lincolnshire Archives Committee, Exchequer Gate, Lincoln.

The Diocesan Record Office, Lincoln, has a few early copy Wills, a number of Inventories, Tuition Bonds, renunciation of probates and other court books.

Also available in print are the following:

Abstracts of some Wills proved P.C.C. 1558-1579. The Northern Genealogist, Vols. 1-6. [Eng. Pub. R Vols. 1-6.]

Abstracts of Lincs. Wills proved P.C.C. 1653-1660 Lincs. Notes and Queries, Vols. 18-21.

Nonconformists: There are records of sixty-two Nonconformist chapels at the General Register Office, London.

Publications: The following publications are of interest:
1. *The Lincolnshire Historian.*
2. *Lincolnshire Notes and Queries.*
3. *Publications* of the Lincolnshire Record Society.
4. *A Handlist of the Records of the Bishop of Lincoln and of the Archdeacons of Lincoln and Stow,* by Kathleen Major. 1953. [Lincs. L4a.]
5. *Archivists' Reports.* (Lincolnshire Archives Committee, since 1948.) [Lincs. 13.]

LONDON

The Metropolis of the United Kingdom, the seat of government, and principal port, being both city and county. It was not, however, until 1888 that the County of London, comprising twenty-eight boroughs (towns), and including the Cities of London and Westminster, was formed from parts of the counties of Kent, Middlesex and Surrey.

(For map, see pages 366-368)

Area: 117 square miles.

Population:

London within the Walls	57,695
London without the Walls	67,878
City and Liberties of Westminster	202,080
Total for the city	327,653
Total for the Metropolis	1,474,069

This figure includes persons living in a number of parishes adjoining the City, but not including all of the twenty-eight boroughs which since 1889 have constituted the County of London.

Main Occupations: Imports, exports, manufactories, administrative.

Ancient Parishes:

London within the Walls	97
London without the Walls	11
City and Liberty of Westminster	10
Borough of Southwark	6
Parishes adjacent to the City	6
	130

Southwark is technically in Surrey, but the total number of parishes in the *Metropolis,* which includes some parishes technically in nearby counties, was 154.

County Hall: at Westminster Bridge, London S.E.1. where is situated the London County Council Record Office. There is a City of London Record Office at the Guildhall, London, E.C.

Ecclesiastically, the City of London formed an archdeaconry in the Diocese of London, and the City of Westminster was in that diocese until 1540, when the Diocese of Westminster was formed. In 1550, however, the latter diocese was abolished, and Westminster reverted to the Archdeaconry of Middlesex, Diocese of London. There were a number of peculiar jurisdictions, as follows:

The Archbishop of Canterbury's Peculiar Deanery of the Arches, (London), covered thirteen parishes in the City of London, and the Dean and Chapter of St. Paul's Cathedral claimed jurisdiction within several parishes. The Dean and Chapter of Westminster claimed jurisdiction within several parishes in Westminster.

Until the Great Fire of London in 1668, there were 108 parish churches in the City of London, but after the rebuilding, this number was reduced to seventy-three.

Southwark, Surrey, on the south bank of the River Thames, was in the Diocese of London from 1846 to 1877. This is mentioned in full under Surrey.

Parish Registers: A number have been printed. Others, such as trans-cript copies and original registers are in various repositories such as the Guildhall Library, the General Register Office, Lambeth Palace and the London County Council Record Office. Percival Boyd's *London and Middlesex Marriage Index*, involving many thousands of marriages, covers a number of parishes for varying periods.

Bishop's Transcripts: These, unfortunately, are almost non-existent. This also applies to Essex and Middlesex. The few that remain are at the Guildhall Library, City of London E.C.2. Those for the Peculiars of the Arches (London), Shoreham (Kent), and Croydon (Surrey) covering around 1750-1800 are at Lambeth Palace Library, London, S.E.1, but they cover only a few parishes in the three Peculiars, and are not available for inspection.

Marriage Licenses: These could be granted by:

1. The Bishop of London, commence in 1520.
   1597-1700, Index Library, British Rec. Soc. Vols 62, 66. [Eng. Pub. AB Vols. 62, 66.] Extracts only 1520-1828, Pub. Harl. Soc. Vols. 25, 26. [Eng. Pub. AC Vols. 25, 26.]

2. The Office of the Vicar-General of the Archbishop of Canterbury, commence in 1660.
   Marr. Lic. from Vicar-General's Office, 1660-1694, Harleian Soc., Vols. 23, 30, 31, 34. [Eng. Pub. A.C. as above.]

3. The Faculty Office of the Archbishop of Canterbury, commence in 1632.
   1632-1714 Index Library, British Rec. Soc. Vols. 33. [Eng. Pub. AB Vol. 33.] Extracts only 1543-1869 Pub. Harl. Soc. Vol 24. [Eng. Pub. AC Vol. 24.]

4. The Dean and Chapter of Westminster.
   Marr. Lic. from Act Books of Dean and Chapter of Westminster, 1558-1678 with a few to 1699, Harleian Soc. Vol. 23. [Eng. Pub. A.C. Vol. 23.]

   The Calendars (Act Books) for these marriage licenses are at the Faculty Office, No. 1, The Sanctuary, Westminster, London, S.W.1. The allegations and bonds for the Bishop of London are at the Guild-hall Library in the City of London, and those for the Office of the Vicar-General (from 1660) and the Faculty Office (1632-1668 and 1696-1929) are at Lambeth Palace Library, London, S.E.1.

5. Those for the Peculiars of the Arches (London), Shoreham (Kent) and Croydon (Surrey), covering Allegations 1707-1802 and Bonds 1684-1804, are at Lambeth Palace Library, London, S.E.1.

6. There is a series of marriage licenses for the Bishop of London's Consistory Court, 1665-1853, kept at the Essex Record Office, Chelmsford, Essex. These are detailed under "Essex."

Probate Records: The following courts were in use:

1. The Archdeaconry Court of London covered about fifty parishes. The records are at the Guildhall Library, the City of London, E.C.2.

2. The Archdeaconry Court of Middlesex covered twenty-seven London and Middlesex parishes. The records are at the Middlesex County Record Office, London S.W.1.

3. The Episcopal Consistory Court of London covered the whole Diocese. The records are at the London County Council Record Office, Westminster Bridge, London, S.E.

4. The Commissary Court of London, London Division, covered about fifty parishes. The records are at the Guildhall Library of the City of London.

5. The Court of Husting being an early court of the Corporation of the City of London. The records are at the City of London Record Office, Guildhall.

> Cal. of Wills and Abstracts, 1258-1688. Library Comm. Corp. of City of London. [London 21.]

6. The Peculiar Court of the Dean and Chapter of St. Paul's, London, covered twelve London and Middlesex parishes. The records are at the Principal Probate Registry, Somerset House, London, but plans for their transfer are under consideration.

7. The Royal Peculiar of the Dean and Chapter of Westminster, covered part of Westminster. They are kept at the City of Westminster Public Library, Buckingham Palace Road, London, S.W.1. There are a few Wills from this court kept in the Muniment Room of Westminster Abbey Library.

> Indexes . . . Testamentary Records of Westminster, by A. M. BURKE, (London, 1913), covers Dean and Chapter of Westminster 1504-1700, Westminster Wills in the Consistory of London 1540-1556, and Muniments at Westminster Abbey 1228-1700. [London Wld.]

8. The Deanery of the Arches, a Peculiar Court of the Archbishop of Canterbury, covered thirteen parishes in the City of London. The records, consisting of Act Books and Registers 1664-1780, 1832 and 1841, and Wills 1620-1766, and Administrations, 1660-1760, are at Lambeth Palace Library, London, S.E.1.

9. The Royal Peculiar Court of St. Katherine-by-the-Tower, covered that parish in the City of London. The records 1689-1775, are at the Guildhall Library of the City of London, E.C.

10. The Court of the Arches of Canterbury, was a court of appeal for the whole Province, excepting the Royal and Archbishop's Peculiars. The records are deposited at Lambeth Palace Library, London, S.E.1, and cover the period 1554-1881. There is an account of them in *Journal of Ecclesiastical History,* Vol. 19. This court should not be confused with the records of the Archbishop of Canterbury's *Ordinary Jurisdiction* in his Peculiar Court of the Deanery of the Arches, London, mentioned in item 8 above. (See I. J. Churchill, *Canterbury Administration* (London, 1933), Vol. 1, pp. 62-78).

11. The Court of the Delegates of England was a court of Appeal from the courts of the provinces and from Peculiar Courts.

> List of Wills and Admons., 1643-1857. The Genealogist, (London). New Series, Vols. 11, 12, and 17. [Eng. Pub. AF., N.S., Vols 11, 12, 17.]

The Muniment Books are at the Principal Probate Registry, Somerset House, London, but the processes are in the Public Record Office, Chancery Lane, London.

12. Miscellaneous Records at Lambeth Palace Library, London. These include probate records extending from about 1313 to 1644, a large portion of which are "Vacancy Wills."

> Cal. of Wills and Admons., (Lambeth), The Genealogist, (London), Old Series, Vols. 5, 6, and 7, and the New Series, Vol. 1. [Eng. Pub. AF., O.S., Vols. 5, 6, 7, and N.S., Vol. 1.]

13. The Prerogative Court of the Archbishop of Canterbury, formerly situated at Doctor's Commons, City of London, covering the whole Province of Canterbury, contains many probate records relating to citizens of London and its immediate localities. These records are at the Principal Probate Registry, Somerset House, London. During Vacancies in the See of London, (i.e., during the time when there was no Bishop of London), the P.C.C. claimed the right of probate. If both the Archbishopric of Canterbury and the Bishopric of London were vacant, then the Dean and Chapter's Court of Canterbury claimed jurisdiction. The printed Calendars for the P.C.C. are listed on page 87.

At the Public Record Office, Chancery Lane, London, there are probate records mixed in with other records, such as Manor Court Rolls. A few items have been indexed from these.

> Wills enrolled on the Close Rolls and the Recovery Rolls, The Genealogist, (London), New Series, Vols. 1, 2, and 3. [Eng. Pub. AF. N.S., Vols. 1, 2, 3,] These indexes are very incomplete.

There are also many probate records for soldiers and sailors, proved in various courts, but filed at the Public Record Office among the "Casualty Returns." These are mentioned in Chapter 7.

For purposes of granting probates, the Borough of Southwark came under the jurisdiction of Surrey, which see.

Nonconformist Registers: There are records of one hundred and seventy-two chapels at the General Register Office, Somerset House, London. Many of these Nonconformist chapels are not in the City itself but are associated with the Metropolis.

Publications: The following publications are of interest:

1. The London and Middlesex Archaeological Society.

2. Publications of the Harleian Society.

> Percival Boyd also made an Index to a Few of the Burials in London Parishes, 1538-1853, and Pedigrees of about 59,000 London Citizens, 1600-1800. There is also a printed Return of [362] Burial Grounds in the County of London, published in 1895. [Lond. 82.] There is an Index to births, deaths, and marriages appearing in the Times of London, 1785-1933. This has been microfilmed for the Genealogical Society, Salt Lake City.

MIDDLESEX   MIDDLESEX

An inland county, and the second smallest county in England. The City of London and the City of Westminster, adjoining Middlesex, have their own independent jurisdiction. Since 1888 southern portions of the county, close to and including the cities of London and West-minster, have been within the Administrative County of London.

(*For map, see page* 370-1)

Area: 282 square miles.

Population: 127,637 not including London enumeration districts.

Ancient Parishes: 67

County Town: There is really no county town. For administrative purposes, Middlesex has County Offices at The Guildhall, West-minster, London, S.W.1. The Middlesex County Record Office is at Queen Anne's Gate Buildings, Dartmouth Street, Westminster, Lon-don, S.W. The Middlesex Registry of Deeds (Land Registry), in-dexes 1709-1837, are at the Middlesex County Record Office, but the registers 1709-1938, are at the L.C.C. County Record Office, Westminster Bridge, London, S.E.

Main Occuptaions: Agriculture and a wide variety of manufactures.

Principal Rivers: Thames, Lea, Coln, Brent.

Ecclesiastically, the county is in the Archdeaconry of Middlesex, Dio-cese of London, Province of Canterbury. See also under "London."

Parish Registers: Some of the marriage registers of certain parishes have been printed for varying periods prior to 1837. These, and the mar-riage registers of many parishes in the Cities of London and West-minster, were used by Boyd in compiling the *London and Middlesex Marriage Index.* There are a few original parish registers deposited at the L.C.C. County Record Office, the Middlesex County Record Office, and the Westminster City Library.

Bishop's Transcripts: Unfortunately these are almost non-existent. See under "London" for mention of those that are at the Guildhall Library of the City of London, E.C.2.

Marriage Licenses: As these could be granted by the same ecclesiastical officials as for London, see under "London" for details.

Probate Records: The following courts were in use:

1. The Archdeaconry Court of Middlesex covered 27 parishes. The records are at the Middlesex County Record Office, West-minster, London, S.W.1.
2. The Commissary Court of London, London Division, covered 44 parishes and the records are at the Guildhall Library of the City of London, E.C.
3. The Peculiar Court of the Archbishop of Canterbury in the Dean-ery of Croydon covered four parishes in Middlesex. The registers of Wills and the Act Books, 1629-1821 and 1841, are at Lambeth Palace Library, London, S.E.1. The bundles of original Wills and Admons., are at Kent County Record Office, Maidstone, Kent.
4. The Peculiar Court of the Dean and Chapter of St. Paul's Cathedral covered eight parishes in Middlesex. The records are at the Principal Probate Registry, Somerset House, London, but plans to transfer them are under consideration.

5. The Royal Peculiar Court of the Dean and Chapter of Westminster covered three places in Westminster. The records are at Westminster Library, Buckingham Palace Road, London S.W.1.
6. The Episcopal Consistory Court of the Bishop of London covered the whole Diocese including all of this county. The records are at the London County Council Record Office, London S.E.1.

Nonconformists: There are records of twenty-eight Nonconformist chapels at the General Register Office, Somerset House, London. A check should also be made in the list of such chapels in London.

Publications: The following publications are of interest:
1. *Transactions* of the London and Middlesex Archaeological Society.
2. *Middlesex and Herts. Notes and Queries.*
3. *Middlesex County Records.*

MERIONETHSHIRE   MERIONETHSHIRE

(Meirionydd or Sir Feirionydd) — a maritime county in North Wales.

(*For map, see page* 369)

Area: 670 square miles.   *Population*: 35,315.

Ancient Parishes: 34.

County Town: Bala, but the County Offices are at Penarlag, Dolgelley,

Main Occupations: Agriculture, mining of lead and copper, quarrying of slate, and various small manufactories.

Principal Rivers: Dee, Mawddach, Dovey.

Ecclesiastically, the county was partly in the Archdeaconry of Merioneth, Diocese of Bangor, and partly in the Archdeaconry and Diocese of St. Asaph. It was in the Province of Canterbury until 1920 when the Province of Wales was created.

Parish Registers: None have been printed or transcribed.

Bishop's Transcripts: These are at the National Library of Wales, Aberystwyth, and range from around 1660 to 1870, but have many gaps.

Marriage Licenses: These are at the National Library of Wales for 1616-1900 for the Diocese of St. Asaph; and 1757-1900 for the Diocese of Bangor.

Probate Records: The following courts covered the county, the records of which are at the National Library of Wales:
1. The Episcopal Consistory Court of St. Asaph.
2. The Episcopal Consistory Court of Bangor.

Nonconformist Registers: There are records of fifty-six Nonconformist chapels at The General Register Office, Somerset House, London. There may be others in local custody, libraries, etc.

Publications: The following publications are of interest:
1. *Publications of the Merioneth Historical and Record Society.*
2. *A List of Merioneth Manuscripts . . . in the National Library of Wales.*

MONMOUTHSHIRE

(Sir Fynwy) — a maritime county in England. Since its creation in 1536, although originally in Wales, it has, for purposes of administration, been accounted within England.

(For map, see page 372)

Area: 498 square miles.   *Population:* 98,126.

Ancient Parishes: 128.

County Town: Monmouth, but the County Hall and County Record Office are in Newport.

Main Occupations: Agriculture, mining of coal, quarrying of limestone, and the manufacturing of iron and steel products.

Principal Rivers: Severn, Wye, Usk, Rhymni.

Ecclesiastically, the county was mostly in the Arch-deaconry of Monmouth and Diocese of Llandaff, except that the parishes of Welsh Bicknor, Newton-Dixton, and St. Mary Monmouth, were in the Archdeaconry and Diocese of Hereford; and Old-castle, Llanthony Abbey and Cwmyoy were in the Archdeaconry of Brecon and Diocese of St. David's. In 1835-1836 the whole of the county was placed in the Diocese of Llandaff. Until 1920 it was in the Province of Canterbury when it became part of the Province of Wales. In 1921 it was formed into the Diocese of Monmouth.

Parish Registers: A few have been printed, and a few others have been transcribed. There are a number of transcript copies, and some of extracts only, in the Bradney Manuscripts at the National Library of Wales. These manuscripts have been microfilmed by the Genealogi-cal Society, Salt Lake City. [F. MONM.2., Parts 1 to 27.]

Bishop's Transcripts: These are at the National Library of Wales for the Diocese of Llandaff, and the Archdeaconry of Brecon and Dio-cese of St. David's. They range from around 1660 to 1870, but have many gaps. Those for the Diocese of Hereford are at the Diocesan Registry, Hereford.

Marriage Licenses: These are at the National Library of Wales for 1665-1900 for the Diocese of Llandaff; and 1661-1867 for the "old" Diocese of St. David's. Some marriage bonds from the St. David's Diocese have been printed 1612-1799 in *West Wales Historical Records,* Vols. 3-12. The Marriage Licenses of the Diocese of Here-ford are at the Diocesan Registry, Hereford.

Probate Records: The following courts covered the county, the records of which are at the National Library of Wales:
1. The Episcopal Consistory Court of Llandaff.
2. The Archdeaconry Court of Brecon in the Diocese of St. David's.
3. The Episcopal Consistory Court of Hereford.

Nonconformist Registers: There are records of fifty-three Nonconformist chapels at The General Register Office, Somerset House, London. There may be others in local custody, libraries, etc.

Publications: The following publications are of interest:
1. S. Lewis, *A Topographical Dictionary of England* (London, 1831 and 1833), 4 Vols. This must be used, 1831 and 1833 editions only, for information on ecclesiastical jurisdiction within Monmouthshire.
2. J. A. Bradney, *A History of Monmouthshire,* (London: 1904-1933). [MONM. 1.]
3. *Publications of the S. Wales and Monmouth Record Society.*
4. *A List of Monmouthshire Manuscripts . . . in the National Library of Wales* (1937).

MONTGOMERYSHIRE   MONTGOMERYSHIRE

(Trefaldwyn) — an inland county in Wales created in 1536.

(For map, see page 373)

Area: 797 square miles.   *Population*: 66,482.

Ancient Parishes: 53.

County Town: Montgomery, but the County Offices are at Welshpool.

Main Occupations: Agriculture, mining of lead and copper, quarrying of slate, and the manufacture of woollen and flannel goods.

Principal Rivers: Severn, Dovey, Wye.

Ecclesiastically, the county was partly in the Archdeaconry and Diocese of St. Asaph; partly in the Archdeaconry of Merioneth and Diocese of Bangor; two parishes were in the Archdeaconry of Brecon and Diocese of St. David's; and partly in the Archdeaconry of Salop and Diocese of Hereford. Since 1835-1836, the county has been partly in the Archdeaconry and Diocese of St. Asaph and partly in the Archdeaconry of Merioneth and Diocese of Bangor. It was in the Province of Canterbury until 1921 when it became part of the Province of Wales.

Parish Registers: A few have been transcribed.

Bishop's Transcripts: These are at the National Library of Wales for the Archdeaconry of Brecon, Diocese of St. David's, and the Diocese of Bangor and St. Asaph. They range from around 1660 to 1870, but have many gaps.
Those for the Diocese of Hereford are at the Diocesan Registry, Hereford.

Marriage Licenses: These are at the National Library of Wales for 1616-1900 for the Diocese of St. Asaph; 1757-1900 for the Diocese of Bangor; 1661-1867 for the "old" St. David's Diocese. There is a separate series for St. John and St. Mary, Brecon, 1666-1867. Those for the Diocese of Hereford are at the Diocesan Registry, Hereford.

Probate Records: The county was covered by the following courts, the records of which are at the National Library of Wales:
1. The Episcopal Consistory Court of St. Asaph.
2. The Episcopal Consistory Court of Bangor.
3. The Episcopal Consistory Court of Hereford.
4. The Archdeaconry Court of Brecon and the Episcopal Consistory Court of St. David's.

Nonconformist Registers: There are records of fifty-seven Noncon-formist chapels at The General Register Office, Somerset House, London. There may be others in local custody, libraries, etc.

Publications: The following publications are of interest:
1. *Collections Historical . . .* Montgomeryshire (Powysland Club), 1888-1942 continued since then as *The Montgomeryshire Col-lections.*
2. *A List of Montgomeryshire Manuscripts . . . in the National Li-brary of Wales.*

NORFOLK   **NORFOLK**

a maritime county of England.

(For map, see page 374-5)

Area: 2,092 square miles.   *Population*: 390,654.

Ancient Parishes: 691, thirty-nine of which are in the City of Nor-wich and three in Thetford.

County Town: Norwich.

Main Occupations: Agriculture, maritime and woven goods. Worsted cloth takes its name from one of the parishes in this county.

Principal Rivers: Greater Ouse, Lesser Ouse, Waveney, Bure, Wensum, Yare and Nar.

Ecclesiastically, the county formed the Archdeaconry of Norfolk and the Archdeaconry of Norwich, both in the Diocese of Norwich, Province of Canterbury. The parish of Emneth is in the Diocese of Ely, and there are several parishes that extend into the adjoining coun-ties or were extra-parochial, as explained in the *Victoria History of the County of Norfolk,* Volume 2.

Parish Registers: This county has the largest number of parishes in any county except Yorkshire, although its size is less than half of that of Yorkshire and its population only one third. Each small group of farms had their own church and formed a parish. The registers of these parishes are, therefore, generally small, with the population moving from parish to parish as they moved from farm to farm. In this situation, searching a number of parishes at once is the more efficient way to locate complete family groups. A number of the marriage registers from the parish registers prior to 1813 have been printed, and Boyd used these in the compiling of his *Norfolk Marriage Index* for certain periods in 146 parishes in the county. Transcript copies of parts of some parish registers are in the possession of the Norwich and Norfolk Archaeological Society at Norwich.

Bishop's Transcripts: These are in the care of the Norfolk Record Society and Central Library, Norwich. Because of neglect, transcripts for the various parishes for periods prior to 1813 have been mixed together and much work still needs to be done to make them available for efficient searching. At the moment, it is not wise to attempt to use them except as a last measure. For the period 1813-1837 the transcripts are reasonably complete and arranged for better searching.

Marriage Licenses: These are at the Central Library, Norwich.
> 1563-1787. Abstracts of some Marriage Bonds (15 notebooks by Frederick Johnson). [Manuscript 1406.]

Probate Records: The following courts were in use:
1. The Episcopal Consistory Court of Norwich covered the county during inhibition of other courts.
   > Index to Wills 1370-1603 Index Library, British Rec. Soc. Vols. 69, 73. [Eng. Pub. AB Vols. 69, 73.] 1370-1686 Norfolk Record Soc. [Norfolk 1. Vol. 16, 21, 28]
2. The Archdeaconry Court of Norwich covered about 300 parishes.
3. The Archdeaconry Court of Norfolk covered about 380 parishes.
4. The Peculiar Court of the Dean and Chapter of Norwich covered sixteen parishes in and near the City of Norwich.
5. The Episcopal Consistory of Ely (for the parish of Emneth) See under "Cambridgeshire."
   All the records in items 1 to 4 are now at the Central Library, Norwich.

Nonconformists: There are records of seventy Nonconformist chapels at the General Register Office, Somerset House, London.

Publications: The following publications are of interest:
1. The Norfolk and Norwich Archaeological Society Publications.
2. *The East Anglian,* or Notes and Queries on Suffolk, Cambridge, Essex and Norfolk.
3. *Publications* of the Norfolk Records Society.

NORTHAMPTONSHIRE   NORTHAMPTONSHIRE

an inland county in the Midlands of England.

(*For map, see page* 378-9)

Area: 1,017 square miles.   *Population*: 179,300.

Ancient Parishes: 292, four of which are in Northampton town and two in Peterboro.

County Town: For administrative and judicial purposes, Northampton- shire is divided into two separate jurisdictions:

1. The County of Northampton with its County Hall at North- ampton and a County Record Office at Delapre Abbey, Northampton.
2. The Soke of Peterborough with County Council Offices at Bridge Street, Peterborough.

Main Occupations: Agriculture and shoe-making.

Principal Rivers: Nene, Wellard, Ouse, Charwell, Avon, Leam.

Ecclesiastically, the county forms the Archdeaconry of Northampton, which was in the Diocese of Lincoln until 1541, when it became part of the Diocese of Peterborough, Province of Canterbury, except for the parishes of Gretton and Nassington which are in the Diocese of Lincoln, and Kings Sutton, a peculiar of the Dean and Chapter of Lincoln.

Parish Registers: Few have been printed. A few others, original parish registers, have been deposited at the County Record Office.

Bishop's Transcripts: These are at the County Record Office. They begin in 1706 and extend to around 1840. They are in fairly good condition.

Marriage Licenses: These are at the County Record Office, North- ampton.

Probate Records: The following courts were in use:

1. The Archdeaconry Court of Northampton covered the parishes in the deaneries of Brackley, Daventry, Higham, Northampton, Preston and Rothwell, roughly, the southern half of the county. The records are at the County Record Office, Northampton.

    Cal. of Wills, 1510-1652, Index Library, British Rec. Soc. Vol. 1. [Eng. Pub. AB Vol. 1.]
    Abstracts of Admons. 1677-1710, Index Library, British Rec. Soc. Vol. 70. [Eng. Pub. AB Vol. 70.]
    Abstracts of Admons. 1546-1641; 1660-1676 Admons. of the Arch- deaconry of Northampton. [Northants. 10.]

2. The Episcopal Consistory Court of the Bishop of Peterborough covered the deaneries in the northern half of the county. The records are at the County Record Office, Northampton.

3. The Peculiar of Banbury, Oxfordshire covered the parish of Kings Sutton. The records are at the Bodleian Library, Oxford.

4. The Peculiar Courts of Gretton and Nassington covered five parishes. The records prior to 1748 are at the Lincolnshire Record Office, Lincoln. Those after that time are at the County Record Office, Northampton.

5. The Peculiar Court of Gretton and Duddington covered those parishes. The records are at the Lincolnshire Record Office, Lin- coln.

Nonconformists: There are records of sixty-two Nonconformist chapels at the General Register Office, Somerset House, London.

Publications: The following publications are of interest:
1. *Northamptonshire Notes and Queries.*
2. *Publications* of the Northampton Record Society.
3. *Records of the Borough of Northampton.*
4. *Northampton and Rutland Clergy.*

NORTHUMBERLAND NORTHUMBERLAND

a maritime county of England bordering Scotland.

(*For map, see pages* 380-383)

Area: 1871 square miles. *Population*: 223,300.

Ancient Parishes: 96, five of which are in Newcastle-upon-Tyne.

County Town: Newcastle upon Type.

Main Occupations: Agriculture, coal and lead mining, shipbuilding, fishing and seafaring.

Principal Rivers: The river Tyne, forming in certain parts the county boundary, gives its name to one of England's important industrial areas, Tyneside. Other rivers are the Coquet, Aln, Blyth, Wansbeck, Till and Tweed.

Ecclesiastically, most of the county formed the Archdeaconry of Northumberland in the Diocese of Durham and Province of York. The parishes of Allendale, Hexham and St. John Lee were Peculiars of Hexhamshire in the jurisdiction of the Archbishop of York. The parish of Thockrington with four townships was in the Peculiar jurisdiction of the Prebendary of Thockrington. In 1882 the new diocese of Newcastle-upon-Tyne was formed, which includes the whole of the county of Northumberland.

The districts of Bedlingtonshire, Norhamshire and Islandshire, formerly part of County of Durham were annexed to Northumberland in 1844. These changes made little difference ecclesiastically as both Northumberland and Durham were in the Diocese of Durham.

Parish registers: The registers of many parishes have been transcribed or printed for periods prior to 1813, and the transcript copies are at the Public Library, Newcastle-upon-Tyne, and have been microfilmed by the Genealogical Society, Salt Lake City. Boyd's *Northumberland Marriage Index* incorporates all these, and covers certain periods in eighty-four parishes.

Bishop's Transcripts: There are none earlier than 1760 and are very spasmodic between 1760 and 1790. From 1790, they are reasonably complete, and housed at the University, Durham, in yearly bundles.

Marriage Licenses: These are at the Diocesan Registry of Durham City. Although none have been printed, a series of marriage bonds 1664-1674 and 1590-1814 is available at the Public Library, Newcastle-upon-Tyne and have been microfilmed for the Genealogical Society, Salt Lake City, Utah. Some marriage bonds filed with the probate records for short periods around 1700-1709 and 1734-1735 also have been microfilmed.

Probate Records: The following courts were in use:
1. The Episcopal Consistory Court of the Bishop of Durham covered most of the county. The records are at the University, Durham. Cal. of Wills and Admons. 1540-1599. Publications of the Newcastle on Tyne Records Commission. [Northu. Pub. C., Vol. 8.] Abstracts of some Wills, 1311-1599. Pub. Surtees Soc. Vols. 2, 38, 112, 116, 121, 142. [Eng. Pub. F., Vols. as above.]
2. The Peculiar Court of the Archbishop of York in Hexham and Hexhamshire covered the parishes of Allendale with West Allen; Ninebanks; Hexham; St. John Lee; St. Oswald Binfield; St. Mary Binfield. The records are at the Borthwick Institute, St. Anthony's Hall, York.
3. The Peculiar Court of the Prebendary of Thockrington (also called Tockerton and Tockerington) covered that parish. Nothing is known as to the whereabouts of these records.

Nonconformist registers: There are records relating to fifty-two nonconformist chapels at the General Register Office, Somerset House, London.

Publications: The following publications are of interest:
1. *Publications of the Newcastle-upon-Tyne Records Committee.*
2. *Publications of the Surtees Society.*
3. The *Transactions* of the Architectural and Archaeological Society Durham and Northumberland.
4. *Archaeologia Aelina.*
5. *Publications* of the Society of Antiquaries of Newcastle-upon-Tyne.
6. *Northern Notes and Queries.*

In the Public Library, Newcastle-upon-Tyne, there are many collections of genealogical interest. The collection, *Pedigrees of Northumberland families* (about 7,000 pages), has been microfilmed for the Genealogical Society, Salt Lake City. A similar copy has been made of *Manuscript Notes on Families of Northumberland and Durham.*

NOTTINGHAMSHIRE

NOTTINGHAMSHIRE

an inland county of England.

(*For map, see page* 384-5)

Area: 837 square miles.   *Population*: 225,400.

Ancient Parishes: 220, of which three are in the town of Nottingham.

County Town: Nottingham, where the County Record Office and Shire Hall are situated.

Main Occupations: Agriculture, coal mining, manufacture of hosiery and lace.

Principal River: Trent.

Ecclesiastically, the county formed the Archdeaconry of Nottingham and the Peculiar of Southwell in the Diocese and Province of York. In

1839 the Archdeaconry of Nottingham was transferred to the Diocese of Lincoln and Province of Canterbury, but it was not until 1841 that the Peculiar of Southwell was transferred from the Archbishop of York to the Archdeaconry of Nottingham and Diocese of Lincoln. In 1884 the Archdeaconry of Nottingham was taken from the Diocese of Lincoln, and, with the County of Derby which was in the Diocese of Lichfield, was formed into a new diocese, the Diocese of South' well, Province of Canterbury. In 1927, Derbyshire was taken from the Diocese of Southwell to form the Diocese of Derby. In 1934, the Diocese of Southwell was transferred to the Province of York.

Parish Registers: The marriage registers for most parishes, for the period prior to 1813, with a few down to 1837, have been printed. Few registers of christenings and burials have been printed. A number of original parish registers have been deposited at the Nottingham County Record Office.

Bishop's Transcripts: These are in fairly good condition and are at the Diocesan Registry, The Minster, Southwell, Notts. They extend from about 1600 to 1812, from which date there is a complete break at Southwell until 1837, after which many extend to as late as 1870. The Bishop's Transcripts for 1813-1837 are at the Borthwick Institute, St. Anthony's Hall, York, mixed with those for the whole Diocese of York, and they are not sorted in parish order. There are as many as thirty bundles of Bishop's Transcripts for each year at York, making the searching of them almost impossible. Work is now in progress arranging these in order of rural deanery.

Marriage Licenses: Those issued in the Archdeaconry of Nottingham, together with those for the Peculiar Court of Southwell, are at Not' tingham University.

> Archd. of Nottingham, 1577-1753. Index Library, British Rec. Soc. Vols. 58, 60. [Eng. Pub. AB Vols. 58, 60.]
> 1754-1770, Thoroton Society Record Series. [Notts. 6 Vol. 10.]
> Peculiar of Southwell, 1588-1853. Index Library, British Rec. Soc. Vols. 58, 60. [Eng. Pub. AB Vols. 58, 60.]

Probate Records: The following courts were in use:

1. The Exchequer Court of the Diocese of York covered (except for Peculiars) the whole of the Archdeaconry of Nottingham. Nearly all grants were made locally by the rural deans.[25] Within the Archdeaconry of Nottingham were the rural deaneries of Bingham, Newark, Nottingham and Retford.[26]

2. The Peculiar Court of the Chapter of the Collegiate Church of Southwell covered about thirty parishes.

> Cal. of Wills, 1470-1541, Camden Soc., New Series, Vol. 48. [Eng. Pub. E., New Series, Vol. 48.]

---

25. "In the case of Exchequer Court [of the Diocese of York] the Wills were proved by the rural dean who had a commission for that purpose from the Commissary of the Exchequer Court." ("Preface", Yorks. Arch. Soc., Vol. 89) [Yorks. 7, Vol. 89]

26. See Deanery Book for a list of Nottinghamshire parishes stating the names of the rural deaneries within which each parish is situated. The original book is among the probate records at York. The microfilm copy at the Genealogical Society is call number 14430, F.Yorks. 9, and the typescript copy is call number Eng. 366.

3. The Peculiar Court of the Manor of Mansfield covered eight parishes.
4. The Peculiar Court of the Manor of Bawtry or Gringley-on-the-Hill, covered four parishes.
5. The Peculiar Court of Kinoulton, covered that parish only.
6. The Court of the Dean and Chapter of York covered seven parishes.
7. The York Peculiar Courts of the Prebends of Apesthorpe or Applesthorpe and Bole covered those parishes.

The records of the courts listed under items 1, 6, and 7 are at the Borthwick Institute, St. Anthony s Hall, York. All others are at the Nottingham County Record Office, Shire Hall, Nottingham, including some probate records for the rural deaneries within the Archdeaconry of Nottingham for 1705-1858. These latter records appear to be copies of the records for the Nottinghamshire rural deaneries kept with the Exchequer Court of the Diocese of York (item 1 above), at York.

Nonconformists: There are records of forty-eight Nonconformist chapels at the General Register Office, Somerset House, London.

Publications: The following publications are of interest:
1. *Notts. and Derby Notes and Queries.*
2. *Transactions* of the Thoroton Society of Nottingham.
3. The Record Series of the Thoroton Society of Nottingham.
4. *Records of the Borough of Nottingham.*

OXFORDSHIRE   **OXFORDSHIRE**

(also called Oxon) — an inland county of England.

(*For map, see page 386-7*)

Area: 752 square miles.   *Population*: 152,000

Ancient Parishes: 217, of which fifteen are in the City of Oxford.

County Town: Oxford, where the Bodleian Library is situated.

Main Occupations: Agriculture, manufacture of blankets and gloves.

Principal Rivers: *Thames* (or Isis), Cherwell, Thame, Evenlode and Windrush.

Ecclesiastically, the county formed the Archdeaconry of Oxford in the Diocese of Lincoln from about 1070 until 1546, when the Diocese of Oxford was formed. It is in the Province of Canterbury.

Parish Registers: Few have been copied.

Bishop's Transcripts: These are deposited at the Bodleian Library, Oxford, and are in fairly good condition, many of them dating from as early as 1640 and extending to as late as 1900. Some have been microfilmed and are available at the Genealogical Society, Salt Lake City, Utah.

Marriage Licenses: These are deposited at the Bodleian Library Oxford. The marriage bonds are indexed for 1618-1856, and this index may be searched in the office of A. H. Franklin and Sons, Solicitors, King Edward Street, Oxford.

Probate Records: The following probate courts were in use:

1. The Episcopal Consistory Court of Oxford over the whole dio-cese.
2. The Archdeaconry Court of Oxford covered most of the county.
3. The Oxford and Bucks Peculiars covered over thirty parishes in the county.
4. The Archdeaconry Court of Berks. covered three parishes.

   Calendar of Wills and Admons., 1508-1652, Index Library, British Record Society, Vol. 8. [Eng. Pub. AB., Vol. 8.]

5. Court of the Chancellor of the University of Oxford, used prin-cipally by persons connected with that University.

   An Index to Wills . . . 1436-1814, (1862). [Oxon. 7.]

   All the records listed above are at the Bodleian Library, Oxford.

6. The Episcopal Consistory Court of Lincoln embraced this area prior to 1546. See under "Lincolnshire" for details of its records.

Nonconformists: There are registers of twenty-six Nonconformist chapels at the General Register Office, Somerset House, London.

Publications: The following publications are of interest:

1. *Publications* of the Oxfordshire Record Society.
2. *Publications* of the Oxfordshire Historical Society.
3. *Alumni Oxoniensis.*
4. *Oxoniensia* published by the Oxford Architectural and Historical Society.

PEMBROKESHIRE   PEMBROKESHIRE

(Benfro) — a maritime county in South Wales created in 1536.

(For map, see page 376)

Area: 532 square miles.   *Population*: 81,425.

Ancient Parishes: 140.

County Town: Pembroke is the historic county town, but Haverford-west has the County Offices.

Main Occupations: Agriculture, shipbuilding and a naval base, coal mining, quarrying of limestone.

Principal Rivers: Cleddy, Gwawn, Nevern, Teify.

Ecclesiastically, most of the county was in the Archdeaconry of St. David's, but there are a few parishes in the Archdeaconries of Cardigan and Carmarthen, all in the Diocese of St. David's. It was in the Province of Canterbury until 1921 when it became part of the Province of Wales.

Parish Registers: A few have been transcribed.

Bishop's Transcripts: These are at the National Library of Wales, Aberystwyth. There are few prior to 1799 but generally they range from 1799 to 1870 but have occasional gaps.

Marriage Licenses: These are at the National Library of Wales for 1615-1900 for the Consistory Court of St. David's; 1661-1867 for "old" St. David's Diocese. Some of the marriage bonds have been printed 1612-1799 in *West Wales Historical Records*, Vols. 3-12.

Probate Records: The county was covered by the Archdeaconry Courts of Pembroke, Carmarthen and Cardigan, all in the Episcopal Consistory Court of St. David's. All the records are at the National Library of Wales.

Nonconformist Registers: There are records of forty Nonconformist chapels at The General Register Office, Somerset House, London. There may be others in local custody, libraries, etc.

Publications: The following publications are of interest:
1. *The Transactions and West Wales Historical Records.*
2. *A List of Pembrokeshire Manuscripts . . . in the National Library of Wales* (1939).

RADNORSHIRE   RADNORSHIRE

(Maesyfed) — an inland county in Wales created in 1536.

(*For map, see page* 377)

Area: 390 square miles.   *Population*: 24,651.

Ancient Parishes: 52.

County Town: Presteigne but the County Hall is at Llandrindod Wells.

Main Occupations: Agriculture.

Principal Rivers: Wye, Teme, Elain.

Ecclesiastically, the county was mostly in the Archdeaconry of Brecon and Diocese of St. David's, but Presteigne, Old and New Radnor, Norton and Knighton were in the Archdeaconry and Diocese of Hereford, all in the Province of Canterbury, but since 1920 the county has been in the Province of Wales. In 1923 the county became part of the Diocese of Swansea and Brecon.

Parish Registers: None have been printed.

Bishop's Transcripts: These are at the National Library of Wales, Aberystwyth for the Archdeaconry of Brecon and Diocese of St. David's. They range from around 1660 to 1870, but have many gaps. Those for the Diocese of Hereford are at the Diocesan Registry, Hereford.

Marriage Licenses: These are at the National Library of Wales for 1661-1867 for the "old" Diocese of St. David's. Some marriage bonds from the St. David's Diocese have been printed 1612-1799 in *West Wales Historical Records*, Vols. 3-12.

There is a series, 1666-1867, for St. John and St. Mary Brecon, that may have Radnorshire references. The marriage licenses of the Diocese of Hereford are at the Diocesan Registry, Hereford.

Probate Records: The following courts covered the county, the records of which are at the National Library of Wales:

1. The Archdeaconry Court of Brecon in the Diocese of St. David's.
2. The Episcopal Consistory Court of Hereford.

Nonconformist Registers: There are records of five Nonconformist chapels at The General Register Office, Somerset House, London. There may be others in local custody, libraries, etc.

Publications: The following publications are of interest:

1. *Transactions of the Radnorshire Society.*
2. Williams, *History of Radnorshire.*
3. W. H. Howse, *History of Radnorshire.*
4. *A List of Radnorshire Manuscripts . . . in the National Library of Wales.*

RUTLAND   RUTLAND

an inland and also the smallest county in England.

(For map, see page 392)

Area: 142 square miles.   *Population*: 19,400

Ancient Parishes: 50.

County Town: Oakham.

Main Occupation: Agriculture.

Pincipal Rivers: Welland, Eyre, Wash, Chater.

Ecclesiastically, the county, from the 13th century until 1876, was a single rural deanery in the Archdeaconry of Northampton. It was in the Diocese of Lincoln until 1541, when it became part of the Diocese of Peterborough. In 1876 it became part of the Archdeaconry of Oakham in the Diocese of Peterborough. It has always been in the Province of Canterbury,

Parish Registers: Transcript copies of a few parish registers are at the Diocesan Registry, Peterboro. A few marriage registers are in typescript form at the Genealogical Society, Salt Lake City, where there is also a partial marriage index, 1780-1837, for this county.

Bishop's Transcripts: None exist for periods prior to 1706. From 1706 to about 1840 they are at the Northampton Record Office, Delapre Abbey, Northampton and are in fairly good condition with customary gaps.

Marriage Licenses: These are at the County Record Office, Northampton.

Probate Records: The following courts were in use:

1. The Archdeaconry Court of Northampton covered most of the county.

   Cal. of Wills, 1510-1652. Index Library, British Rec. Soc. Vol. 1. [Eng. Pub. AB Vol. 1.]
   Cal. of Admons. 1546-1641; 1660-1676. Administrations of the Archdeaconry of Northampton. [Northants. 10.]
   Cal. of Admons. 1677-1710, Index Library, British Rec. Soc. Vol. 70. [Eng. Pub. AB Vol. 70.]

2. The Episcopal Consistory Court of the Bishop of Peterboro covered most of the county.

   Records in items 1 and 2 above are at the Northampton Record Office.

3. The Prebendal Courts of Liddington, Caldecott and Ketton with Tixover covered those parishes.

   There are records for Liddington (1723-1820), Caldecott (1669-1820) and Ketton with Tixover (1574, 1722-1820) at the Leicester County Record Office.

   Cal. of Wills prior to 1821, Index Library, British Rec. Soc. Vol. 51. [Eng. Pub. AB Vol. 51.]

   Other records for Gretton (1657-1832), Liddington (1668-1810), and Ketton (1666-1667) are kept by the Lincolnshire Archives Committee.

4. The Peculiar of Empingham covered that parish. The records 1669-1835 are kept by the Lincolnshire Archives Committee.

   Probate records for Rutlandshire also appear among the records of Lincoln, the courts of which are detailed under Lincolnshire.

Nonconformists: There are records of six Nonconformist chapels at the office of the Registrar General, Somerset House, London.

Publications: The following publications are of interest:
1. *The Leicestershire and Rutland Magazine.*
2. *Leicestershire and Rutland Notes and Queries.*
3. *Northampton and Rutland Clergy.*

SHROPSHIRE SHROPSHIRE

(Salop)—an inland county of England on the borders of Wales.

(For map, see page 388-9)

Area: 1341 square miles.   *Population*: 222,800

Ancient Parishes: 229, five of which are in Shrewsbury.

County Town: Shrewsbury, where the County Record Office is situated.

Main Occupations: Agriculture; mining of coal, iron ore, lead ore, and stone quarrying.

Principal Rivers: Severn, Camlet, Vyrnwy, Tern, Clun, Ony, Teme.

Ecclesiastically, the following arrangements existed:
1. Part of the Archdeaconry of Salop, Diocese of Hereford, covered the southern half of the county.
2. One parish in the Archdeaconry of Hereford, Diocese of Hereford.
3. Three parishes in the Diocese of Worcester.
4. Several parishes in the north-west of the county were in the Archdeaconry of St. Asaph, Diocese of St. Asaph.
5. Part of the Archdeaconry of Salop, Diocese of Lichfield covered the northern half of the county.
6. Five parishes are in the Archdeaconry of Stafford, Diocese of Lichfield.

Parish Registers: A great many of the parish registers for periods prior to 1813 have been printed. These were used by Percival Boyd in compiling the *Shropshire Marriage Index* which covered marriages for varying periods from 127 parishes. The registers of a number of other parishes are available in transcript form at the Borough Library, Shrewsbury.

Bishop's Transcripts: Depending upon the ecclesiastical jurisdiction by which the individual parishes were covered, the Bishop's Transcripts are at the National Library of Wales (Diocese of St. Asaph); the Diocesan Registry, Hereford (Diocese of Hereford); and the Diocesan Registry, Lichfield (Diocese of Lichfield). Those at the National Library of Wales extend from about 1600 to about 1850 but many years are missing. Those at the Diocesan Registry at Hereford exist up to 1812 and are in fair condition. Those at Lichfield extend to about 1840 and are in fair condition.

Marriage Licenses: These are at the same repositories as are the Bishop's Transcripts, namely the National Library of Wales, the Diocesan Registry, Hereford, and the Diocesan Registry, Lichfield, depending upon the diocese in which the license was granted.

Probate Records: The following courts were in use:
1. The Episcopal Consistory Court of Lichfield and Coventry covered the northern part of the county and the records are at the Public Library, Lichfield, Staffordshire.
   Cal. of Wills and Admons. 1516-1652, Index Library, British Rec. Soc. Vol. 7. [Eng. Pub. AB Vol 7.] (additional documents were found later.)
2. Various Shropshire Peculiar Courts covered about twenty parishes and the records are at the National Library of Wales.
   Cal. of Wills, Shrops. Arch. Soc. 4th Series, Vols. 12, 13. [Shrops. Pub. A., Vol. 46.]
3. The Episcopal Consistory Court of Hereford covered those parishes within that Diocese. The records are at the National Library of Wales.

4. The Episcopal Consistory of the Diocese of St. Asaph covered parishes within that Diocese. The records are at the National Library of Wales.
5. The Manorial Court of Ruyton-of-the-Eleven-Towns covered the parishes of Ruyton and Felton. The records, 1666-1816 only, are at the Public Library, Shrewsbury.

> Cal. 1665-1709, Trans Shrops. Arch. Soc. Vol. 52. [Shrops. Pub. A Vol. 52.]

6. Episcopal Consistory Court of Worcester covered three parishes. See Worcestershire for details.

Nonconformist Registers: There are records of fifty-five Nonconformist chapels at the office of the Registrar General, Somerset House, London.

Publications: The following publications are of interest:
1. *Transactions* of the Shropshire Archaeological and Natural History Society.
2. *The Antiquities of Shropshire*.
3. *Shropshire Parish Documents* (Salop County Council) lists all the parish registers existing about 1900. [Shrops. 11.]

SOMERSETSHIRE   SOMERSETSHIRE

(*For map, see page* 390-1)

a maritime county in the south of England.

Area: 1642 square miles.   *Population*: 402,500.

Ancient Parishes: 486, three of which are in Bath, two in Glastonbury, two in Taunton and three associated with the City of Bristol.

County Town: Taunton, where the Somerset Record Office in the Shire Hall is situated.

Main Occupations: Agriculture, coal mining and the manufacture of wool and silk.

Principal Rivers: Lower Avon, Parnet, Tone, Brue and Ax. The Bristol Channel is an important waterway.

Ecclesiastically, the county forms three archdeaconries, Bath, Wells and Taunton. All are in the Diocese of Bath and Wells in the Province of Canterbury. Three parishes which prior to 1542 were in that diocese are in the Diocese of Bristol. The parish of Holwell, including the tithing of Buckshaw, was transferred in 1836 from Somerset to Dorset.

Parish Registers: Many of the marriage registers have been printed for periods prior to 1813, and these were used by Percival Boyd in his *Somerset Marriage Index* that contains marriage for varying periods from 120 parishes. A number of transcript copies of parish register extracts together with a few original parish registers are at the Public Library, Bath. A few other original parish registers are at the Castle, Taunton.

The County Council has printed a complete list of the existing registers in *Inventory of Parochial Documents in the Diocese of Bath and Wells.* [Somerset 14.]

Bishop's Transcripts: Those prior to 1813 are in parish order but are very incomplete and should only be used as a last measure. Some of the very early Bishop's Transcripts have been printed but they repre-sent only a few years for any one parish. The Bishop's Transcripts for periods after 1812 are arranged in years rather than by parish, making a search for the transcript of any one parish a lengthy matter. These records are at the Diocesan Registry, Wells.

Marriage Licenses: These are at the *Diocesan Registry, Wells.*

> 1645-1755, Marriage Licenses in the Diocese of Bath and Wells. [Som. B3.] An additional copy is printed in The Genealogist, Vols. 15-26, New Series. [Eng. Pub. AF, N.S., Vols. as above.]

Probate Records: The following courts were in use, although those records that were stored at the District Probate Registry, Exeter, were destroyed by enemy action in World War II. It would be well to read *Somerset Wills from Exeter* in the Publications of the Somerset Record Society, 1952, Vol. 62.

1. The Consistory Court of the Bishop of Bristol in the Deanery of Bristol covered the parishes of Abbotts Leigh, St. Mary Redcliff, and Temple or Holy Cross, all in Somerset but adjacent to Bristol. These wills were not destroyed and are at the Council House, Bristol. See "Gloucester" also.

2. *The Episcopal Consistory Court of Bath and Wells covered the whole Diocese.

> Cal. of Wills, 1529-1600. Publications of the Somerset Record Society, Vol. 62 [Som. Pub. C., Vol. 62.]
> Abstracts of some Wills, 1543-1546; 1554-1556. [ibid. Vol. 40.]

3. *The Consistorial Court of the Archdeaconry of Wells covered all parishes in that Archdeaconry except those parishes having peculiar jurisdiction.

4. *The Consistorial Court of the Archdeaconry of Taunton covered all parishes in that Archdeaconry except those parishes having peculiar jurisdiction.

> Cal. of Wills and Admons. 1537-1799, Index Library, British Rec. Soc. Vols. 45 & 53. [Eng. Pub. AB Vols. 45 & 53.]

5. *The Consistory Court of the Dean and Chapter of Wells covered eleven parishes.

6. *The Consistory Court of the Dean of Wells covered fourteen parishes.

7. *The Royal Peculiar Court of Ilminster covered that parish.

> Cal. of Wills and Admons. 1690-1857. Index Library, British Rec. Soc. Vol. 53. [Eng. Pub. AB Vol. 53.]

8. *Various other peculiar courts covered over thirty parishes.

An asterisk indicates that the original Calendars, Wills and Admons., and other probate records were destroyed.

Among the records of the diocese, kept at the Diocesan Registry, Wells, are many Wills and Admon. Bonds, and references to Probate and Admon. Acts entered in act books and license books. These rec-ords were not surrendered with the main collections of Probate records.

A number of other probate records have beeen printed as follows:

Abstracts of some Somerset Wills proved P.C.C., 1383-1558, Publica-
tions of the Somerset Record Society, Vols. 16, 19, 21. [Som. Pub. C
Vols. 16, 19, 21.]
Abstracts of some sixteenth and seventeenth century Wills proved P.C.C.
Somersetshire Wills. [Som. 8 Vols. 1-6.]
Abstracts of sixteenth century Chew Magna Wills Publications of the
Somerset Record Society, Vol. 62. [Som. Pub. C Vol. 62.]
Frederick Wm. Weaver: Wells Wills, (London: 1890). These are
extracts from the whole of the approximately 600 Wills in the first
two books of Registered Wills formerly kept at the District Probate
Registry, Exeter, and which were destroyed. They cover 1528-1536.
[SOM. W 3 A.]

Nonconformists: There are records of ninety-six Nonconformist chapels
kept by the Registrar General, Somerset House, London.

Publications: The following publications are of interest:

1. *Publications* of the Somerset Record Society.
2. *Somerset Archaeological and Natural History Society.*
3. *Somerset and Dorset Notes and Queries.*
4. *Inventory of Parochial Documents in the Diocese of Bath and
   Wells.* [Som. 14.]
5. *Handlist . . . Documents . . . Somerset Record Office, Shire Hall,
   Taunton,* 1947. [Somerset 13.]

STAFFORDSHIRE STAFFORDSHIRE

(*For map, see page 393-5*)

Area: 1,148 square miles. *Population*: 410,400

Ancient Parishes: 183, three of which are in the town of Stafford and
four in the City of Lichfield.

County Town: Stafford, where the County Record Office is situated.

Main Occupations: Agriculture, coal and iron mining, the manufacture
of pottery and hardware.

Principal Rivers: Trent, Dove, Tame, Blythe, Penk, Sow.

Ecclesiastically, the county was mostly in the Archdeaconry of Stafford,
Diocese of Lichfield, Province of Canterbury. A few parishes are now
in the Diocese of Worcester, and since 1905, when the Diocese of
Birmingham was created, several parishes near Birmingham have been
in that Diocese.

Parish Registers: A number have been printed for periods prior to
1812 by the Staffordshire Parish Register Society, and a number of
others are available in transcript form at the William Salt Library,
Stafford.

*Bishop's Transcripts:*These are at the Diocesan Registry, Lichfield and
range from 1665 to around 1840. They are in average condition with
the customary gaps. For a list of the Bishop's Transcripts of the
Peculiar parishes see *Historical Collections of Staffordshire,* Part 2
of Volume 6, pp. 82-85. [Staffs. Pub. A., Vol. 6.]

Marriage Licenses: These are at the Diocesan Registry, Lichfield.

Probate Records: The following probate courts were in use:
1. The Episcopal Consistory Court of Lichfield and Coventry covered most of the county.
   > Cal. of Wills and Admons. 1516-1652, Index Library, British Rec. Soc. Vol. 7. [Eng. Pub. A.B., Vol. 7.]
   > (additional documents were found after printing.)
2. The Court of the Dean and Chapter of Lichfield covered seven parishes.
3. The Courts of the Lichfield Peculiars covered sixty-eight parishes.
   > Cal. of Wills and Admons. 1529-1652, [Ibid.]
   All of the above records are at the Public Library, Lichfield, Staffordshire.
4. The Peculiar Court of Prees or Pipe Minor covered the parish of St. Chad, Lichfield, and the parish of Tipton. The records relating to these two parishes are kept with the Lichfield Peculiars probate records at the Public Library, Lichfield.
   > Calender of Wills, Admons., [Ibid.]

Nonconformists: There are registers of seventy-two Nonconformist chapels at the General Register Office, Somerset House, London.

Publications: The following publications are of interest:
1. *Publications of the William Salt Archaeological Society.*
2. *Publications of the Staffordshire Record Society.*
3. *Publications of the Old Staffordshire Society.*
4. *Historical Collections of Staffordshire.*

SUFFOLK   **SUFFOLK**

(*For map, see page* 396-7)

a maritime county on the east coast of England.

Area: 1512 square miles.   *Population*: 296,000.

Ancient Parishes: 504, of which twelve are in Ipswich, two in Bury St. Edmunds and three in Sudbury.

County Town: The historic county town is Ipswich but for administrative purposes Suffolk has been divided into two parts, East Suffolk and West Suffolk. Bury St. Edmunds is the administrative capital of West Suffolk, where is situated the West Suffolk Record Office. Ipswich is the administrative capital of East Suffolk where is situated the East Suffolk Record Office.

Main Occupations: Agriculture and fishing.

Principal Rivers: Stour, Orwell, Deben, Waveney, Little Ouse, Lark.

Ecclesiastically, the county consists, since 1126, of the Archdeaconry of Sudbury that covers the western half of the county, and the Archdeaconry of Suffolk that covers the eastern half. Both were in the Diocese of Norwich until the creation, in the 1900's, of the modern Diocese of St. Edmundsbury and Ipswich. A few parishes are also in the modern Diocese of Chelmsford. The whole county is in the Province of Canterbury.

Parish Registers: A good number have been transcribed for periods prior to 1813, and these copies are at the Borough Library, Ipswich. These were used by Percival Boyd to compile the *Suffolk Marriage Index* that covers about 500 parishes. Although this index extends from 1538-1837 most of the parishes involved are indexed for periods prior to 1754 only. Both the East Suffolk Record Office, Ipswich, and the West Suffolk Record Office, Bury St. Edmunds, have a number of original parish registers in their care.

Bishop's Transcripts: Those for the Archdeaconry of Sudbury are at the West Suffolk Record Office. They cover the period 1560-1853. The period 1560-1640 is arranged in parish order but for all other years they are arranged in yearly bundles by deanery arranged alphabetically by parish within each deanery.

Those for the Archdeaconry of Suffolk are at the East Suffolk Record Office. They commence in 1711 but few exist until 1723. From that year until 1812 they are an almost complete series. For the most part they are arranged in yearly bundles in deanery order. In 1959 about one-third of them were still in yearly bundles for the whole Archdeaconry but plans were being prepared to have these arranged in yearly bundles arranged by deanery.

In this county the Bishop's Transcripts are sometimes called Archdeacon's Transcripts, Register Bills and Indented Bills. Many of the Bishop's and Archdeacon's Transcripts belonging to this county were at the Diocesan Registry, Norwich, but an effort is being made to sort these into the groups listed above.

Marriage Licenses: Those for the Archdeaconry of Sudbury are at the West Suffolk Record Office, Bury St. Edmunds 1684-1839.

> 1684-1839, Pub. of Harleian Soc. Vols. 69-72. [Eng. Pub. AC, Vols. 69-72.]

Those for the Archdeaconry of Suffolk are at the East Suffolk Record Office, Ipswich.

> 1663-1750, Marriage Licence Bonds at Ipswich. [Suff. 8.]
> Those deposited at the Probate Registry 1613-1674, Marriage Licences at the Ipswich Probate Court. [Suff I 3g.]

Probate Records: The following courts were in use:

1. The Archdeaconry Court of Suffolk covered 288 parishes in East Suffolk. The records are at the East Suffolk Record Office, Ipswich.

   > Cal. of Wills 1444-1600; 1751-1793, Calendar of Wills at Ipswich. [Suff. I 3a and Suff. I 3h.]

2. The Archdeaconry Court of Sudbury and Commissary of Bury St. Edmunds covered 229 parishes in West Suffolk. The records are at the West Suffolk Record Office, Bury St. Edmunds.

   > Wills . . . Commissary of Bury St. Edmunds (abstracts from about fifty selected Wills between 1370 and 1650.) Pub. Camden Soc., Old Series, Vol. 49. [Eng. Pub. E., Old Series, Vol. 49.] This volume also contains a list of the deaneries in this archdeaconry and names each parish within each deanery.
   > Cal. of Pre-Reformation Wills 1354-1535, Proceedings Suffolk Institute of Arch. and Natural History, Vol. 12, 13. [Suff. Pub. A., Vol. 12, 13.]

3. The Episcopal Consistory Court of Norwich covered the county during the inhibition of the other courts. The records are at the Central Library, Norwich. (See also Norfolk.)

> Cal. of Wills 1370-1603, Index Library, British Rec. Soc., Vols. 69 & 73. [Eng. Pub. AB., Vols. 69 & 73.]

4. The Peculiar Court of Isleham, Cambridgeshire covered the parish of Freckenham. The records are at the West Suffolk Record Office.

5. The Peculiar Court of the Archbishop of Canterbury in the Peculiar Deanery of Bocking, covered three parishes in Suffolk. The records are at the Essex Record Office, Chelmsford.

6. The Peculiar Court of the Deanery of South Elmham prior to 1540. The records are at the East Suffolk Record Office.

> See Publications of the Suffolk Institute of Archaeology and Natural History, Vol. 14 (Ipswich: 1912), "South Elmham Deanery", page 326, concerning probate book numbered VI.A., then at the District Probate Registry, Ipswich.

Nonconformists: There are records of sixty-six Nonconformist chapels at the General Register Office, Somerset House, London.

Publications: The following publications are of interest:

1. *Publications and Proceedings* of the Suffolk Institute of Archaeology and Natural History.
2. *East Anglian or Notes and Queries.*
3. *The Manors of Suffolk.*

SURREY   SURREY

—an inland county of England. Since 1888 the northern portion of the county, close to London, has been within the Administrative County of London.

(For map, see page 398-9)

Area: 758 square miles.   *Population*: 485,700. This figure includes that part of the Metropolis of London lying south of the River Thames, including the boroughs or places Lambeth, Southwark, Rotherhithe, Bermondsey, Newington, Camberwell, Clapham, Battersea and Wandsworth.

County Town: The historic county town is Guildford, but Kingston-upon-Thames is the center of the county administration and where the Surrey Record Office and the County Hall are situated.

Ancient Parishes: 146, of which six are in Southwark and three in Guildford.

Main Occupations: Agriculture, except for small manufactories near London, seafaring and import and export trade.

Principal Rivers: Thames, Wey and Mole.

Ecclesiastically, the county formed the Archdeaconry of Surrey, Diocese of Winchester, with the exception of eleven parishes in the Peculiar of the Archbishop of Canterbury in the Deanery of Croydon

that were in the Diocese of Canterbury. In 1837 the parishes of Ad-
dington and Lambeth were transferred to the Diocese of Canterbury.
In 1846 all the parishes in Southwark, with Battersea, Bermondsey,
Camberwell, Clapham, Lambeth, Rotherhithe, Streatham, Tooting,
Wandsworth, and Merton, were transferred to the Diocese of London. In 1877 parts of Surrey that were within the Dioceses of London
and Winchester were transferred to the Diocese of Rochester. In
1905 part of Surrey and part of the County of London south of the
River Thames were made into the Diocese of Southwark. Additional
information is given in *The Victoria History of Surrey,* Vol. 2, pages
49-53. In 1927 a portion of the county was formed into the Diocese
of Guildford.

Parish Registers: A few have been printed for periods prior to 1813.
There are a number of others in transcript form at the Minet Branch
Library, Lambeth, London, S.E. 5, and these have been microfilmed
for the Genealogical Society, Salt Lake City. A number of original
parish registers have been deposited with the London County Council
Record Office, County Hall, London, S.E. 1, as that record office
is the official repository for records of the Diocese of Southwark.

A list of pre-1813 parish registers is given in the "Abstract of
Parish Records," (Surrey Record Soc., 1928), Vol. 1., [Surrey Pub.
C., Vol. 1.], and a list of copied parish registers is given in "List
of Transcripts," (Surrey Achaeol. Soc., 1938), Vol. 46. [Surrey Pub.
A., Vol. 46.]

Bishop's Transcripts: Those for the old Archdeaconry of Surrey are
at the L.C.C. Record Office, London, S.E. 1. There are very few
prior to 1800, the main period extant being 1800-1850, and some
extend to as modern as 1919. Those for the Peculiars of Arches
(London), Shoreham (Kent) and Croydon (Surrey), covering around
1750 to 1800 are at Lambeth Palace Library, London, S.E. 1, but they
cover only a few parishes in the three Peculiars, and are not available
for inspection.

Marriage Licenses: Those for the old Archdeaconry of Surrey, 1674-
1830, are at the L.C.C. Record Office, London, S.E. 1. Those for
the Peculiars of the Arches (London), Shoreham (Kent), and Croydon (Surrey), covering Allegations 1707-1804 and Bonds 1684-1804,
are at Lambeth Palace Library, London, S.E. 1. Because Surrey is
close to London, residents might have obtained marriage licenses from
the Bishop of London's Registry, and the Archbishop of Canterbury's
Faculty Office and Vicar General's Office. The records of these three
offices are detailed under London.

> 1674-1770, Commissary Ct. Surrey (copy at the Society of Genealogists,
> London).

Probate Records: The following courts were in use:

1. The Archdeaconry Court of Surrey covered the county, except
   Peculiars.

   > Some abstracts 1484-1490 and 1595-1608. Pub. Surrey Rec. Soc., Vols.
   > 3, 7, 15, 17. [Surrey Pub. B., Vols. 3, 7, 15, 17.]

2. The Commissary Court of the Bishop of Winchester in the Archdeaconry of Surrey, covered the county, except Peculiars.

The above records are at the Principal Probate Registry, Somerset House, London, but plans for their transfer elsewhere are under consideration.

3. The Peculiar Court of the Archbishop of Canterbury in the Deanery of Croydon covered twelve places in Surrey. After 1821 there is only one grant, recorded in 1832.

   The above records are deposited as follows:

   1. The consolidated Registers of Copy Wills and Act Books for the Archbishop of Canterbury's Peculiars of the Deaneries of Arches (London), Shoreham (Kent), and Croydon (Surrey), are at Lambeth Palace, London, S.E. 1.

   2. The bundles of original Wills and Admons., together with a few volumes of probate records, are deposited at the Kent Record Office, Maidstone, Kent.

4. Printed abstracts of *Surrey* probate records 1593-1611 filed in the P.C.C., are in the *Surrey Arch. Collections,* Volumes 10 to 35. [Surrey Pub. A. Vols. 10-35.]

Nonconformist Registers: There are records of forty-seven Nonconformist chapels at the General Register Office, Somerset House, London. A check should also be made under London in the printed list of Non-Parochial Registers for Surrey chapels listed within the Metropolis.

Publications: The following publications are of interest:

1. *Publications* of the Surrey Record Society.
2. *Publications* of the Records Committee of the Surrey County Council.
3. *Publications* of the Surrey Archaeological Society.

SUSSEX   SUSSEX

—a maritime county on the south coast of England.

(*For map, see page* 400-1)

Area: 1463 square miles.   Population: 272,300

Ancient Parishes: 305, eight of which are in Chichester, six in Lewes and two in Hastings.

County Towns:
1. Lewes for East Sussex where there is an East Sussex Record Office.
2. Chichester for West Sussex where there is a West Sussex Record Office.

Main Occupations: Agriculture and seafaring.

Principal Rivers: Arum, Rother, Ouse, Adur.

Ecclesiastically, the county is comprised of the Archdeaconries of Chichester and Lewes, both within the Diocese of Chichester. The exempt Deaneries of Pagham and South Malling and the parishes of All Saints, Chichester and St. Thomas-at-Cliffe, Lewes, were in the Peculiar jurisdiction of the Archbishop of Canterbury. All are in the Province of Canterbury.

Parish Registers: Very few parish registers have been printed or transcribed. A few original parish registers have been deposited at the West Sussex Record Office, Chichester.

Bishop's Transcripts: These are kept at the West Sussex Record Office for the whole county and are a good series extending to around 1870. *Sussex Notes and Queries*, Vol. 10, [Suss. Pub. A., Vol. 10] has helpful lists of existing Bishop's Transcripts, although every parish is not included in any one list.

Marriage Licenses: These are at the West Sussex Record Office, Chichester, for the whole county.

> Consistory Court of Chichester for the Archdeaconry of Chichester, 1575-1800. Pub. of the Sussex Record Soc. Vols. 9, 32, 35. [Suss. 2, Vols. 9, 32, 35.]
> Consistory Court of Chichester for the Archdeaconry of Lewes, 1586-1642; 1670-1728; 1764; 1768; 1773-1837. Pub. of the Sussex Rec. Soc., Vols. 25, 26. [Suss. 2, Vols. 25, 26.]
> Peculiar Deanery of South Malling 1620-1732, ibid. Vol. 6. [Ibid. Vol. 6.] 1772-1837, ibid. Vols. 25, 26. [Ibid. Vols. 25, 26.]
> Peculiar Court of the Deanery of Chichester 1582-1730 and the Peculiar Deaneries of Pagham and Tarring 1579-1730, ibid. Vol. 12. [Ibid. Vol. 12.]

Probate Records: The following courts were in use:

1. The Consistory Court of the Bishop of Chichester for the Archdeaconry of Lewes covered 142 parishes in East Sussex and the records are at the East Sussex Record Office, Lewes.

   > Cal. of Wills and Admons., 1518-1642, Index Library, British Rec. Soc. Vol. 24. [Eng. Pub. AB., Vol. 24.]

2. The Episcopal Consistory Court for the Archdeacon of Chichester covered 135 parishes in West Sussex. The records are at the West Sussex Record Office, Chichester.

   > Cal. of Wills, 1482-1800, ibid. Vol. 49. [Ibid. Vol. 49.]
   > Cal. of Admons., 1555-1800, ibid. Vol. 64. [Ibid. Vol. 64.]

3. The Deanery of South Malling, a Peculiar Court of the Archbishop of Canterbury had jurisdiction over a few parishes adjoining Chichester. The records are at the East Sussex Record Office, Lewes.

   > Cal. of Wills and Admons., 1558-1660, ibid. Vol. 24. [Ibid. Vol. 24.]

4. The Peculiar Court of the Deanery of Battle covered the parish of Battle. The records are at the East Sussex Record Office, Lewes.

   > Cal. of Wills and Admons., 1530-1617, ibid. Vol. 24. [Ibid. Vol. 24.]

5. The Peculiar Court of the Dean of Chichester covered part of the city of Chichester, and the parishes of Fishborne, Wike and Rumboldswick. The records are at the West Sussex Record Office, Chichester.

   > Cal. of Wills and Admons., 1577-1800, ibid. Vol. 64. [Ibid. Vol. 64.]

6. The Peculiar Court of the Archbishop of Canterbury in the Deaneries of Pagham and Tarring covered eight parishes in the vicinity of Chichester. The records are at the West Sussex Record Office, Chichester.

   > Cal. of Wills and Admons., 1520-1670, ibid. Vol. 64. [Ibid. Vol. 64.]

Nonconformist Registers: There are records of fifty-six Nonconformist chapels at the General Register Office, Somerset House, London.

Publications: The following publications are of interest:
1. *Publications* of the Sussex Archaeological Society.
2. *Publications* of the Sussex Record Society.

WARWICKSHIRE

WARWICKSHIRE

(pronounced Worrickshire)—an inland county in the midlands of England.

(For map, see page 402-3)

Area: 902 square miles.   *Population*: 335,988.

Ancient Parishes: 208, of which four are in Birmingham, three in Coventry and two in Warwick.

County Town: Warwick, where the County Record Office is situated.

Main Occupations: Agriculture, coal mining, tool and machine making.

Principal Rivers: Avon, Tame.

Ecclesiastically, the county consisted of the Archdeaconry of Worcester in the Diocese of Worcester and the Archdeaconry of Coventry in the Diocese of Lichfield and Coventry from A.D. 680 to 1836 when in the latter year, the Archdeaconry of Coventry was transferred to the Diocese of Worcester. The county is now in the Diocese of Coventry, except for a few parishes in and adjoining the City of Birmingham and parts of north Warwickshire that were transferred to the Diocese of Birmingham when that diocese was formed in 1905.

Parish Registers: The marriage registers of a few parishes have been printed for periods prior to 1813. A number of the original parish registers have been deposited at County Record Office, Warwick. Transcript copies of a few parish registers are at the Shakespeare Library, Stratford-on-Avon.

Bishop's Transcripts: Those for the Diocese of Lichfield are at the Diocesan Registry, Lichfield, Staffordshire. They range from 1665 to around 1840, most parishes having missing periods. For those parishes in the Diocese of Worcester the Bishop's Transcripts are at the Worcestershire Record Office, Worcester and are arranged in yearly bundles, deanery by deanery.

Marriage Licenses: Those for the parishes in the Diocese of Lichfield and Coventry are at the Diocesan Registry, Lichfield, Staffordshire. Those for the parishes in the Diocese of Worcester are at the Worcestershire Record Office, Worcester.

Probate Records: The following courts were in use:
1. The Episcopal Consistory Court of Lichfield covered those parishes that were in the Diocese of Lichfield and Coventry.

   Cal. of Wills, 1516-1652, Index Library, British Rec. Soc., Vol. 7. [Eng. Pub. AB Vol. 7.] (additional documents were found later.)
2. The Episcopal Consistory Court of Worcester covered those par-

ishes that were in the deaneries of Kington and Warwick.

> Cal. of Wills and Admons., 1451-1652, ibid. Vol. 31 & 39. [Ibid. Vol. 31 & 39.]

3. The Court of the Dean and Chapter of Lichfield covered two parishes.
4. The Lichfield Peculiars covered seventeen parishes.

> Cal. of Wills and Admons., 1529-1652, ibid. Vol. 7. [Ibid. Vol. 7.]

5. The Worcester Peculiars covered one parish in this county.

> Cal. of Wills 1675-1790, ibid. Vol. 7. [Ibid| Vol. 7.]

The records listed in items 1, 3, and 4 are at the Public Library, Lichfield. Those listed in items 2 and 5 at the Worcestershire Record Office, Worcester.

Nonconformists: There are registers of fifty-five Nonconformist chapels at the General Register Office, Somerset House, London.

Publications: The following publications are of interest:

1. *Publications* of the Dugdale Society.
2. *The County of Warwick, a Handbook . . . Administrative County of Warwick,* (Warwick: 1939)

WESTMORLAND   WESTMORLAND

(also spelled Westmoreland)—an inland county in the north-west of England.

(For map, see page 404-5)

Area: 763 square miles.   *Population*: 55,000.

Ancient Parishes: 68, of which two are in Appleby.

County Town: Kendal, where there is a County Record Office.

Main Occupation: Agriculture.

Principal Rivers: Eden, Eamont, Lowther, Lune, Kent.

Ecclesiastically, the county was divided as follows:

1. The Barony of Appleby, sometimes called the Barony of Westmorland, which was in the Diocese of Carlisle.
2. The Barony of Kendal. Prior to 1541 this Barony was in the Diocese of York but from 1541 to 1856 it was in the Archdeaconry of Richmond, Diocese of Chester. On 5 February 1856 the Barony of Kendal was transferred to the Diocese of Carlisle.

Parish Registers: A few have been printed, mainly for periods prior to 1813.

Bishop's Transcripts: These are at the County Record Office, Kendal. A microfilm copy is at the Genealogical Society, Salt Lake City. The Bishop's Transcripts range from 1640 to around 1900, although for many parishes there are none before 1700 and others cease around 1870. The earlier periods have many gaps and are in poor condition.

Marriage Licences: Those for the Diocese of Carlisle (affecting parishes in the Barony of Appleby) are at the County Record Office, Carlisle.

A microfilm copy is at the Genealogical Society, Salt Lake City, Utah. Those for the Archdeaconry of Richmond, (affecting parishes in the Barony of Kendal) are at the Lancashire Record Office, Preston, Lancs. In addition to the period available in print (see under "Lancashire.") a microfilm copy 1746-1799 is at the Genealogical Society, Salt Lake City, Utah.

Probate Records: The following courts were in use:

1. The Episcopal Consistory Court of Carlisle covered a few parishes.

   Abstracts of some Wills 1353-1386, Papers and Pedigrees Mainly Relating to Cumberland and Westmorland, Vol. 9. [Cum. Pub. A., Extra Series, Vol. 9.]

   The records are at the County Record Office, Carlisle, Cumberland.

2. The Archdeaconry Courts of Richmond, which was in the Diocese of York until 1541 when it became part of the Diocese of Chester. This covered all parishes in the barony or rural deanery of Kendal in Westmorland. The following is the situation with regard to the records of this archdeaconry:

   A The Records of Westmorland Wills and Admons. that received grants in the Western Deaneries (and the rural deanery of Kendal is in the Western Deaneries) are at the Lancashire Record Office, Preston, Lancs. To avoid confusion it should be noted that the *printed* Calendar, *The Lancashire Wills Proved Within the Archdeaconry of Richmond, 1457-1858,* does *NOT* include references to Westmorland estates in the deanery of Kendal.

   B The records of Westmorland Wills and Admons. that received grants in the Eastern Deaneries at Richmond are at the Archives Department, Central Library, Leeds, Yorks.

   Abstracts of some Wills, 1458-1579. Pub. Surtees Soc. [Eng. Pub. F., Vol. 26.]

3. The Manorial Court of Temple Sowerby covered that place. The records are at the County Record Office, Carlisle.

4. The Manorial Court of Ravenstonedale covered that place. The records are at the County Record Office, Carlisle.

   Prior to 1541 Westmorland Wills may also be found at Lichfield.

   Cal. of Wills, Consistory Court of Lichfield 1516-1541, Index Library, British Rec. Soc., Vol. 7. [Eng. Pub. AB., Vol. 7.]

   Westmorland Wills may also be found in the Prerogative Court of York and in the Prerogative Court of Canterbury.

   Some North Country Wills proved P.C.C., Pub. Surtees Soc. Vols. 116, 121. [Eng. Pub. F., Vols. 116, 121.]

Manuscript 1692 at the Genealogical Society, Salt Lake City, Utah, is a photostat copy of a map that clearly indicates the boundaries of the Diocese of Carlisle before and after 1856. The map shows the parishes within the Diocese and is entitled *A Map to Illustrate the Annals of Carlisle.* Another map entitled *A Map of the Diocese of Chester Divided into Deaneries, etc.,* published about 1750, shows the parishes and rural deaneries within the Archdeaconry of Richmond, Diocese of Chester. The original is at the Lancashire Record Office, Preston and a copy is available at the Genealogical Society, Salt Lake City, Utah.

Nonconformist Registers: There are records of nine Nonconformist chapels at the General Register Office, Somerset House, London.

Publications: The following publications are of interest:
1. *Publications* of the Cumberland and Westmorland Antiquarian and Archaeological Society.
2. *Publications* of the Surtees Society.
3. *The Northern Genealogist.*
4. *Northern Notes and Queries.*

WILTSHIRE   WILTSHIRE

—an inland county in the south of England.

(For map, see page 406-7)

Area: 1379 square miles.   *Population*: 240,200.

Ancient Parishes: 318, of which four are in Salisbury, two in Devizes and two in Marlboro.

County Town: The historical county town is Salisbury but Trowbridge is the administrative capital. The Wiltshire Record Office is at Trow-bridge.

Main Occupations: Agriculture, and the manufacture of carpets and woollen goods.

Principal Rivers: Isis, Thames, Lower Avon, Kennett, Wiltshire Avon.

Ecclesiastically, the county formed two archdeaconries. The Archdea-conry of Sarum or Salisbury, covered the south of the county and the Archdeaconry of Wiltshire covered the north of the county. Both archdeaconries are in the Diocese of Salisbury. Exceptions are the parishes of Kingswood in the Diocese of Gloucester and the parish of Whitchbury in the Diocese of Winchester. The county is wholly in the Province of Canterbury.

Parish Registers: The marriage registers of a number of parishes for periods prior to 1813 have been printed. A number of transcribed parish register copies are available at the Society of Genealogists, London. There are also a number of transcript copies of parish regis-ters at the Museum, Devizes. Original registers of a few parishes are at the Wiltshire Record Office, Trowbridge.

Bishop's Transcripts: These are at the Diocesan Registry, Salisbury and extend to around 1840. They are in fairly good condition and are arranged by parish.

Marriage Licenses: These are at the Diocesan Registry, Salisbury, but only the bonds are now available.

> Bishop of Salisbury 1615-1682. The Genealogist, New Series, Vols. 24-38. [Eng. Pub. AF., New Series, Vols. 24-38.]
> Peculiar Court of the Dean and Chapter of Sarum 1629-1690. Wilts. Notes and Queries, Vols. 6-8. [Wilts. Pub. C., Vols. 6-8.]

Probate Records: The following courts were in use:
1. The Episcopal Consistory Court of Sarum (i.e. Salisbury) covered

ten parishes and had jurisdiction over the archdeaconry courts during inhibitions.

2. The Archdeaconry Court of Sarum covered the parishes in the south of the county.
3. The Archdeaconry Court of Wiltshire covered the parishes in the north of the county.
4. The Peculiar Court of the Dean of Sarum covered nine parishes.
5. Eight other Sarum Peculiars covered forty-three parishes.

All of the records listed above are at the Wiltshire Record Office, Trowbridge. The names of parishes that came under peculiar jurisdiction are listed at the Wiltshire Record Office, Trowbridge.

Some of the Wiltshire Wills proved P.C.C. have been listed in print:

> Wiltshire Wills proved P.C.C., 1383-1604, Wilts. Notes and Queries, Vols. 1, 2, 5, 6, 7, 8. [Wilts. Pub. C., Vols. as above.]

Nonconformist Registers: There are records of seventy-one Nonconformist chapels at the General Register Office, Somerset House, London.

Publications: The following publications are of interest:

1. *Wiltshire Magazine.*
2. *Wiltshire Notes and Queries.*

WORCESTERSHIRE

WORCESTERSHIRE

(pronounced Wustershire)—an inland county in the south midlands of England.

(*For map, see page 408-9*)

Area: 780 square miles. *Population*: 211,356.

Ancient Parishes: 209, ten of which are in the City of Worcester, two in Droitwich, two in Evesham and two in Pershore.

County Town: Worcester, where the Worcester Record Office is situated.

Main Occupation: Agriculture, the manufacture of glass, iron and steel goods.

Principal Rivers: Severn, Upper Avon, Teme, Stour.

Ecclesiastically, the county formed the Archdeaconry of Worcester in the Diocese of Worcester except for fifteen parishes and eight chapelries that were in the Diocese of Hereford. All are in the Province of Canterbury. Several parishes near Birmingham, Warwickshire, have since 1905, been in the modern Diocese of Birmingham.

Parish Registers: The marriage registers of a few parishes have been printed for periods prior to 1813. Transcript copies of a few other parish registers are at the Shakespeare Library, Stratford-on-Avon.

Bishop's Transcripts: These are at the Worcester Record Office, Worcester. The earliest transcript is dated 1599 but there are many gaps up to 1700. From 1700 they are a fairly regular series until 1812.

Prior to 1700 they are arranged in parish order and from 1700 to 1812 they are arranged in yearly bundles in deanery order. Those for the Diocese of Hereford are at the Diocesan Registry, Hereford. (For details see "Herefordshire").

Marriage Licences: These are at the Worcester Record Office 1684-1942.

Some 1446-1662; 1676-1698; 1712-1717; 1720-1722, The Genealogist, Old Series, Vols. 6, 7. New Series, Vols. 1, 2. [Eng. Pub. AF., Old Series, Vols. 6, 7. New Series, Vols. 1, 2.]

A few others are with the Calendar of Wills and Admons. listed below. Those for the Diocese of Hereford are at the Diocesan Office, Hereford.

Probate Records: The following probate courts were in use:

1. The Episcopal Consistory Court of Worcester covered most parishes in the county.

   Cal. of Wills and Admons. 1451-1652, Index Library, British Rec. Soc. Vols. 31, 39. [Eng. Pub. AB, Vols. 31, 39.]

2. The Court of the Dean and Chapter of Worcester covered the parishes of Berrow, Kempsey, Norton, St Michael-in-Bedwardine, Stoulton, Tibberton, Wolverley and the College Precincts of Worcester City.

3. The Peculiar Courts of Alvechurch, Bredon, Evesham, Fladbury, Hampton Lucy, Hanbury, Hartlebury, Knowle, Ripple, Stratford-on-Avon and Tredington covered those parishes.

All the above are at the Worcestershire Record Office, Worcester.

4. Episcopal Consistory Court of Hereford for places that were in the Diocese of Hereford. These records are at the National Library of Wales, Aberystwyth, Cardiganshire.

Nonconformist Registers: There are records of thirty-nine Nonconformist chapels at the General Register Office, Somerset House, London.

Publications: The following publications are of interest:

1. *Publications* of the Worcestershire Historical Society.
2. *Worcester County Records.*
3. A *Digest of the Parish Registers,* printed for the Committee of Parish Registers under the authority of the Worcester Diocesan Conference, gives details of the parish registers and their condition for the whole county. It also indicates the number of Bishop's Transcripts available for each parish prior to 1700.

YORKSHIRE   YORKSHIRE

—is the largest county in England, containing areas that are maritime and inland. The ancient County of York is divided into three Ridings or thirdlings that are separate adminstrative counties, and the City of York with its own civil administration. The total area of the county is 5,961 square miles, that had a population of 1,371,296 residing within 751 ancient parishes, and is divided for administrative purposes as follows:

(For maps, see pages 410-419)

1. West Riding of Yorkshire:

Area: 2450 square miles. *Population*: 976,415

Ancient Parishes: 307, two of which are in Wakefield, two in Halifax, and eleven in Leeds.

County Town: Wakefield, where the County Hall and the West Riding Registry of Deeds are situated.

Main Occupations: Agriculture, industries concerned with coal and iron mining and allied productions; the manufacture of cutlery, machine tools, woollen cloth, etc.

Principal Rivers: Ouse, Aure, Don, Humber.

2. North Riding of Yorkshire:

Area: 2048 square miles. *Population*: 190,873

Ancient Parishes: 227, two of which are in New Malton.

County Town: Northallerton, where the County Hall, the County Record Office, and the North Riding Registry of Deeds are situated.

Main Occupations: Agriculture and the manufacturing of cloth. Seafaring and shipbuilding along the north-east coast.

Principal Rivers: Hertford, Derwent, Ouse, Tees, Rye.

3. East Riding of Yorkshire:

Area: 1280 square miles. *Population*: 204,008
(including the city of York)

Ancient Parishes: 193, two of which are in Beverley, and two are in Kingston-upon-Hull, the latter place generally being referred to as Hull.

County Town: Beverley, where the County Hall and the East Riding Registry of Deeds are situated.

Main Occupations: Agriculture and seafaring.

Principal Rivers: Hertford, Hull, Derwent, Ouse, Humber.

4. The City of York:

The City of York and the Ainsty of the City of York is a special division of the county. There are thirty-nine ancient parishes within this division, twenty-four of which are within the City itself. The City has its own civil administration and archives, and is also the seat of the Archbishop of York who has an Archdiocesan Record Office and Archivist.

Ecclesiastically, except for a few parishes, the whole of Yorkshire was, at one time, wholly within the Diocese and Province of York. As far back as the 12th century, there were four ancient archdeaconries containing seventeen rural deaneries. The rural deaneries are listed later in this section under the heading "Probate Records." The following are the ecclesiastical jurisdictions and the major changes that have taken place:

1. The Archdeaconry of York, also known as the Archdeaconry of the West Riding, comprised the City of York and most of the Ain-sty of York, together with the whole of the West Riding, with certain exceptions. A list of these exceptions is in the *Victoria History of York*, Vol. 3, pp. 81-83. It was wholly in the Diocese of York until 1836, when, at the creation of the Diocese of Ripon, a portion of this archdeaconry was transferred to that new diocese. In 1888, when the Diocese of Wakefield was created, a part of the Diocese of Ripon was transferred to the Diocese of Wakefield.

2. The Archdeaconry of the East Riding, comprises the whole of the East Riding, with certain exceptions that are listed in the *Victoria History of York*, Vol. 3, pp. 84-86. It is wholly in the Diocese of York.

3. The Archdeaconry of Cleveland, comprises the eastern and major portion of the North Riding, a small portion of the Ainsty of York, and prior to 1896, a small part of the East Riding. Certain excep-tions are listed in the *Victoria History of York*, Vol. 3, pp. 86-87. It was wholly within the Diocese of York.

4. The Archdeaconry of Richmond was within the Diocese and Province of York until 1541 when it was trans-ferred to the Diocese of Chester which was created in that year. In 1836, when the Diocese of Ripon was created, that portion of the Archdea-conry of Richmond which was in Yorkshire was made into the Arch-deaconry of Richmond in the Diocese of Ripon.

In 1888, when the Diocese of Wakefield was created, a part of the Diocese of Ripon was transferred to it.

Within the limits of Yorkshire, the Archdeaconry of Richmond comprised certain places in the western half of the North Riding, and a small portion of the West Riding. Information concerning the Archdeaconry will be found in the *Victoria History of York*, Vol. 3, p. 88.

5. Saddleworth, Yorkshire, was an ancient chapelry in the parish of Rochdale, Lancashire. Whitewell, Yorkshire, was an ancient chap-elry in the parish of Whalley, Lancashire. Both ancient chapelries are within the West Riding of Yorkshire, and were in the Diocese of Lichfield and Coventry, Province of Canterbury, until 1541, when they became part of the Archdeaconry and Diocese of Chester in the Province of York. Since 1836 they have been in the Diocese of Manchester.

6. The Diocese of Durham contained Over Dinsdale and Girsby, Yorkshire. They are portions of the parish of Sockburn, a parish in County Durham but chiefly in the County of York.

7. The Diocese of Durham contained the parish of Crayke (or Craike) until 1837, when Crayke was transferred to the Arch-

deaconry of Cleveland, Diocese of York, and freed from the Peculiar Jurisdiction of the Dean and Chapter of Durham. In 1844 Crayke was completely annexed to Yorkshire.

8. The Archdeaconry of Nottingham contained several Yorkshire places that were in the extreme south of the West Riding. This archdeaconry was in the Diocese and Province of York until 1839, when it was transferred to the Diocese of Lincoln, Province of Canterbury. In 1844 it was taken from the Diocese of Lincoln to form part of the Diocese of Southwell. In 1934, the Diocese of Southwell was transferred to the Province of York. The places in Yorkshire are as follows:

A. Chapelries of Bawtry and Austerfield, Yorks., that were parts of the parish of Blyth, Notts.

B. Townships of Auckley or Aulkey and Blaxton, Yorks., that were part of the parish of Finningley, Notts.

C. The parish of Rossington, Yorks., that was transferred in 1856, from the Archdeaconry of Notts. to the Archdeaconry of York or West Riding, in the Diocese and Province of York.

Since 1888, when the Diocese of Wakefield was created, Yorkshire has been further divided, and portions of it are now within the Dioceses of Sheffield and Bradford.

Parish Registers: The Yorkshire Parish Register Society has published well over one hundred volumes of printed parish registers. Other parish registers have also been printed. Others have been transcribed and are available in the Library of the Yorkshire Parish Register Society and the Yorkshire Archaeological Society in Leeds. Most of these have been microfilmed for the Genealogical Society, Salt Lake City, Utah. Other transcribed copies are available at the Society of Genealogists, London. These represent, however, less than half of the parishes in the county.

Percival Boyd's *Yorkshire Marriage Index* covers about 170 parishes for varying periods. Parish registers transcribed or printed since 1938 are not included in this.

The Yorkshire Archaeological Society has published information on the condition and dates of the parish registers in the Archdeaconry of the East Riding of York.[27] This covers 269 parishes in the county.

Bishop's Transcripts: Those for the Archdeaconry of York or the West Riding, the Archdeaconry of the East Riding, and the Archdeaconry of Cleveland are at the Borthwick Institute, St. Anthony's Hall, York. They are arranged 1600-1813 in yearly bundles in *deanery order*. For some of the earlier years they are in need of re-sorting. For the period 1813-1837 they are in yearly bundles, not arranged in any order whatever. The Bishop's Transcripts for Yorkshire *and* Nottinghamshire are mixed together 1813-1837, and work has commenced to place these transcripts in deanery order. Until that has been completed they are almost impossible to search for the period 1813-1837. The Bishop's Transcripts of the parishes of Rossington, Bawtry and

---

27. *Parochial Documents in the Archdeaconry of the East Riding,* published by the Yorkshire Arch. Society as Volume 99 of their Record Series. (1939)

Austerfield are at the Diocesan Registry at Southwell, Notts. (except for the period 1813-1837) arranged in parish order.

The Bishop's Transcripts of the Archdeaconry of Richmond relating to those rural deaneries (the Eastern Deaneries) that are in the County of York, namely Boroughbridge, Catterick and Richmond, are at the Archives Department, Central Library, Leeds, 1. The transcripts for those parishes that were added to this archdeaconry in 1836, when the Diocese of Ripon was created are, for dates later than 1836, in the same archives. The publications of the Yorkshire Parish Register Society, Volume 101, *Richmond Register Transcripts,* gives a list of the parishes involved. A copy of a more accurate and complete list is available at the Archives Department, Central Library, Leeds and at the Genealogical Society, Salt Lake City, Utah. This collection has few transcripts prior to 1700 and then extends to the 1840s with customary gaps. This collection has been microfilmed for the Genealogical Society, Salt Lake City.

The Bishop's Transcripts for Saddleworth and Whitewell are assumed to be at the Lancashire Record Office, Preston, Lancashire.

Those Bishop's Transcripts that exist for the parishes of Sockburn and Craike (Crayke) are at the University, Durham.

The Bishop's Transcripts for the many parishes in this county classed as Peculiars are very few. Those that exist are at the Borthwick Institute, York.

Marriage Licenses: As the right to issue marriage licenses fell within the jurisdiction of the ecclesiastical authorities, a record of a particular marriage license issued in Yorkshire may be difficult to find, the following jurisdictions should be considered:

1. The Archbishop's Registry at York. As practically the whole of the county was in the Province of York, marriage licenses were obtainable from the Archbishop.

   1567-1630. Yorks. Arch. Journal, Vols. 7, 9, 10-14, 16, 17, 20. [Yorks. Pub. A., Vols. as above.]
   1630-1714. Yorks. Arch. Soc., Vols. 40, 43, 46. [Yorks. 7, Vols. as above.]

   According to the *Northern Genealogist* (1896), there are no records of marriage bonds in the Archbishop's Registry prior to 1660. The marriage allegations begin to be filed with the bonds in 1723. The records are at the Borthwick Institute, St. Anthony's Hall, York.

2. The Archdeaconry of Richmond. There are about 2,000 marriage bonds for the three Yorkshire (Eastern Deaneries) at the Archives Department, Central Library, Leeds. In this series very few exist prior to 1740 and a number are missing around 1770. Many persons from Yorkshire parishes will be found recorded in the series covering the Western Deaneries of this Archdeaconry. These records are at the Lancashire Record Office, Preston, Lancs.

   1648-1745 Lancs. & Chesh. Rec. Soc., Vols. 74, 75, 80, 81, 83, 100. [Chesh. 1. Vols. as above.]

   The period 1746-1799 has been microfilmed for the Genealogical Society, Salt Lake City, Utah.

3. The Archdeaconry of Nottingham. Persons residing in certain parishes on the south-east border came within this jurisdiction.
     1577-1753, Index Library, British Rec. Soc., Vols. 58, 60. [Eng. Pub. AB., Vols. 58, 60.]
     1754-1770, Thoroton Society Record Series Vol. 10. [Notts. 6, Vol. 10.]

   The records are at the University, Nottingham.

4. The Archdeaconry of Chester. See "Cheshire" regarding persons connected with Saddleworth and Whitewell.

5. Peculiar Jurisdictions. Records of marriage licenses issued for the many parishes that had peculiar jurisdiction are very few, and in some cases, the whereabouts of the records has not been established. They may be part of the regular series kept at the Archbishop's Registry (see item 1). Those for the Peculiar of Selby, 1710-1800, are at the Borthwick Institute, St. Anthony's Hall, York.
     Pec. Court of Selby. 1664-1726. [Yorks. 7. Vol. 47.]
     Pec. of Dean and Chapter of York, extracts only 1660-1777. [Eng. Pub. R., Vols. 3-5.]

Probate Records: The situation with regard to probate records in York-shire is complicated, and presents an unusual state of affairs that genealogists must face. York is the seat of the Archbishop of York, head of the Province of York, but who is also head of the Diocese of York, as he exercises the power of Bishop within that Diocese. This diocese anciently included four Yorkshire archdeaconries comprising seventeen rural deaneries and about 750 ancient parishes, and one Nottinghamshire archdeaconry. The details concerning the archdeaconries have already been detailed earlier. As certain of the probate records are filed under the names of the rural deaneries, the following list will help:

Archdeaconries and Dioceses	*Rural Deaneries (Yorkshire)*
1 The Archdeaconry of York or the West Riding, Diocese of York.	1. Christianity or City of York. 2. Ainsty. 3. Craven with Ripon. 4. Doncaster. 5. Pontefract with Halifax.
2. The Archdeaconry of the East Riding, Diocese of York.	1. Beverley (a Provostry). 2. Buckrose, Old and New. 3. Dickering. 4. Harthill with Hull. 5. Holderness, with part of Hull.
3. The Archdeaconry of Cleveland, Diocese of York.	1. Bulmer. 2. Cleveland. 3. Ryedale.
4. The Archdeaconry of Nottingham, Diocese of York.	1. Retford, containing five places in Yorkshire.
5. The Archdeaconry of Richmond, formerly in the Diocese of York, later in the Diocese of Chester.	1. Boroughbridge, an Eastern Deanery. 2. Catterick, an Eastern Deanery.

3. Richmond, an Eastern Deanery

4. Lonsdale, one of the Western Deaneries, but containing sev' eral Yorkshire parishes.

Out of the approximately 750 parishes situated in above rural dean' eries and archdeaconries, more than 135 of them were situated within 35 ecclesiastical Peculiars and several Manorial jurisdictions. These Peculiars exercised testamentary jurisdiction, and were exempt from the Exchequer Court of the Diocese of York and the Commissary Court of the Archdeaconry of Richmond.

When an estate was *solely* within the Diocese of York (excluding Peculiars) it was usual for the local rural dean, acting by commission from the Exchequer Court of the Diocese of York, to make the grant of probate, etc. The records were then transmitted to the Exchequer Court in York where an entry was made in the Calendar or Index (if one was kept), the grant was then entered in the Act Book for the *particular deanery* concerned, the Wills copied into the Registers of Copy Wills, and the original documents, including the Admon. Bonds, were filed in the bundles or boxes.

When an estate was *solely* within the Archdeaconry of Richmond (excluding Peculiars) it was usual for the local rural dean, acting by commission from the Commissary of the Archdeaconry of Richmond, to make the grant of probate, etc. If within the three Eastern Dean' eries, the records were transmitted to Richmond Registry, York. If within the Rural Deanery of Lonsdale (one of the Western Deaner' ies) the records were transmitted to Lancaster Registry, Lancs. There are, however, some Yorkshire estates in Lonsdale Rural Deanery that received grants at Richmond Registry, most of which were by Decree of Court, and these are listed in the Calendars or Indexes for the Eastern Deaneries only.[28]

The *Victoria History of York*, Vol. 3, pp. 81-88, lists details of ecclesiastical divisions, stating information on each of the archdeacon' ries, and listing the Peculiar Jurisdictions and the parishes involved. Reference should also be made to Bouwen's *Wills and their where' abouts*, pp. 71-75. Among the probate records at York there is a *Deanery Book* that lists the names of all Yorkshire and Nottingham' shire parishes, stating the name of the rural deanery within which each is situated, and whether the parish is within a Peculiar jurisdiction.[29]

The following probate courts were in use:

1. The Prerogative Court of the Archbishop of York, (abbreviated

---

28. A map showing the parishes within the Archdeaconry of Richmond to' gether with boundaries of the rural deaneries is *A Map Of The Diocese of Chester Divided Into Deanries, &c.,* published about 1750. The map is at the Lancashire Record Office, Preston. A photo'copy is available at the Genealogical Society, Salt Lake City, Utah.

29. *Deanery Book.* This book has been microfilmed, and the microfilm at the Genealogical Society, Salt Lake City, has the Library call number 14430, F.Yorks. 9. A typescript copy of this book has the call number Eng. 366.

to P.C.Y.), covered the whole province, which, incidentally, covered the Isle of Man.[30]

2. The Exchequer Court of the Diocese of York, also known as the
Exchequer Court of the Dean, because probates were granted by
the rural deans, covered the whole Diocese of York, excluding,
however, the Peculiars.[31] The archdeaconries and rural deaneries
involved are listed above.

> Cal. for both the above courts, 1389-1688. Pub. Yorks. Arch. Soc.,
> Vols. 4, 6, 11, 14, 19, 22, 24, 26, 28, 32, 35, 49, 60, 68 and 89.
> [Yorks. 7, Vols. as above.]
> Abstracts of some Yorkshire Wills 1316-1616; 1623-1659. Pub. Surtees
> Soc., Vols. 2, 30, 45, 53, 79, 106, 111, 121. [Eng. Pub. F., Vols. as
> above.] and Pub. Yorks. Arch. Soc. Vol. 9. [Yorks, 7, Vol. 9.]

3. The Court of the Dean and Chapter of York covered eleven parishes within the City of York and at least sixteen others within
the county. During vacancies, in the Prerogative and Exchequer
Courts, the grants were made in this court.

> Cal. 1321-1724. Pub. Yorks. Arch. Soc., Vols. 38, 60. [Yorks. 7,
> Vols. 38, 60.]

4. The Peculiar Court of the Dean of York covered a few parishes
in the vicinity of Pocklington and Pickering.

> Cal. 1604-1722, ibid. Vol. 73. [Ibid. Vol. 73.]

5. The Peculiar of the Precentor of the Cathedral covered three
parishes.
The Peculiar of the Treasury of the Cathedral covered several
places.
The Peculiar of the Sub-Dean of the Cathedral covered one parish.
The Peculiar of the Archdeacon of the East Riding covered one
parish.
The Peculiar of the Succentor of the Cathedral covered one parish.
The Peculiar of the Archdeacon of York covered two places.
The Peculiar of St. Leonard's Hospital.

6. The Peculiar of the Chancellor of the Cathedral with the Prebend
of Laughton-en-le-Morthen covered eleven parishes in the vicinity
of Laughton.

7. The Episcopal Consistory and Chancery Courts. The Episcopal
Consistory Court had jurisdiction ver certain clergy and over
Peculiars during their inhibition. The Chancery Court concerned
itself with probates subject to litigation.

> Cal. 1316-1822, ibid. Vols. 73, 93. [Ibid. Vols. 73, 93.]

8. The Peculiar Court of the Archbishop of York in Hexham and
Hexhamshire covered five parishes.

> Cal. 1593-1602, ibid. Vol. 73. [Ibid. Vol. 73.]

9. The Peculiar Court of the Archbishop of York in Ripon (Liberty
of Ripon) covered twenty parishes in the vicinity of Ripon.

All the above records are at the Borthwick Institute, St. Anthony's
Hall, York.

---

30. See Yorks. Arch. Soc. Pub. (Record Series), Vol. 89, and read the Preface
for additional information on the procedure of the P.C.Y. and the Exchequer Court. [Yorks., 7, Vol. 89.] See also the Northern Genealogist, Vol. 2,
where it states "Where there are no official indexes to Wills . . . [1688-
1731] . . . the Act Books [of the Prerogative Court or of the Rural
Deaneries] . . . must be searched." [Eng. Pub. R., Vol. 2.

31. See footnote 30.

10. The Consistorial Court of the Commissary of the Archdeaconry of Richmond. The records for the rural deaneries of Borough-bridge, Catterick, and Richmond covering parishes within those three rural deaneries, and also covering estates where the grant was by Decree of Court anywhere within the Archdeaconry, including the rural deanery of Lonsdale, a part of which covered parishes in Yorkshire. These records are at the Archives Department, Central Library, Leeds.

> Cal. A to G only, prior to 1617. Northern Genealogist, Vol. 2. Supp. [Eng. Pub. R., Vol. 3, Supp.]
> Abstracts of some Wills 1442-1578. Pub. Surtees Soc. Vol. 26. [Eng. Pub. F., Vol. 26.]
> Abstracts of some Wills 1438-1601, Northern Gene, Vols. 2, 3, 4. 6. [Eng. Pub. R., Vols. 2, 3, 4, 6.]

The records for the rural deanery of Lonsdale, one of the Western Deaneries, a part of which covered parishes in Yorkshire, are at the Lancashire Record Office, Preston, Lancs. The Record Society . . . Lancashire and Cheshire, has published the Calendars or Indexes to some of the records of the Western Deaneries of this archdeaconry. In searching these printed books, care is needed, as these relate to *Lancashire estates only,* and do not refer to the records of estates within the Archdeaconry but outside of Lancashire.

11. The Peculiars of the Bishop of Durham and of the Dean of Allerton and Allertonshire covered fifteen parishes in the vicinity of Northallerton. The records are at the University, Durham.

12. The Peculiar of Crayke (Craike) was in the Diocese of Durham until 1837 and the records are at the University, Durham. Since 1837 this parish has been in the Archdeaconry of Cleveland, Yorkshire, and the records since 1837 are at the Borthwick Institute, St. Anthony's Hall, York.

13. There are more than 135 parishes in over 35 Peculiar and Manorial jurisdictions. For a complete listing of these see B. G. Bouwens, *Wills and Their Whereabouts.*

> Cal. Pec. of Aldborough. 1610-1700. Pub. Yorks. Arch. Soc. Vol. 60. [Yorks. 7 Vol. 60.]
> Cal. Pec. of Beeford 1586-1768, ibid. Vol. 68. [Ibid. Vol. 68.]
> Cal. Pec. of Provost of Beverley 1539-1552, ibid. Vol. 60. [Ibid. Vol. 60.]
> Cal. Pec. of St. Leonard's Hospital, York. 1410-1533, ibid. Vol. 60. [Ibid. Vol. 60.]
> Cal. Pec. of Altofts in Normanton 1622-1677. Northern Genealogist, Vol. 1. [Eng. Pub. R., Vol. 1.]
> Cal. Pec. of Barnoldswick 1660-1794, ibid. Vol. 1. [Ibid. Vol. 1.]
> Cal. Pec. of Marsden, 1654-1855, ibid. Vol. 2 [Ibid. Vol. 2.]
> Cal. Pec. of Crossley, Bingley, Pudsey, 1580-1676, ibid. Vol. 1. [Ibid. Vol. 1.]
> Cal. Pec. of Masham, A to R only. 1654-1855, ibid. Vol. 2. [Ibid. Vol. 2.]
> Cal. Pec. of Silsden 1587-1737, ibid. Vol. 1. [Ibid. Vol. 1.]
> Cal. Pec. of Templenewsum 1612-1701, ibid. Vol. 1. [Ibid. Vol. 1.]
> Cal. Pec. of Warmfield and Heath 1613-1691, ibid. Vol. 1. [Ibid. Vol. 1.]

All the records listed in item 13 are at St. Anthony's Hall, York.

14. The Episcopal Consistory Court of Chester covered Saddleworth and Whitewell. See under "Cheshire" for complete details.

Histories of parishes and towns should be read as they may contain references to probates of residents. For example:

1. Michael Sheard, Residents of Batley, mentions probates of parish residents, 1391-1768.
2. Hull, List of Wills enrolled in the Liber Rubeus. 1309-1426. Pub. Yorks. Arch. Soc., Vol. 2. [Yorks. 7, Vol. 2.]

The Prerogative Court of Canterbury, should of course be considered, especially during the Commonwealth Period, 1649-1660.

Cal. of Wills proved P.C.C. 1649-1660, ibid. Vol. 1. [Ibid. Vol. 1.]
Abstracts of Some Yorkshire Wills proved P.C.C. 1649-1660, ibid. Vol. 9. [Ibid. Vol. 9.]

Nonconformist Registers: There are records of four hundred and twenty-three Nonconformist chapels at the General Register Office, Somerset House, London.

Publications: The following publications are of interest:

1. *Transactions* of the Hunter Archaeological Society.
2. *Transactions* of the East Riding Antiquarians Society.
3. *Publications* of the North Riding Record Society.
4. *Collection of Historical Notes Relating to Yorkshire.*
5. *Publications* of the Thoresby Society (Leeds locality).
6. *Publications* of the Surtees Society.
7. *The Northern Genealogist.*
8. *Publications* of the Yorkshire Archaeological Society.
9. *Publications* of the Yorkshire Parish Register Society.

MAPS

ANGLESEY

Reference to the Unions

1 *Anglesea*

2 *Carnarvon Part*

3 *Bangor and Beaumaris Part*

BRECKNOCKSHIRE

Scale of Miles

Reference to the Unions

1   *Rhaiadr Part*
2   *Llandovery Part*
3   *Builth Part*
4   *Brecknock*
5   *Hay Part*
6   *Neath Part*
7   *Merthyr Tydvil Part*
8   *Crickhowel*

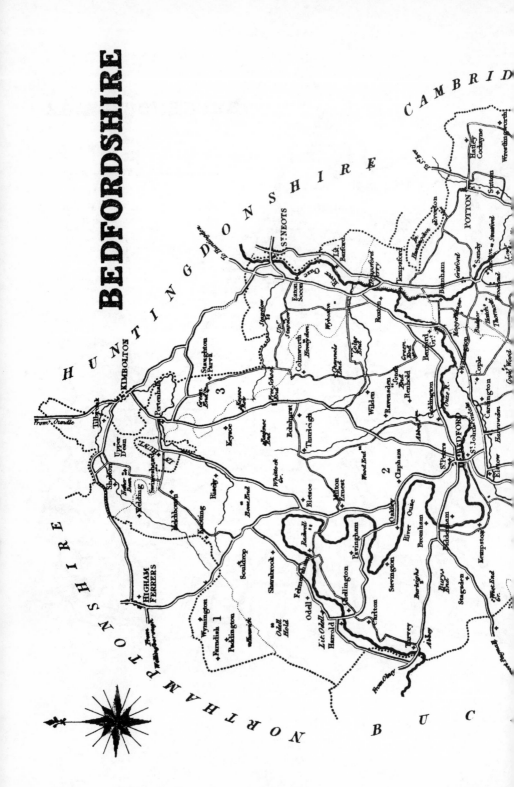

BEDFORDSHIRE

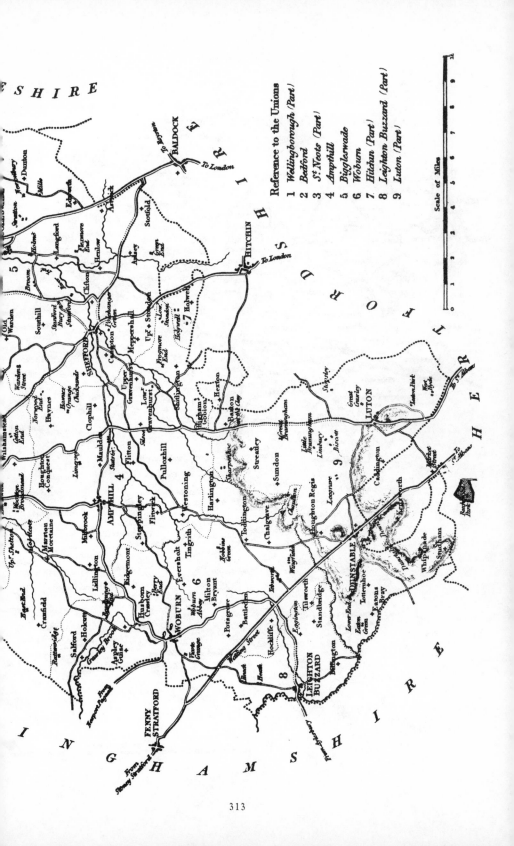

Reference to the Unions

1 Wellingborough (Part)
2 Bedford
3 St. Neots (Part)
4 Ampthill
5 Bigglswade
6 Woburn
7 Hitchin (Part)
8 Leighton Buzzard (Part)
9 Luton (Part)

Scale of Miles

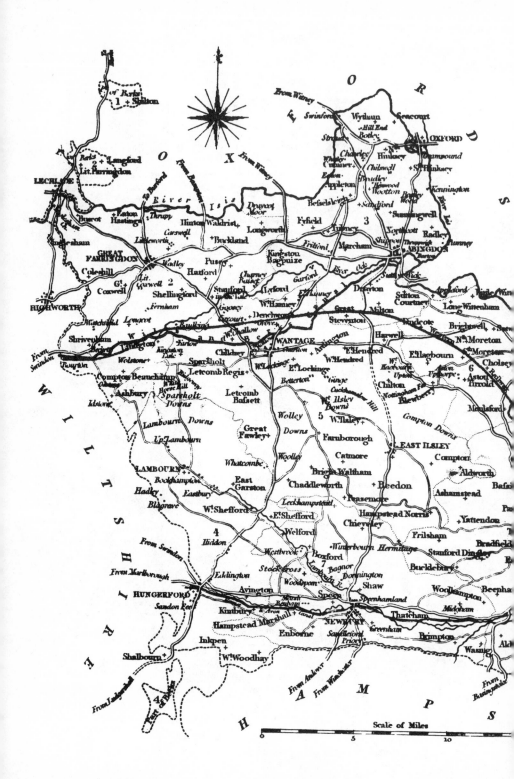

BERKSHIRE

Reference to the Unions

1	*Witney (Part)*	8	*Bradfield (Part)*
2	*Farringdon (Part)*	9	*Reading*
3	*Abingdon (Part)*	10	*Basingstoke (Part)*
4	*Hungerford (Part)*	11	*Henley (Part)*
5	*Wantage*	12	*Wokingham*
6	*Wallingford (Part)*	13	*Cookham*
7	*Newbury*	14	*Easthampstead*
		15	*Windsor (Part)*

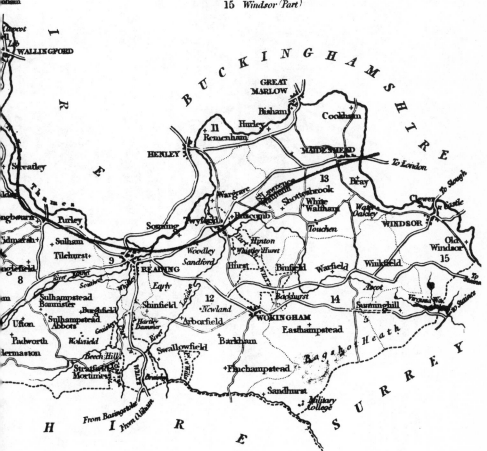

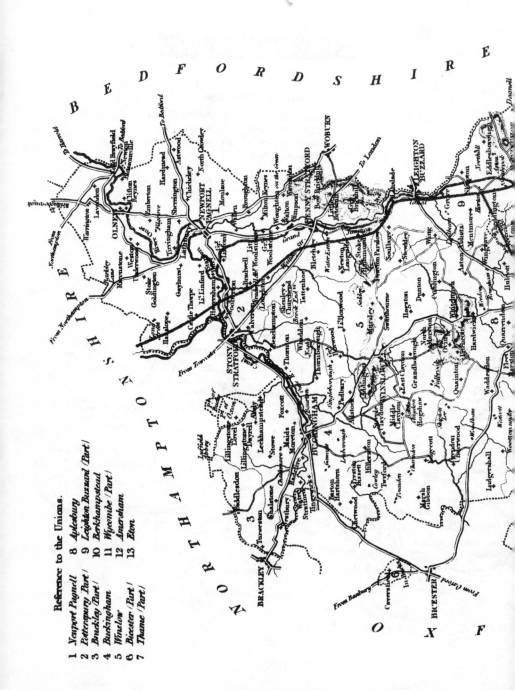

Reference to the Unions.

1 Newport Pagnell
2 Potterspury (Part)
3 Brackley (Part)
4 Buckingham
5 Winslow
6 Bicester (Part)
7 Thame (Part)
8 Aylesbury
9 Leighton Buzzard (Part)
10 Berkhampstead
11 Wycombe (Part)
12 Amersham
13 Eton

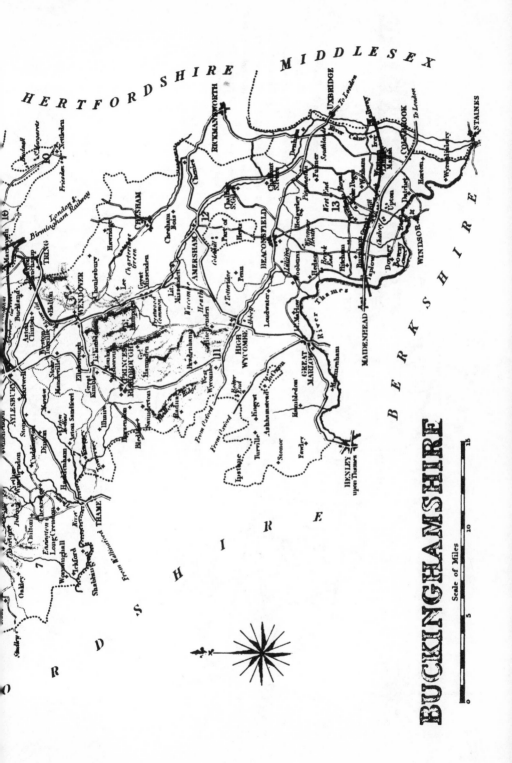

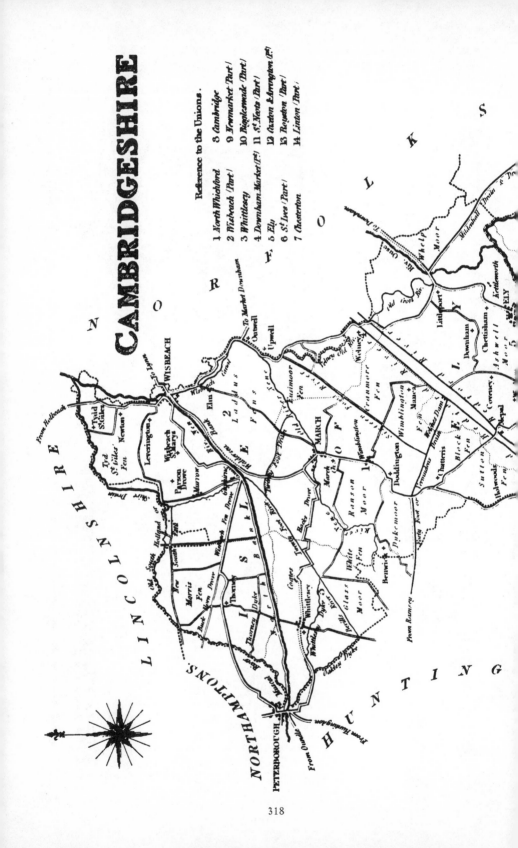

CAMBRIDGESHIRE

Reference to the Unions.

1 North Whichford
2 Wisbeach (Part)
3 Whittlesey
4 Downham Market (Pt.)
5 Ely
6 St. Ives (Part)
7 Chesterton

8 Cambridge
9 Newmarket (Part)
10 Bigglesworde (Part)
11 St. Neots (Part)
12 Caxton & Arrington (Ft.)
13 Royston (Part)
14 Linton (Part)

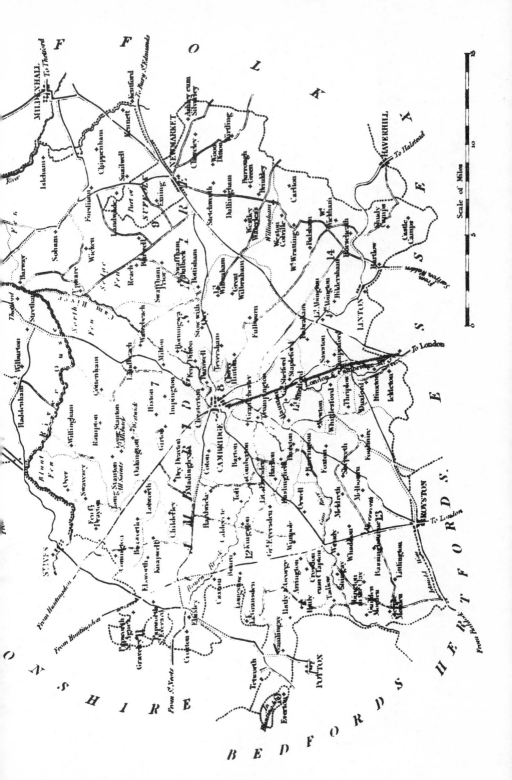

CARNARVONSHIRE

Reference to the Unions

1 Bangor and Beaumaris (Part)
2 Conway (Part)
3 Carnarvon (Part)
4 Llanrwst (Part)
5 Pwllheli
6 Festiniog (Part)

CARDIGANSHIRE

Reference to the Unions

1 Machynlleth (Part)
2 Aberystwith
3 Aberaeron
4 Tregaron
5 Cardigan (Part)
6 Newcastle Emlyn (Part)
7 Lampeter (Part)

Scale of Miles

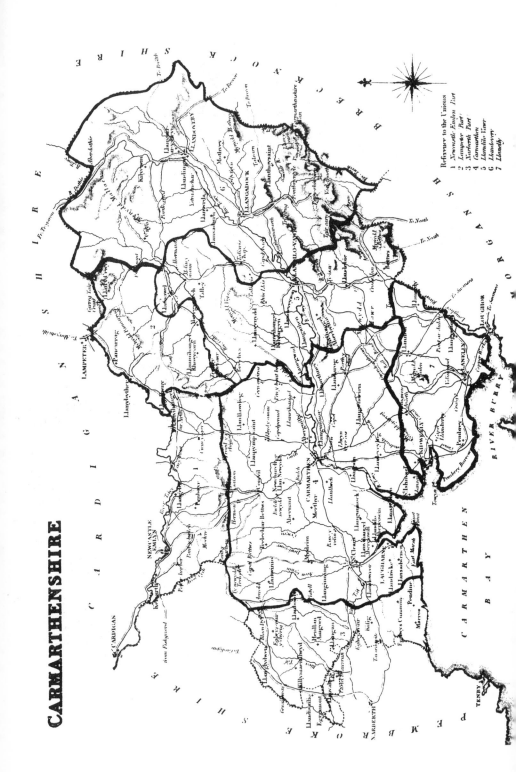

CARMARTHENSHIRE

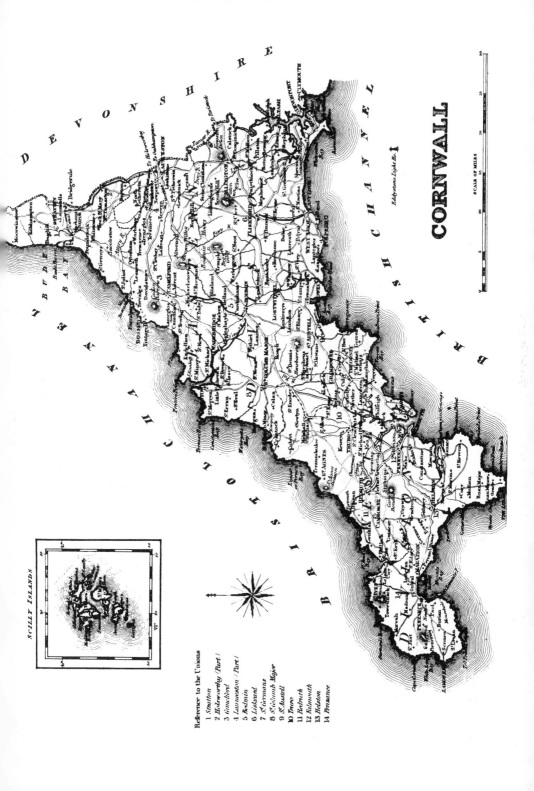

CORNWALL

SCALE OF MILES

DEVONSHIRE

BRISTOL CHANNEL

BRITISH CHANNEL

Eddystone Light Ho.

BUDE BAY

SCILLY ISLANDS

Reference to the Unions

1 Stratton
2 Holsworthy (Part)
3 Camelford
4 Launceston (Part)
5 Bodmin
6 Liskeard
7 S.Germans
8 S.Columb Major
9 S.Austell
10 Truro
11 Redruth
12 Falmouth
13 Helston
14 Penzance

323

CHESHIRE

Scale of Miles

Reference to the Unions.

1 Wirrall   8 Hayfield (Part)
2 Chester (local act)   9 Northwich
3 Gr.! Boughton (Part) 10 Macclesfield
4 Runcorn   11 Congleton (Part)
5 Altrincham   12 Wrexham (Part)
6 Stockport (Part) 13 Nantwich
7 Ashton under line (P.t) 14 Drayton (Part)

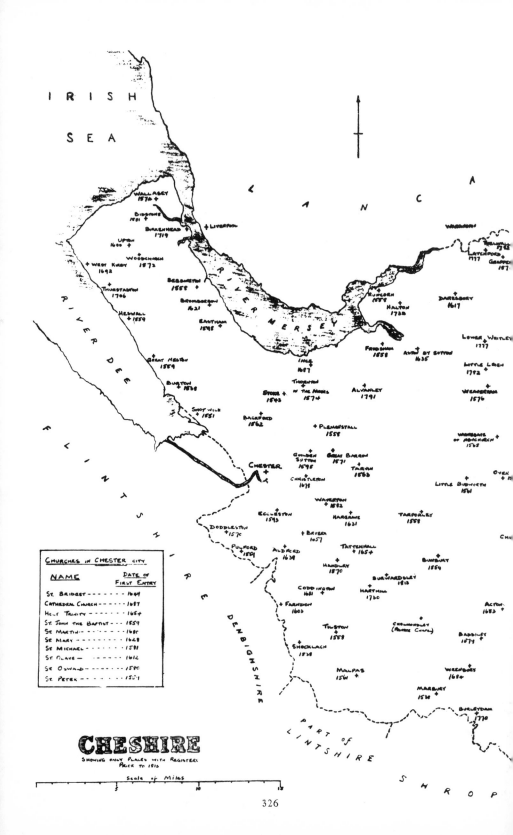

CHESHIRE

Showing only places with Registers prior to 1812

Scale of Miles

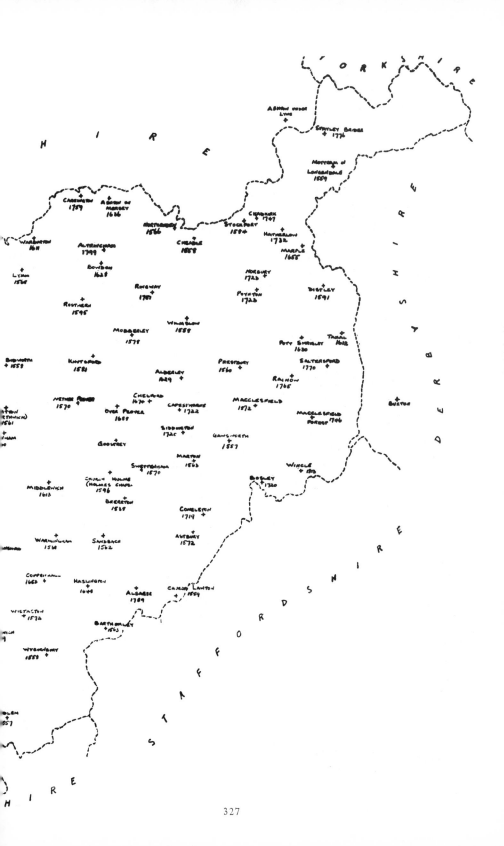

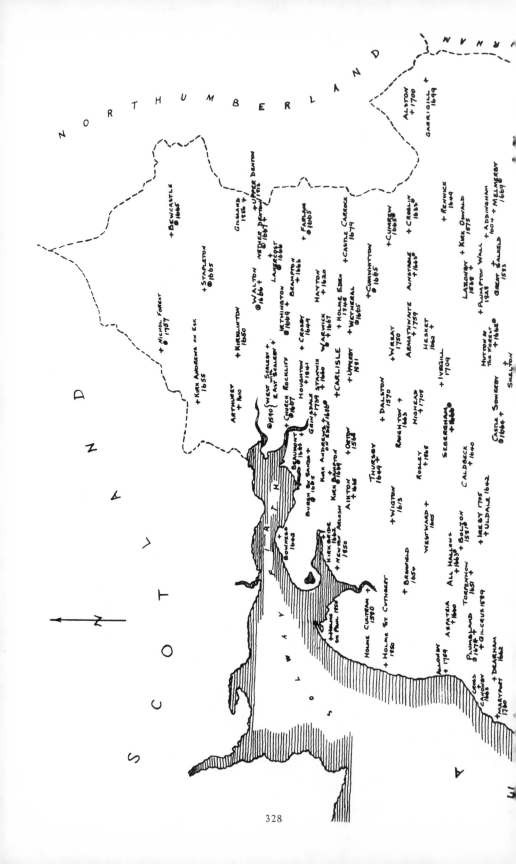

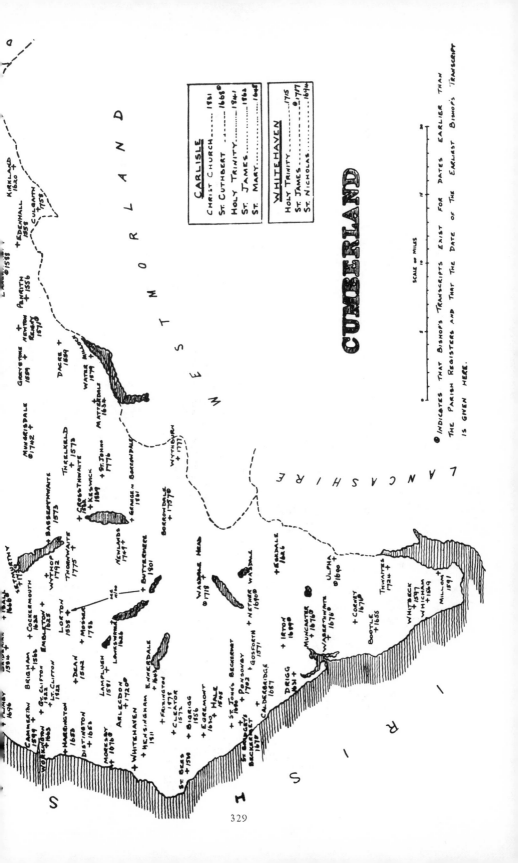

CUMBERLAND

CARLISLE

CHRIST CHURCH 1851
ST. CUTHBERT ...... 1668●
HOLY TRINITY 1841
ST. JAMES 1862
ST. MARY ...... 1668●

WHITEHAVEN

HOLY TRINITY 1715
ST. JAMES ...... ●1717
ST. NICHOLAS ... 1694●

SCALE OF MILES

● INDICATES THAT BISHOP'S TRANSCRIPTS EXIST FOR DATES EARLIER THAN THE PARISH REGISTERS AND THAT THE DATE OF THE EARLIEST BISHOP'S TRANSCRIPT IS GIVEN HERE.

S C O T L A N D

W E S T M O R L A N D

L A N C A S H I R E

I R I S H   S E A

KIRKLAND 1620 +
+ EDENHALL 1558
CULGAITH 1758
PALACE RIGG ●1588
PENRITH + 1556
GREYSTOKE 1559 +
NEWTON REIGNY 1571/2 +
DACRE + 1559
WATER MILLOCK +
MATTERDALE 1634 +
WYTHBURN + 1771
MUNGRISDALE ●1742 +
THRELKELD + 1578
+ CROSTHWAITE
KESWICK 1589
+ ST. JOHNS 1776
+ GRANGE IN BORROWDALE 1901
BORROWDALE + 1570
SETMURTHY +
BASSENTHWAITE 1573 +
+ WYTHOP 1792
THORNTHWAITE 1775 +
NEWLANDS 1547 +
+ BUTTERMERE 1901
BRIDEKIRK + 1584
ISALL + 1568
+ COCKERMOUTH +
EMBLETON 1658 +
LORTON 1538 +
+ MOSSER 1740
+ DEAN 1548
LAMPLUGH 1581 +
LOWESWATER 1628 +
WADDALE HEAD ●1718 +
+ NETHER WASDALE 1690●
ESKDALE 1626 +
CAMERTON 1844 +
WORKINGTON + 1665
+ HARRINGTON 1653
+ DISTINGTON 1658
MORESBY 1676 +
+ WHITEHAVEN
ARLECDON + 1720●
ENNERDALE 1511 +
+ FRIZINGTON
+ HENSINGHAM
+ CLEATOR 1675
+ EGREMONT 1600●
HALE 1645 +
+ ST. JOHN'S BECKERMET
+ PONSONBY 1700
+ GOSFORTH 1571
CALDER BRIDGE 1687
ST. BEES + 1538
BIGRIGG 1856 +
ST. BRIDGET'S BECKERMET 1639 +
DRIGG + 1811 +
IRTON 1694 +
MUNCASTER + 1676●
WABERTHWAITE + 1676●
ULPHA ●1690
+ CORNEY 1676
BOOTLE + 1655
WHITBECK 1597 +
WHICHAM 1649 +
MILLOM + 1591
THWAITES 1724 +

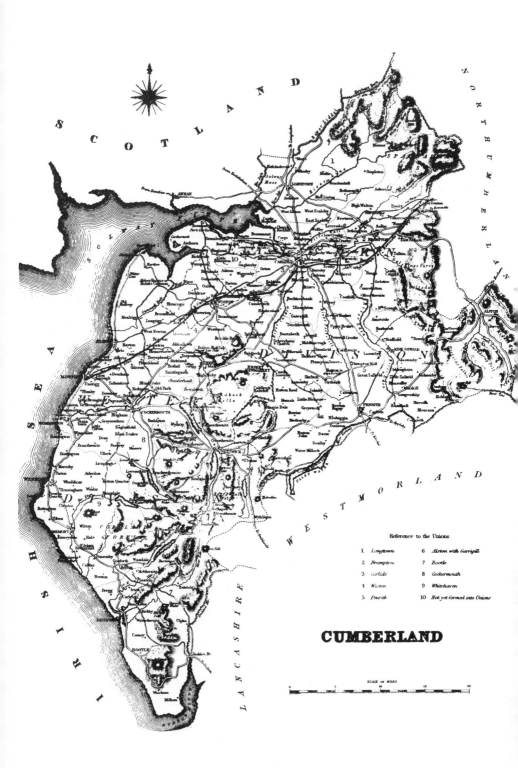

Reference to the Unions

1	*Longtown*	6	*Alston with Garrigill*
2	*Brampton*	7	*Bootle*
3	*Carlisle*	8	*Cockermouth*
4	*Wigton*	9	*Whitehaven*
5	*Penrith*	10	*Not yet formed into Unions*

CUMBERLAND

SCALE OF MILES

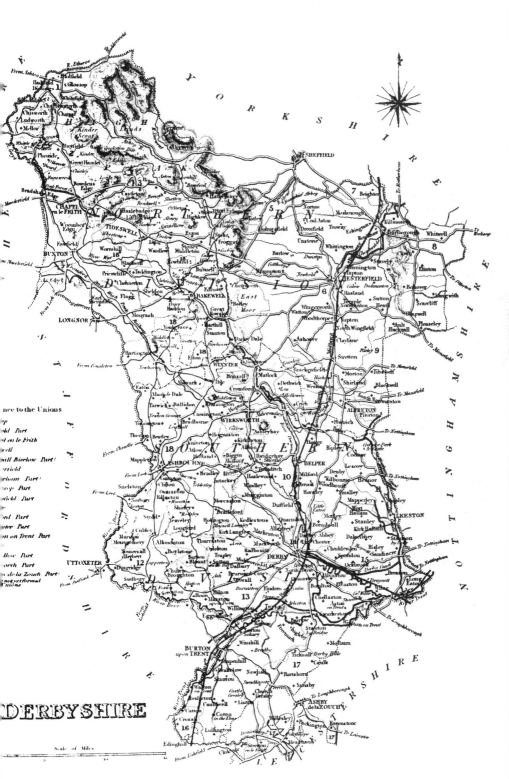

DERBYSHIRE

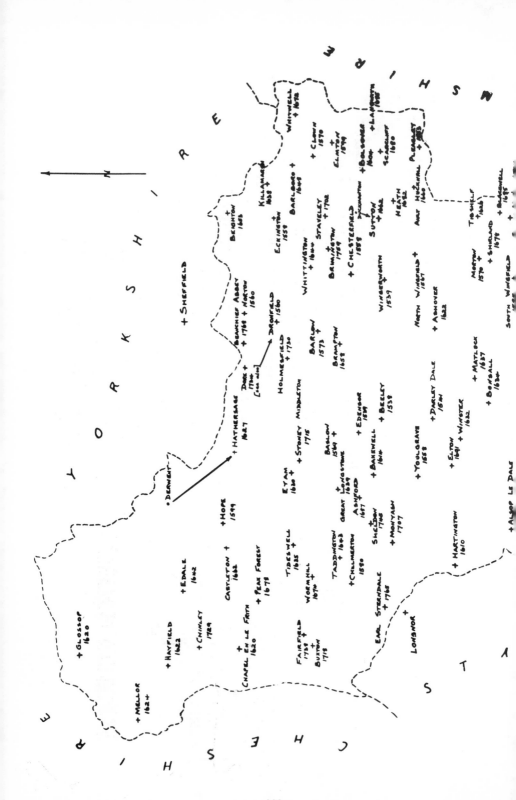

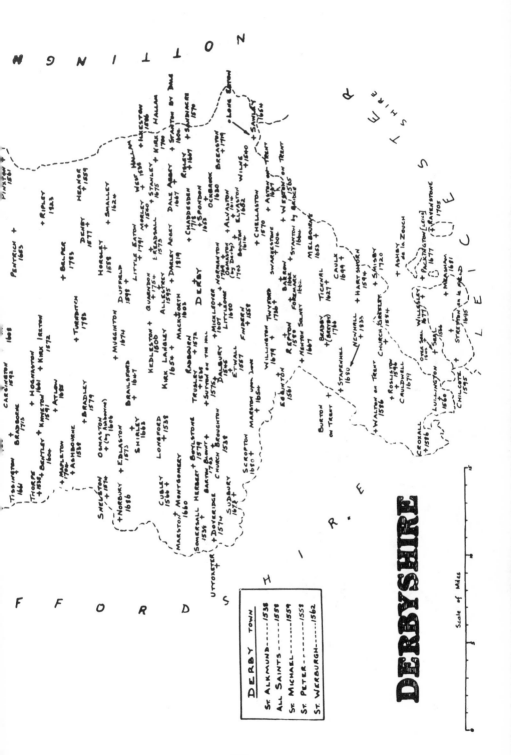

DERBYSHIRE

DERBY TOWN
St. Alkmund------1538
All Saints------1559
St. Michael------1558
St. Peter------1558
St. Werburgh------1562

Scale of Miles

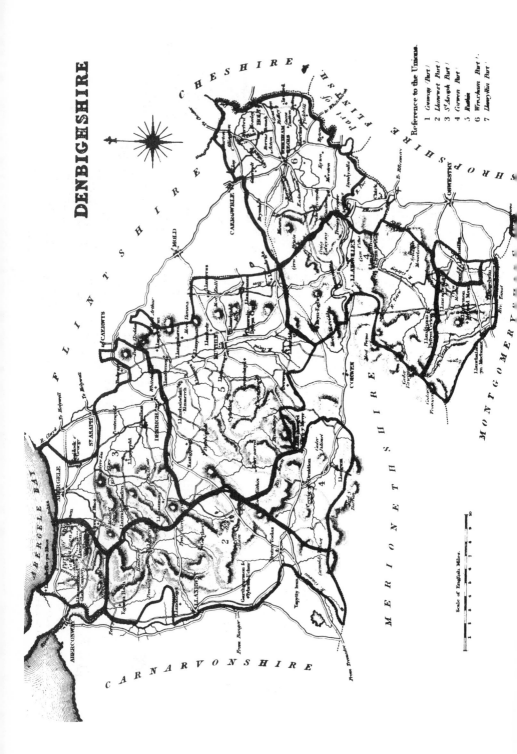

DENBIGHSHIRE

Reference to the Unions.

1 (Conway (Part)
2 Llanrwst Part)
3 St Asaph Part)
4 Corwen Part
5 Ruthin
6 Wrexham Part).
7 Llanfyllin Part)

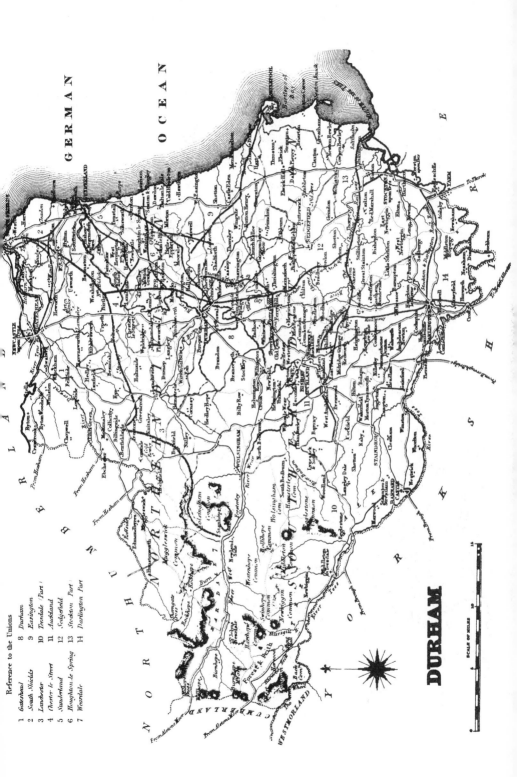

DURHAM

Reference to the Unions

1 Gateshead
2 South Shields
3 Lanchester
4 Chester-le-Street
5 Sunderland
6 Houghton-le-Spring
7 Weardale
8 Durham
9 Easington
10 Teesdale (Part)
11 Auckland
12 Sedgefield
13 Stockton Part
14 Darlington Part

SCALE OF MILES

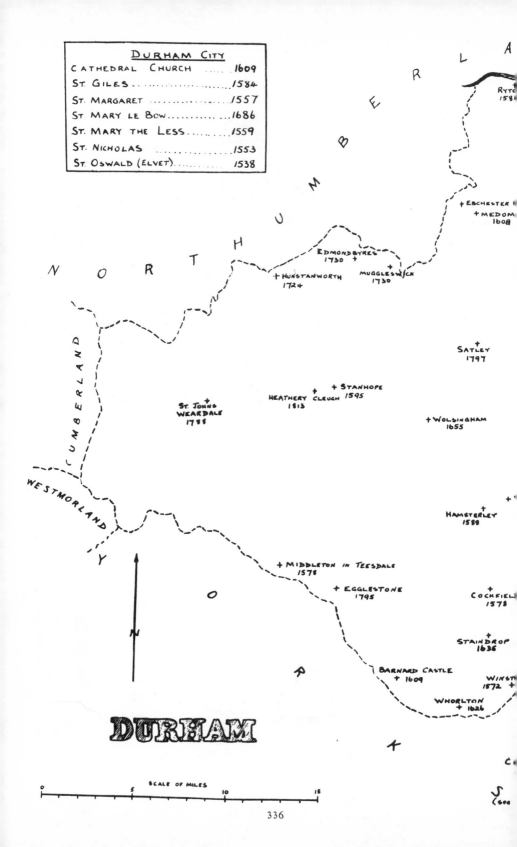

DURHAM CITY

CATHEDRAL CHURCH	1609
ST. GILES	1584
ST. MARGARET	1557
ST. MARY LE BOW	1686
ST. MARY THE LESS	1559
ST. NICHOLAS	1553
ST. OSWALD (ELVET)	1538

N O R T H U M B E R L A

RYTO
158

+ EBCHESTER
+ MEDOM
1608

EDMONDBYRES
1730 +

+ HUNSTANWORTH
1724

MUGGLESWICK
1730 +

C U M B E R L A N D

SATLEY
1797

+ STANHOPE
HEATHERY CLEUGH 1595
1813

ST. JOHNS
WEARDALE
1788

+ WOLSINGHAM
1655

WESTMORLAND

Y

HAMSTERLEY
1588

N

O

+ MIDDLETON IN TEESDALE
1578

+ EGGLESTONE
1795

COCKFIEL
1578

+ STAINDROP
1636

BARNARD CASTLE
+ 1609

WINST
1572 +

R

WHORLTON
+ 1626

K

C

DURHAM

SCALE OF MILES

0   5   10   15

S
(600

D

NORTH SHIELDS

NEWCASTLE
ON TYNE
GATESHEAD FELL
1825

SOUTH
SHIELDS
1653

JARROW
1572

GATESHEAD
1559

WHICKHAM
1516

HEWORTH
1808

see also

BOLDON
1571

WHITBURN
1579

NORTH

MONK
WEARMOUTH
1708

LAMESLEY
1603

WASHINGTON
1603

BISHOP
WEARMOUTH
1567

SUNDERLAND
1719

IELD
1719

PAINSHAW
1754

RYHOPE
1825

CHESTER LE STREET
1582

HOUGHTON LE
SPRING
1563

SEAHAM
1646

SEA

TER

WEST RAINTON
1825

DALTON LE DALE
1653

SM
567

WITTON GILBERT
1571

PITTINGTON
1574

EASINGTON
1571

DURHAM

SHERBURN HOSPITAL
1678

SHINCLIFFE
1826

BRANCEPETH
1599

CROXDALE
1696

CASTLE EDEN
1720

MONK
HESLEDEN
1578

KELLOE
1643

WHITWORTH
1564

TRIMDON
1720

HART
1577

HARTLEPOOL
1566

WEAR

MERRINGTON
1578

BISHOP MIDDLEHAM
1559

ELWICK HALL
1592

STRANTON
1580

ESCOMBE
1543

St ANDREWS AUCKLAND
1558

SEDGEFIELD
1580

EMBLETON
1650

St HELENS AUCKLAND
1593

GRINDON
1565

GREATHAM
1559

WOLVISTON
1759

HEIGHINGTON
1570

GREAT
AYCLIFFE
1560

GREAT STAINTON
1561

Stillington

Carlton

BILLINGHAM
1570

BISHOPTON
1653

REDMARSHALL
1559

NORTON
1574

DENTON
1586

STOCKTON
ON TEES
1621

AINFORD
1560

HOUGHTON LE SKERNE
1569

SADBERGE
1662

ELTON
1573

LONG NEWTON
1564

CONISCLIFFE
1590

DARLINGTON
1590

EAGLESCLIFFE
1539

E

MIDDLETON St. GEORGE
1616

YARM

HURWORTH
1559

DINSDALE
1556

R

ing of Yorks.)

H

SOCKBURN
1588

337

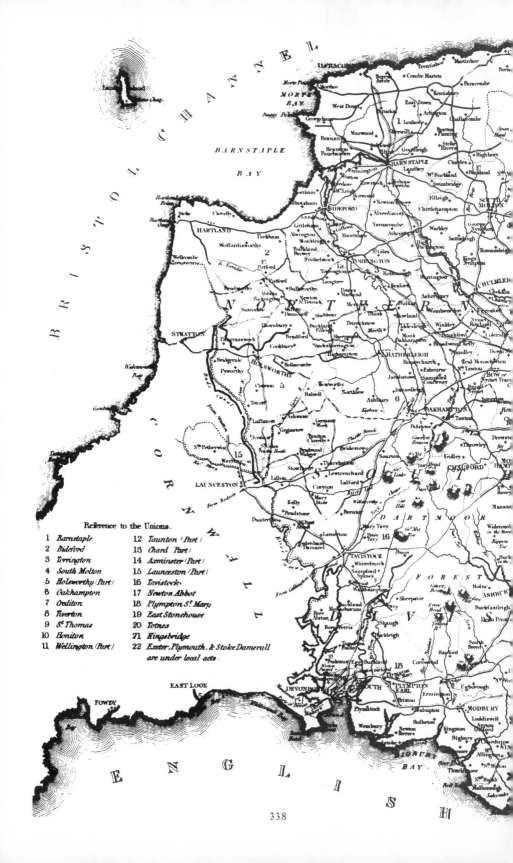

Reference to the Unions.

1	*Barnstaple*	12	*Taunton (Part)*
2	*Bideford*	13	*Chard (Part)*
3	*Torrington*	14	*Axminster (Part)*
4	*South Molton*	15	*Launceston (Part)*
5	*Holsworthy (Part)*	16	*Tavistock*
6	*Oakhampton*	17	*Newton Abbot*
7	*Crediton*	18	*Plympton St. Mary*
8	*Tiverton*	19	*East Stonehouse*
9	*St. Thomas*	20	*Totnes*
10	*Honiton*	21	*Kingsbridge*
11	*Wellington (Part)*	22	*Exeter, Plymouth, & Stoke Damerall are under local acts.*

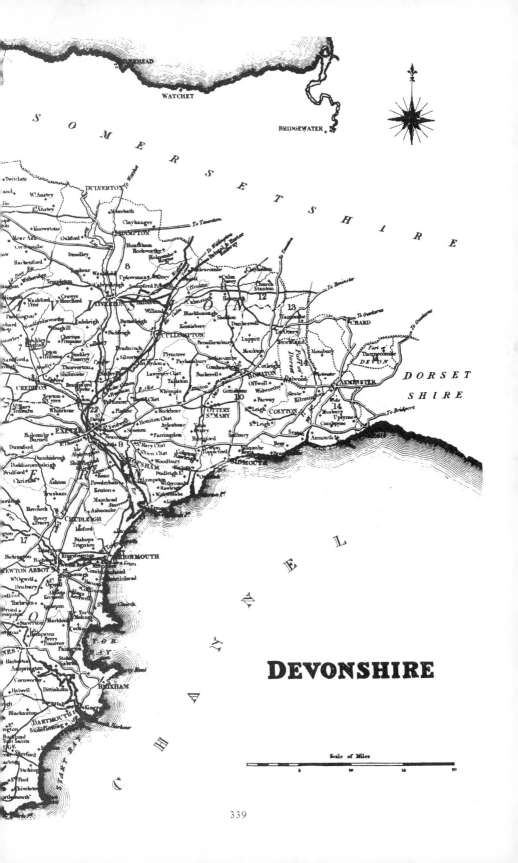

DEVONSHIRE

Scale of Miles

DORSETSHIRE

Scale of Miles

Reference to the Unions

1 Axminster
2 Chard (Part)
3 Beaminster (Part)
4 Bridport
5 Sherborne
6 Cerne
7 Dorchester
8 Weymouth

9 Mere (Part)
10 Wincanton (Part)
11 Sturminster
12 Shaftesbury
13 Blandford
14 Wareham & Purbeck
15 Wimborne & Cranborne
16 Poole

Reference to the Unions

1 *Royston (Part)*	12 *Braintree*
2 *Saffron Walden*	13 *Witham*
3 *Linton (Part)*	14 *Edmonton (Part)*
4 *Risbridge (Part)*	15 *Epping*
5 *Halstead*	16 *Chipping Ong*
6 *Sudbury (Part)*	17 *Chelmsford*
7 *Lexden & Winstree*	18 *Maldon*
8 *Colchester*	19 *West Ham*
9 *Tendring*	20 *Romford*
10 *Bishop Stortford (P.)*	21 *Billericay*
11 *Dunmow*	22 *Rochford*
23 *Orsett*	

ESSEX

SCALE OF MILES

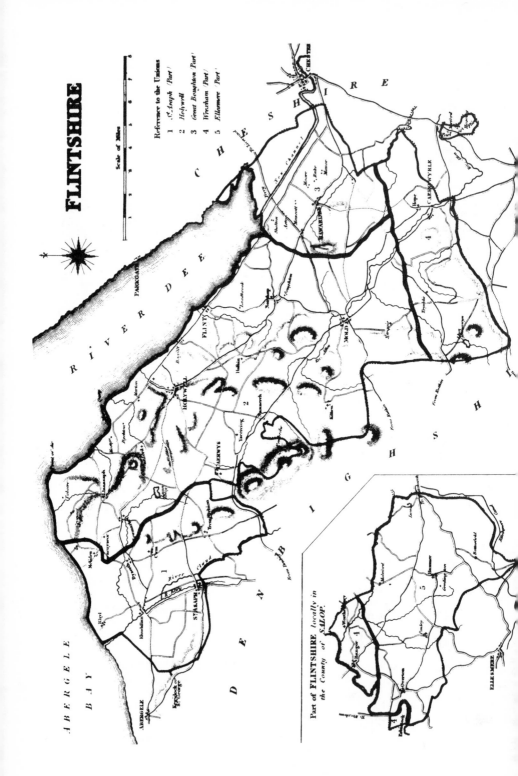

FLINTSHIRE

Scale of Miles

Reference to the Unions
1   S.t Asaph (Part)
2   Holywell
3   Great Boughton Part
4   Wrexham Part
5   Ellesmere Part

Part of FLINTSHIRE locally in
the County of SALOP.

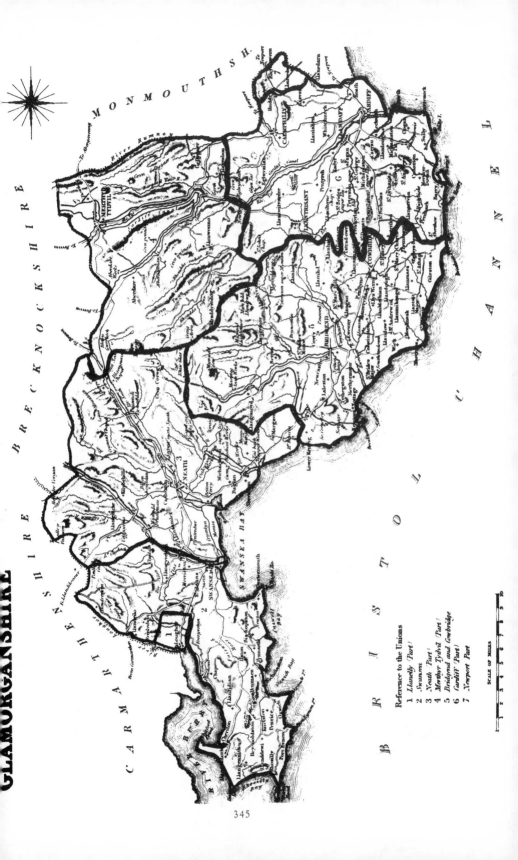

GLAMORGANSHIRE

Reference to the Unions

1 Llandly (Part)
2 Swansea
3 Neath (Part)
4 Merthyr Tydvil (Part)
5 Bridgend and Cowbridge
6 Cardiff (Part)
7 Newport Part

SCALE OF MILES

Reference to the Unions.

1 Evesham (Part)
2 Stratford on Avon (Part)
3 Shipston on Stour (Part)
4 Banbury (Part)
5 Tewkesbury (Part)
6 Winchcombe (Part)
7 Stow on the Wold
8 Newent (Part)
9 Monmouth (Part)
10 Chepstow (Part)
11 Westbury on Severn
12 Gloucester
13 Cheltenham
14 Northleach
15 Witney (Part)
16 Wheatenhurst
17 Stroud
18 Cirencester (Part)
19 Malmesbury (Part)
20 Thornbury
21 Dursley
22 Tetbury (Part)
23 Chipping Sodbury
24 Clifton
25 Bristol (local act)
26 Keynsham (Part)
27 Farringdon (Part)
28 Ross (Part)

GLOUCESTERSHIRE

Scale of Miles

SOUTHAMPTON

Reference to the Unions

1 Hungerford (Part)
2 Kingsclere
3 Newbury (Part)
4 Bradfield (Part)
5 Andover
6 Whitchurch
7 Basingstoke
8 Hartley—Witney
9 Stockbridge (Part)
10 New Winchester
11 Alresford
12 Alton
13 Romsey
14 Hursley
15 Fordingbridge (Pt.)
16 Ringwood
17 Christchurch
18 New Forest (Part)
19 Lymington
20 South Stoneham
21 Fareham
22 Droxford
23 Petersfield
24 Catherington
25 Portsea Island
26 Havant
27 Midhurst (Part)
28 Parts not yet formed into Unions

Scale of Miles

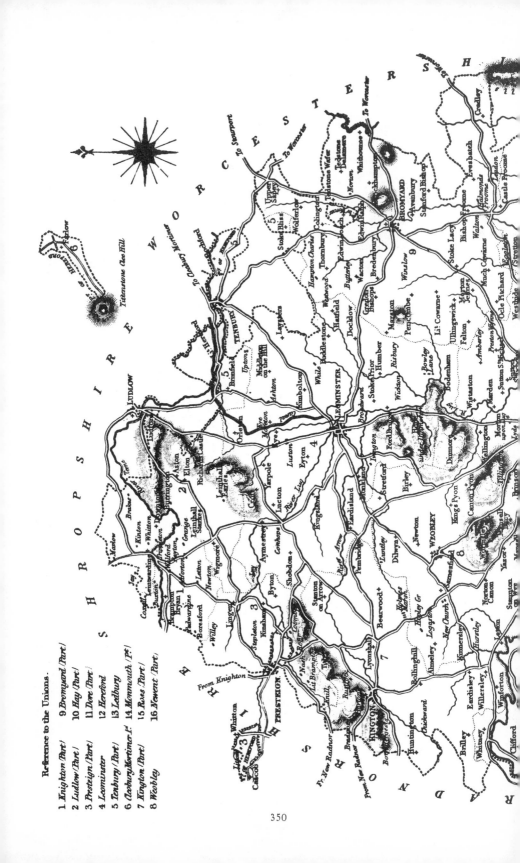

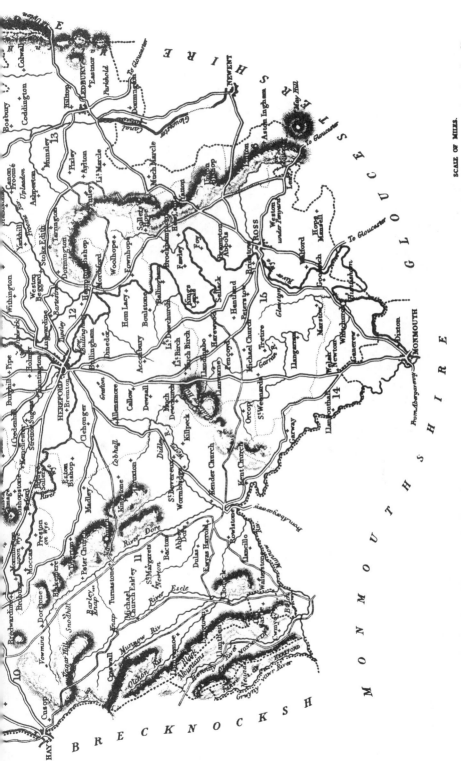

HEREFORDSHIRE

SCALE OF MILES.

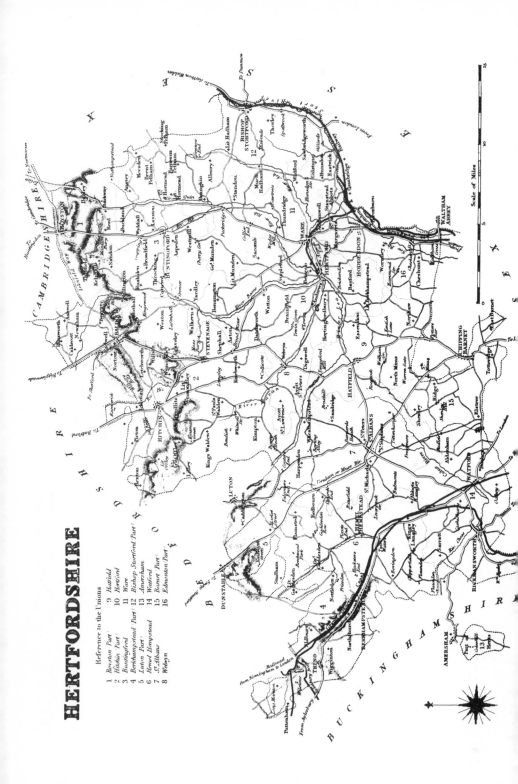

HERTFORDSHIRE

Reference to the Unions

1	Royston (Part)	9	Hatfield
2	Hitchin (Part)	10	Hertford
3	Buntingford	11	Ware
4	Berkhampstead (Part)	12	Bishop Stortford (Part)
5	Luton (Part)	13	Amersham
6	Hemel Hempstead	14	Watford
7	St Albans	15	Barnet (Part)
8	Welwyn	16	Edmonton (Part)

Scale of Miles

ISLE of MAN

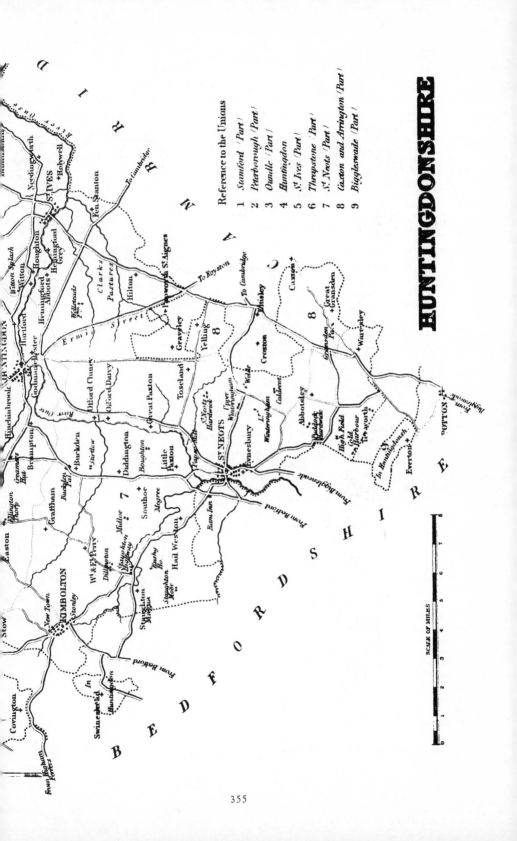

HUNTINGDONSHIRE

Reference to the Unions

1 Stamford (Part)
2 Peterborough (Part)
3 Oundle (Part)
4 Huntingdon
5 St Ives (Part)
6 Thrapstone (Part)
7 St Neots (Part)
8 Caxton and Arrington (Part)
9 Biggleswade (Part)

SCALE OF MILES

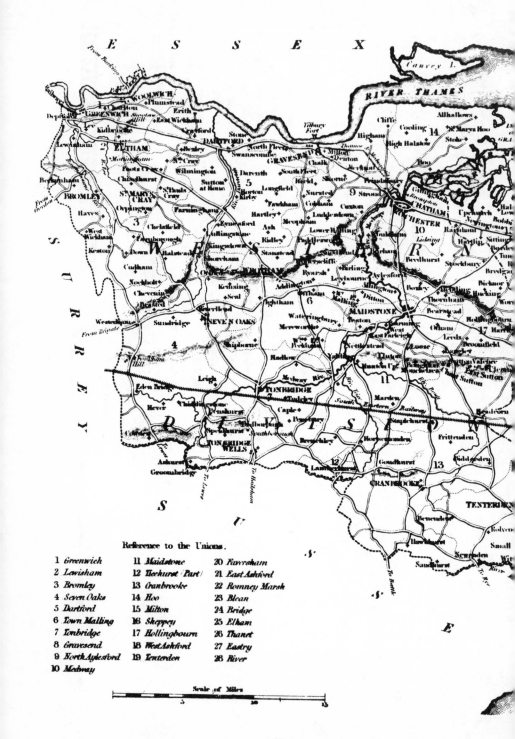

Reference to the Unions.

1 Greenwich
2 Lewisham
3 Bromley
4 Seven Oaks
5 Dartford
6 Town Malling
7 Tonbridge
8 Gravesend
9 North Aylesford
10 Medway

11 Maidstone
12 Tiehurst (Part)
13 Cranbrooke
14 Hoo
15 Milton
16 Sheppey
17 Hollingbourn
18 West Ashford
19 Tenterden

20 Faversham
21 East Ashford
22 Romney Marsh
23 Blean
24 Bridge
25 Elham
26 Thanet
27 Eastry
28 River

Scale of Miles

KENT

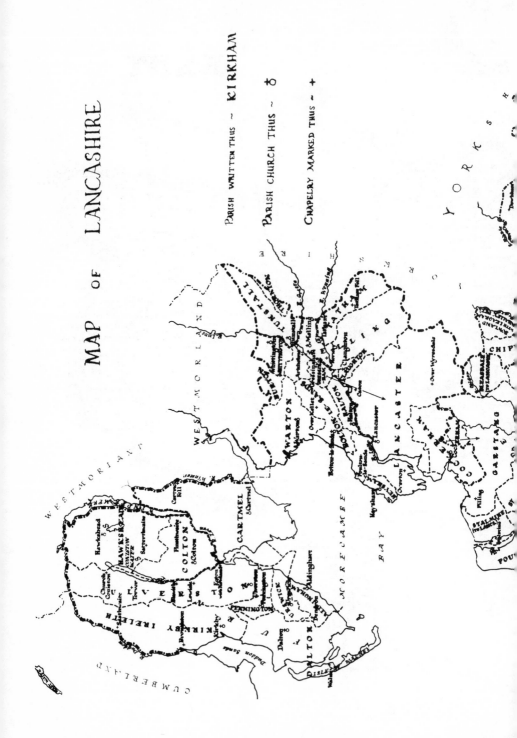

MAP OF LANCASHIRE

PARISH WRITTEN THUS ~ KIRKHAM

PARISH CHURCH THUS ~ ☩

CHAPELRY MARKED THUS ~ +

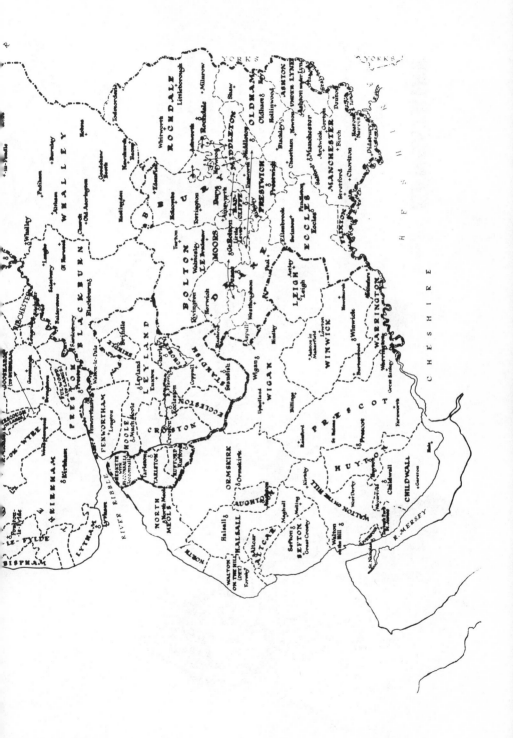

LANCASHIRE

Scale of Miles

Reference to the Unions.

1 Ulverstone
2 Garstang
3 The Fylde
4 Clitheroe (Pt.)
5 Preston
6 Blackburn
7 Burnley
8 Ormskirk
9 Chorley
10 Wigan
11 Bolton
12 Haslingden
13 Bury
14 Rochdale
15 Oldham
16 West Derby
17 Prescot
18 Warrington
19 Leigh
20 Salford
21 Chorlton
22 Stockport (Pt.)
23 Ashton under Line (Pt.)
24 Todmorden (Pt.)
25 Parts not yet formed into Unions

360

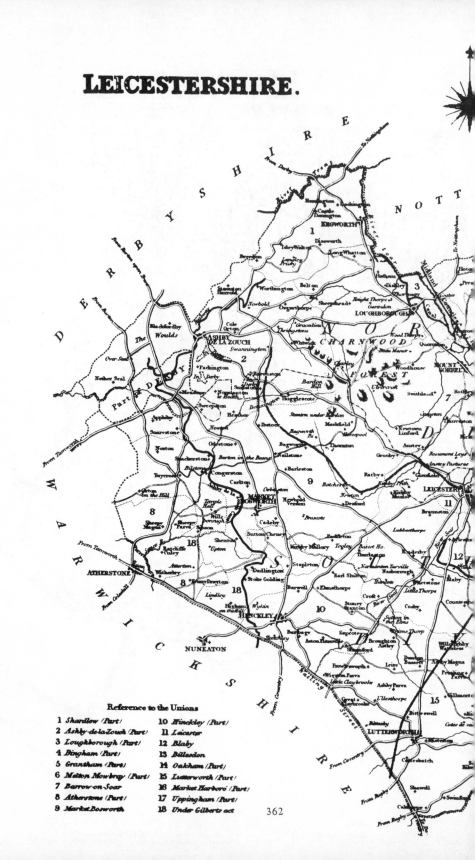

LEICESTERSHIRE.

362

Scale of Miles

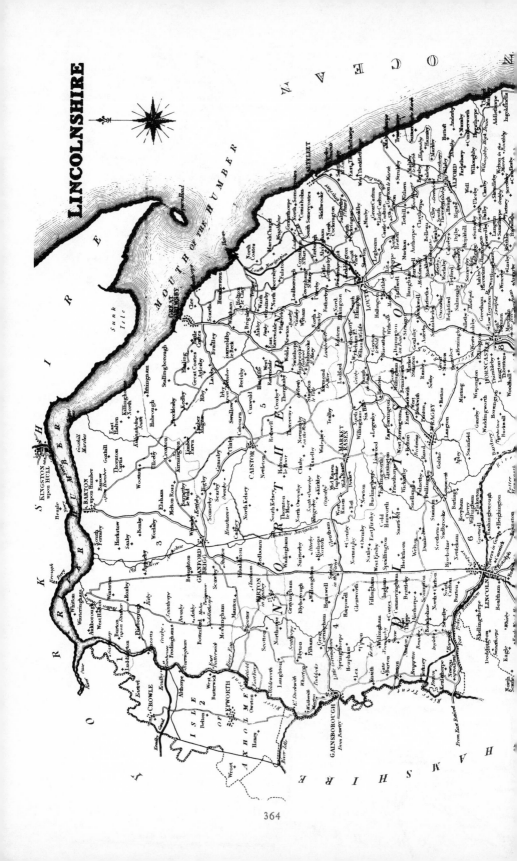

LINCOLNSHIRE

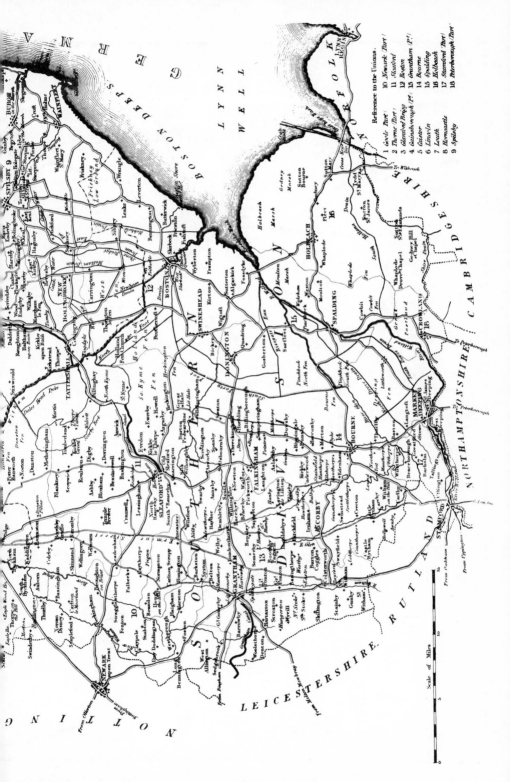

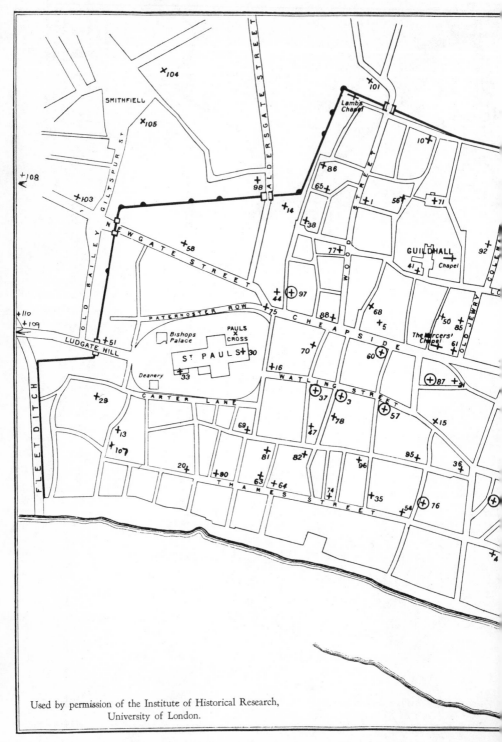

Used by permission of the Institute of Historical Research,
University of London.

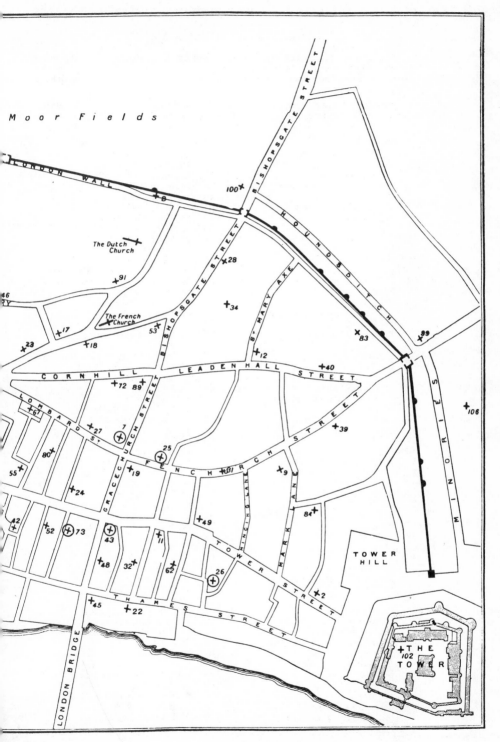

Moor Fields

The Dutch Church

The french Church

LONDON WALL

BISHOPSGATE STREET

HOUNDSDITCH

CORNHILL   LEADENHALL   STREET

ST. MARY AXE

GRACECHURCH STREET

FENCHURCH   STREET

LOMBARD ST.

MINCING LANE

MARK LANE

TOWER   STREET

THAMES   STREET

LONDON BRIDGE

TOWER HILL

MINORIES

THE TOWER

CITY OF LONDON DURING THE PERIOD BETWEEN THE REFORMATION AND THE GREAT FIRE

REFERENCE TO LONDON MAP

The sites of parish churches are indicated by a square cross +, the numbers appended referring to the accompanying list. Those belonging to the Deanery of Bow (peculiars of the Archbishop of Canterbury) are marked by a circle round the cross ⊗.

Outside the area shown in the map, but within the bars, were the parish churches of St. Andrew Holborn, St. Dunstan in the West, and St. Bride.

1. St. Alban.
2. All Hallows Barking.
3. All Hallows Bread Street.
4. All Hallows the Great.
5. All Hallows Honey Lane.
6. All Hallows the Less.
7. All Hallows Lombard Street.
8. All Hallows London Wall.
9. All Hallows Staining.
10. St. Alphage.
11. St. Andrew Hubbard.
12. St. Andrew Undershaft.
13. St. Andrew by the Wardrobe.
14. S. S. Anne and Agnes.
15. St. Antholin.
16. St. Augustine.
17. St. Bartholomew Exchange.
18. St. Benet Fink.
19. St. Benet Gracechurch.
20. St. Benet Paul's Wharf.
21. St. Benet Sherehog.
22. St. Botolph Billingsgate.
23. St. Christopher le Stocks.
24. St. Clement Eastcheap.
25. St. Dionis Backchurch.
26. St. Dunstan in the East.
27. St. Edmund the King.
28. St. Ethelburga.
29. St. Anne Blackfriars.
30. St. Faith.
31. St. Gabriel Fenchurch.
32. St. George Botolph Lane.
33. St. Gregory.
34. St. Helen
35. St. James Garlickhithe.
36. St. John the Baptist, Walbrook.
37. St. John the Evangelist.
38. St. John Zachary.
39. St. Katharine Colman.
40. St. Katharine Cree.
41. St. Laurence Jewry.
42. St. Laurence Pountney.
43. St. Leonard Eastcheap.
44. St. Leonard Foster
45. St. Magnus.
46. St. Margaret Lothbury.
47. St. Margaret Moses.
48. St. Margaret New Fish Street.
49. St. Margaret Pattens.
50. St. Martin Iremonger.
51. St. Martin Ludgate.
52. St. Martin Orgar.
53. St. Martin Outwich.
54. St. Martin Vintry.
55. St. Martin Abchurch.
56. St. Mary Aldermanbury.
57. St. Mary Aldermary.
58. Christchurch Newgate.
59. St. Mary Bothaw.
60. St. Mary le Bow.
61. St. Mary Colechurch.
62. St. Mary at Hill
63. St. Mary Mounthaw.
64. St. Mary Somerset.
65. St. Mary Staining.
66. St. Mary Woolchurch.
67. St. Mary Woolnoth.
68. St. Mary Magdalen Milk Street.
69. St. Mary Magdalen Old Fish St.
70. St. Matthew Friday Street
71. St. Michael Bassishaw.
72. St. Michael Cornhill.
73. St. Michael Crooked Lane.
74. St. Michael Queenhithe.
75. St. Michael le Querne.
76. St. Michael Royal or Paternoster.
77. St. Michael Wood Street.
78. St. Mildred Bread Street.
79. St. Mildred Poultry.
80. St. Nicholas Acon.
81. St. Nicholas Coleabbey.
82. St. Nicholas Olave.
83. St. James Duke's Place.
84. St. Olave Hart Street.
85. St. Olave Jewry.
86. St. Olave Silver Street.
87. St. Pancras Soper Lane.
88. St. Peter Cheap.
89. St. Peter Cornhill.
90. St. Peter Paul's Wharf.
91. St. Peter le Poor.
92. St. Stephen Coleman Street.
93. St. Stephen Walbrook.
94. St. Swithin.
95. St. Thomas Apostle.
96. Holy Trinity the Little.
97. St. Vedast or Foster.
98. St. Botolph Aldersgate.
99. St. Botolph Aldgate.
100. St. Botolph Bishopsgate.
101. St. Giles Cripplegate.
102. St. Peter in the Tower.
103. St. Sepulchre.
104. St. Bartholomew the Great.
105. St. Bartholomew the Less.
106. Holy Trinity Minories.
107. St. Anne Blackfriars.
108. St. Andrew Holborn.
109. St. Bride Fleet Street.
110. St. Dunstan in the West.

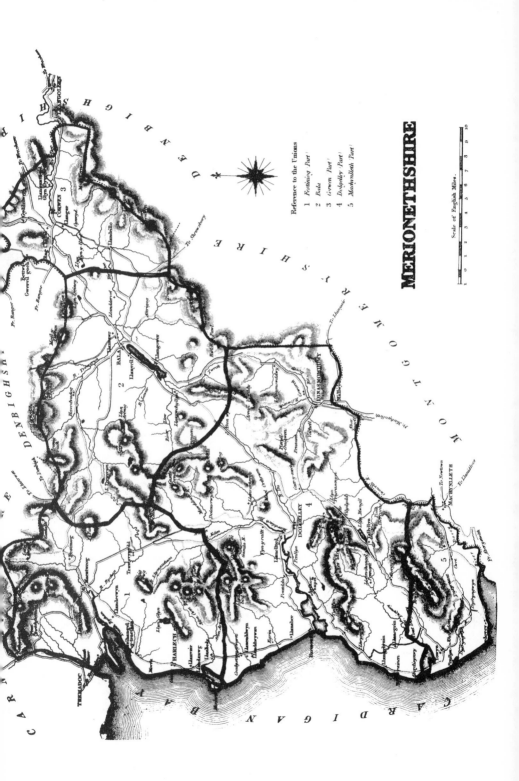

MERIONETHSHIRE

Reference to the Unions

1 Festiniog Part
2 Bala
3 Corwen Part
4 Dolgelley Part
5 Machynlleth Part

Scale of English Miles.

Reference to the Unions.

1 Uxbridge
2 Hendon
3 Barnet (Part)
4 Edmonton (P.t)
5 Staines
6 Brentford

7 Kensington
8 Hackney
9 Kingston (Part)
10 Including the city of
   London and unions
   adjacent, and several
   parishes under local acts.

HERTFO

HERTFORDSHIRE

BUCKINGHAMSHIRE

From Amersham
From Watford
RICKMANSWORTH
From Watford
From Watford
From St Albans

Great Stanmore
Lit. Stanmo
Harefield
Hatch End
Harrow Weald
Hodgetts Hill
Pinner
Eastcot
Ruislip
Greenhill
Preston Gr.
Ken
Harefield Ho.
Ickenham
Harrow on the Hill
From Beaconsfield
Grand Junction Canal
River Colne
UXBRIDGE
Greenford Green
Wembley
Hillingdon
Northolt
App
Cowley
Hayes End
Court Farm
Perrivale
The
Iver
Great Hayes
Yeading
Greenford
West End
Western
SOUTHALL
Hanwell Railway
West Drayton
Old Hatts
Harlington
Ealin
Southal
Norwood
6
The
COLNBROOK
Harmondsworth
Cranford
Heston
River Brent
Harlington Corner
Lampton
New Brentford
BRENTFORD
Poyle
Perry Oaks
HOUNSLOW
Hatton
Isleworth
River Colne
Stanwell Moor
West Bedfont
Babers Br.
Review Ground
Whitton
RICH
Staines Moor
Stanwell
5
The Old River
East Bedfont
Twickenham
From Basingstoke
STAINES
Ashford
Feltham
The Len river
Egham
Withycroft Field
Hanworth
ddington
Laleham
Littleton
Kempton
Hampton
Hampton Wic
9
KINGS
Sunbury
Up.r Halliford
River Thames
Hampton Court
CHERTSEY
Low Halliford
Shepperton
Walton
S
U

MIDDLESEX

MONMOUTHSHIRE

HEREFORDSHIRE

BRECKNOCKSHIRE

GLAMORGANSHIRE

GLOUCESTERSHIRE

RIVER SEVERN

BRISTOL CHANNEL

CALDICOT LEVEL

ABERGAVENNY

MONMOUTH

PONT-Y-POOL

USK

CAERLEON

NEWPORT

CARDIFF

CAERPHILLY

Scale of Miles

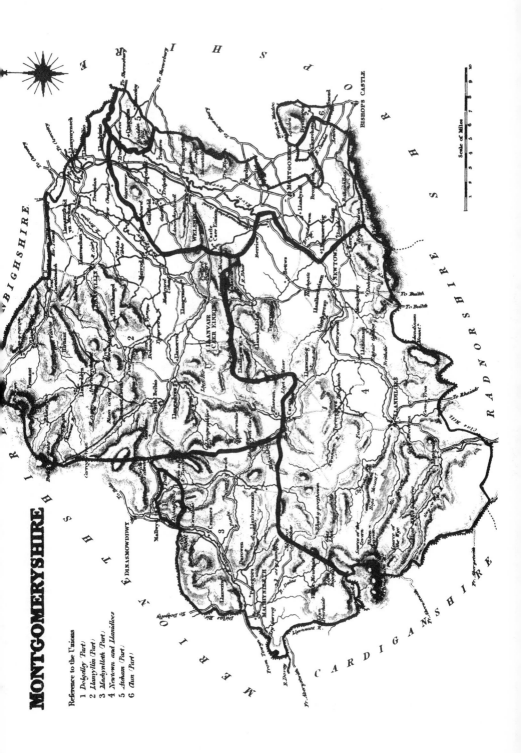

MONTGOMERYSHIRE

Reference to the Unions

1 Dolgelly (Part)
2 Llanvyllin (Part)
3 Machynlleth (Part)
4 Newtown and Llanidloes
5 Axham (Part)
6 Clun (Part)

Scale of Miles

NORFOLK

Scale of Miles

N O R T H

S E A

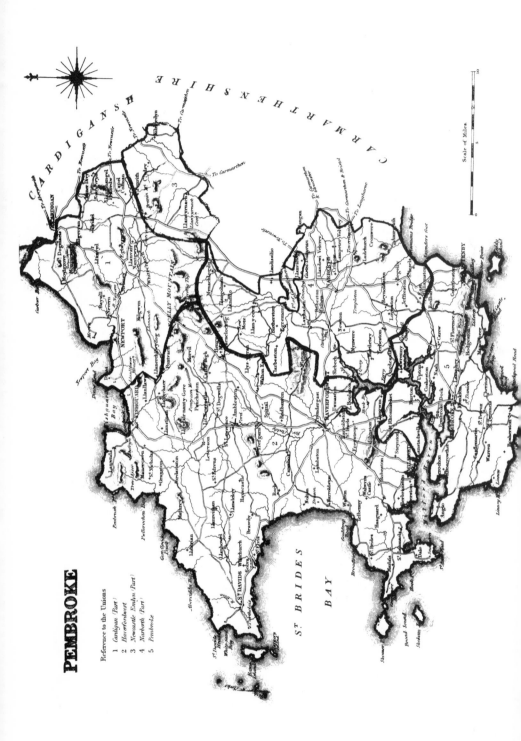

PEMBROKE

Reference to the Unions

1 Cardigan (Part)
2 Haverfordwest
3 Newcastle Emlyn (Part)
4 Narberth (Part)
5 Pembroke

Scale of Miles

ST. BRIDES BAY

CARDIGANSHIRE

CARMARTHENSHIRE

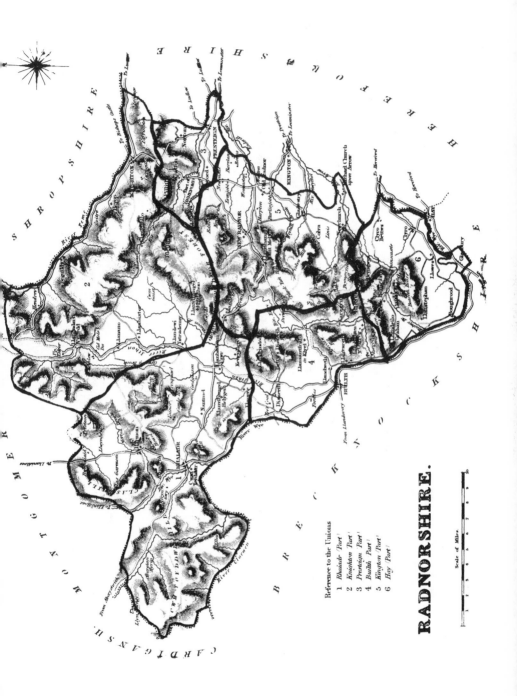

RADNORSHIRE.

Reference to the Unions

1 Rhaiadr Part
2 Knighton Part
3 Presteign Part
4 Builth Part
5 Kington Part
6 Hay Part

Scale of Miles

Reference to the Unions

1 Stamford (Part)	10 Brixworth
2 Peterborough (Part)	11 Wellingborough (Part)
3 Uppingham (Part)	12 Daventry
4 Oundle (Part)	13 Northampton
5 Market Harborough (Part)	14 Hardingstone
6 Kettering	15 Banbury (Part)
7 Thrapstone (Part)	16 Brackley (Part)
8 Lutterworth (Part)	17 Towcester
9 Rugby (Part)	18 Potters Pury
	19 Buckingham (Part)

NORTHAMPTONSHIRE

Scale of Miles

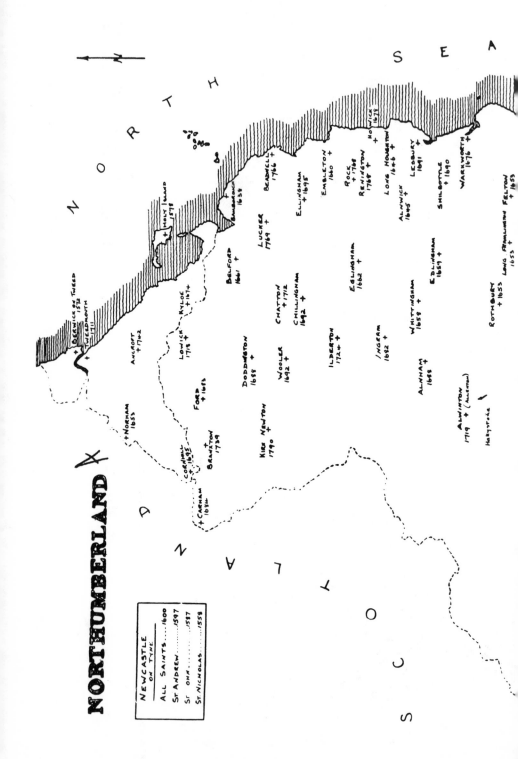

NORTHUMBERLAND

NORTH SEA

NORTHUMBERLAND

SCOTLAND

NEWCASTLE
ON TYNE
ALL SAINTS......1600
ST ANDREW.......1597
ST OHN...........1587
ST NICHOLAS......1558

HOLY ISLAND 1578

BAMBURGH 1639

BERWICK on TWEED 1572
TWEEDMOUTH 1711

NORHAM 1653

CORNHILL 1695
BRANXTON 1739

CARHAM 1644

ANCROFT 1742

LOWICK KYLOE 1718 1674

FORD 1685

KIRK NEWTON 1740

DODDINGTON 1688

BELFORD 1661

LUCKER 1769

WOOLER 1692

CHATTON 1712
C MILLINGHAM 1692

ILDERTON 1724

INGRAM 1682

ALNHAM 1688

ALWINTON 1719 (ALNETON)
HALYSTONE

RADCLIFFE 1766

ELLINGHAM 1695

EMBLETON 1660

HOWICK 1678

ROCK 1768
RENNINGTON 1768

LONG HOUGHTON 1668

LESBURY 1691

ALNWICK 1645

EGLINGHAM 1662

WHITTINGHAM 1659

SHILBOTTLE 1690

WARKWORTH 1676

EDLINGHAM 1659

LONG FRAMLINGTON FELTON 1653 1655

ROTHBURY 1653

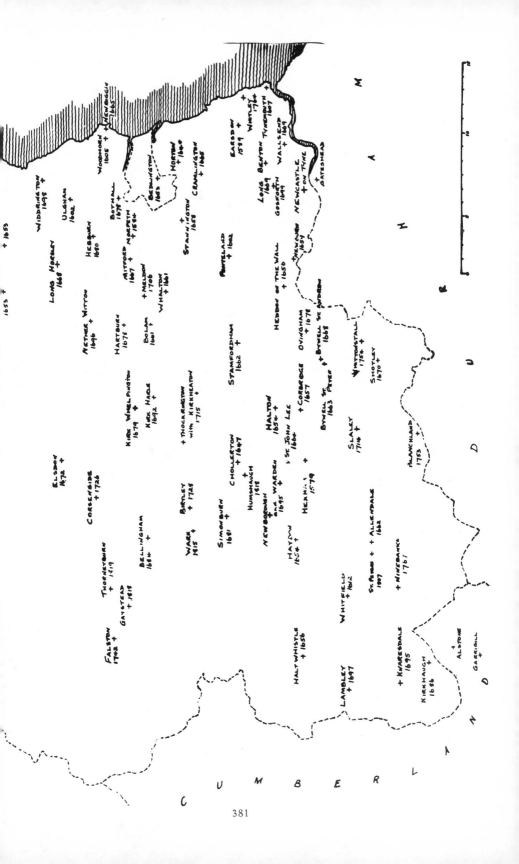

(Map of Northumberland showing parish locations with dates)

1653 +
1653 + 1653

WIDDRINGTON 1698 +
LONG HORSLEY 1668 +
ULGHAM 1662 +
WOODHORN 1605 +
NEWBIGGIN 1665 +
HEBBURN 1690 +
NETHER WITTON 1696 +
BOTHAL 1670 +
BEDLINGTON 1655 +
HORTON 1665 +
EARSDON 1599 +
WHITLEY 1764 +
TYNEMOUTH 1657 +
WALLSEND 1669 +
MITFORD 1607 + MORPETH 1584 +
MELDON 1706 +
WHALTON 1661 +
STANNINGTON 1658 +
PONTELAND 1602 +
LONG BENTON 1669 +
GOSFORTH 1649 +
NEWCASTLE ON TYNE
GATESHEAD

ELSDON 1672 +
THORNEYBURN 1819 +
GAYSTEAD 1818 +
FALSTON 1762 +
CORSENSIDE 1726 +
BELLINGHAM 1684 +
KIRK WHELPINGTON 1679 +
KIRK HAGLE 1692 +
HARTBURN 1674 +
BOLAM 1661 +
+ THOCKRINGTON with KIRKHEATON 1715 +
STAMFORDHAM 1662 +
HEDDON or THE WALL 1650 +
OVINGHAM 1678 +
BYWELL ST ANDREW 1668 +
WHITTONSTALL 1756 +
SHOTLEY 1670 +

WARK 1815 +
BIRTLEY 1726 +
SIMONBURN 1681 +
HUMSHAUGH 1818 +
CHOLLERTON 1647 +
NEWBOROUGH and WARDEN 1695 +
HALTON 1654 +
ST JOHN LEE 1666 +
CORBRIDGE 1657 +
BYWELL ST PETER 1663 +
HEXHAM 1579 +
SLALEY 1714 +
BLANCHLAND 1753 +

HAYDON 1654 +
WHITFIELD 1612 +
ST ANNES + ALLENDALE 1607 +
NINEBANKS 1761 +
HALTWHISTLE 1656 +
LAMBLEY 1647 +
KNARESDALE 1695 +
KIRKHAUGH 1686 +
ALSTONE
GARRIGILL

C U M B E R L A N D

D U R H A M

(scale bar)

NORTHUMBERLAND

Reference to the Unions
1 Berwick on Tweed
2 Glendale
3 Belford
4 Bellingham
5 Rothbury
6 Alnwick
7 Morpeth
8 Haltwhistle
9 Hexham
10 Castle Ward
11 Tynemouth
12 Newcastle upon Tyne

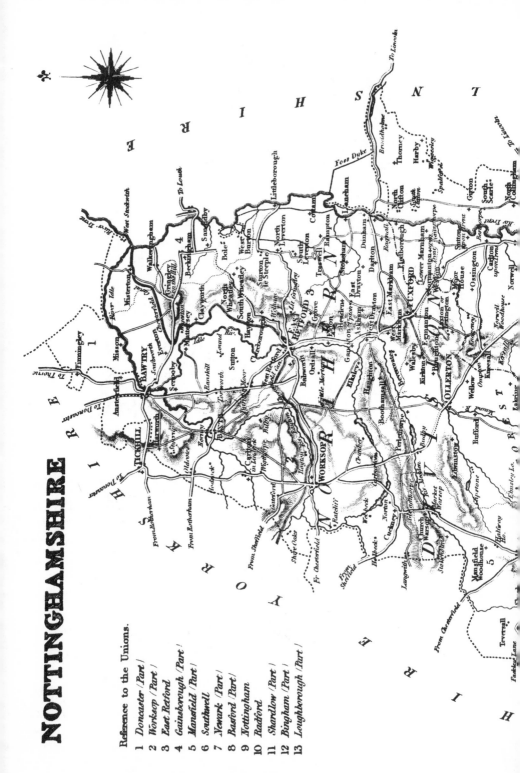

NOTTINGHAMSHIRE

Reference to the Unions.

1 Doncaster (Part)
2 Worksop (Part)
3 East Retford
4 Gainsborough (Part)
5 Mansfield (Part)
6 Southwell
7 Newark (Part)
8 Basford (Part)
9 Nottingham
10 Radford
11 Shardlow (Part)
12 Bingham (Part)
13 Loughborough (Part)

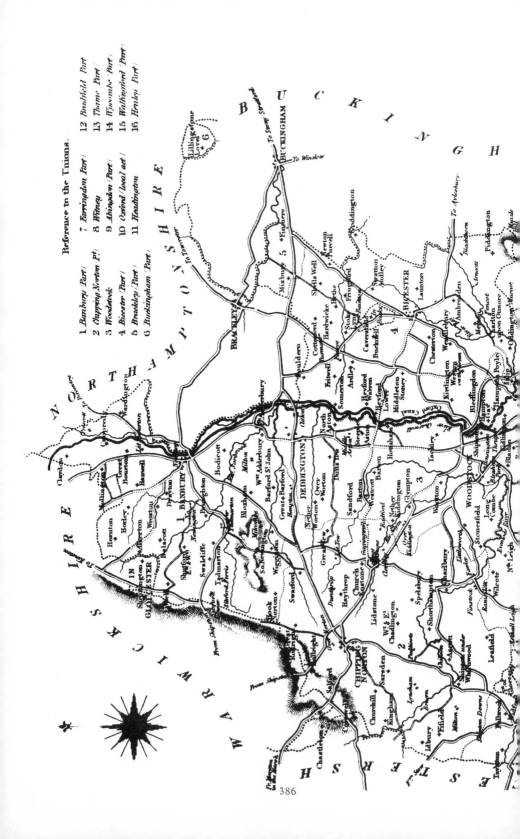

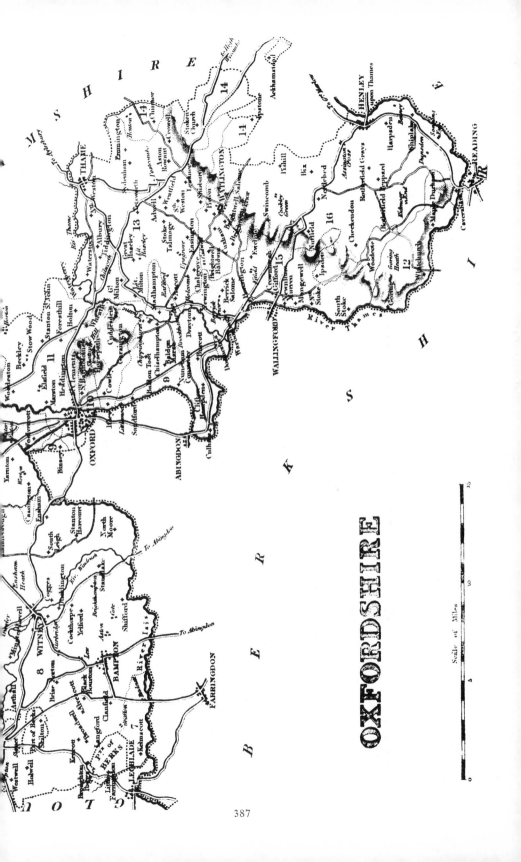

OXFORDSHIRE

Scale of Miles

SHROPSHIRE

Part of SHROPSHIRE.
Locally in Worcestershire.

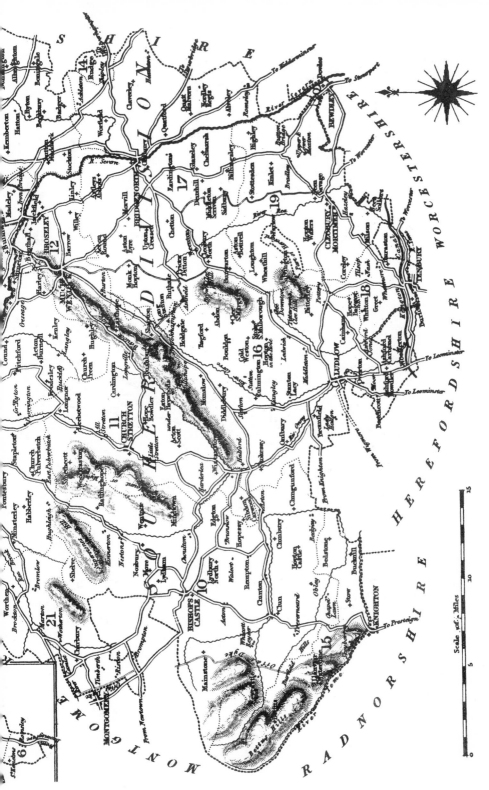

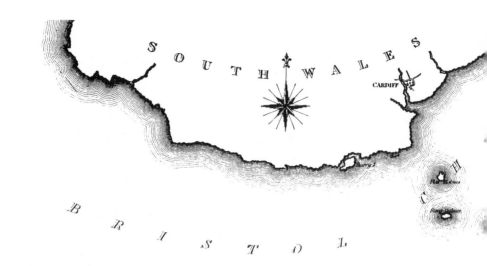

Reference to the Unions

1	Dulverton	11	Frome
2	Williton	12	Wellington Part
3	Bridgwater	13	Taunton Part
4	Axbridge	14	Langport
5	Bedminster	15	Wincanton Part
6	Keynsham Part	16	Mere Part
7	Bath	17	Chard Part
8	Clutton	18	Yeovil
9	Wells	19	Sherborne Part
10	Shepton Mallet	20	Bradford Part

Scale of Miles

SOMERSETSHIRE

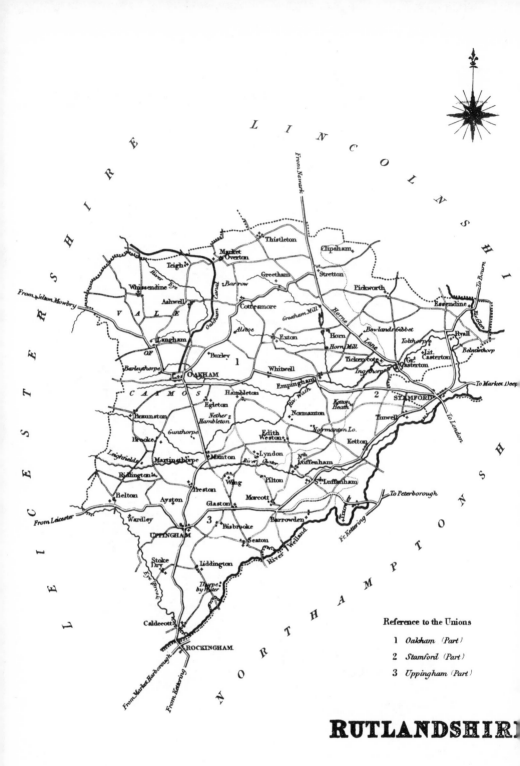

Reference to the Unions

1 *Oakham* (Part)

2 *Stamford* (Part)

3 *Uppingham* (Part)

RUTLANDSHIRE

Scale of Miles

1 2 3 4 5 6 7 8

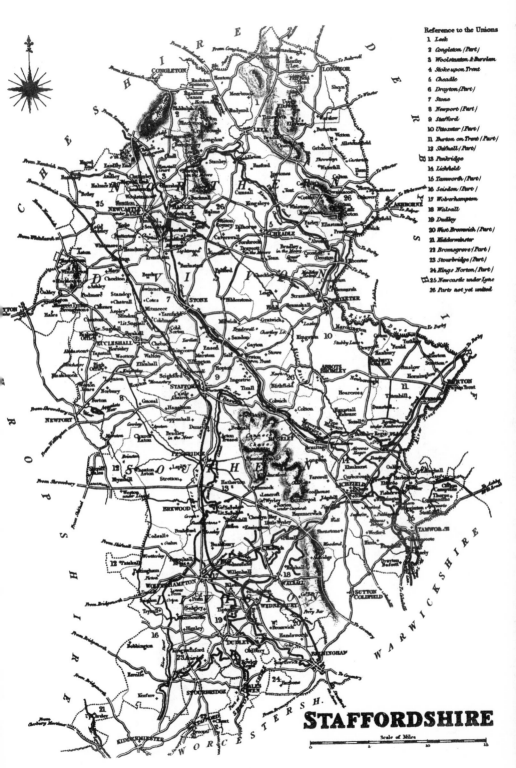

STAFFORDSHIRE

Scale of Miles

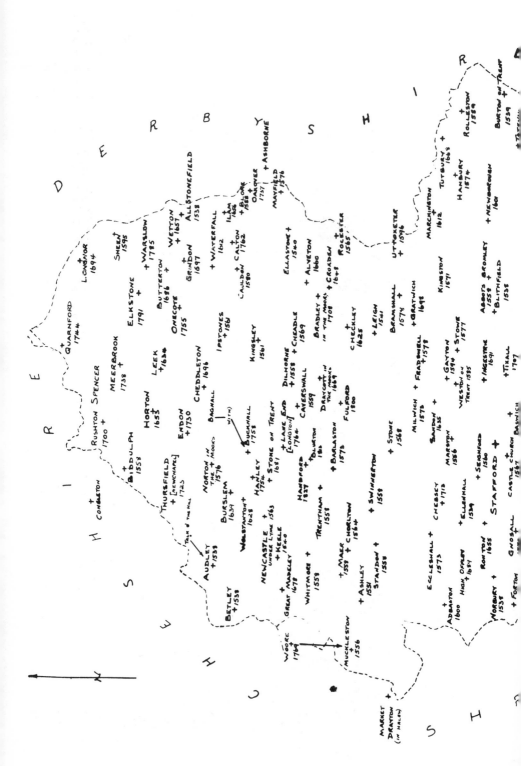

D E R B Y S H I R E

C H E S H I R E

S H R O P S H I R E

QUARNFORD 1744
LONGNOR 1694
SNEAD 1595
WARSLOW 1785
ELKSTONE 1791
BUTTERTON 1696
WETTON 1657
ALLSTONEFIELD 1538
OMECOTE 1755
GRINDON 1697
WATERFALL 1662
ILAM 1666
BLORE 1558
CALTON 1762
CAULDON 1580
OAKOVER 1737
MAYFIELD 1576
ASHBORNE

ROLLESTON 1584
BURTON on TRENT 1539
HANBURY 1574
NEWBROUGH 1602
TUTBURY 1665
MARCHINGTON 1612
UTTOXETER 1596
ROCHESTER 1565
CROXDEN 1608
ALVETON 1600
ELLASTONE 1540
BRADLEY in THE MOORS 1708
CHECKLEY 1625
LEIGH 1541
BRAMSHALL 1574
GRATWICH 1648
ABBOTS BROMLEY 1559
BLITHFIELD 1538
KINGSTON 1571
STOWE 1577
GAYTON 1574
WESTON on TRENT 1585
INGESTRE 1691
TIXALL 1707
MILWICH 1578
FRADSWELL 1578
SANDON 1635
MARSTON 1556
SEIGHFORD 1560
STAFFORD 1557
CASTLE CHURCH 1547
BASWICH

IPSTONES 1561
KINGSLEY 1561
DILHORNE 1558
CHEADLE 1569
CAVERSWALL 1559
DRAYCOTT in THE MOORS 1707
FULFORD 1800
STONE 1568
CHEDDLETON 1696
BAGNALL
WETLEY
BUCKNALL 1755
STOKE on TRENT 1581
HANLEY 1754
MILTON 1841
NORTON in THE MOORS 1576
BURSLEM 1634
HANFORD 1837
BARLASTON 1578
SWINNERTON 1558
LEEK 1634
EADON 1730
HORTON 1653
BIDDULPH 1558
MEERBROOK 1738
RUSHTON SPENCER 1700
THURSFIELD [NEWCHAPEL] 1725
WOLSTANTON 1628
TRENTHAM 1558
MAER 1559
CHORLTON 1564
CHEBSEY 1713
ECCLESHALL 1573
ELLENHALL 1554
RONTON 1655
GNOSALL 1572
ADBASTON 1600
HIGH OFFLEY 1691
FORTON 1589
MORBURY 1655
CONGLETON
AUDLEY 1538
BETLEY 1538
GREAT MADELEY 1678
NEWCASTLE UNDER LYME 1563
KEELE 1640
WHITMORE 1559
ASHLEY 1551
STANDON 1558
MUCKLESTON 1556
WOORE 1764
MARKET DRAYTON (in HALES)
CHESHIRE

TALK o THE HILL

N

394

SUFFOLK

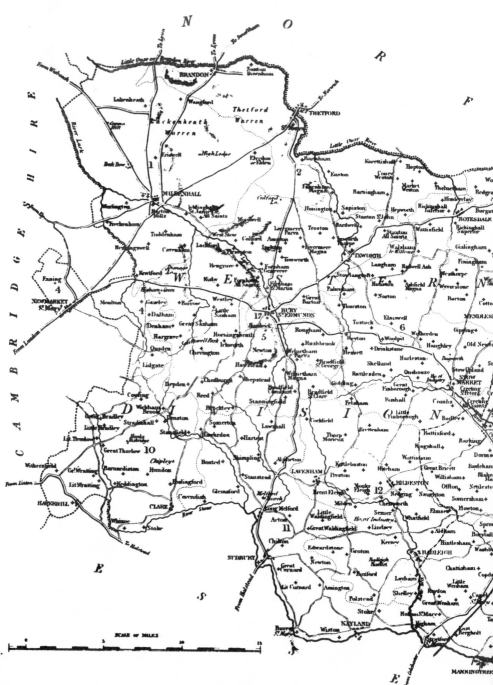

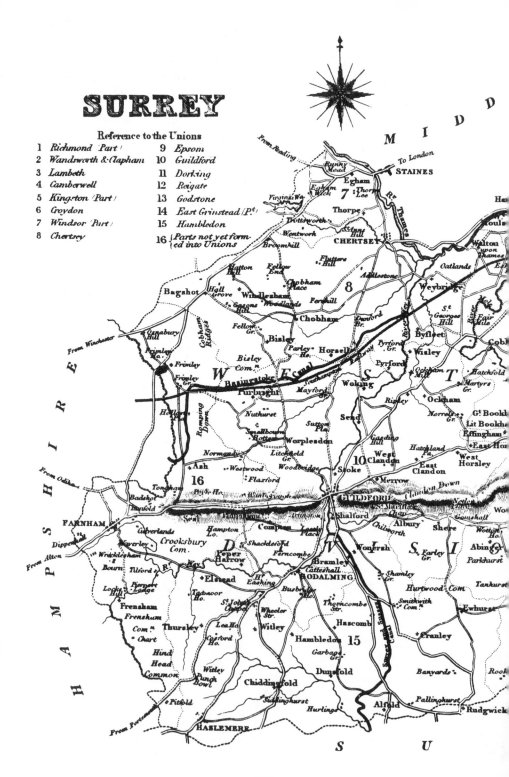

SURREY

Reference to the Unions

1 Richmond (Part)
2 Wandsworth & Clapham
3 Lambeth
4 Camberwell
5 Kingston (Part)
6 Croydon
7 Windsor (Part)
8 Chertsey
9 Epsom
10 Guildford
11 Dorking
12 Reigate
13 Godstone
14 East Grinstead (P.t)
15 Hambledon
16 { Parts not yet form
     ed into Unions

Scale of Miles

0 1 2 3 4 5 6 7 8 9 10

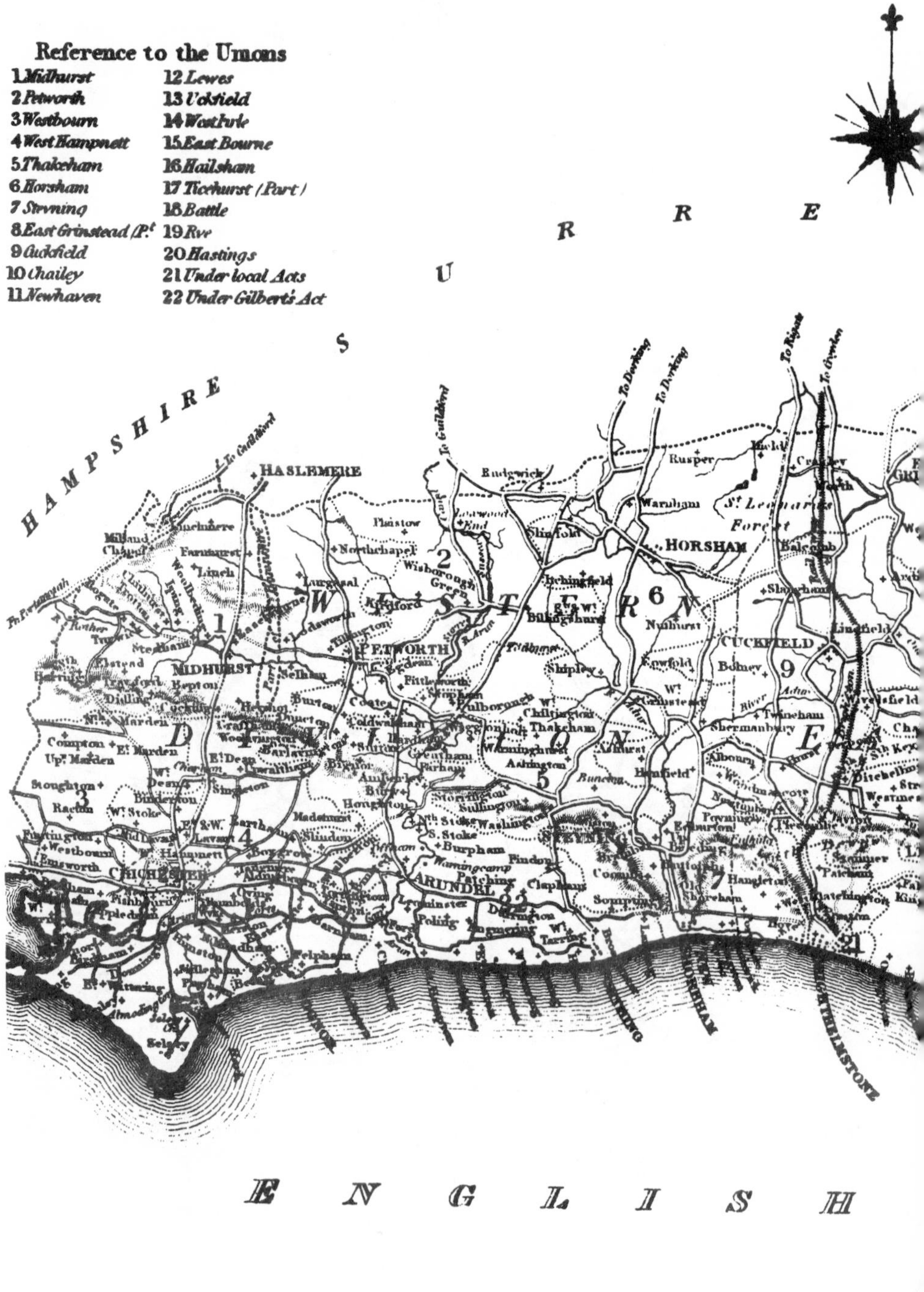

Reference to the Unions
1 Midhurst
2 Petworth
3 Westbourn
4 West Hampnett
5 Thakeham
6 Horsham
7 Steyning
8 East Grinstead (Pt
9 Cuckfield
10 Chailey
11 Newhaven
12 Lewes
13 Uckfield
14 West Firle
15 East Bourne
16 Hailsham
17 Ticehurst (Part)
18 Battle
19 Rye
20 Hastings
21 Under local Acts
22 Under Gilbert's Act
S U R R E
HAMPSHIRE
HASLEMERE
HORSHAM
PETWORTH
MIDHURST
CUCKFIELD
CHICHESTER
ARUNDEL
STEYNING
SHOREHAM
BRIGHTHELMSTONE
E N G L I S H
Scale of Miles

SUSSEX

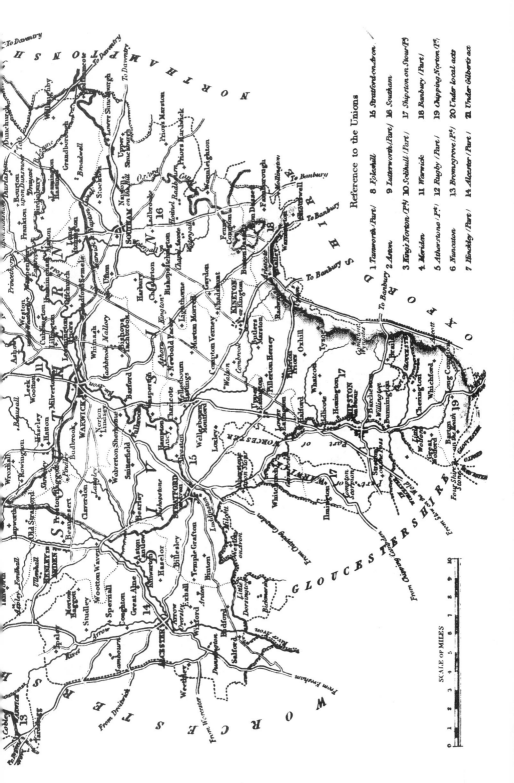

Reference to the Unions

1 Tamworth (Part) 8 Foleshill 15 Stratford-on-Avon.
2 Aston. 9 Lutterworth (Part) 16 Southam.
3 King's Norton (Pt.) 10 Solihull (Part.) 17 Shipston-on-Stour (Pt)
4 Meriden 11 Warwick. 18 Banbury (Part.)
5 Atherstone (Pt.) 12 Rugby (Part.) 19 Chipping Norton (Pt.)
6 Nuneaton. 13 Bromsgrove (Pt.) 20 Under local acts
7 Hinckley (Part.) 14 Alcester (Part.) 21 Under Gilbert's act

SCALE OF MILES

0 1 2 3 4 5 6 7 8 9 10

403

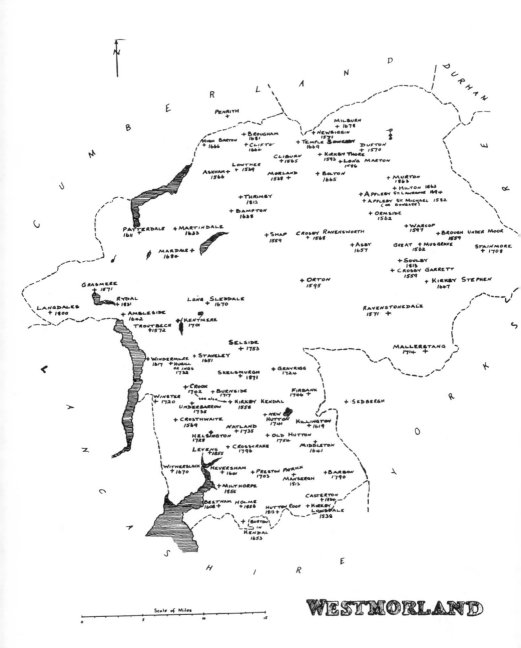

C U M B E R L A N D DURHAM

PENRITH
+

MILBURN
+ 1678

+ BROUGHAM
1681
+ NEWBIGGIN
1571
HIGH BARTON
1666
+ CLIFTON
1664
+ TEMPLE SOWERBY
DUFTON
+ 1570

CLIBURN
+ 1565
+ KIRKBY THORE
1593
LOWTHER
+ 1529
+ LONG MARTON
1486

ASKHAM +
1566
MORLAND
1528 +
+ BOLTON
1665
+ MURTON
1863
+ HILTON 1863
+ APPLEBY ST. LAWRENCE 1694
+ APPLEBY ST. MICHAEL 1582
(OR BONGATE)

+ THRIMBY
1813
+ ORMSIDE
1562

+ BAMPTON
1628

PATTERDALE
1611
+ MARTINDALE
1633
+ SHAP
1559
CROSBY RAVENSWORTH
+ 1568
+ WARCOP
1597
+ BROUGH UNDER MOOR
1559

MARDALE +
1684
+ ASBY
1657
GREAT + MUSGRAVE
1502
STAINMORE
+ 1708

+ SOULBY
1813
+ CROSBY GARRETT
1559

GRASMERE
+ 1571
+ ORTON
1595
+ KIRKBY STEPHEN
1647

RYDAL
+ 1831
LONG SLEDDALE
1670
RAVENSTONEDALE
1571 +

LANGDALES
+ 1800
AMBLESIDE
1642
+ KENTMERE
1701

TROUTBECK
+ 1572

MALLERSTANG
1714 +

SELSIDE
+ 1753

+ WINDERMERE
1617
+ STANELEY
1651
+ HUGILL
OR INGS
1732
SKELSMURGH
+ 1871
+ GRAYRIGG
1724

+ CROOK
1742
+ BURNSIDE
1717
FIRBANK
1744 +

WINSTER
+ 1720
+ KIRKBY KENDAL
1558
see also
UNDERBARROW
1735
+ NEW
HUTTON
1744
KILLINGTON
+ 1619
+ SEDBERGH

+ CROSTHWAITE
1569
NATLAND
+ 1735

HELSINGTON
1728
+ OLD HUTTON
1754
MIDDLETON
+ 1641

LEVENS
+1855
+ CROSSCRAKE
1796

WITHERSLACK
+ 1670
HEVERSHAM
+ 1601
+ PRESTON PATRICK
1703
+ BARBON
1790

+ MILTHORPE
1556
MANSERGH
1813

CASTERTON
+ 1844
BEETHAM
1608 +
HOLME
+ 1666
HUTTON ROOF
1813 +
+ KIRKBY
LONSDALE
1538

+ IBURTON
IN
KENDAL
1653

L A N C A S H I R E
Y O R K S

Scale of Miles
0   5   10   15

WESTMORLAND

404

Reference to the Unions

1   West Ward
2   East Ward
3   Kendal

Scale of Miles

WESTMORLAND

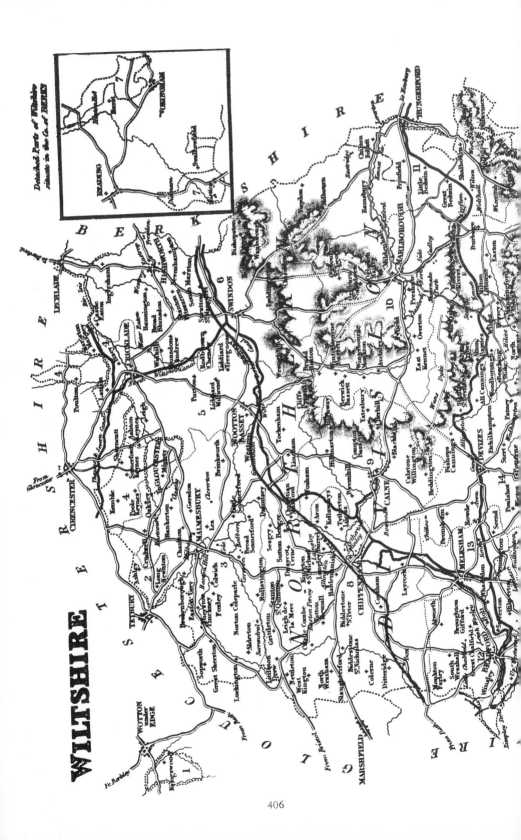

WILTSHIRE

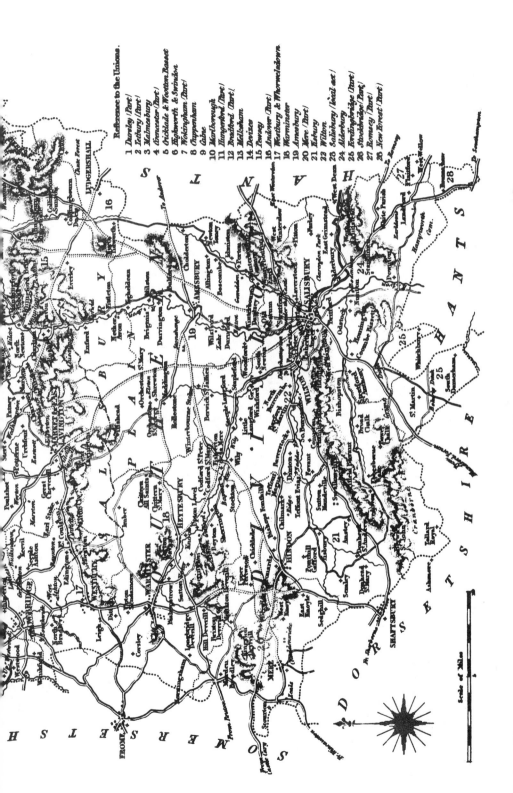

Reference to the Unions.

1 Dursley (Part)
2 Tetbury (Part)
3 Malmesbury
4 Cirencester (Part)
5 Cricklade & Wootton Basset
6 Highworth & Swindon
7 Wokingham (Part)
8 Chippenham
9 Calne
10 Marlborough
11 Hungerford (Part)
12 Bradford (Part)
13 Melksham
14 Devizes
15 Pewsey
16 Andover (Part)
17 Westbury & Whorwelsdown
18 Warminster
19 Amesbury
20 Alresford (Part)
21 Ketbury
22 Wilton
23 Salisbury (local act)
24 Alderbury
25 Fordingbridge (Part)
26 Stockbridge (Part)
27 Romsey (Part)
28 New Forest (Part)

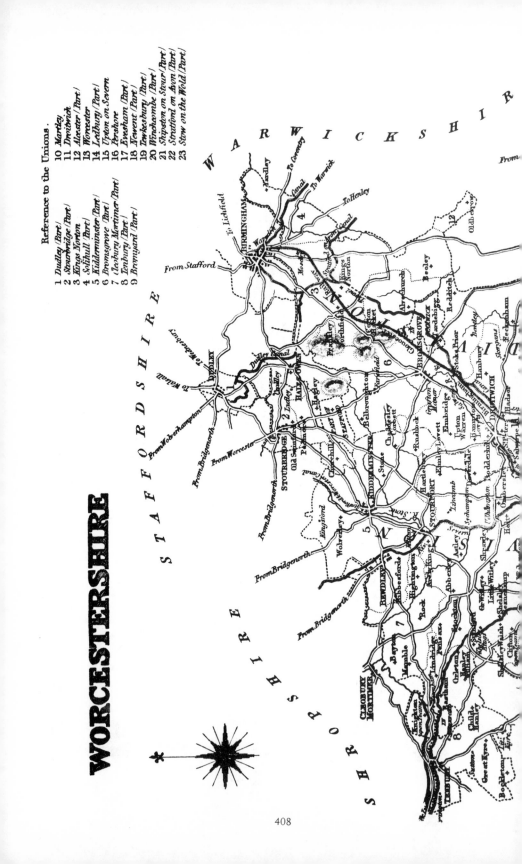

WORCESTERSHIRE

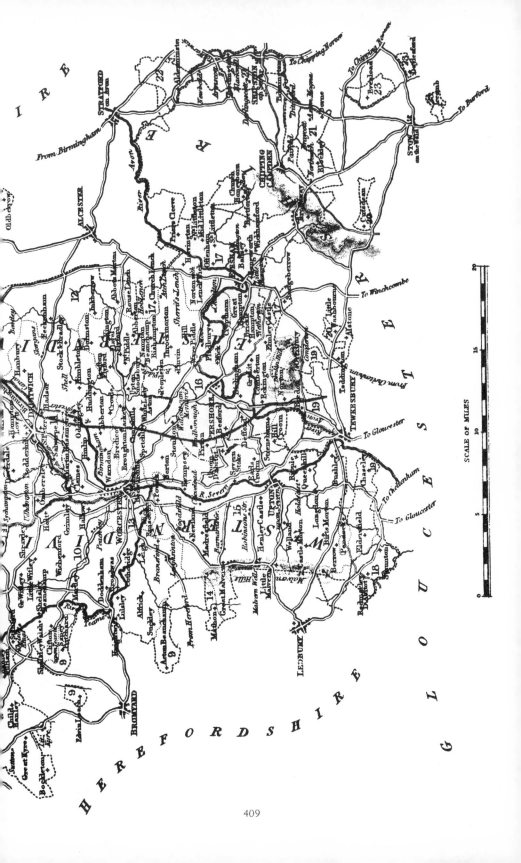

EAST RIDING
OF YORKSHIRE

FILEY 1573

FOLKTON 1655

MUSTON 1842

WILLERBY 1655

HUNMANBY 1584

WOLD NEWTON 1709

FORDLES 1654

BURTON FLEMING 1538

THWING 1691

RUENTON 1597

SPECTON

GRINDALE 1592

BEMPTON 1577

FLAMBOROUGH 1564

BOYNTON 1565

BRIDLINGTON 1564

LANGTOFT 1571

KILHAM 1653

RUDSTON 1550

BESSINGBY

GREAT DRIFFIELD 1556

LITTLE DRIFFIELD 1658

NAFFERTON 1655

HARPHAM 1720

BURTON AGNES 1700

CARNABY 1596

GT. KELK

LT. KELK

LOWTHORPE

BARMSTON 1571

FOSTON-ON-THE-WOLDS 1653

ULROME 1765

SKERNE 1561

BEEFORD 1564

SKIPSEA 1720

HUTTON CRANSWICK 1653

NORTH FRODINGHAM 1677

NUNKEELING 1559

NORTH SEA

WATTON 1558

ATWICK

BRANDESBURTON 1558

HORNSEA 1654

1592

BESWICK 1557

SCARBOROUGH 1653

LEVEN 1628

CATWICK 1583

SIGGLESTHORNE

FOXHILL 1561

LECONFIELD 1551

ROUTH 1633

RISTON 1653

RISE 1559

MAPPLETON 1683

WITHERNWICK 1658

BEVERLEY ST. MARY 1561 ST. NICH. 1561

ST. JOHN (MINSTER) WITH ST. MARTIN 1558

SKIRLAUGH 1719

WAWNE 1653

SWINE 1706

ALDBROUGH 1538

COTTINGHAM 1563

SUTTON ON HULL 1558

SKIDBY 1655

KIRK ELLA 1558

SCULCOATES 1576

HULL

HILTON 1571

PRESTON 1551

BURSTWICK

SPROATLEY 1647

HUMBLETON 1577

BURTON 1662

BURTON PIDSEA 1908

ROOS 1571

NORTH FERRIBY 1695

HESSLE 1561

MARFLEET 1711

SKECKLING 1747

HALSHAM 1563

OWTHORNE 1574

HOLLYM 1564

HOLMPTON 1739

EASINGTON 1585

PAULL 1657

KEYINGHAM 1618

OTTERINGHAM 1566

WINESTEAD 1579

PATRINGTON 1570

WELWICK 1650

SKEFFLING 1585

SUNK ISLAND (EXTRA PAROCHIAL LIBERTY)

◆ KINGSTON upon HULL:
ST. MARY - 1564
HOLY TRINITY - 1558

N S H I R E

411

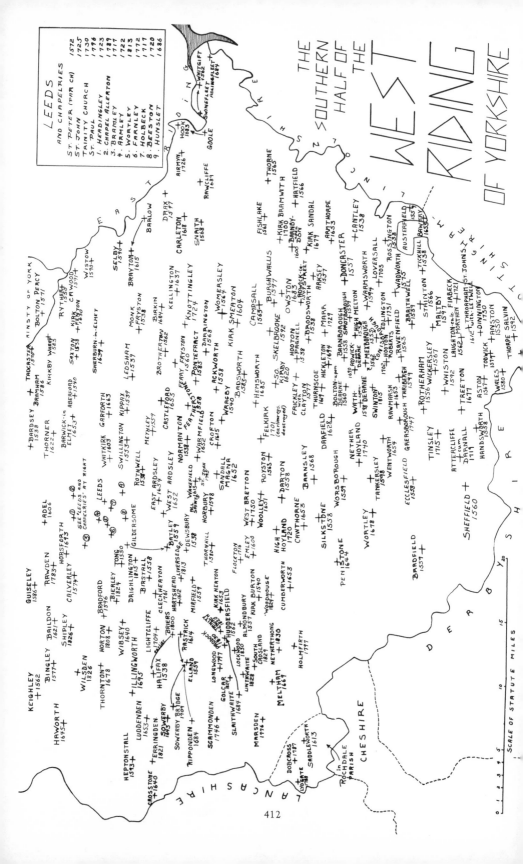

THE SOUTHERN HALF OF THE WEST RIDING OF YORKSHIRE

LEEDS
AND CHAPELRIES

St. Peter (Par Ch)	1572
St. John	1730
Trinity Church	1725
St. Paul	1796
1. Headingley	1723
2. Chapel Allerton	1737
3. Bramley	1717
4. Armley	1722
5. Wortley	1813
6. Farnley	1772
7. Holbeck	1717
8. Beeston	1720
9. Hunslet	1686

LANCASHIRE

CHESHIRE

DERBYSHIRE

NOTTINGHAMSHIRE

LINCOLNSHIRE

SCALE OF STATUTE MILES

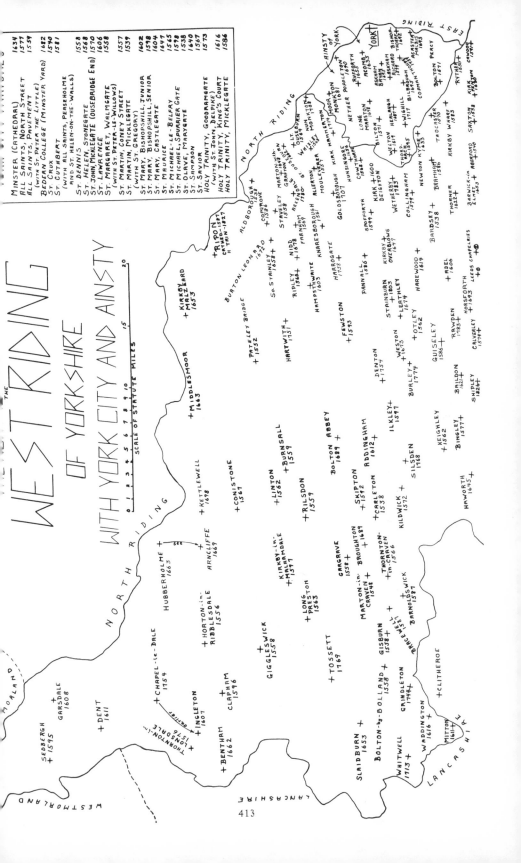

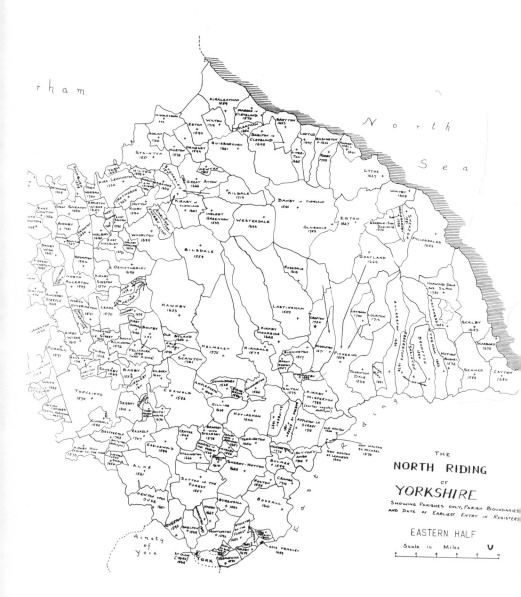

THE
NORTH RIDING
OF
YORKSHIRE

SHOWING PARISHES ONLY, PARISH BOUNDARIES
AND DATE OF EARLIEST ENTRY IN REGISTERS

EASTERN HALF

Scale in Miles

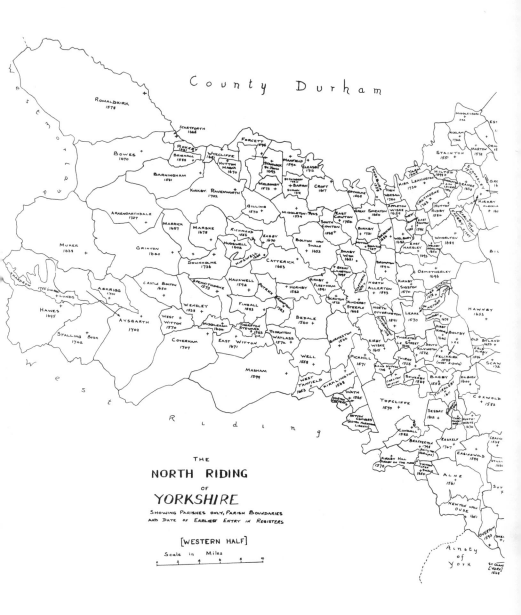

County Durham

THE
NORTH RIDING
OF
YORKSHIRE

SHOWING PARISHES ONLY, PARISH BOUNDARIES
AND DATE OF EARLIEST ENTRY IN REGISTERS

[WESTERN HALF]

Scale in Miles

415

416

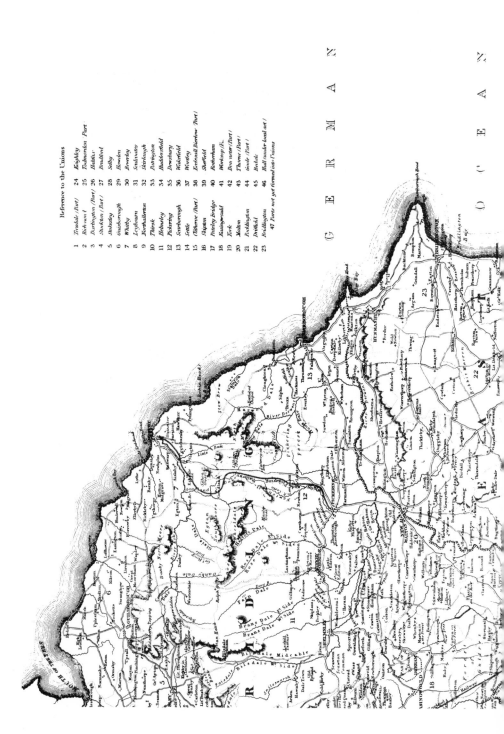

Reference to the Unions

1	Teesdale (Part)	24	Keighley
2	Richmond	25	Todmorden (Part)
3	Darlington (Part)	26	Halifax
4	Stockton (Part)	27	Bradford
5	Stokesley	28	Selby
6	Guisborough	29	Howden
7	Whitby	30	Beverley
8	Leyburn	31	Sculcoates
9	Northallerton	32	Skirlaugh
10	Thirsk	33	Patrington
11	Helmsley	34	Huddersfield
12	Pickering	35	Dewsbury
13	Scarborough	36	Wakefield
14	Settle	37	Wortley
15	Aldwarke (Part)	38	Ecclesall Bierlow (Part)
16	Skipton	39	Sheffield
17	Pateley Bridge	40	Rotherham
18	Knaresborough	41	Worksop (Pa...)
19	York	42	Don caster (Part)
20	Malton	43	Thorne (Part)
21	Pocklington	44	Goole (Part)
22	Driffield	45	Bedale
23	Bridlington	46	Hull (under local act)

47 Parts not yet formed into Unions

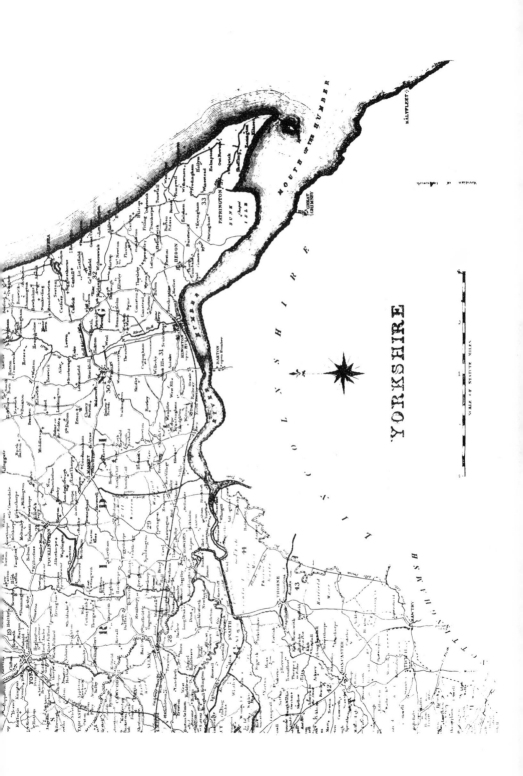

YORKSHIRE

MOUTH OF THE HUMBER

LINCOLNSHIRE

NOTTINGHAMSHIRE

SCALE OF STATUTE MILES

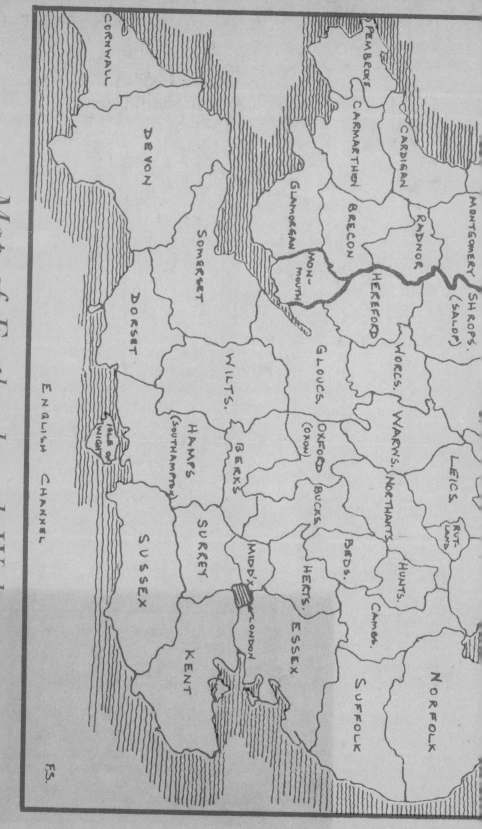

Map of England and Wales

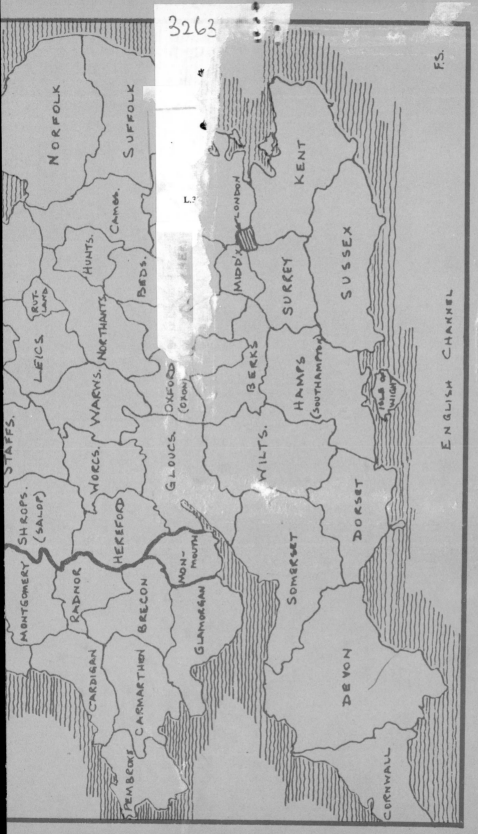

Map of England and Wales